SACRED AND PROFANE: SECULAR AND DEVOTIONAL INTERPLAY IN EARLY MODERN BRITISH LITERATURE

edited by

HELEN WILCOX
RICHARD TODD
ALASDAIR MACDONALD

VU University Press
Amsterdam 1996

VU University Press is an imprint of
VU Boekhandel/Uitgeverij bv
De Boelelaan 1105
1081 HV Amsterdam
The Netherlands

Layout by: Sjoukje Rienks, Amsterdam
Cover by: Neroc, Amsterdam
Cover illustration: Henk Helmantel
Printed by: Wilco, Amersfoort

isbn 90-5383-367-6

SACRED AND PROFANE

CONTENTS

ACKNOWLEDGEMENTS

The editors are indebted to a number of individuals and institutions whose assistance, both financial and practical, has made this publication possible. The conference out of which the volume grew was supported by the Royal Netherlands Academy of Sciences (KNAW), the British Council, the Groningen University Fund (GUF) and the Arts Faculty of the University of Groningen. The English Department at the University of Groningen facilitated both the conference and this publication by providing financial, scholarly and secretarial support; the editors would like to thank in particular Christien van der Werff, Koos Gräper, Miralda Meulman, Sheila Ottway, Elizabeth Waltheer and Hilary Martin for their help with 'Sacred and Profane'. The contributions of Henk Helmantel, in giving permission for the reproduction of his painting 'Nieuw Leven' ('New Life') on the cover of this book, and of Arina Vermaas and Jeroen Kans at the VU University Press, are also gratefully acknowledged.

HELEN WILCOX
RICHARD TODD
ALASDAIR MACDONALD

Groningen/Amsterdam, May 1995

INTRODUCTION

HELEN WILCOX

The painting which you see reproduced on the cover of this book—'Nieuw Leven' ('New Life') by the Groningen artist Henk Helmantel—is an emblem of the issues explored in the following pages. It is, like the essays in this collection, a late twentieth-century representation of a prominent early modern theme, the interrelation of the sacred and the 'profane', in the widest sense of the word as that which is before ('pro'), thus outside, the temple or holy place ('fanum').

The sacred element in the painting is an early seventeenth-century Bible, a copy of the Dutch translation authorised at the Synod of Dordrecht in 1618-1619. The water in the vase standing on the opened Bible acts as a magnifying glass over the word 'Jesu', focusing—as did the sixteenth and seventeenth-century writers discussed in the subsequent chapters—on the name at the centre of the New Testament, the word (which is also the Word) and the textuality of the sacred. The parallel with George Herbert's poem 'Jesu', in which the enlarged letters of the saviour's name are 'carved' on the speaker's heart and take on an expressive life of their own in the course of the lyric, is very striking.[1] This, then, is the first sense of 'New Life' in the picture: the life of the resurrected Christ on whom the 'New' Covenant was founded and who gives textual and spiritual inspiration to those who, like our early modern writers, read and use the Bible.

There is, of course, a second and equally prominent kind of 'New Life' in the painting, which is that of the fresh young leaves on the sprig in the vase. This is the life of the natural world outside the 'temple', the potentially pagan energies of the natural cycles of birth, growth and death. Does this new life come from the Bible—with Christ symbolically suggested as the new green shoot on the old tree of Jesse—or is the earthly vitality of the plant independent of, or even in defiance of, the sacred page on which it stands? There is perhaps a direct contrast implied between the old dry leaves of the book and the living leaves of the plant, which signify the more vibrant and tangible 'New Life'.

These thoughts on Henk Helmantel's painting have drawn us into a consideration of the central concerns of this volume. What was the nature of the interplay between the sacred and the profane in texts of the early modern period? Though these two principles are inherently in opposition to one another—they are located metaphorically inside and outside the 'temple'—they are inevitably interconnected as part of human culture and experience, even at times sharing the very same vocabulary. As Donne commented, God 'stoops even to the words of our foul and unchaste love, that thereby he might raise us to the heavenly love of himself'.[2] Donne's assumption here is that the higher influence of the divine 'raises' the earthly in the direction of God. But the influence can be in the other direction, too: sacred echoes can be used to empower the secular, the passionate or the political. The pattern of interplay, however, is rarely so clear-cut as this binary structure suggests; the following pages demonstrate the complex and fascinating interconnections of secular and devotional energies in the early modern period.

One of the effects of this collection of essays is to expand our definitions of the sacred and the profane. In addition to the central importance of the Bible as source and resource for writers in the sixteenth and seventeenth centuries, the sacred signifies traditions of thought and teaching, structures of church authority and liturgy, a system of symbols with enormous flexibility in their application, and a variety of written forms and modes of rhetoric such as sermon, hymn and prophecy. The richness of the profane is also extended by these essays, so that the term comes to suggest not only the 'foul and unchaste', as Donne put it, but also the traditions of classical thought and metaphor, the urgency of history and immediacy of sexual politics, and the call of art itself.

This volume is divided into three sections, on a broadly chronological basis. The first part, under the heading of 'Sacred and Profane in Renaissance Contexts', establishes some of the fundamental elements in the relationship between the secular and the devotional in texts from sixteenth and early seventeenth-century Britain. Political and spiritual pressures, the language of love and the practice of sacred parody of worldly texts are analysed in essays which range across the period from Wyatt and Surrey to Aemilia Lanyer. The title of the central section of the book, '"Nor ever chast...": John Donne, Amorous and Divine', recalls the paradoxes of Donne's 'Holy Sonnet' XIV in which he claims, in the startling vocabulary of physical love, that he will never be 'chast' unless God 'ravish' him.[3] This sonnet and a range of other works by Donne in prose as well as verse are discussed in a major reconsideration of the interplay of secular and sacred worlds in Donne's art and theology. The volume ends with a section on 'Religion, Rhetoric and Revolution in the Seventeenth Century', extending the analysis of sacred and profane interaction into the classical aesthetics and radical politics of the later part of the period. The issue of martyrdom—for the sake of art, faith, freedom or lust—is one of several themes woven through these final chapters.

It is impossible in a brief introduction to do justice to the complexity and variety of approaches and questions with which the contributors address the interplay of the sacred and the profane in early modern British literature. What emerges from the range of texts considered and the stimulating discussions which ensue is the undoubted vitality and crucial centrality of this theme in early modern art and life. It offered a source of wit as well as anxiety, and a framework for expression as well as a challenge for change.

The texts under discussion in this volume are refreshingly varied: not only English but also Scottish (and Dutch) works, not only poetry but also drama and prose, and including many less familiar texts in addition to the writings of figures such as Spenser, Shakespeare, Donne and Milton. However, there would appear to be one major ommission, that is, the absence of an essay on the work of George Herbert, in which secular love lyrics were transformed into 'window-songs' for God.[4] The justification for this peculiar lack is the fact that we are simultaneously publishing a sister volume entirely devoted to the ways in which worldly and spiritual matters are creatively interwoven in Herbert's writing.[5] It is the editors' hope that, together, the two volumes will stimulate continuing discussion and new perceptions of the interplay of the sacred and profane, in their fullest meanings, in early modern literature.

Notes

1   The speaker 'sat me down to spell' the letters of the name 'Jesu', finding that they contain in compacted form the message of salvation; see *The English Poems of George Herbert*, edited by C.A. Patrides (London, 1974), 125.

2   *The Sermons of John Donne*, edited by George R. Potter and Evelyn M. Simpson (Berkeley, 1953-62), 3: 313.

3   *The Complete English Poems of John Donne*, edited by C.A. Patrides (London, 1985), 443.

4   'Dulnesse', in *The English Poems*, 128.

5   *George Herbert: Sacred and Profane*, edited by Helen Wilcox and Richard Todd (Amsterdam, 1995).

PART I

SACRED AND PROFANE IN RENAISSANCE CONTEXTS

LUTE AND HARP IN WYATT'S POETRY

ELIZABETH HEALE

Artlessness is a recurring theme in Wyatt's poetry; spontaneity is true and sincere, art is craft (with its more manipulative shades of meaning). A rondeau (Wyatt's version of a probable French version of a Petrarchan original), states the theme with particular clarity:

> I must goo worke, I se, by craft and art,
> For trueth and faith in her is laide apart;
> Alas, I cannot therefore assaill her
> With pitefull plaint and scalding fyer,
> That oute of my brest doth straynably stert:
>   Goo, burning sighes![1]

'Craft and art' are set in opposition to 'trueth and faith' and to the spontaneous plaint and sighs which 'straynably stert' out of the lover's heart.[2] 'Straynably' suggests the painful constrictions of the lover's feeling heart, but it is also, of course, a musical metaphor (*OED* strain, vb. II.b: 'to tighten up the strings of a musical instrument so as to raise the pitch'), which may be compared with Herbert's line 'Oh take thy lute, and tune it to a strain'.[3] This doubleness draws attention to a familiar pun, latent in the Wyatt poem, which equates the strings or 'cords' of the musical instrument with the Latin word for heart, *cor, cordis*. At the moment when this crafty (conceited, carefully wrought) poem declares the spontaneity of the lover's sighs, it depends on a pun which likens the heart, the source of spontaneity, to a stringed instrument af art. In this essay I want to explore, in Wyatt's courtly and devotional poems, some aspects of such a collapsing of the opposition between spontaneity and craft, through the image of a musical instrument.

Wyatt uses the image of the lute in a number of his courtly poems ('My lute awake', 'Blame not my lute', 'Sins you will nedes', 'All hevy mindes', 'At moost myschief'). Such courtly verses ('ballets' would be the contemporary term) have seemed, in the past, to resist critical analysis because of their apparent slightness; they have been described as 'verse of lighter weight' ... 'the most ephemeral of courtly poems' or, in a well-known judgement of H.A. Mason, 'not poems at all'.[4] This perceived slightness may be in part a consequence of their social function: they circu-

lated, were copied into albums, perhaps on occasion sung, as part of a
social world of dalliance and pastime, 'gambits in a "game of love", half-
mocking, half-serious'.[5] We may perhaps detect in critical judgements of
their slightness, the same ambivalence about such arts of courting that Castiglione registered in *Il Libro del Cortegiano*. There the egregious Count
Lodovico advised the aspiring courtier to 'exercise him selfe in Poets ...
especially in this our vulgar tongue [because] ... he shall by this meanes
never want pleasant entertainements with women'[6] and in the same vein he
praises the art of singing and playing on an instrument 'and principally in
courtes, where.many things are taken in hand to please women withall,
whose tender and soft breastes are soone pierced with melodie, and filled
with sweetnesse' (75). The other side of this coin for the courtier is
articulated by the more explicitly misogynist Pallavicino: 'I believe musick
... together with many other vanities is meet for women, and peradventure
for some also that have the likenesse of men, but not for them that be men
in deede: who ought not with such delicacies to womanish their mindes,
and bring themselves in that sort to dread death' (75).

Such a valuation of the courtly lyric as an art of dalliance, tainting its
practitioner and its kind with insubstantiality and effeminacy, is written into
Wyatt's use of the genre, and, particularly, the figure of the lute which
represents the voice of the lover/poet as spontaneous, ephemeral, and inef-
fective. As such, the figure deflects our attention, with a gesture of artlessness (Castiglione's 'sprezzatura')[7], from the considerable artifice and
aggressive misogynism which actually characterise the verse.

In 'My lute awake' the lover picks up his lute, as a final act, to com-
plain of his mistress' cruelty:

> My lute, awake! perfourme the last
> Labour that thou and I shall wast
> And end that I have now begon;
> For when this song is sung and past,
> My lute be still, for I have done.   (M&T no. 66, ll. 1-5)

The conceit is of a spontaneous, private performance, the lover's swan-
song to this lute. The frailty and ephemerality of this self is intensified by
the impermanence and insubstantiality of his song, mere vibrating air,
which, when pitted against the impenetrable hardness of the lady (she is
imaged as 'marbill stone' and rock) is wholly powerless. Concluding his
'playnyng in vain' in the final stanza, the poet calls on his lute to be still,
bringing to a close this song, perhaps all performances on his lute, perhaps
his life as a lover, perhaps even his life itself:

Now cesse, my lute; this is the last
Labour that thou and I shall wast,
And ended is that we begon;
Now is this song, boeth sung and past;
My lute, be still, for I have done.   (ll. 36-40)

However, the poem's refrain, with its varying repetitions 'for I have done',
'and I have done', 'as I have done' has, by the last stanza, altered the possibilities of words that in the first stanza seemed wholly plaintive; the final
phrase 'for I have done' introduces the possibility that he has both 'done
with' and 'done for' (*OED* II. e) the lady. These altered possibilities depend
on stanzas 6 and 7, the only two which do not mention the lute in the
refrain. These stanzas turn upside down the scenario of cruel lady and fading lover established in the previous stanzas, placing in its stead, an ageing,
fading lady, and a cruel, masculine world:

Perchance the lye wethered and old,
The wynter nyghtes that are so cold,
Playnyng in vain vnto the mone;
Thy wisshes then dare not be told;
Care then who lyst, for I have done.   (ll. 26-30)

This vision only partially reverses the previous roles of the lover and his
lady. The desired vengeance is actually only a wish which betrays its own
powerlessness, 'perchance'; the lover cannot enforce his particular vision of
this lady's lonely fate, he just hopes it will be as he envisages it. But
although this lover has only a wished for power over this particular woman,
the poem displays a confident verbal power over women in general, telling
all who read his poem, male and female, by means of the death's head
image of the decayed beauty burning with unrequited passion, of women's
value and function as seen from the cruellest male perspective. The plaintive song of the lover evaporates, or so runs the conceit, but on the manuscript page there is left a powerful and indelible misogynism. The apparently artless spontaneity of the lover's song, wrung from his heart, and
articulated by the lute, masks the careful and retaliatory craft of the poem.

   This posture of powerlessness masking a confident assertion of male
verbal power frequently uses the figure of the insubstantiality of sound in
Wyatt's courtly verse. In another poem which uses the image of the lute,
'All hevy myndes / Do seke to ese their charge' (M&T no. 84), the lover
claims to be addressing 'My faithfull lute / Alone', emphasising the
insubstantiality of his effort: 'In vain oft in the ayre / To say Alas'. The

pose of spontaneity and intimacy are, of course, poetic figures functioning
in part at least to construct the lover as passionate and powerless, even
while the poem purveys to the courtly circle within which it was no doubt
intended to circulate, a representation of women as unkind and perversely
cruel, incapable of appreciating 'trouth and faithfull mynd'.

A similar doubleness with the lover/poet as both victim and aggressor
is apparent in 'Blame not my lute' (M&T no. 205). The poem enacts a verbal, and indeed supposedly physical struggle between the lover and the lady
over the lute. The lady seeks to stop the song by breaking the lute's strings,
while the lover exonerates the lute from blame:

> Blame not my lute, for he must sownd
> Of thes or that as liketh me;
> For lake of wytt the lutte is bownd
> To gyve suche tunes as plesithe me;
> [Then] Tho my songes be sume what strange
> And spekes such words as toche they change
>   Blame not my lutte.   (ll. 1-7)

Here the lover/poet seems to assert overt control; the lute only sounds the
tunes the lover wishes to sing 'as liketh me' and those are designed 'To
qwytt thy chainge with Rightfull spight' (l. 20) recording the lady's faults
of spite and 'falsyd faith'. But as the poem progresses, it becomes apparent
that the poem is constructing the lute as a figure for the poet himself. As
the lute's chords/cords reflect the poet's heart (*cor, cordis*) and its passions,
so the poet is played upon by the lady:

> Blame but thy selfe that hast mysdown
> And well desaruid to haue blame;
> Change thou thy way so evyll bygown
> And then my lute shall sownd that same;
> But if tyll then my fingeres play
> By thy desartt their wontyd way,
>   Blame not my lutte.   (ll. 29-35)

Blame not my lute, and blame not me. As the lady touches the strings of his
heart so he touches the strings of his lute; both, it seems, are innocent instruments of a song for which the lady is the originating source, and both
are vulnerable to the lady's aggression. But instrument and lover escape in
the last stanza, with a display of just such faithlessness and spite as he
accuses the lady of showing: 'Yet haue I fownd owt for thy sake / Stringes

for to strynge my lute agayne'. Under the pose of innocent victim, the lover's actions are remarkably similar to those of which he accuses the lady: both struggle to control the lute's 'discourse' but there is really no contest; the poet may ascribe the lute's notes to her as she plays on the player's heart, but the song speaks only the lover's words of 'blame', not those of the lady. The image of the lute song figures the supposed insubstantiality and innocence of the voice which sings the song. The tune is nothing in itself; why waste time breaking the cords? They are merely the audible vibrations of the poet's heart, but that itself (*cor, cordis*) merely vibrates to the fingers of an unknown lady. Under the guise of artlessness, of insubstantiality and of an ever receding responsibility, the poet aggressively reasserts a threatened masculinity.

What kind of performance, if any, might the poems be evoking? John Stevens, in his study of early Tudor music and poetry, arguing from admittedly 'negative evidence' (that is, the absence of any evidence to the contrary) surmises that 'there could hardly have been in England a tradition of courtier poets singing extempore to their lutes, comparable to the Italian, without it leaving some traces; and it is certain that the *composition* of songs specifically for solo voice and instrument was a new thing in the middle of the sixteenth century'.[8] He does accept that some of Wyatt's courtly poems may have been sung to existing (popular) tunes. Aristocratic amateur playing of the lute does not seem, as far as I can gather, to have been very common in England in the 1520s and 30s. The royal family, Henry VIII and his sisters, could play, as could Anne Boleyn, but these were exceptionally highly cultivated people—Anne Boleyn having been trained in the musically very advanced courts of the Netherlands and France.[9] A tradition of virtuoso singing to the lute (by both men and women), sometimes with solo voice, often improvisatory or at least designed to give the effect of spontaneous improvisation did exist in the early sixteenth century, originating in Italy in the late fifteenth century, spreading less robustly to France, and, in spite of Stevens, probably to England via professional Italian musicians at court by the second decade of the sixteenth century. This is the fashion for Italian *frottola* singing, the preferred poetic forms for which were *strambotti* (a form Wyatt often translates and imitates) and *barzellette* (stanzaic songs, with often mocking refrains, which characteristically took a 'popular', decidedly unidealising view of love).[10] I suggest that it is in fact this style which Wyatt's conceit of lute singing invokes, adding, to its other connotations, a frisson of fashionable Italianate styles marked by a sardonic chauvinism. It is this style of singing and performing that Castiglione recommends to the accomplished courtier:

> But to sing to the lute [*viola da braccio*] is much better, because all the
> sweetnes consisteth in one alone [solo singing] ... singing to the lute
> with the dittie [*il cantar alla viola recitare*—the style associated with
> *frottola* singing] ... is more pleasant than the rest, for it addeth to the
> wordes such a grace and strength, that it is a great wonder.   (101)

But, as we have seen, such courtly singing to the lute was also liable to the
charge of effeminacy, 'meet for women, and peradventure for some also
that have the likenesse of men, but not for them that be men in deede'
(75).[11]

Thus the conceit of lute song epitomises many of the characteristics of
Wyatt's verse: the vibrating air of the imaginary lute song helps to construct the poet/lover's voice as spontaneous, ephemeral and powerless, even
while the artful form belies the artless pose, and even while the poems'
circulation in ink on paper helps to preserve more permanently their powerful reassertion of a threatened masculinity, threatened less by women, surely, than by the 'womanish' arts of courtiership. The conceit of fashionable,
ephemeral lute song confronts that threat by masking craft and effort as
spontaneity, and aggression as plaintiveness.[12]

While the lute is the profane instrument of the lover, the harp's associations with David make it traditionally the instrument of devotional and
sacred music.[13] In the prologues to Wyatt's verse paraphrases of the seven
penitential psalms, it is a crucial image. Wyatt links each of his psalms with
a narrative prologue modelled, closely at first, on those in Aretino's *I Setti
Salmi* (first published in 1534). Aretino's prose introductions specifically
located each psalm as a stage in the penitence of David after his adultery
with Bathsheba.[14] Wyatt borrows Aretino's emphasis on David's use of
his harp, but, as we shall see, he soon begins to develop it in ways that
Aretino does not.

In the introduction to the first of the seven psalms, psalm 6, Aretino
tells the story of David's adultery up till the point when the prophet Nathan
confronts the king with his sin. Overwhelmed by fear of due punishment,
David takes his harp, wet from the tears which flow from his heart, and
retires into a dark cave ('presa la cetera, la quale immollaua tuttauia il
pianto, che distillaua il core per bear l'anima'), where, kneeling, he takes
the instrument to his breast and looking up to the sky, he touches the strings
('toccando le *corde*' [my italics]) and sings the words of psalm 6.[15] It has
been noted that at this point David seems more like a pleading lover than a
sinner.[16] This effect is even more apparent in Wyatt's version, in which
David

    frawtyd with disese
Off stormy syghes, his chere colourd lyk clay,
Dressyd vpryght, sekyng to conterpese
His song with syghes, and towching of the strynges
With tendre hert, lo thus to god he synges.   (M&T no. 108 ll. 68-72)

As Wyatt wrote in one of his sonnets 'If waker care if sodayne pale
Coulour / If many sighes with litle speche to playne / ... Be signe of love
then do I love agayne' (M&T no. 97).

    The singing of the psalm does calm David; the soothing power of
David's harp, most notably on King Saul, was a commonplace.[17] Calmer
and more hopeful, David, in the link (both in Aretino and in Wyatt) between the first and second penitential psalms, takes up the harp again.
Wyatt, even more than Aretino, and in a way different from his own use of
the lute in the secular verse, emphasises David's technical effort and mastery of voice and instrument—in other words, his artfulness:

His harp agayne in to his hand he rowght.
Tunyng accord by Jugement of his ere:
His hertes botum for a sigh he sowght,
And there withall apon the holow tre
With straynid voyce agayne thus cryth he.   (ll. 212-216)

'Straynid' here draws attention to the musical connotations of the word,
suggesting a careful tuning of the voice as well as the instrument.

    As David finishes the second penitential psalm, Wyatt, following Are-
tino, describes a silence in which David's mind seems to enter into an
unspoken dialogue with the cave about the mercy attributed to God in the
psalm he has just sung. As David prays, a ray of light illuminates the cave
and glances across the cords of the harp making the instrument glow like
gold, 'The torne wheroff into his Iyes did sterte, / Surprisd with Joye by
penance off the herte' (ll. 315-316). Wyatt is following Aretino closely
though he concentrates his readers' attention more exclusively on the effect
of the light striking the harp, and through the compression of his grammar
on the identity of the beam of light and the sudden inner penitence that
surprises the poet at the very moment the light 'starts' into his eyes.[18]
David's response to this apparently miraculous sign does not seem wholly
in keeping. He renews his efforts with his harp in a spirit that seems more
appropriate to the amorous lutenist than the harpist:

He then Inflamd with farr more hote affect
Of god then he was erst of Bersabe,
His lifft fote did on the eyerth erect,
And just therby remaynth the tothr kne;
To his lifft syde his wayght he doth direct.
Sure hope of helth, and harpe agayne takth he;
His hand, his tune, his mynd sowght his lay,
Wyche to the Lord with sobre voyce did say.   (ll. 317-24)

On this occasion, David's playing brings him no comfort. In the narrative link between the third and fourth penitential psalms, we are told he breaks off weary, weeping and nigh insensible. His fingers still play over the cords of the harp but 'Withowt heryng or Jugement off the sownd' (ll. 404). The 'Jugement' is Wyatt's addition to the Italian and ironically recalls the confident artfulness that David brought to his harp-playing in the prologue to the second psalm 'Tunyng accord by jugement of his ere' (l. 213). It is now possible to detect a developing independent theme in Wyatt's use of the harp imagery. The instrument and the songs he has tuned to it have soothed his passions, voiced his penitence, and raised ideas of mercy which have given him hope, but his own best efforts and skill seem unable to take him further, indeed his most striking moment of joy so far comes from an outer agency, the divine light striking on the cords.

It is therefore significant that at the end of this introduction to the fourth psalm, when David resumes his song, he seems to abandon his harp altogether, a detail to which Wyatt far more dramatically calls attention than Aretino's simple 'esclamando cantò':

His voyce he strains, and from his hert owt brynges
This song that I not wyther he crys or singes.   (ll. 425-426)

The heart/string (*cordis*/cord) pun is at work here; David is turning from his wooden instrument to a living one, his own heart, as a fit vehicle for his penitence. The artful tuning of the harp of the earlier prologues has been abandoned.

In the next narrative link, between the fourth and fifth psalms, Wyatt continues to move away from his earlier close dependence on Aretino, and part of the reason appears to be Wyatt's now independent development of the musical imagery. Aretino's David continues to play his harp and fit his voice to the music, but Wyatt's has not only by now abandoned the instrument, but is moving away from control of the song. As he concludes the fourth penitential psalm, Wyatt's narrator comments:

> Of diepe secretes that David here did sing,
> Off mercy, off fayth, off frailte, off grace,
> Off goddes goodnes and off Justyfying,
> The grettnes dyd so astonne hymselff a space,
> As who myght say who hath exprest this thing?   (ll. 509-513)

David goes on to ponder silently 'ech word that erst his lypps might forth aford' as though he were analysing some new previously unseen text: 'He poyntes, he pawsith, he wonders, he praysyth ...'. Unlike his own 'lay' in the third penitential psalm, the result of a tuneful fitting of his hand and tune and mind (l. 323), which left him exhausted and despairing, this fifth psalm, for which David himself has been the passive instrument, gives him new and lasting hope.

Wyatt's development of the musical imagery in the psalms has moved from the profanity of David's use of the harp as though it were a lute in the first prologue, to the metaphor, widespread in Christian thought, of the well-tuned body as an instrument upon which God or the soul can play. St. John Chrysostom in his 'Exposition' of Psalm XLI, gives particularly clear expression to the idea:

> What is here sought for is a sober mind, an awakened intelligence, a contrite heart, sound reason, and clear conscience. If having these you have entered into God's sacred choir, you may stand beside David himself.
>
> Here there is no need for the cithera, or for stretched strings, or for plectrum, or for art, or for any instrument; but, if you like, you may yourself become a cithera, mortifying the members of the flesh and making a full harmony of mind and body. For when the flesh no longer lusts against the Spirit, but has submitted to its orders and has been led at length into the best and most admirable path, than you will create a spiritual melody.[19]

The conceit of David as an instrument for God is made explicit in the narrative link between the fifth and sixth psalms, albeit that this image is now that of a blown instrument:

> When David had perceyvid in his brest
> The sprite off god retournd that was exild,
> Be cause he knew he hath alone exprest
> Thes grete thinges that greter spryte compilde,

> As shalme or pype letes owt the sownd inprest
> By musikes art forgid to fore and fyld,   (ll. 632-637)

Wyatt is like a pipe not only in having become an instrument on which 'a greter spryte' plays, but in having been 'forgid to fore and fyld' by 'musikes art'. Penitence is seen as to some extent a collaborative act: David's skilful playing could not, by itself, effectuate much; it did not persuade God to pity. But it was necessary to David in the implementation of his penitence, in helping to tune his own heart and mind so that his body might become an instrument through which God could play.

The direction in which Wyatt is developing the conceit of song is suggested by the significant differences between the poses adopted by Aretino's David and his own, in the introduction to the sixth penitential psalm. Aretino's David assumes a striking pose before turning again to his musical efforts:

> ma statosi alquanto con la mano destra nella barba, e col dito ch'è allato al piu grosso attrauersato alla bocca, essendo certo che solo il salmeggiare la sua penitenza lo poteua riporre in gratia di Dio, ritornato à lui col core, col uolto, con le parole, e col suono prontamente disse.

> (but he stayed for a little with his right hand in his beard, and with the finger which is next to the largest [his index finger?] placed crosswise over his mouth, being certain that only by singing in psalms his penitence could he return to God's grace, turned again to him with his heart, with his face, with his words, and with his music, he readily said ...)[20]

Aretino's psalmist turns from pondering his plight in a pose in which he could not possibly sing, to assuming the pose, with face uplifted, of the first prologue. Wyatt's remains in the cramped position of the thinker, his song no longer a matter of performance or technical art:

> And whilst he ponderd thes thinges in his hert,
> His knee, his arme, his hand, susteind his chyn,
> When he his song agayne thus did begynn.   (ll. 661-663)

St. John Chrysostom, after the passage quoted above, goes on to say: 'One may also sing without voice, the mind resounding inwardly. For we sing, not to men, but to God, who can hear our hearts and enter into the silences of our minds'.[21] The final introduction, to Wyatt's seventh penitential psalm, gives no indication that the final psalm is said or sung aloud. The narrator tells us of David's unspoken words as he silently 'frames this reson [the significance of Christ] in his hert', and the unvoiced monologue described in the prologue continues into the psalm itself as David puts his suit, now 'with suryd confidence' (l. 725), to God: 'Here my prayer o lord, here my request' (l. 727). Within the fiction of the poem, David has moved beyond song, beyond even the voice as an instrument, to an apparently unmediated communication with God in the 'silences of [his] mind.'

A stubborn materiality, however, belies this fiction of immanence. David's 'unvoiced' psalm is brought to us via multiple texts and many voices, fictional and historical—those of David, the narrator, Wyatt. The text itself is a palimpsest of other versions, commentaries, and translations into Latin and Italian of the original Hebrew.[22] The mediation of presence through multiple texts points us to a paradox that is apparent through all Wyatt's musical conceits; it calls attention to the craft which the conceits are deployed to disguise and devalue. The more artful David is seen to be, tuning his voice to his hand, the more distant he is from that ideal of un-mediated communication in which a perfectly tuned David can meet an unveiled God in a fantasy of full presence. In the courtly lyrics, singing to the lute is similarly designed to give the illusion, however transparent, of spontaneity and presence through the 'I' of the innocent performer, an effect produced, as we have seen, by the vengeful craft of the poem. The unmediated and spontaneous voice of truth and innocence never in fact gets a hearing in Wyatt's verse which, in spite of such claims to transparency, must always 'go worke ... by craft and art'.

Notes

1   *Collected Poems of Sir Thomas Wyatt*, edited by Kenneth Muir and Patricia Thomson (Liverpool, 1969) no. 20. All quotations from Wyatt's poems will be from this edition, and poems will be identified, in parenthesis in the text, by a reference to M&T's numbering.

2   Jonathan Crewe in an essay on 'Wyatt's Craft' describes the poem as 'charged with contradictory instructions', *Trials of Authorship: Anterior Forms and Poetic Reconstruction from Wyatt to Shakespeare*, The New Historicism: Studies in Cultural Poetics, 9 (Berkeley, 1990), 35.

3   'Ephes. 4. 30. Grieve not the Holy Spirit' 1.19. Quoted from *The Works of George Herbert*, edited by F.E. Hutchinson, corrected edition (Oxford, 1945).

4   John Stevens, *Music and Poetry in the Early Tudor Court* (London, 1961), 207; and H.A. Mason, *Humanism and Poetry in the Early Tudor Period* (London, 1959), 168.

5   Stevens, pp. 207-208.

6   Baldassare Castiglione, *The Book of the Courtier*, translated by Sir Thomas Hoby [1561] (London, 1971), 70. Future references to this edition will be in parenthesis in the text.

7   Hoby describes Castiglione's '*sprezzatura*' as 'that verie arte, that appeareth not to be arte' (46).

8   Stevens, p. 282. The italics are his.

9   For Anne Boleyn's education, see E.W. Ives' *Anne Boleyn* (Oxford, 1986), esp. pp. 36 and 62 for her skill at music. See also Edward E. Lowinsky, 'A Music Book for Anne Boleyn' in *Florilegium Historiale: Essays presented to Wallace K. Ferguson*, edited by J.G. Rowe and W.H. Stockdale (Toronto, 1971), 160-235.

10   For the *frottola* see Gustave Reese, *Music in the Renaissance* (London, 1954), 156-165, and *The Renaissance. From the 1470s to the end of the 16th century*, edited by Iain Fenlon, Man and Music Series (Basingstoke and London, 1989), 145. James Haar remarks that 'the frottola repertory appears in part to be designed as a reflection of improvised song' in *Essays on Italian Poetry and Music in the Renaissance, 1350-1600* (Berkeley, 1986), 88. For the popularity of the *frottola* in France, see Daniel Heartz 'Les Gouts Réunis or The Worlds of the Madrigal and the Chanson Confronted' in: J. Haar (ed.), *Chanson and Madrigal 1480-1530*, (Cambridge, Mass., 1964), 118-120. The poet and virtuoso lutenist, Serafino d'Aquila, whose *strambotti* Wyatt often translates and imitates, had been one of the most renowned of the poet/performers at the court of Mantua where the *frottola* developed at the end of the fifteenth century. For discussions of Wyatt's possible debts to Italian musical settings, see especially two articles by Ivy L. Mumford, 'Sir Thomas Wyatt's Verse and Italian Musical Sources', *English Miscellany* 14 (1963): 9-26, and 'Petrarchism and Italian Music at the Court of Henry VIII' *Italian Studies* 26 (1971): 49-67.

11   The view of music, especially amorous music, as morally relaxing was widespread. See, for example, Sir Thomas Elyot, *The Book Named The Governor*, edited by S.E. Lehmberg (London, 1962), 22. See also John Hollander, *The Untuning of the Sky. Ideas of Music in English Poetry 1500-1700* (Princeton, 1961), 103-105.

12   For an illuminating discussion of the very different use made by a woman, of the conceit of a lute-playing, see Line Pouchard, 'Louis Labé in dialogue with her lute: silence constructing a poetic subject,' *History of European Ideas* 20 (January, 1995).

13   Hollander, p. 46.

14   For discussions of Wyatt's debt to Aretino, see Mason, *Humanism and Poetry* 206-215; the notes in Muir and Thomson's edition; Robert G. Twombly, 'Thomas Wyatt's paraphrase of the Penitential Psalms of David,' *Texas Studies in Literature and Language* 12 (1970): 345-380 passim; Rivkah Zim, *English Metrical Psalms. Poetry as Praise and Prayer 1535-1601* (Cambridge, 1987), 48-74, and Helen V. Baron, *Sir Thomas Wyatt's Seven Penitential Psalms: A Study of Textual and Source materials*, PhD dissertation (Cambridge, 1977), 221-235.

15   I quote the Italian from the Helen V. Baron's thesis (260), which gives extensive quotations from the sources alongside Wyatt's text. She uses the 1534 Venice

edition of *I Sette Salmi* which is, she argues, the edition Wyatt himself probably used.

16 On the eroticism of Aretino's vocabulary, see Twombly, p. 354 and Stephen Greenblatt, *Renaissance Self-Fashioning* (Chicago, 1980), 122-123. For Wyatt's, see Stephen Merriam Foley, *Sir Thomas Wyatt* (Boston, 1990), 88.

17 See, for example, Elyot, *The Governor*, p. 20 and Hollander, p. 239.

18 The relevant passage by Aretino is 'e percuotendo su le corde della cetera che egli si hauea riposta in grembo, la fece lampeggiare nella guisa che lampeggia l'oro al cui splendore accresce luce il lume; e feriti i suoi occhi dal lampo, sentì da quello confortarsi l'anima, tutta lieta per la contritione del core.' Quoted from Baron, p. 279.

19 St. John Chrysostom, quoted in *Source Readings in Music History. From Classical Antiquity to the Romantic Era*, selected and annotated by Oliver Strunk (London, 1952), 69-70. See also Hollander, p. 270.

20 Baron, p. 309. The English translation is my own.

21 Strunk, p. 70; Hollander, p. 270.

22 See the discussions of the multiple sources for Wyatt's psalms in Mason, pp. 206-221 and Baron, pp. 218-254.

2

SURREY'S PSALMS IN THE TOWER

W.A. SESSIONS

I

Of the major Psalm translations in Renaissance England, none has so dramatic an interplay of the sacred and the profane as those composed by Henry Howard, the earl of Surrey, in the Tower of London in December 1546 and January 1547.[1] He was writing them, it would appear, up until his beheading on January 19, 1547. Surrey was the last of the long procession of Henry VIII's executions, the old king himself dying within a week. After Surrey's sudden arrest by the king's halberdiers in the early afternoon of December 2, 1546, as he was emerging from dinner at Whitehall Palace, he had been secretly taken by boat and kept at Ely House.[2] Then on Sunday, December 12, he had been forced to march through Holburn to the Tower before large crowds who may have lamented aloud with him, according to the *Greyfriars Chronicle* observer (possibly an underground Franciscan monk).[3] Once in the Tower, Surrey did not cease to write during his last forty days, and the formal ingenuity of the inventor of the English sonnet, the heroic quatrain, and blank verse did not fail him here. In fact, it was probably in his solipsistic inscribing of fury and anger that Surrey could come to terms, if at all, with what was not only the greatest dynastic breakdown of the Tudor world but a personal disaster.

Once more in the Tower, as throughout his short life, Henry Surrey wrote out the tension and painful dialectic of his life as nobleman and poet, pouring into six psalms or paraphrases the effects of his constant examinations, trial and humiliation. Driving all these texts was the terror of annihilation that would soon come to him at age thirty in a matter of weeks, then days, then hours. Here, as in all his Biblical paraphrases at the end of his life, Surrey was still seeking the answer to the question he had translated from the second Book of Virgil's *Aeneid* a few years before, Aeneas' question of how to retell the story of disaster, the burning city, the night Troy fell: 'Who can express the slaughter of that night?'[4] To express his own slaughter in 1547, Surrey translates six psalms in the Tower, 31, 51, 73, 88, 55, and a final poem that takes its origin from a line of a psalm. At least four of these can be dated with some accuracy in these last days because two are addressed to figures at court who he thought might be instrumental in helping him; another has a direct reference to Surrey's entrapment and betrayal; and one is dated in a letter of forty years later to Elizabeth I by Surrey's son, Henry Howard, later James I's earl of Northampton and member of the Privy Council.

Surrey had earlier translated one other psalm, No. 8, that is as serene as the original text. He had also paraphrased during his last year of life five chapters from the Book of Ecclesiastes, taking his cue from Erasmus' edition in 1536 to develop an original series English poets had not tried. Yet all the major editors of Surrey from the Romantic Nott to Padelford and Jones and the biographer Casady agree that most of Surrey's Biblical paraphrases occurred in the last part of his life, even in his last weeks. All these Biblical paraphrases form, as a unit, the final phase in Surrey's literary career. He had moved from the Petrarchan texts to the Virgilian experiments and Wyatt elegy to these Biblical translations. As such, they are the first deliberate experiments that followed in the wake of two events: Wyatt's own spectacular achievement in his *Penitential Psalms*, the work for which Wyatt was primarily known, and the increasing Biblical and theological shift in the Henrician court toward reformed Christianity. As David Starkey has noted, by the 1540s the new Christians had won the day as the modish and innovative force in court circles, especially the circle around the Queen Catherine Parr (where even Surrey's younger brother Thomas had been reprimanded for being such an outright evangelical).[5] In that victory of the reformed Christianity, text and language became paramount: linguistic inscription became the new form of icon. The moment was ripe politically for the leading poet of England after Wyatt's death in 1542 to display his immense talent and translate the Bible. Thus, the first Biblical experiments were texts such as his even-tempered Psalm 8 and some of the Ecclesiastes poems, exercises that were like avant-garde piano pieces for a special salon, a politically powerful coterie.

But with his arrest, Surrey faced his own annihilation. New tactics were needed. In such desperation, what could conceivably impress the reformed Christians who had won was the Howard heir's mastery of the new English poetic line. It could serve the true God and its revealed instrument, the English state and its church, both metonymised in its Supreme Head. In this political strategy that involved Surrey's genius as text-maker, Surrey's Davidic persona (and in the Ecclesiastes paraphrases, the Solomonic) could be about as *au courant* as any English poet could become. Henry VIII had chosen, in fact, just such personae for himself, not only in Holbein's massive mural at Whitehall Palace of Solomon and Sheba and in stained glass windows at King's College Chapel (where Solomon's face is Henry's) but in the illuminations of Henry VIII's own last Psalter. As Pamela Tudor-Craig has shown in detail, the Davidic pose of Henry VIII fitted in with

Henry's imperial inscription of self and gradually became 'his only satisfactory archetype' dating generally from Henry's first use of the word 'conscience' in its Lutheran meaning. If in the 1530s Henry saw his Davidic pose as the rightful role of a crowned king of England and its empire, in the 1540s the inscriptions became more personal, as his marginalia and annotations of Biblical texts reveal. Especially in his notes on the actual Psalter (BL MS Royal 2 AXVI), the king is 'consistently self-congratulatory. The King aligns himself with the author at every turn' without the slightest trace of irony. He is, in this sense, in Tudor-Craig's analysis, 'a Psalter Christian—convinced of direct cause and effect between conduct and fate. God's enemies are his enemies—more, his enemies are God's'. Nowhere is this solipsism clearer than in the images of David as the king himself, whether harping with his fool Will Sommers or sitting in his bedroom reading and studying his Psalter (not mindlessly reciting as in the old religion) or, in a bizarre distortion, himself as little David with slingshot against a giant Goliath (looking amazingly like Charles V) or, most amazingly, of himself with arms outstretched and kneeling, his crown on the floor beside him. If in this last plate, Henry VIII identifies himself with King David in penitence, he is more clearly like Christ in agony in the Garden of Gethsemane, and an angel does come out of the heavens with a sword of justice for the suffering hero.[6]

Given the familiarity of such images to the court, Surrey's solipsistic Psalm translations had a precedent. For both Henrys, Tudor and Surrey (and the old Henry probably godfather to the younger), narcissism meant a collective and social gesture. Indeed, in Tyndale's Lutheran inscription of the king that Parliament had promulgated and all bishops but one had signed, Henry VIII was, at the least, Christ's intercessor for his people. In the same way, Surrey could only be, in his last days, a representative for a blood-nobility, an ancient class, and then, after his revolutionary elegy on Wyatt, a figuration for a new type of honour and nobility centered on the power of text-making. In both cases, the self could become an instrument of history beyond self. Its identity could only be social and communal.

After Surrey's arrest and his concomitant growing consciousness of annihilation, such inscription of self could only accelerate. As in the beginning of his career with his elegies on his beloved friend Henry Fitzroy, for which he had invented the English sonnet and the heroic quatrain, so now at the end of his career Surrey abandons the attempts at objectivity of his middle period (although even there personal suffering actualised most texts) and turns to solipsistic outbursts in the communal frame of the Davidic lyric. Thus, the psalms in the Tower reveal constant interplay between new verse forms, original personal music, and Surrey's own meditations on his own situation, his own version of Lutheran 'internalising' on a text. The result generates a painful dialectic between actualising self and history. The dialectic metonymises the energies of Surrey's whole life and earlier texts, and acts as closure to that life.

That dialectic was to express itself in a special music. It was typical of Surrey to realise that such a unique situation—his own—needed a new form, a more collective and less lyric voice. To dramatise the terror of his situation in the Tower of London, Surrey needed an English musical form that was both free and discursive. He found it in Wyatt's recent invention, poulter's measure (used by Wyatt to translate a passage from the *Aeneid* and reflecting perhaps Wyatt's own search for a long epic line in English). The succinct Latin of the Vulgate Psalms had given Surrey a resource in exact brevity that allowed for expansion, and his use of the Latin commentaries of the Lutheran humanist Campensis and the English translations of Coverdale and other English compilers of the new Christian Bible gave him the latest intellectual and linguistic directions. But Surrey wanted a special music that would release his rambling solipsistic energies. Thus, six of the eight psalm translations by Surrey are in his friend Wyatt's poulter's measure. This metre C.S. Lewis has described as 'labouring up a steep hill in bottom gear for the first line, and then running down the other side of the hill, out of control, for the second'.[7]

For Surrey and his audience, however, poulter's measure, the fourteen syllables in one line balancing in rhyme with the twelve syllables in the next, carried an inherent ballad measure (and would become, when broken into shorter lines, the basis for the popular 'common metre' of the English Christian hymn). Surrey obviously understood the desire of audiences, for the form of his translations and the texts themselves became very popular for the next fifty years. In fact, in just the summer before his execution, a remarkable act of transfer had occurred when one of Surrey's paraphrases from Ecclesiastes was used by the most famous new Christian martyr of that period. For her poem about her own terror, one which Bale published immediately in 1546, Anne Askew borrows a passage directly from Surrey (the manuscript lent to her in prison probably by her friends at court, the Dennys and the Catherine Parr circle). It describes the figure of an Apocalyptic tyrant that Surrey's translation had seemed to point towards Henry VIII, the killer of them both.

II

If the Davidic texts work for Surrey as a kind of diary during his own imprisonment, they also perform as political instruments in the self-inscribing
mode of the king himself and with the same royal dialectic of solipsism and
collectivity. Thus in four psalm texts that illustrate the tensions of a dramatised self trapped in history, Psalms 88 and 73 have dedicatory poems to
specific persons, Sir Antony Denny and George Blage, now powerful reformed Christians; Psalm 55 has direct attack on an unnamed but known
person, his betrayer Sir Richard Southwell; and the last psalm paraphrase
encircles chaotically the self, personal and collective, just before its annihilation.

It is probable that in mid December 1546 Surrey sent to Denny his
dedicatory poem and the paraphrase of Psalm 88. This figure of immense
power may earlier have expressed admiration for Surrey's texts; now in his
political fall, and especially just after he had entered the Tower, Surrey had
to manipulate that admiration for survival. Sir Anthony Denny controlled
the old king's privy chamber (and therefore the body of the king) and certainly knew by mid-December there was little or nothing he could do for
the Howard heir, whatever his personal disposition. Surrey knew—and this
was the basis of his hope—that Denny combined, like Henry's last queen, a
'sincere affection to God and his holy word' with a love of Erasmian humanism and ancient texts.[8] In short, Denny had that combination of humanism and power that drove the late Henrician and Edwardian courts, and
Surrey's Davidic text could thus serve, with its careful Erasmian equival-
ency of translation, as medium for his real message. Denny was the man
who in 1546 controlled, with his brother-in-law, Sir John Gates, the dying
King's 'dry stamp' for the royal signature. He could conceivably control
executions.

It is hardly surprising, therefore, that Surrey's poem to Denny acts as
as *apologia* (but, notably, not the outright confession legally required for
his execution). The work recounts an act of contrition. For this act, David,
the perfect warrior and knight and, simultaneously, the contrite composer of
the Penitential Psalms, was a model, says Surrey's poem to Denny. Because
of the reformation of the court, writing a Davidic text of contrition could
deliver an important political statement, especially if expressed with the
humanist wit of a syllogism:

> When reckless youth in an unquiet breast
> Set on by wrath, revenge and cruelty,
> After long war patience had oppressed,

> And justice wrought by princely equity;
> My Denny, then mine error, deep impressed,
> Began to work despair of liberty,
>   Had not David, the perfect warrior, taught
>   That of my fault thus pardon should be sought.   (56)

The one-sentence poem, in the musical form of a *strambotto* borrowed by both Wyatt and Surrey from the Petrarchan Seraphino, begins with a long subordinate clause of self-justification. Although the grammar is ambiguous, the centre and subject of the clause appear to be 'patience', and almost parenthetically, 'justice'. In Surrey's insistent contextualisation of this classical topos, patience has finally conquered 'after long war' the deliberately set-upon 'unquiet breast', a phrase that recalls Wyatt's only prose work, his 1528 *Plutarckes boke of the Quyete of mynde*. Furthermore, with patience comes recognition of the justice that has within it the equity or mercy of the king himself. This justice too has calmed down the 'reckless youth' who has been 'set on', and its power of equity remains a hope for his freedom. In the form of an Aristotelian enthymeme, the poem heads immediately, after the introductory major premise, to its conclusion, when, in an apostrophe, Surrey speaks directly: 'My Denny, then mine error, deep impressed' by these self-recognitions and weeks of humiliation and imprisonment, has begun to 'work' within the Howard heir the new Christian downside of 'despair of liberty'—in this case, despair of ever being freed from the Tower and his fear of annihilation. On the field and in the cave (as Wyatt's Penitential Psalms had powerfully and recently dramatised) David had fought to find internal patience in the midst of despair. Now the figure of David teaches as model *vir armatus*, Surrey's most recent role at court, and David teaches the former 'Lieutenant General' he should seek pardon. The upside of grace, in Davidic military-hero shape, thus returns at the end of the poem as a kind of encapsulated self-congratulation. The implicit question is asked: what can you do for a penitent noble 'youth' who is trapped?

The real question is whether Surrey achieves in his actual text of Psalm 88 the intention, stated in his prologue to Denny, of Davidic and public penitence. He does ask the Lord to 'Grant that the just request of this repentant mind / So pierce thine eares that in thy sight some favor it may find' (57: 3-4). Further, Rivkah Zim is probably right to see this poem as 'a particular prayer', a paraphrase where Surrey analogises more completely the subject and themes of his Biblical text to those of his own life.[9] But Surrey's images of repentance ring with a sound of rage beyond autobiography. The centre of Surrey's paraphrase emerges angrily with the question: 'Within this careful mind, burdened with care and grief, / Why dost thou not appear, Oh Lord, that shouldst be his relief?' (35-36) It is not only the precise linguistic talents of Surrey that are burdened but the sense of vocation and history he holds; he is overwhelmed by this loss of historical identity among the 'blind endured [hardened] hearts' where 'light of thy lively name / Cannot appear' because they 'can not judge the brightness of the same' (25-26). Surrey then evokes the consequences that such blindness to a poet and nobleman can bring:

> Nor blasted [blazoned] may thy name be by the mouth of those
> Whom death hath shut in silence so as they may not disclose.
> The lively voice of them that in thy word delight
> Must be the trump that must resound the glory of thy might.   (27-30)

III

As prefatory to his translation of Psalm 73, Surrey also wrote an *apologia*, this time to George Blage, Wyatt's close friend and fervent reformed Christian who had particularly disliked the conservatives (and therefore the Howards) who had recently tried to execute him. In what appears a shortened sonnet of twelve lines (a totally new form, as Ringler notes)[10], Surrey delivers a calculated exercise in sincerity, perhaps genuine in its traditional three-fold performance of contrition. Faced with the ever-increasing prospect of his death and the demise of his family, total uncertainty in every direction, Surrey is writing a text of survival. In fact, the whole of his Psalm 73 recapitulates Surrey's vacillations in the Tower between despair and hope. Because Surrey will use any device to dramatise the moral righteousness of his life and therefore his right to survive, here, indirectly but clearly, the common friend Wyatt is called on in this poem that Mason is right to see as catching the humble tone of Wyatt's own *strambotto* to Surrey.[11] Blage himself (and all the court readers) would have observed more than a modern reader like Mason, however: from its opening ship image to its final allusion to King David, Surrey's text to Blage evokes Wyatt and reminds Blage of another freer world where they had shared a friend. The poem dramatises a world of the noble voyaging knight, another questing Ulysses or Lancelot, who is now despairing until he is redeemed by a text, that is, by reading the Psalms. Although in his text contrite and new Christian enough, Surrey admits only 'error,' one more strategic than sinful. His new textualising of the Psalm will soon set any 'error' straight. Thus, if failure to find the proper 'port' finally 'bred despair' and from this, 'such

doubts did grow / That I gan faint, and all my courage fail,' now 'my
Blagge, mine error well I see, / Such goodly light King David giveth me'
(54).

The psalm that follows in Wyatt's invention of Poulter's Measure—
Psalm 72 in the Vulgate, Surrey's principal source for the ensuing paraphrase—can only be read as the most lucid text Henry Howard wrote about
his last days. In this clarity, language moves with abruptness and violent
motion. Linguistic shifts render the terrorising psychological situation that
has led to Surrey's entrapment; they point toward the death, the annihilation
of self, setting into his consciousness. For this reason, Hughey's analysis of
the freedom of Surrey's text, 'with so many interpolations of the poet's
thoughts, and so many departures from the strict sense of the Latin' leads to
her correct conclusion of the poem as a special self-invention.[12] Within
that invention, Surrey builds a more dichotomous structure than in any of
his sources. He contrasts the wicked to the suffering 'elect' whose gifts of
language may blazon forth God's 'secret works' in public and in social occasion, 'in sight of Adam's race' (55: 66). If penitence is built into the
basic poetic structure in the original Hebrew and Latin, it is dramatically
shifted here into a long solipsistic discourse. Here not only does the 'self-
righteousness' Hughey sees as the tenor of the poem dominate, but also the
distinct sense that, for this prisoner of the Tower, enough nobility still survives within himself.

The contrast of the wicked and 'elect' begins with generalisation—the
Lord gives 'graces plenteous' to 'such with pure intent as fix their trust in
thee' (1-2)—and develops logically into two bitter stages of negative
examples before a final affirming apotheosis of the poet-prophet. The
greatest of the negative examples is, as Hughey suggests, another portrait of
Henry VIII himself. The line 'Whose glutton cheeks sloth feeds so fat as
scant their eyes be seen' (14) evokes the last known portrait of Henry
Tudor, the drawing by the Flemish Cornelys Matsys.[13] The whole passage
finally indicts the Henrician court as that of Sardanapalus, the royal subject
of Surrey's most satiric sonnet, and here the monster

> Unto whose cruel power most men for dread are fain
> To bend and bow with lofty looks, whilst they vaunt in their reign.
> And in their bloody hands, whose cruelty doth frame
> The wailful works that scourge the poor without regard of blame,
> To tempt the living God they think it no offence,
> And pierce the simple with their tongues, that can make no defence.
>
> (55: 15-20)

Against such a figure, the speaker offers his own struggle in a world where he is isolated in total alienation: 'For I am scourged still, that no offence have done' and this is by 'wrath's children' (adapted from Campensis' 'ungodly') so that 'from my birth my chastising began' (31-1). Bewailing 'the woeful state wherein thy chosen stand', Surrey's persona finds 'no wit could pierce so far' God's 'holy dooms', the purpose in all this pain and slaughter, and he is confused 'Till I come to the holy place, the mansion of the just, / Where I shall see what end thy justice shall prepare' (34-39). Of all the new Christian diction that permeates this poem, the word 'chosen' appears as a deliberate sign to Blage and others of Surrey's sympathetic reformist ideology (the Vulgate 'filiorum tuorum' becomes Campensis' 'thyne owne chyldren' becomes Surrey's 'thy chosen'—a significant shift). The final vision in Surrey's poem leads to a scene of Apocalyptic revenge: 'Oh, how their ground is false and all their building vain! / And they shall fall, their pow'r shall fail, that did their pride maintain' (41-42). In this fantasy, the wicked men shall see 'their glory fade, thy sword of vengeance shall / Unto their drunken eyes in blood disclose their errors all' (45-46). This aggression leads to a dizzying height, the judgment passage of the sheep and goats from the Gospel of Matthew. It is transposed by Surrey, in a completely original image, into a bitter new key: 'And when their golden fleece is from their back yshorn, / The spots that underneath were hid, thy chosen sheep shall scorn' (47-48). Now the speaker/poet sees his own role in history. While the wicked who 'for dread or gain ... thy name refuse' and 'perish with their golden gods, that did their heart seduce' (61-62), language will save, says Surrey in his closure. This new poet-prophet's 'word' will redeem him[14]:

> Where I that in thy word have set my trust and joy,
> The high reward that 'longs thereto shall quietly enjoy.
>   And my unworthy lips, inspired with thy grace,
> Shall thus forspeak thy secret works in sight of Adam's race.   (63-66)

IV

For the more directly emotional translation of Psalm 55, Surrey abandoned the melody of poulter's measure and used a blank verse, but of hexameters. The occasion originated a new form in English poetry. Thus, Surrey's was the first use in English of a consciously imitated classical alexandrine he may have already heard and read at Fontainebleau.[15] What Surrey sought in such a steady unrhymed line of twelve syllables, recalling Virgil's own prosody, is a Roman inscription of history found in the imperial narratives of Suetonius and Tacitus: catastrophe, terror, and human evil. However implicit the anguish in the original psalm, the effect in Surrey's text represents now his own reduction not just at court but in the scale of being. He and his family, the Howard dynasty, are going to be annihilated. Thus, Surrey begins his translation of Psalm 55 with direct apostrophe and petition 'Give ear to my suit, Lord, fromward hide not thy face' (53: 1). In drumming end-stopped lines that also typify his blank verse, Surrey combines alliterative Anglo-Saxon diction, strong verbs, and a terrifying combination of abstract subjects with concrete modifiers. They all render the basic image of the trapped animal:

> My foes they bray so loud, and eke threpe on so fast,
> Buckled to do me scathe, so is their malice bent.
> Care pierceth my entrails and travaileth my spirit;
> The grisly fear of death environeth my breast;
> A trembling cold of dread clean overwhelm'th my heart.   (3-7)

In this 'cold of dread', Surrey recognises it was not his 'declared foe'—Seymour or Henry VIII himself?—that 'wrought' him 'all this reproach'. All this 'harm so looked for, it weigheth half the less' (19-20). Surrey had become cunning; he knew how to fight such a 'foe'. 'For though mine en'mies hap had been for to prevail, / I could have hid my face from venom of his eye' (21-22). Rather, his betrayal came from a beloved friend, in Surrey's Chaucerian oxymoron, 'a friendly foe' (23). This figure has been traditionally identified with Sir Richard Southwell, who in the very year that Holbein had painted him at age thirty-three was sent to the Tower by Cromwell to take away all the books from Thomas More so that More would have nothing left.

Such betrayal had marked all of Surrey's last days, and in his paraphrase Surrey circles round and around this personal treason. The circling builds to the disjunction of the last lines and a final breakdown in the language itself. A closure almost as painful as that of his last poem takes the form of the original Latin hexameter in the Vulgate that Surrey took as the psalmist's cry for help. Although the ending in Latin does not transmute Surrey's fury into the contrition demanded by fastidious later readers, it does offer a solace. Indeed, the closure of Psalm 55 puts its trust as much in Latin as in God. Latin, the humanist source of reality, will heal in a rhythm where the English alexandrines have not been able to control or reduce the rising fury. The Latin Surrey uses at the end becomes a final resource that cannot itself end the violence but can universally express it, however momentarily.

V

Surrey's very last text—a fragment that resembles a Petrarchan sonnet—
carries the same prophetic self-fashioning and rage. It is far from the
patience that Surrey as Davidic poet had described for himself to Denny. In
fact, this last poem ends more like an incoherent scream than anything else.
The solipsistic Latin title, 'Bonum est mihi quod humiliasti me' is taken
almost verbatim from the Vulgate Psalm 118: 71-72 (It is good for me that
you have humiliated me), its next line—73 in the Psalm—continuing with
'because I may learn your justifications'. In fact, the title of this poem
marks the texts as Surrey's last, as Surrey's second son, the long-surviving
Henry, earl of Northampton, is at pains to indicate.[16]

If the title of the poem reflects Surrey's intent, the progression of the
poem reveals no such humiliation. Surrey becomes more and more enraged
as he moves to his end. At the beginning of this last Psalm paraphrase, he
may announce:

> The storms are past, these clouds are overblown,
> And humble cheer great rigor hath repressed;
> For the default is set a pain foreknown,
> And patience graft in a determined brest. (42: 1-4)

This way of patience may indeed lead in the text to Cicero's famous description of the noble Scipio Africanus in *De officiis* (III, i), a crucial text
for English Renaissance aristocrats, and offer another self-definition (and
self-deception):

> And in the heart where heaps of griefs were grown
> The sweet revenge hath planted mirth and rest;
> No company so pleasant as mine own. (5-7)

Surrey may even remark how 'Thraldom at large hath made this prison
free' (8) in a poem built on the basic cultural image of the imprisoned Boe-
thius lamenting and then accepting his shameful condition. Surrey may
even echo Aeneas's cry of encouragement to his desperate survivors 'forsan
et haec olim meminisse iuvabit' (I, 203) in 'Danger well past remembered
works delight' (9). But such serenity can barely make it through ten lines.
By the closure of the poem (and thus of his life and all his texts) Surrey
launches into a final gesture of outrage.

In this absolute last moment of any Surrey text, Henry Howard looks
into a mirror, not surprisingly. Obsessed with the historical roles subjectiv-

ity as deep as his must play, he recognises his loss, 'the curelesse wound that bleedeth night and day' (13). If a Boethian discourse is behind such self-discovery, Surrey's use of the mirror, a logical theatrical prop for such medieval discourse, gave a new Renaissance inscription as Sackville's *Induction* to the *Mirrour for Magistrates* soon showed in its borrowing from Surrey. This mirror of Surrey's last text thus reveals the continually bleeding wound of intimate self in a history where the Howard loss and the possible extinction of the Howard line in himself is metonymic for the disappearance of English blood-nobility itself. For Surrey, that loss of blood signals the death of hope for any renewed English culture or higher new civilisation: 'To spill that blood that hath so oft been shed / For Britain's sake, alas, and now is dead' (16-17). Instead of despairing or smashing the mirror as Shakespeare's Richard II does, Surrey is simply angered by what he sees. Looking, Surrey compares himself to another courtier, probably his betrayer Southwell, whom he had challenged at his trial, 'a wretch that hath no heart to fight' (15), as the Howards had fought with 'heart' and honour for England for over two centuries. The young poet still cannot comprehend why this should be happening to himself: 'To think, alas, such hap [success] should granted be' to the 'wretch' and to the new society created by Henry VIII, the 'thraldom at large'.

Such final anger before the oblivion of self and family, of cultural vision, carries no nostalgic resignation. Above all, it offers no leap to transcendence, no prayer of any kind. Whatever else their sorrowing may be, Surrey's lines witness to a pure defiance before oblivion. He is angry that loss will mean not only obliteration of personal texts like the Petrarchan sonnets he and Wyatt had already adapted into English but of communal and national texts, like his translations of Virgil, a new heroic line. Precisely these texts would have conveyed what Surrey's *renovatio* of English nobility might have been—if only he could not disappear but live, first, as the new Duke of Norfolk, the possible Protector of the new young King Edward, the new Earl Marshal, head of the College of Arms, succeeding his father, and then as the master of a new complex humanist language, the maker of the Virgilian epic in his time and place and its English heroic metre. With such making, he would have redefined the whole nature of nobility, revealing the honour of the poet that he had himself defined in his elegy on Wyatt. His own 'blood'—the blood of the poet as well as of the Howards—had prepared him for that role as leader of a new civilisation like the promised Renaissance he had viewed unfolding at Fontainebleau.

Indeed, as Surrey's last poem reveals, this shed blood—'the cureless wound that bleedeth day and night'—is his last testament, the historical testament of a poet as well as of a Howard. In an irony of textuality, Surrey's psalms would continue to 'bleed'. They would set the stage for new English psalms, inscriptions of self and historical vocation by Sidney or Southwell's own grandson Robert Southwell (to be canonised in 1972 like his friend Philip Howard, the earl of Arundel, Surrey's grandson) or by Donne or Herbert. Following Wyatt, Surrey is the first to reveal how the new Erasmian and Lutheran method of 'internalising' on a text can generate an utterly original text of self in history. Furthermore, Surrey shows the self as representative of his time and history because of that very 'internalised' linguistic text. The result was that English lyric poetry had found a new voice and a new genre. Most remarkable of all, this discovery and these texts that 'bleedeth day and night' originated in the Tower as the young poet faced his own annihilation, his own loss in time.

Notes

1   The essay by Susan Brigden, 'Henry Howard, Earl of Surrey, and the "Conjured League"' *The Historical Journal* 37, 3 (1994): 507-537, should be read in tandem with this essay. It appeared after this essay was edited, but its meticulous historical detailing supports, I believe, my argument. It provides a full context for political forces at work as Surrey wrote his last texts.

2   This account is based on the details in *Chronicle of King Henry VIII of England Being a Contemporary Record of Some of the Principal events of the Reigns of Henry VIII. and Edward VI. Written in Spanish by an Unknown Hand*, translated and edited by Martin A. Sharpe Hume (London, 1889), 144. The authenticity of the *Chronicle* has been questioned, but Hume's lengthy introduction, with its discussion of the possibility of a Spanish observer at the Tudor court during this period and the provenance of the manuscript in the Spanish archives in Madrid, has the effect of preventing any easy dismissal of the *Chronicle*'s prolific detail, whatever its flamboyance or the tendentiousness of the observer. Furthermore, the eminent historian James Gairdner helped in the preparation of the Victorian edition for the press, an act that may not imply an imprimatur but certainly one that could have been refused an unreliable text. For the last days of Surrey, the *Chronicle* remains one of the best guides, and Hume notes (142) in his own continuation of the cult of the earl of Surrey: 'The barbarous sacrifice of the noble Surrey, the last effort of the dying despot, is told here with many small touches which reveal the eye-witness or deeply interested spectator.'

3   The anonymous figure wrote down a single entry for the day in the strangely continuous *Chronicle of Grey Friars* of this period, edited by J.G. Nichols (London, 1852), 57: 52. Just who this observer was—a former Franciscan grey-robed monk (their great monastery had been quite near Ely House) forced underground, as were many formerly cloistered men and women when a decade earlier Henry VIII had abolished religious orders, or someone simply keeping a record—is not clear. 'This yere the XIIth day of December', the observer writes, 'the dewke of Norffoke and the yearle of Sorre hys sonne were comyttyd unto the tower of London:

and the dewke went be watter from the Lorde chaunseler's place in Holborne, and soo downe unto the wattersyde and so be [by] watter unto the tower; and hys sonne the yerle of Sorre went thorrow the cytte of London makynge grete lamentacion.' The grammar of the terse final phrase caps the episode of the forced march of shame. The ambiguous reference of the single participle marks the intensity of the event. If Surrey were himself lamenting, was it with anger and fury, an unPuritan hero like Achilles bellowing on the beaches before Troy? Or was it the outcry of 'the most proud foolish boy in England', as one of Henry's new religious deans had said about Surrey in 1539, finally confronted with the results of his dangerous and silly game-playing? It was certainly not silent suffering. Words and sounds poured out loud enough to still a holiday crowd or at least be heard above it. Or does the phrase, closer to a French or Latin placement, refer to the crowds of the City of London? Is it possible they were themselves captured, as Bapst writing his 19th-century *belle-époque* biography of Surrey believes, by the sight of this descendant of Plantagenet kings reduced to such injustice, a scene of dishonour increased in Bapst's phrase 'par ses allures de grand seigneur ... de temperament si chevaleresque' (by his allure of the grand aristocrat ... with a temperament so chivalric)? Whatever the ambiguity of language, the event did not pass unnoticed by the people of London. There is also a record by Antony Antony, another mysterious observer of Henry VIII's last days (Bodleian Library Delta 264). Antony is less ambiguous: both Surrey and his father were locked up in the Tower by four o'clock that Sunday afternoon, that is, by nightfall in the northern European winter.

4   Poem 58, line 464. I use for this essay a manuscript edition of Surrey's poems being completed by William McGaw and forthcoming from Oxford University Press. I list the poem and the page number as McGaw gives it.

5   David Starkey, *The Reign of Henry VIII: Personalities and Politics* (London, 1985), 141-142.

6   Pamela Tudor-Craig, 'Henry VIII and David' in Daniel Williams (ed.), *Early Tudor England: Proceedings of the 1987 Harlaxton Symposium* (Woodbridge, 1989), 191; 196. The use of 'conscience' can be found in Hall's *Chronicle* (New York, 1968), 754. Tudor-Craig appends to her essay plates from Henry VIII's Psalter as well as a plate from the lid of Henry's reading desk in which the painter made Henry an armed Roman soldier in the exactly the same pose as Michelangelo's David.

7   C.S. Lewis, *English Literature in the Sixteenth Century Excluding Drama* (Oxford, 1954), 233.

8   The phrase is from the entry on Denny in the *Dictionary of National Biography*.

9   Rivkah Zim, *English Metrical Psalms: Poetry As Praise and Prayer, 1535-1601* (Cambridge and New York, 1987), 88-96.

10   Cited in Charles Willison Eckert, 'The Poetry of Henry Howard, Earl of Surrey' (doctoral dissertation, Washington University, 1960), 51.

11   H. A. Mason, *Humanism and Poetry in the Early Tudor Period* (London, 1959), 160.

12   *The Arundel-Harington Manuscript of Tudor Poetry*, edited by Ruth Hughey (Columbus, 1960), 2: 106.

13   British Museum Prints 1868-8-22-2394.

14 As proof that Surrey is envisioning such a role for himself, a comparison of this final passage with the paraphrase of Campensis, itself elaborate when compared with the simple Vulgate inscription that it is good to trust the Lord, shows the first stage of such a role that Surrey would make his own: 'Wherefore when I had persuaded my selfe that it shulde be very profytable for me to come in to fauoure wyth the true God I set all my confydence in the Lorde God, trustynge that in tyme to come he wolde gyue me lycence to wrytte those dyuerse and most perfyte workes whyche he hath contynually in hande' (sig. K4r). Taking Campensis' ideas a step further, Surrey becomes the voice of God.

15 As Hughey notes, pp. 429-430, within a year, the tutor of King Edward, Sir John Cheke, the teacher of Roger Ascham, used this same metre in four poems, the first and fourth as elegies. The first was the first English elegy on Surrey (I accept Hughey's argument that Surrey is the subject), and proves how soon Surrey's own manuscript passed through court circles to act as a model for other humanists and new Christians. Cheke is the model humanist and a proper authorising source for the fame of Surrey. The extraordinarily ascetic Edwardian portrait of Cheke depicts him holding in his right hand two such manuscript volumes and in his left, a roll. In front of his massive black gown (that contrasts with the long red beard and rectangular white face) is a table with a large book on it and, in it, a passage marked by a piece of paper. In the background, to Cheke's right, is a dawning light and in front, brilliantly outlined, an austere Doric column. The founder of modern Greek studies in England (at Cambridge), Cheke adapts, eulogising Surrey, a classical metre to his own English. Surrey has shown him the way. Even the strong Anglo-Saxon language of Surrey's poem may have influenced Cheke's own plain-style adaptations and the theory of language that Cheke insisted on in his preface to Sir Thomas Hoby's translation of Castiglione's *The Book of the Courtier*: diction should be 'pure, unmixt and unmangeled with borowing of other tunges' (Baldwin, I, 428-431). The length and gravity of Surrey's alexandrines gave Cheke the right example for such diction, for Surrey's long lines balanced rhythmically with a diction constructed on monosyllables and alliterative effects.

16 Bodleian Library MS 2958. Arch. A. 170, f. 6r. Henry Howard, earl of Northampton, says in the Dedicatory Epistle of his *Dutiful Defense of the Royal Regimen of Woman*, written to Elizabeth, his father's second cousin: this poem was 'the last thinge that he [his father] wrote before his ende.'

3

CONTRAFACTA AND THE GUDE AND GODLIE BALLATIS

A.A. MACDONALD

Throughout the history of Christian verse the technique of *contrafactum* has been one of the more important of creative resources. This technique implies that the poet takes an already existing secular work as the starting-point for his own composition, removes from that earlier work any elements that might be judged to be in conflict with Christian faith or morality, and gives to it instead a clear Christian cast. The resulting work thenceforth counts in its own way as an original composition. A *contrafactum*, therefore, may be considered as a special kind of parody, in that it is dependent for its existence upon a prior work of art; however, unlike most parodies, it does not aim to generate amusement at the expense of either the original work or the original author. A *contrafactum*, rather, aims to subvert, and ultimately to replace, its model by imitating it closely and exploiting its most attractive features. In the case of lyric verse, the process of conversion normally entails that the melody of the original song will be retained; as a consequence, the structure (and not infrequently even the very number) of the stanzas of the original will be respected, involving the retention of as many as possible of the original phrases and rhymes. As a genre, then, the *contrafactum* is both parasitic and antithetic in its relation towards its model, paradoxically displaying resemblance and difference in equal measure.

Before all else, the *contrafactum* is essentially a derivative kind of composition, of which the express function is to supplant that of an original work, with which it shares a formal identity. The *contrafactum* employs the strategies of both paraphrase and generic extension: it is more than paraphrase, however, in that it changes not only the outward dress of words, but also the inward structure of thought; the *contrafactum*, moreover, goes further than merely developing the possibilities inherent in the genre of its model, since it usually implies a shift into a new genre while still clinging to features of that model. One witnesses this, for example, when a courtly lyric expressing the honour of an earthly mistress is transformed into a lyric in praise of Our Lady. One of the earliest collections of English lyric verse, BL Harley MS 2253, contains a pair of such poems, sacred and profane, and also several specimens where the generic and stylistic conventions of courtly love are applied to religious ends.[1] The poetic *contrafactum* may be in a language other that that of its exemplar, although this does not have to be the result of translation. Where the *contrafactum* is primarily intended to supplant its model, the new words do not need to show *any* connection with that original, but may be completely new. In such cases the resemblance remains exclusively at the level of form, and does not impinge upon content.

The *contrafactum* tends to be the child more of will rather than of inspiration. The religious controversies of the sixteenth and seventeenth centuries gave a powerful impetus to this kind of composition—though the *contrafactum* is by no means an invention of the age of Reformation: indeed, a multitude of examples might be given, from both before and after this very productive period. One famous specimen from medieval English verse is this thirteenth-century lyric:

> Sumer is icumen in —
> lhudë sing, cuccú!
> Groweþ sed and bloweþ med
> and springþ þe wudë nu.
> Sing, cuccú![2]

This secular song has become a classic of English literature—so much so that Ezra Pound even composed a parody of his own upon it.[3] This twentieth-century work cannot be considered as a *contrafactum*: it depends for its effect of humour on a thorough awareness of the medieval original, and it can thus hardly be said to be artisitcally autonomous. Almost totally forgotten is the medieval Latin lyric, 'Perspice, Christicola', intended to be sung to the music now familiar from 'Sumer is icumen in'. Since the Latin and the English lyrics are quite independent of each other in terms of subject-matter, one might of course wonder which was the chicken and which the egg. The most recent editors, Dobson and Harrison, are convinced that the Latin version is the earlier; this is important, since it indicates that, despite the general sketch of the normal genesis of the *contrafactum* given above, it is also possible for a religious poem to serve as the model for a secular counterpart.[4]

Transformation in this direction, however, is much less common than in the opposite direction. It is noticeable that, in the case of 'Sumer is icumen in', it is only the external features of form (stanza and music) that are adopted for the vernacular song. Given the privileged position of religion in the culture of the Middle Ages, it is difficult to imagine that a poet would compose a *contrafactum* in order deliberately to subvert the message of a religious lyric; that, however, does not mean that a good tune might not be conveniently taken over for a new purpose. While a simplistic definition of the *contrafactum* as 'new words to an old tune' contains a modicum of truth, it is also clearly inadequate, since it leaves out of consideration the possibilities of: 'old words to a new tune', 'new words for old words' (where there never was any tune, or where the presumed original music no longer survives), and 'old words adapted to express new thoughts' (with or without music).

Since the essence of the *contrafactum* as a literary and cultural phenomenon is the relationship between the original text and the revision thereof, it is hardly surprising that *contrafacta* should to some extent betray their models. If we leave out of account here the purely musical connections, the verbal trace-elements can be of several kinds: secular-sounding phrases in religious poems; echoes of Catholic verse in Protestant hymns; medieval turns of expression in Renaissance lyrics. With complete ease the *contrafactum* can disregard incompatibilities of genre, ideology and time. Indeed, this is one of the greatest points of interest for the student of *contrafacta*: where the critic can discover which earlier poem served as the starting-point for the *contrafactum*, he can gain an interesting insight into at least some aspects of the process of poetic composition.

The above remarks are preliminary to a discussion of one sixteenth-century anthology of verse. The latter is known by various names: *A Compendious Book of Godly and Spiritual Songs*; the 'Dundee Psalms'; the 'Wedderburn Psalms'; and, most commonly, the *Gude and Godlie Ballatis* (*GGB*).[5] This book, printed at Edinburgh, first appeared in 1565, and was reissued with additions and some deletions in 1567, and with other additions and deletions in 1578. Thereafter the contents remained stable, and there were reprints in 1600 and 1621.[6] There was also at least one other edition, of which only an undated fragment survives; the latter may represent the edition alleged to have been published in 1597.[7] The collection is generally said to be the work of the brothers John, Robert and James Wedderburn, who came from Dundee. It is possible that some, if not all, of the poems in this colection circulated in Scotland in manuscript form even as early as the 1540s: John Knox, in his *Historie of the Reformatioun in Scotland*, refers to one item in connection with the arrest of George Wishart, in 1546.[8]

There are essentially four sections within the *Gude and Godlie Ballatis*. First, there is a catechism, in prose and then in verse: this contains fundamental religious texts such as the Ten Commandments, the Creed, the Lord's Prayer, the Sacraments of Baptism and Communion. Second, there come the 'Spiritual sangis'—a collection beginning with Biblically-based poems on the topic of sin and redemption (including verse paraphrases of the stories of the Prodigal Son and of Dives and Lazarus) and concluding with poems on the Passion, Nativity, Nunc Dimittis and Resurrection. Third, there follow 'Certane ballatis of the Scripture', another sequence of religious lyrics less directly based upon the Bible. The fourth and final division of the book contains the 'Psalmes of Dauid, with vther new plesand ballatis'—a selection of some twenty psalms and twice as many lyrics.[9]

The literary and aesthetic assumptions fundamental to the *Gude and Godlie Ballatis* are boldly announced in the Prologue:

> Paule, writand to the Colloss*ians* in his thrid Chap*ter* sayis, let the word of God dwel in yow plenteouslie in all wisdo*me*, teiching and exhorting your awin selfis with Psalmes, *and* hymnis, and spirituall sa*n*gis, quhilkis haue lufe to God *and* fauouris his word. We haue heir ane plane Text, that the word of God incressis plenteouslie in vs, be singing of the Psalmes and spiritual sangis, and that speciallie ama*n*g young personis, and sic as ar not exercisit in the Scriptures, for thay wil soner consaue the trew word nor quhen thay heir it sung in Latine, the quhilks thay wait not quhat it is. Bot quhen they heir it sung into thair vulgar tou*n*g or singis it thame selfis with sweit melodie, then sal thay lufe thair Lord God with hart and minde, and cause them to put away baudrie *and* vnclene sangis. Prays God. Amen.[10]

The enterprise of evangelisation is clear. The compilers intended that a mass audience of theologically naive people should assimilate the word of God as this was packaged and presented by the supporters of the Protestant Reformation; to make the religious message easier and more palatable, Latin words were to be replaced by the vernacular, and familiar tunes were to be retained. Attractive melodies were the unavoidable means to the doctrinal and moral end.[11]

Despite this initial declaration, there is much in the *Gude and Godlie Ballatis* which one would not wish to classify as *contrafactum*. In this context one might mention the vernacular psalms contained in the book, and also the Scots translations from German, French, and English. An example from German would be Martin Luther's *Vom himel hoch da kom ich her*, rendered as *I come from heuin to tell*.[12] From French we have a poem by one Mathieu Malingre, native of Normandy and subsequently pastor in Neuchatel, in French Switzerland, *O! prebstres, prebstres*; this is rendered as *Preistis, Christ beleue*.[13] One of the notable facts about the *Gude and Godlie Ballatis* is that it contains the earliest version, in any form of English, of the fifteenth-century macaronic (German and Latin) lyric, *In dulci jubilo*.[14] Scotticisations of English poems—such as those by Myles Coverdale, Bible-translator and bishop of Exeter—also fall into the category of translations rather than of *contrafacta*, since the final products, despite the necessary adjustments for language (often merely of spelling), differ from the originals only in a superficial way.[15]

One would also have to exclude from the category of *contrafacta* those poems which lack any earlier models; such poems demand to be considered as original, Scottish lyrics. Unfortunately, the mere absence of a known exemplar is no guarantee that the Scottish poem is not a *contrafactum*: as always, any argument *ex silentio* is dangerous. The poem, 'Rycht sore opprest I am with panis smart', together with certain others which accompany it in the collection, was said by the Victorian editor, A.F. Mitchell, to be 'either original, or ... derived from some English or Scottish source unknown to [him]'.[16] Subsequent research has shown that the latter possibility is indeed the case, and the secular words have been printed by Helena Shire from Robert Edwardes' musical manuscript, of the seventeenth century.[17] Also to be disregarded is a poem where drastic remodelling of the known source quite transcends what one normally understands by *contrafactum*. An example is the 'carrail contrair idolatrie', beginning 'We suld beleue in God abufe'; this poem of five short stanzas, each of four lines, is a reworking of three stanzas from the lengthy, fifteenth-century English allegorical and encyclopaedic poem, *The Court of Sapience*.[18]

A *contrafactum*, as we have defined it above, is intended to supplant its model. In the case of one religious lyric included in the 1567 edition of the *Gude and Godlie Ballatis*, however, the original secular poem was—perhaps by oversight—preserved on the final page of the book. For the student of the *contrafactum* such an thing is *gefundenes Fressen*. The original lines:

> Welcum, Fortoun, welcum againe,
> The day and hour I may weill blis,
> Thow hes exilit all my paine,
> Quhilk to my hart greit plesour is.
>
> For I may say, that few men may,
> Seing of paine I am drest,
> I haif obtenit all my pay,
> The lufe of hir that I lufe best. [etc.]

were adapted to give the following:

Welcum, Lord Christ, welcum againe,
My joy, my confort, and my bliss,
That culd me saif from hellis paine,
Bot onlie thow nane was, nor is.

Thairfoir, I may rycht bauldlie say,
Geue Christ, the quhilk hes me redrest,
Be on my syde, quhilk hes done pay
My ransoun, quha can me molest? [etc.][19]

The printer's *faux pas*, amusing to the modern reader, is interesting, since it demonstrates that both the profane and the sacred versions (at least of this poem, but very possibly of more) were present in the workshop at the time when the book was set up in print. Furthermore, it would seem that not every poem was destroyed immediately after conversion to a religious lyric took place. The Church authorities, however, were less than amused by this oversight, and the General Assembly ordered all copies of the book to be called in, in order that the offending poem might be deleted.[20] This ordinance, incidentally, shows that it remained the intention that the printed copies should be sold. It is therefore highly ironic that the only extant copy of this 1567 edition of the *Gude and Godlie Ballatis* should be one which survives in the uncensored state. Perhaps the politically correct copies were so popular as to be read to pieces. 'Welcum, Lord Christ', like a true *contrafactum*, adheres to the stanza pattern of its model, and even maintains the rhymes wherever possible; there is no doubt that it could be sung to the original tune. Even the pattern of thought is not dissimilar: where the secular poet rejoices at the beneficent effect of the presence of his beloved, and can want for no more, the religious poet rejoices at the uniquely valid sacrifice of Christ, in which he reposes all his faith.

Some of the *contrafacta* in the *Gude and Godlie Ballatis* betray their origins through the repetition of the opening lines of the respective secular poems; this was, of course, a convenient way of indicating the tune to which the new poems were to be sung. On one page we find what is obviously a *Ständchen*-like song:

Quho is at my windo, quho, quho?
Go from my windo, go go.
Quha callis thair, sa lyke ane stranger,
Go from my windo, go.[21]

After this enigmatic opening, it emerges that it is the sinner who is outside, like the suitor in many a love-poem, and he is calling to Christ to let him in. Later in the poem, however, the words spoken by Christ tend towards a different idiom, and adopt the reproachful tone common in the medieval lyric genre of the 'complaint of Christ':

> Remember thy sin, and als my smart,
> And als for the quhat was my part,
> Remember the speir that thirlit my hart,
> And in at my dure thow sall go.

The poem, however, concludes with a suggestive linking of the imagery of entering heaven with that of being admitted to the chamber of the beloved:

> I ask nathing of the thairfoir,
> Bot lufe for lufe to lay in stoir,
> Gif me thy hart, I ask no moir,
> And in at my dure thow sall go.

The abruptness of the opening of another item in the collection is altogether startling, in terms of the conventions of the religious lyric:

> Johne, cum kis me now,
> Johne, cum kis me now,
> Johne, cum kis me by and by,
> And mak no moir adow.[22]

These are, of course, the first lines of the relevant secular model, and the *contrafactum* immediately thereafter embarks upon its message concerning the Atonement:

> The Lord thy God I am,
> That Johne dois the call,
> Johne representit man
> Be grace celestiall.

The poet makes a brave attempt to harness to his purpose the erotic elements of the original ('This kis of faith will justifie the'), but the result is not uniformly happy:

> My prophetis call, my preichouris cry,
> Johne cum kis me now, [...]

Several secular versions of this same song are known, and there also exists
a satirical, political parody, quoted by Knox in reference to the Catholic
forces which in 1546 recaptured the castle of St Andrews from the
Reformers:

> Preasts content you now,
> Preasts content you now,
> For Normond and his cumpany
> Hes filled the galayis fow.[23]

For its part, the poem, With huntis vp, with huntis vp', is a *contrafactum* of
an English hunting song dating from the time of Henry VIII (a different
religious *contrafactum* of this poem, by John Thorne, appears in BL Addit.
MS 15233). The Scottish poet applies his words with gusto:

> The hunter is Christ, that huntis in haist,
> The hundis ar Peter and Paull,
> The Paip is the fox, Rome is the rox,
> That rubbis vs on the gall.[24]

It is difficult to resist the rhythmic force of such a poem, which is eminent-
ly suited to the task of spreading religious propaganda.

The *contrafacta* in the *Gude and Godlie Ballatis* are not always so
successful, however. Sometimes they only work as long as they closely
follow their models—as is the case with a lyric mentioned above:

> Rycht sore opprest I am with panis smart,
> Baith nicht and day makand my woful mone
> To God, for my misdeid, quhilk hes my hart
> Put in sa greit distres with wo begone;
> Bot gif he send me sum remeid anone,
> I list not lang my lyfe for till indure,
> Bot to the deide bowne, cairfull creature.[25]

The courtly-love connotations of many of the terms employed in this godly
lyric are clear enough, and comparison with the secular original confirms
the impression:

> Richt soir opprest am I with paines smart,
> Both night and day makand my wofull moan
> To Venus quein, that ladie hes my heart
> Put in to so gret distres with wo begone.
> Bot gif that she send me remeid anone
> I list no langer my lyf till induir,
> Bot to the death bound cairfull creatour.[26]

Venus has had to make way for the one true God, and the pain of frustrated love for that of frustrated devotion. But there are dangerous limitations to the points of equivalence: for example, a Christian is not expected despairingly to long for death, especially since he ought to recall that he is justified through the sacrifice of the Son of God. Again, unlike the courtly lover, the sinner cannot hope to 'deserve' mercy; in any case the mercy in question is very different. In this *contrafactum*, the quality of the writing—within its necessary constraints—may nevertheless be said to be rather successful; but this obtains only up to the point at which the poet ponderously attempts a stanza all of his own, for which, significantly, he has no secular model:

> Remember, Lord, my greit fragillitie,
> Remember, Lord, thy Sonnis Passioun,
> For I am borne with all iniquitie,
> And can not help my awin saluatioun;
> Thairfoir is my justificatioun
> Be Christ, quhilk cled him with my nature,
> To saif from schame all sinfull creature.[27]

Such halting rhythms prompt one to conclude that the requirements of the *contrafactum* could actually benefit the less gifted versifier.

When one compares the religious verse of the *Gude and Godlie Ballatis* with that of the Scottish poets of the pre-Reformation period, one is struck by several things. First, many traditional topics are no longer available for poetry: this applies most obviously, but not exclusively, to verse referring to Mary, who becomes a *persona non grata*. Second, there is a perceptible simplification in style and rhetoric: gone, for example, is such a formal device as alliteration, used in a Marian lyric by the fifteenth-century poet Sir Richard Holland (contained in the *Buke of the Howlat*), and also used for the invocation of God's blessing at the opening of the play, *Ane Satire of the Thrie Estaitis*, by the sixteenth-century poet, Sir David Lindsay of the Mount.[28] Third, the elaborate stanza-forms favoured by William Dunbar and his contemporaries of the age of James IV (1488-1513) are no longer in evidence, and the abiding impression is of a marked decline in the level of poetic artistry. It is perhaps unreasonable to expect many courtly graces in the lyrics of the Protestants, since during the personal reign of the Catholic Mary Queen of Scots Protestant verse was of necessity anti-courtly. In any case, whereas the religious poetry of Dunbar and his fellows was often honorific in tone, that of the *Gude and Godlie Ballatis*—with the exception of some of the translated items—is characteristically penitential, moralistic, satirical and propagandistic.[29]

Rosemary Woolf has praised the *Gude and Godlie Ballatis* for the way in which the collection transmits an echo of the popular devotional idiom of the later Middle Ages.[30] One example would be the following, with its quasi-medieval feel:

> My saull and lyfe stand up and se
> Quha lyis in ane cribbe of tre:
> Quhat babe is that, sa gude and fair?
> It is Christ, Goddle Sone and air.[31]

These charming lines, which derive from Luther, are, however, the product of translation, not of contrafaction. They serve to illustrate that the appreciation of the literary qualities of the *Gude and Godlie Ballatis* is a complex and tricky affair, wherein the critic has to do justice to the various styles and periods of the original poems, before he can properly assess the virtues (or lack of them) of the resulting items in the Scottish anthology. Another critical difficulty here is the unfortunate result of significant gaps in the literary record. For example, as far as the tradition of surviving Scottish verse is concerned, courtly styles predominate over popular ones before the Reformation, and Protestant verse over Catholic thereafter. It will be obvious, however, that this is unlikely to be a true reflection of the actual contemporary production. In a curious way, therefore, the *Gude and Godlie Ballatis* might be said to occupy a pivotal position from the point of view of literary history, containing as it does such a diversity of poetic styles and traditions: while some of the poems which it contains exhibit literary affinities with late-medieval devotion, others may be related to the most strident and modern productions of the age of Reform.

In conclusion, attention may be called to one poem in this collection, 'Till Christ, quhome I am haldin for to lufe', which displays all the hallmarks of a *contrafactum*, even though no source-model has so far been discovered. In this work the idiom of erotic devotion, redirected to a religious end, has resulted in a felicitous composition, which may be said even to approach the mystical:

> Quhome suld I serue bot him, that did me saue?
> Quhome suld I dout bot him, that dantis deide?
> Quhome suld I lufe bot him, attour the laif?
> Of all my wo he is the haill remeid;
> How suld I fle, and can not find na feid?
> Quhome suld I lufe but him, that hes my hart?
> How suld we twin that na man can depart?[32]

Although the secular original is unknown, there can scarcely be any doubt that this lyric, which in poetic power is one of the most effective in the collection, is a *contrafactum* of a courtly love-lyric; such words as 'serue', 'wo', 'remeid' and 'twin' (i.e. separate) are a sufficient guarantee of that. Indeed, one could almost reconstruct the original on the basis of the *contrafactum*. Within the context of the *Gude and Godlie Ballatis* the tone of this lyric is preternormally intense, and it demonstrates that *contrafacta* of this sort, provided they retain from their models sufficient 'sweet phrases and lovely metaphors', are not predestined to be crude or inelegant.

Notes

1   *The Harley Lyrics*, edited by G.L. Brook (Manchester, 1956).
2   Text quoted from *Medieval English Songs*, edited by E.J. Dobson and F.Ll. Harrison (London, 1979), 143-145.
3   'Ancient Music'—perhaps most easily consulted in: *The Faber Book of Parodies*, edited by Simon Brett (London, 1984), 38.
4   The Latin text is given in *Medieval English Songs*, ibid.
5   *A Compendious Book of Godly and Spiritual Songs, commonly known as 'The Gude and Godlie Ballatis'*, edited by A.F. Mitchell, STS (Edinburgh, 1897; reprint New York, 1966).
6   On the *GGB* see: introduction to Mitchell's edition; D. Hay Fleming, *The Hymnology of the Scottish Reformation* (Edinburgh and Perth, 1884); Shire, *Song, Dance and Poetry*, pp. 25-33; A.A. MacDonald, *The Middle Scots Religious Lyrics,* PhD dissertation, University of Edinburgh, 1978, pp. 409-450.
7   A.A. MacDonald, 'The *Gude and Godlie Ballatis* (1597): a ghost no more?', *Edinburgh Bibliographical Society Transactions*, forthcoming.
8   *The Works of John Knox*, edited by David Laing, Bannatyne Club, 6 vols. (Edinburgh, 1846-1864), I, 139.
9   These numbers are necessarily indicative, considering the differences between the three early editions.
10 *GGB*, edited by Mitchell, p. 1.
11 On music in Reformed Scotland see, most recently: D James Ross, *Musick Fyne: Robert Carver and the Art of Music in Sixteenth Century Scotland* (Edinburgh, 1993), 81-88.

12 *GGB*, edited by Mitchell, pp. 49-51.

13 *GGB*, edited by Mitchell, pp. 49-51 (249-250); 195-199 (290-291), respectively.

14 *GGB*, edited by Mitchell, p. 53 (250-251).

15 *GGB*, edited by Mitchell, pp. lxvi-lxxii, cxiv-cxxv, 65-66, 136-137, 143-144, 145-146; *Remains of Myles Coverdale*, edited by George Pearson, Parker Society (Cambridge, 1846), 560-562, 580-581, 565-566, 553-554, respectively.

16 *GGB*, edited by Mitchell, pp. 62-63, 254.

17 *Musica Britannica XV = Music of Scotland 1500-1700*, edited by Kenneth Elliott and Helena Mennie Shire, 3rd edition (London, 1975); Helena Mennie Shire, *Song, Dance and Poetry of the Court of Scotland under King James VI* (Cambridge, 1969), 38-39. See the quotations below.

18 *GGB*, edited by Mitchell, pp. 71-72; *The Court of Sapience*, edited by Ruth Harvey (Toronto, 1984), 77-78 (lines 2290-2310). See: A.A. MacDonald, 'The *Court of Sapience* and the *Gude and Godlie Ballatis*', *Neophilologus*, 74 (1990): 608-611.

19 *GGB*, edited by Mitchell, pp. 222, 171-172, respectively. On this and some others of the *GGB* poems here discussed see: Edward J. Cowan, 'Calvinism and the Survival of Folk', in *The People's Past*, edited by Edward J. Cowan (Edinburgh, 1980), 32-57 (esp. 38-42).

20 *GGB*, edited by Mitchell, pp. lxxv-lxxvi; *The Booke of the Universall Kirk of Scotland*, Bannatyne Club (Edinburgh, 1839), 125-126.

21 *GGB*, edited by Mitchell, pp. 132-136.

22 *GGB*, edited by Mitchell, pp. 158-161.

23 For texts of these versions see: *GGB*, edited by Mitchell, pp. 277-278.

24 *GGB*, edited by Mitchell, pp. 174-177.

25 *GGB*, edited by Mitchell, pp. 62-63.

26 *Music of Scotland*, edited by Elliott and Shire, pp. 160-161.

27 On this poem see: Shire, *Song, Dance and Poetry*, pp. 38-39.

28 In Holland's alliterative poem, *The Buke of the Howlat* (1450) we find a lyric addressed to Mary: *Longer Scottish Poems*, Vol. I, edited by Priscilla Bawcutt and Felicity Riddy (Edinburgh, 1987), 43-84 (lines 718-754). Lindsay used the Scottish alliterative stanza for the opening of his political drama (1552): *Ane Satyre of the Thrie Estaitis*, edited by R.J. Lyall (Edinburgh, 1989), 1. On Middle Scots alliterative verse see Felicity Riddy, 'The Alliterative Revival', in *The History of Scottish Literature*, Vol I, edited by R.D.S. Jack (Aberdeen, 1988), 39-54.

29 A.A. MacDonald, 'Religious Poetry in Middle Scots', in *The History of Scottish Literature*, Vol. I, edited by R.D.S. Jack (Aberdeen, 1988), 91-104.

30 Rosemary Woolf, *The English Religious Lyric in the Middle Ages* (Oxford, 1968), 357-358.

31 *GGB*, edited by Mitchell, pp. 50, 249-250.

32 *GGB*, edited by Mitchell, pp. 59-61.

4

THE SIXTEENTH-CENTURY SCOTTISH LOVE LYRIC

THEO VAN HEIJNSBERGEN

It is difficult to find examples of Scottish lyrics of the sixteenth century that provide a combination of sacred and profane elements similar to that found in contemporary English poems that figure more prominently in twentieth-century anthologies and editions. It is therefore useful to establish some common ground first, and recapitulate a few dominant critical notions concerning the sixteenth-century *English* lyric. This may involve preaching to the converted, but it is important that one should start by indicating explicitly by what tradition the Scottish lyrics are to be measured here.

In England, late medieval vernacular poetry, consisting of a mix of religious, popular and courtly elements, gradually evolved a new set of poetic conventions, especially through Wyatt's development of the Petrarchan conceit into a multifaceted vehicle for psychological analysis within the lyric. Barely a generation after Wyatt, Surrey turned the English language into a flexible medium for confident lyric expression in smooth, self-assured English. The publication of many poems by these two poets in Tottel's miscellany of *Songs and Sonets* in 1557 meant that their achievements could be picked up and redefined by later writers. The most crucial role among these later writers was played by Philip Sidney, whose insistence on the value of poetry as a mutually reinforcing combination of interior logic and eloquent expression (thus combining the achievements of Wyatt and Surrey) completed the conversion of the lyric into an organic unit of language and meaning that could scrutinise human psychology more sensitively than any other form of verbal art. As such a major analytical tool, it negotiated within its own literary field of reference—among other things—the interplay between elements of the sacred and the profane.

In the hands of these English poets, the love lyric thus turned from a public celebration of love into a private, interiorised and interiorising form of address, and the dialectics of abandonment and fulfilment that had characterised the public, profane form of worship now known as courtly love gradually developed into a pattern for internal dialogue within the love lyric. This interiorisation or spiritualisation of the love lyric transferred elements from a quasi-sacred register of self-analysis to a more purely profane one. It had already been a prominent feature of the medieval courtly lyric, but in the sixteenth century, under the influence of forces such as those mentioned above, it blossomed into a form of poetry with a radically different reach. The love lyric developed into a paradigm of private heuristics, an evolution that profoundly altered the range and direction of lyric poetry and eventually led to a dominant mode of negotiating existential questions through primarily amatory discourse. In this process, antitheses like foreign and native, Catholic and Protestant, secular and devotional (or even retrospective notions such as plain and golden, medieval and modern) were generally interactive rather than mutually exclusive. Thus, in the sixteenth century the courtly love lyric in England emancipated itself from its quasi-sacred, courtly origins while at the same time retaining and even intensifying elements of introspection from such a devotional tradition.

In Scotland, however, there was no comparable fusion between secular and devout registers of lyric that led to a concentrated use of metaphor from the sacred tradition in profane, amatory poetry. By contrast, the most interesting as well as the most perplexing aspect of sixteenth-century Scottish lyric poetry is its bewildering diversity in genre, tone and register; the poems involved display an energy that moves away from a notion of the lyric as having an indivisible autobiographical core, and present instead a poetic persona spread over many different genres and contradictory modes. There are many vernacular poets in sixteenth-century Scotland who, like Wyatt and Surrey, wrote devotional poetry as well as secular love lyrics in the more traditional manner, but, unlike Surrey and Wyatt, these same poets also produced bawdy or even obscene lyrics that clearly relish dealing with human sexuality before its acculturation to any of the idealised or at least highly stylised ways of depicting sexual relations as provided by non-popular literature, be it courtly, moral or divine. These poems reflect a type of self-confidence and self-consciousness that is difficult to comprehend for the modern mind which is traditionally brought up with a fairly selective conception of 'the lyric' as polished, autonomous and introspective utterance, and which would therefore consider 'paradoxical' what to a contemporary Scottish mind—or indeed to any medieval consciousness—were complementary modes of expression in art as well as in life. Early sixteenth-century Scottish poets wrote in a context in which a firm belief in one model for the universe and for society was shared by all; consequently, they could present homiletic modes next to quasi-goliardic ones without causing embarrassment or giving offence, and they could also address their sovereign with a remarkable degree of familiarity. Throughout the century we find Scottish men of letters dealing with their sovereign in a refreshingly self-assertive way: Dunbar's begging poems addressed to James IV are exacting rather than reverential, James V's less than chaste lifestyle is openly criticised by his former tutor David Lindsay, while a few decades later another royal tutor and renowned poet, George Buchanan, repeatedly boxed the royal ears when his pupil, the young James VI, had failed to do his homework. The latter king's sensitivity was not spared by his subjects in later life either, when Andrew Melville, a leading Presbyterian, called him 'but God's silly vassal'.[1] One wonders what English poetry now as well as then would have looked like if, for example, Wyatt or Surrey had approached *their* king in a similar spirit; the 'Complete Works of Sir Thomas Wyatt' would no doubt be a somewhat cheaper volume.

In the context of the poems by Wyatt, Surrey and early Elizabethan poets, contemporaneous Scottish lyrics reflect an ordering of experience that is much closer to the spirit of Huizinga's later Middle Ages than to the contemporary English, more Renaissance-focused culture. As a result, they are frequently received by a modern reading public with a mixture of disbelief and perplexity. To a Petrarchist, a humanist or a (post-)Romantic reader the Scottish juxtaposition within one poem of bawdy as well as devout elements or of stark realism and aureation may appear schizophrenic, but in a late medieval, Burgundian spirit of sophisticated chivalry such diversity was not only considered perfectly acceptable but even a sign of health. What in these Scottish lyrics may to a modern audience seem contradictory modes were not recognised as such by their contemporary readers, who were not looking for the signs of poetic individuality as defined by later readers; these poems derive their *raison d'être* and their unity from a much more public, communally-defined understanding of poetry.

In this way, the separation—through the juxtaposition of extremes—of the secular from the devout within one author's output or even within one poem remained a common phenomenon in Scotland for a much longer period than in England, where lyric poetry capitalised on the *coalescence* and *mutually reinforcing* potential of these two registers, and during the sixteenth century the two national literatures gradually moved further and further apart in their conceptions of literature and of the lyric mode. If we look at the period from the 1540s to the 1560s, Alexander Scott (*c.* 1515-1582/3) is the one Scottish poet who comes closest, both in output and intention, to the type of lyricist presented by his contemporaries Wyatt and, to a lesser extent, Surrey. Although mainly a poet of erotic verse, Scott also wrote a few vernacular psalms, including Psalm 51, one of the penitential psalms also translated by Wyatt. As has been pointed out, Wyatt in his version reveals an intense 'inwardness', a mix of humility and militancy that has been said to be characteristic of English Protestantism; at the same time, however, he does not surrender his identity entirely to the paradigms of the sacred tradition but fuses them with those of a secular, profane convention, which yields a set of metaphors that is now most frequently identified with the royal court, the context of Wyatt's *profane* self-fashioning. In his version of Psalm 51, Wyatt turns the historical sites of Zion and Jerusalem into the 'inward Zion, the Zion of the Ghost' and into the 'heart's Jerusalem'; true contrition and knowledge can only be found in these private seats of the heart and mind. The identities of the latter are shaped and intensified by associations that originate in or derive from rhetorical embellishment but those in the more modern of Wyatt's poems have become truly organic, 'literary' metaphors within an autonomous text.[2] In contrast, instead of turning these historical places and events into components of a personal, inwardly-gravitating crisis of consciousness, Scott makes them part of a more traditional, communal and ritual confession of sin, one that celebrates the experience of a whole community rather than that of one single person. This, for example, is a stanza from his metrical version of Psalm 51:

>   Sweit lord, to Syon be suave,
>   And strenth the wallis of thy conclave,   strengthen; walls
> 75   Ierusalem, thy haly grave,
>   Quhilk makis ws ransone fre.   which redeems us
>   This sacrifice than thow salt have
>   Off thy iust pepill, and ressave   receive
>   Thair laill trew hairtis with all the lave: rest, remainder
> 80   Lord God, deliuer me.

Scott's psalms remain collective utterances that follow ancient texture; he does not turn such traditional material into interior dialogue and he does not add typically 'Wyatty' phrases such as the 'heart's Jerusalem'; his text is clearly concerned with the redemption of a society and a community rather than with that of an individual poet.[3] Compared to Wyatt, Scott provides a different distribution of the sacred and the profane, due to a different notion of poetry; Scott treats the lyric as an act of collective celebration or of poetic and emotional effect rather than as emotional expression or self-dramatisation.[4] Such a conception of poetry is generally ranked as inferior to Wyatt's creative adaptations of *his* cultural heritage, but this judgement requires modification, if only because it relies on definitions of 'poetry' and 'lyric' that are culturally defined rather than intrinsic.

When we turn to love lyrics, we encounter another element that widened the distance between the two national literatures, notably a different concept of 'the court'. Whereas in England courtiers acted as *Kulturträger* or vehicles of culture, at the Scottish royal court the Chapel Royal and similar institutions such as cathedral or burgh song schools, rather than aristocratic individuals, functioned as the cultural intermediaries, and the

Scottish poets of the middle of the sixteenth century emerge mainly from the ranks of Chapel Royal personnel, song school masters and related circles. In other words, Scottish poetry of this period was produced largely by and for men who were professionals rather than courtiers, musicians rather than politicians, and aural craftsmen rather than verbal dissimulators.[5] All this greatly impeded the development towards self-analysis in secular Scottish verse; most of these poets were first and foremost musicians or clergymen, and their efforts were unlikely to originate primarily in purely literary concerns or to be in any way directly expressive of an autobiographical individuality. More closely tied to a medieval tradition, sixteenth-century Scottish verse is generally more interested in the typical than the individual; love is among its topics, but considering the semi-religious identity of many of these Scottish poets it comes as no surprise that their lyric personae often act as observers of or commentators on the game of love—frequently in the familiar role of eavesdroppers—rather than as participants. One of these Scottish poets was John Fethy (*c.* 1490-*c.* 1570), and stanzas 1, 3, 5 and 8 of his *Pansing in hairt with spreit opprest* exemplify how such Scottish lyrics, even those in which the first-person 'protagonist' is meant to represent a sincere and loyal lover, do not develop into an intensely emotional and individual love experience but remain rational and rather iconographic:

Pansing in hairt with spreit opprest	musing; spirit
This hindirnycht bygon,	the other night
My corps for walking wes molest	waking
For lufe only of on.	one
Allace, quhome to suld I mak mon,	complain
Sen this come to lait?	too late
Cauld, cauld culis the lufe that kendillis our het.	kindles; too hot
Hir first to luf quhen I began,	
I trowd scho luvit me,	believed, trusted
Bot I, allace, wes nocht the man	
That best pleisit hir e.	eye
Thairfoir will I lat dolour be	
And gang ane vthir gett:	go another way
Cauld, cauld culis the lufe that kendillis our het.	

Hir proper makdome so perfyt,   appearance
    Hir visage cleir of hew,
Scho raissis on me sic appetyte
    And caussis me hir persew.
    Allace, scho will nocht on me rew
Nor gre with myne estait: agree
Cauld, cauld culis the lufe that kendillis our het.

No, no, I will nocht trow as yit
    That scho will leif me so,   leave
Nor yit that scho will chenge or flit
    As thocht scho be my fo.   as though
    Thairfoir will I lat dolour go
And gang ane vthir gait: go; way
Cauld, cauld culis the lufe that kendlis our haitt.

Moreover, Fethy was not only a clergyman but also a professional musician, and the fact that this particular poem was set to music is reflected by
its repetitive nature as well as by its rather bewildering lack of logic, bewildering until one looks for a logic of sound or music. We do not move by
any mental, linear process from A to B in the poem; instead, every individual stanza generally moves from a statement that indicates that the love for
the lady is still alive to its opposite in the penultimate stanza-line, before
the stanza is rounded off with a haunting refrain that rings in our ears like a
kind of death-knell; the latter effect is in itself another indication that the
intended impact of this type of verse was primarily aural rather than emotional.[6]

   This particular interest in the stanza rather than in the poem as a whole
as a unit of thought is typical of Scottish poetry of this period, something
which is linked to the fact that these texts frequently functioned as the verbal component in a larger, complex structure of words, part-song and
dance. Within a Scottish context, the extra dimension that such a prevalence
of aural over verbal logic brings to a poetic text can also be found in
William Dunbar's 'parodies' of various liturgical offices, and the best
example of an aural effect similar to Fethy's is provided by Dunbar's
equally haunting use of the well-known line from the Office of the Dead,
Timor mortis conturbat me (*i.e.* 'fear of death perturbs me'), which he uses
in his list of fellow poets that have been carried off by Death personified:

81   In Dunfermelyne he has done roune
       With Maister Robert Henrisoun;
       Schir Johne the Ros enbrast has he:
       Timor mortis conturbat me.

85   And he has now tane last of aw   taken; all
       Gud gentill Stobo and Quintyne Schaw
       Of quham all wichtis has pete: of whom; everyone
       Timor mortis conturbat me.

       Gud Maister Walter Kennedy
90   In poynt of dede lyis veraly-   death
       Gret reuth it wer that so suld be: shame, regret
       Timor mortis conturbat me.

       Sen he has all my brether tane
       He will naught lat me lif alane;
95   On forse I man his nyxt pray be: inevitably; must; prey
       Timor mortis conturbat me.

       Sen for the ded remeid is none
       Best is that we for dede dispone   make ready, prepare ourselves
       Eftir our deid that lif may we: death
100   *Timor mortis conturbat me.*

Of course, neither the thought itself nor the use of this particular liturgical echo in poetry is new; what makes the poem singularly effective is the aural context provided by Dunbar, the rhythm of the poem sparking off associations between the text and the ancient, communal ritual of life and death that lies around and behind it. The achievement of Dunbar has been acknowledged outside Scotland, but Fethy's role in transferring such quasi-liturgical echoes to purely secular part-song is as yet barely noticed even in Scotland itself.[7]

Another element that separated poets such as Fethy more and more from the English lyric tradition is the fact that, even though they were the producers of part-song and accompanying court poetry, the mid sixteenth-century Scottish poets were also, due to their relatively humble social status and occupations, more likely to show influences from popular vernacular poetry. Moreover, the increasingly unstable position and role of courtly patronage in Scotland meant that, compared to their English contemporaries, these Scottish poets in the period from the 1540s until well into the

1580s experienced a smaller degree of exposure to the literary fashions that
(at least in hindsight) dominated European literature in this period, particularly those of the Italian Renaissance. As the editor of a recent anthology of
late medieval Scottish poetry was remarked: 'Behind, under, around and
through the art poetry of court and cloister ... was the eternal poetry of the
folk'.[8] Such a popular tradition is present in the diction of sixteenth-century Scottish poetry and in its relish in verbal effects and grotesque
imagery, a predilection which is tied in with a general preference for
imagery over metaphor, and it is yet another element that kept the Scottish
lyric from developing along the same lines as the contemporary English
lyric with its centripetal drive towards a problematisation of personal identity.

A brief look at a poem attributed to the late sixteenth-century Scottish
poet Alexander Montgomerie will illustrate this point; it shows how the
above-mentioned forces shaped a distinctly *Scottish* poetics of the lyric, a
poetics which in itself carried the ingredients that kept it from changing in
the same fashion as its English equivalent. Moreover, it contrasts nicely
with one of the best-known poems from that rival English tradition, Wyatt's
They fle from me that sometime did me seek, notably the final two stanzas[9]:

> Thanked be fortune it hath been otherwise
> Twenty times better, but once in special,
10 In thin array after a pleasant guise,
> When her loose gown from her shoulders did fall
> And she me caught in her arms long and small,
> Therewithal sweetly did me kiss
> And softly said, 'Dear heart, how like you this?

15 It was no dream: I lay broad waking.
> But all is turned thorough my gentleness
> Into a strange fashion of forsaking.
> And I have leave to go of her goodness
> And she also to use newfangleness.
20 But since that I so kindly am served
> I would fain know what she hath deserved.

In these lines, Wyatt's poem clearly dramatises the persona's existential
crisis in terms of individual sexuality. The poem attributed to Montgomerie,
however, is characteristic of many Scottish lyrics that deal with the same
topic in that, even if sexual love is the dominant metaphor, it is either sub-
ordinated to a moral or devotional superstructure or expressed in purely

physical or highly ambiguous terms, or even straightforwardly parodied; the intense inwardness or self-transcendence of the profane English lyric 'I' is in Scottish lyrics usually grounded in one of these formal rather than dramatic realities.[10] This is the sonnet attributed to Montgomerie[11]:

	I dreamit ane dreame, o that my dreame wer trew!	
	Me thocht my maistris to my chalmer came,	
	And with hir harmeles handis the cowrteingis drew,	curtains
4	And sueitlie callit on me be my name:	
	'Art ye on sleip,' quod sche, 'o fy for schame!	
	Haue ye nocht tauld that luifaris takis no rest?'	lovers
	Me thocht I ansuerit, 'Trew it is, my dame,	
8	I sleip nocht, so your luif dois me molest.'	
	With that me thocht hir nicht-gowne of sche cuist,	cast
	Liftit the claiss and lichtit in my armis;	bedclothes; alighted
	Hir rosie lippis me thocht on me sche thirst,	thrust
12	And said, 'May this nocht stanche yow of your harmes!'	sufferings
	'Mercy, madame,' me thocht I menit to say,	
	Bot quhen I walkennit, alace, sche was away.	awoke

Instead of turning inward into a private discourse of self, the poem moves away from a 'lyrical' centre (lyrical in the modern sense) and instead points towards its own margins and to the formal and generic expectations it raises, taking delight especially in subverting these. The first line leaves no doubt as to what sort of generic conventions the reader is supposed to activate in the poem he is about to read—that of the dream vision—but at the same time this line already sets the tone of parody by its repetition of the key-word 'dreame', which is as deliberately rhetorical as the stopgap filler 'me thocht', a phrase repeated no less than six times within fourteen lines. It is through their accumulation that these repetitions surcharge the conventional, hyperbolic diction in this poem, with parodic effect.

Another conventional courtly and Christian notion, 'mercy', *i.e.* a plea for compassion, is used in the penultimate line in a way in which it also ironically invokes the meaning of 'thank you', as in French 'merci'; in a courtly setting, these were opposites in terms of the consummation of physical love, and this subversive word-play, juxtaposing rather than blending rival conceptions of human love, is more than coincidental. There is a strong suggestion that the would-be lover is merely playing for time while desperately trying to remember the lady's name, and the pun on 'mercy' again reflects an inclination within the Scottish lyric to move away from the self-analytical tendency as found in many of Wyatt's lyrics. Moreover, the poet's 'maistris' is the opposite of the courtly ideal of the distant lady; she briskly handles the whole situation with a very physical aim in mind, and although she uses the jargon required by courtly convention (ll. 4-6) her actions are quite unladylike, and her officiousness in presenting herself to her 'lover' constitutes a reversal of the roles as prescribed by courtly poetry. The persona's behaviour falls similarly short of traditional expectations in that he fails to live up to a conventional claim he had apparently subscribed to himself on an earlier occasion, namely that 'luifaris takis no rest' (l. 6): not only is the scene as a whole a dream, but within that dream the persona appears to be asleep as well.[12] In the same vein, the mechanical claim that love 'molests' him is doubly undermined: this standard verb from the courtly love tradition is used in a subversive way here, for it is not his unrequited love for the lady (as courtly convention prescribed) but, on the contrary, her highly physical appetite for *him* that is doing the 'molesting'.

This Scottish poem stresses the humorous, erotic and narrative energy of text, language and situation rather than moving authorial subjectivity into a central position as organising principle, and in doing so focuses on exploiting the formal and generic potential of the poem, a potential that is provided by assumptions concerning preconceived setting and genre that the poet shares with his audience. The view of the lyric as the verbal representation of 'the heart's forest', as in Wyatt's most well-known poems, is thus frequently undercut in Scottish lyrics in ways that show affinities instead with the counter-culture of shared laughter that characterises late medieval literature in general. The Scottish *Dreame* is a parody of courtly love, of courtly lovers, and of courtly love poetry itself, expressed within an art form—courtly lyric—that usually celebrated or even sublimated these same phenomena; in this way, it presents a sophisticated, paradoxical act of self-denial, that of its own art, and creates the illusion that the source of the self-denial is purely authorless. Such a parody of poetic activity is in itself indicative of a mature literary awareness; furthermore, with regard to the present purpose, it is important to realise that in such a parodic tradition the registers of sacred and profane remain separate rather than coalesce.[13]

Poems that have been 'canonised' by later generations of readers and that have thus in retrospect shaped the identity of the English lyric frequently exploit not only the capacity of art to provide stylised representations of human experience but also the potential of art to question and to 'figure forth' human existence. The sixteenth-century Scottish lyric tradition, however, traced different patterns. Both the poem of Wyatt and that of Montgomerie are developments of, as well as reactions against, a courtly heritage, and both poets considered its fancies unreal. However, whereas the central concern of Wyatt's poem—the onset of an abandonment, of an absence—implies that at an earlier stage there was a presence (that of an idealised beloved), the Scottish poem denies that there ever *was* such a presence. Whereas in Wyatt's poem the projection of the woman serves to draw attention to the narrator's existential predicament, in the sonnet attributed to Montgomerie the lady is an occasion for the makar to display his skill in manipulating language, genre, style, situation and audience, and on an existential level the relation between persona and author remains tangential. In subsequent eras, the dominant notions regarding literature were to privilege Wyatt's lyric practice; recent literary criticism, however, is gradually retracing its steps, not only through its revaluations of the canon, but also, more particularly, by focusing on the dismantling of codified attitudes in texts and on the playful, open-ended nature of language and signs rather than on the naturalisation of them by individual, historical subjects. In this sense, Middle Scots literature may profit from the notion of 'the death of the author'.

Such Scottish denials of 'life imitating art' lay bare discontinuities in the communication of a text from author to reader that bring out the essentially medieval origins of such texts, the intertextual drive of these texts—*i.e.* their meaning—located primarily on a formal and generic level. The active poetic principle in the sixteenth-century Scottish lyric should therefore be located in its margins, in the area of form and genre, in the music it accompanies or is accompanied by, in its rhythms, in its parody of poetic activity, and, *inter alia*, in its surplus of unbridled, so-called 'eldritch' fantasy. On the level of contents, the latter has provided us with poems that are as fascinating as the margins of medieval illuminated manuscripts or cathedral sculptures; it has yielded poems in which drunken personae roast strawberries on a fire of fresh green snow or in which God appears as a boisterous human being who joins in with communal laughter on the subject of thirsty ale-wives and who is an amused participant, while out for a walk in Argyll with Saint Peter, in the scene in which the first Highlander is created out of horse droppings.[14] At the same time, on the level of language this type of fantasy found verbal expression in 'flytings', poems of abuse that violently oppose what modern readers have been generally taught to expect (or even demand) from poetry. In these different ways, the Scottish lyrics of this period show that such modern expectations are of fairly recent origin, within a British context only beginning to occur in English verse of the sixteenth century.

Within the Scottish lyric there was thus a stubborn resistance against the dominant trend in English literature to set up love, Petrarch or even literary activity *per se* as the one standard which poets and poems ought to measure themselves by. The Scottish lyricist was primarily a 'makar', a craftsman, as opposed to the *vates* or visionary that Sidney describes in his *Defense of Poesie*, the latter view eventually giving love poetry sufficient self-confidence to claim semi-divine status for its lyric 'I' in a mixture of the sacred and the profane, of the mystic and the *troubadour*. From such a sophisticated perspective, the more exclusively 'profane' Scottish lyric might be censured for its lack of introspection and for its reluctance to define its own version of the lyric 'I' in similar terms. However, such a verdict exposes an *interpretational* handicap, rather than any inherent defect of these Scottish lyrics: Scottish poetry of this period is a phenomenon with predominantly medieval features in a century that has been earmarked 'modern', and it is therefore frequently approached with anachronistic critical tools and assumptions. However, if we follow the signs that these Scottish poets themselves have set out for us to follow, we are able to reconstruct a body of literature that is in danger of being neglected simply because it celebrated a different, more frequently communal liturgy of self and self-hood, of sacred and profane.

A recent, happy instance of a similar literary excavation is John Skelton, the one English poet who might be said to echo Scottish poets such as Dunbar. Skelton's poetry, largely neglected for more than four centuries, has in the recent past been rehabilitated by attempts to look at it on its own conditions, in its own 'ritual' context. His work has been described as typically medieval 'in that the system of ideas on which it is based is external to it. It is not, in the language of Coleridgean criticism, an organic whole; on the contrary, it is manifestly incomplete without the co-operation of an audience of informed readers. It is designed for a community of Christian readers, and like most medieval art, it cannot be wholly alive apart from such a community'; this dependence on the reader 'refutes our aestheticisms' in that poetry conceived in such a context does not present 'an allegory of the artist's life, nor a poem about poetry; [but] it reminds us that art imitates life, and that works of art belong to the history of mankind, not to the history of art'.[15] Scottish poetry of the kind discussed above prescribes the same critical starting-points; like Skelton's verse, it belongs to a tradition in which the secular and the devout were still part of one and the same human experience and in which the audience engaged in a conspiracy with the author that differs from that between a modern author and his or her reader, but which is not therefore any the less sophisticated. If anything, it is the lack of interpretational skills on the part of later generations of readers that causes these texts to appear defective; we have, therefore, to rehistoricise ourselves into informed readers of Scottish poems if we want to appreciate more accurately the impact of such a poem as Fethy's song or

Scott's translation of Psalm 51. The latter may seem to pale in comparison
with Wyatt's version, but a re-contextualisation of our own cultural paradigms within sixteenth-century Scottish terms will make us better readers of
stanzas such as the following, from Scott's version of Psalm 51:

	Only to the I did offend,	
	May non my miss bot thow amend,	
	As by thy sermondis thow art kend,	known
20	Ourcum all contrarie.	subdue
	In filth, lo! I begyn and end;	
	By syn maternall I am send,	
	With vyce I vaneiss, and mon wend:	must; go, pass away
	Lord God, deliuer me.	

* * *

This general outline of the sixteenth-century Scottish lyric would be incomplete without a short epilogue that covers the last decade and a half of the
century. In the introductory paragraphs above, a brief indication has been
given of how the medieval lyric is generally said to have developed in
England into a tool for psychological self-scrutiny in the domain of the love
lyric under the combined influences of the court, Petrarchism and Protestantism. In the contemporaneous Scottish lyric, only rudimentary traces of
such a development can be found. The post-Reformation dismantling of the
Chapel Royal and of other collegiate churches under lay patronage robbed
Scottish literature of important centres of poetic activity, and made the love
lyric increasingly defenceless against more powerful, exclusively religious
or political discourses. As a consequence, the attempt by James VI at the
end of the sixteenth century to create a court-centred band of poets in Scotland (known as the Castalian band) that would function as the native equivalent of the *Pléiade*, which represents the belated arrival of Italian and
Renaissance fine literature in Scotland, made but a brief impact. James
mustered both court culture and Petrarchism, but historical developments
turned Protestantism into a formidable opponent rather than ally. Protestantism settled in Scotland some three decades later than in England—a delay
that in itself enabled the prolonged existence of medieval ways of producing and enjoying poetry—but, once firmly established, Scottish Calvinism
was less prepared to compromise on the subject of secular literature than
the more political type of Protestantism that was dominant in England.
Moreover, from at least the 1550s onwards, the Scottish court had enjoyed

an uneasy relationship with kirk and town (*i.e.* Edinburgh). Its unifying and epitomising role was curbed by these other institutions and handicapped by a string of minority reigns, and in the long run, such a state of affairs, in conjunction with the waning influence of a decentralised aristocracy, meant that the Scottish court was much less of a dominant ideological force than its English equivalent. This lack of a culturally prevalent secular identity in Scotland prevented a synthesis of the vernacular love poem and the religious lyric within a profane, courtly tradition, and as a result the Scottish love lyric became increasingly separated from what eventually came to be called 'the lyric tradition'. This difference in profane identity, caused by the dissimilar roles played by the respective national institutions of court and church as cultural and ideological influences, lies at the heart of the different relation between the sacred and the profane in sixteenth-century Scottish lyrics as compared to their English equivalents. The 'profane' in the sixteenth-century Scottish lyric frequently represents the 'popular' tradition, whereas in an English context it refers to a much larger extent to a 'courtly' type of literature, in which not the text but the author has become the self-conscious element, *i.e.* the organising principle and the generator of 'meaning'. In the 'profane' sphere, poetry in Scotland thus generally remained either earthy or moralising, grounded in an extra-literary context, while its essentially public nature precluded the interiorisation as found in English poetry from Wyatt onwards. The Scottish religious lyric did develop a dialogic potential, but under the influence of a dogmatic rather than pragmatic type of Protestantism this always involved the use of verbal material as a closed index to an exclusively *divine* love, not to the sexual politics of individual men and women—let alone of individual poets—and the lyric centre of these poems remains 'sacred' in a purely religious sense. As a result of all this, the sacred and the profane, 'mercy' and 'merci', continued to be exploited by Scottish love poets as opposites rather than as cognates, there being no common field of reference within which to merge them.

It is significant that when modern literary criticism traces the roots of the poet who put Scottish poetry back on the map (Robert Burns), it does not point to the Castalian poets but, in atavistic fashion, to poets such as William Dunbar and Alexander Scott, the products of an indigenous late medieval culture. Indications such as these should stimulate and guide the re-evaluation of sixteenth-century Scottish poetry on its own conditions and within its own context; this will yield a more truthful picture of a national cultural poetics.

Notes

1   For Dunbar, see *The Poems of William Dunbar*, edited by James Kinsley (Oxford, 1979), esp. the poems 'To the King' in the section of 'Poems of Court Life'; for Lindsay, see *The Works of Sir David Lindsay of the Mount, 1490-1555*, edited by Douglas Hamer (Scottish Text Society, Third Series 1, 2, 6 and 8, 1930-1936), esp. *The Dreme of Schir Dauid Lyndesay, The Complaynt of Schir Dauid Lindesay* and *Ane Satyre of the Thrie Estaitis*. On Buchanan as tutor, see I.D. McFarlane, *Buchanan* (London, 1981), 448, where it is noted how Buchanan added spice to the physical punishment by telling the young prince, future successor of Elizabeth I, that 'he was a true bird of the bloody nest to which he belonged'; see also the *Dictionary of National Biography*, vii, 191, and Eric Stair-Kerr, *Stirling Castle. Its Place in Scottish History*, 2nd edn (Stirling, 1928), 86. On Melville, see *Dictionary of National Biography*, xxxvii, 234.

2   Stephen Greenblatt, *Renaissance Self-Fashioning. From More to Shakespeare* (Chicago and London, 1980), 115-116. In England, the conjunction of an earlier Reformation and a stronger monarchy is another factor that led to differences in the developments of the Scottish and English lyric persona; for one thing, the political situation and the fear of betrayal were instrumental in leading to poetical innovations and modes of introspection that bear a direct relation to the precarious situations of the individual authors concerned: see, for example, the account of the development of vernacular psalm paraphrases in Rivkah Zim, *English Metrical Psalms. Poetry as Praise and Prayer, 1535-1601* (Cambridge, 1987). By contrast, Scottish poets had fewer incentives to investigate, in isolation, the shadows within the self. Not until the turn of the century, when they were in different ways cut off from their national, communal bedding and when the influence of the Italian Renaissance became more tangible, did Scottish poets such as Alexander Montgomerie, Robert Aytoun and William Drummond of Hawthornden begin to follow the same signs.

3   Scott's poems have been edited for the Scottish Text Society by James Cranstoun, *The Poems of Alexander Scott* (STS, First Series, 36, 1896) and for the Early English Text Society by Alexander Karley Donald, *The Poems of Alexander Scott* (EETS, Extra Series, 85, 1902). The texts by Scott provided in the present paper are my own transcriptions from the Bannatyne manuscript (1568), with added punctuation, transliteration and capitalisation; Denton Fox and William A. Ringler (eds), *The Bannatyne Manuscript* (London, 1980), provides a facsimile edition of this manuscript.

4   The fundamental distinction between poetry as emotional effect and poetry as emotional expression is derived from John Stevens, *Music and Poetry in the Early Tudor Court* (London, 1961), 65.

5   On this, see Theo van Heijnsbergen, 'The Interaction between Literature and History in Queen Mary's Edinburgh: The Bannatyne Manuscript and its Prosopographical Context' in A.A. MacDonald, Michael Lynch and Ian B. Cowan (eds), *The Renaissance in Scotland. Studies in Literature, Religion, History and Culture* (Leiden, 1994), 183-225. As such, the identity of mid sixteenth-century Scottish makars bears a much closer resemblance to late fifteenth-century and early six-

teenth-century English lyric poets, a similarity which is also reflected in the
poems: see E.K. Chambers and F. Sidgwick (eds), *Early English Lyrics. Amorous,
Divine, Moral and Trivial* (London, 1907, reprt. 1921), 280-282 and (notes to)
poems 25, 33, 34, 39 and 123.

6   Fethy's poem appears in full in John MacQueen (ed.), *Ballattis of Luve*
     (Edinburgh, 1970), 59-61.

7   Kinsley, *Dunbar*, pp. 180-181. Note that C.S. Lewis, in his *English Literature in
     the Sixteenth Century Excluding Drama* (Oxford, 1954), 99-100, claimed that the
     quality of rhythm of Fethy's poem is 'quite unlike' Dunbar; however, this judge-
     ment does not take into account the liturgical element shared by Dunbar with
     Fethy in this particular poem. Similar use of this particular liturgical line can be
     found in 'As I me walked in one morning', No 83 in Chambers and Sidgwick,
     Early English Lyrics, while No 82 in the same collection ('*Illa juventus* that is so
     nise') provides a humorous parody; both are taken from Richard Hill's common-
     place book. For an intriguing new reading of Dunbar's poem, see A.A. Mac-
     Donald, 'Alliterative Poetry and its context: the case of William Dunbar', in:
     L.A.J.R. Houwen and A.A. MacDonald (eds), *Loyal Letters: Studies on Mediaeval
     Alliterative Poetry and Prose* (Groningen, 1994), 261-279 (274-278).

8   Tom Scott (ed), *Late Medieval Scots Poetry. A Selection from the Makars and
     their Heirs down to 1610* (London, 1967), 32.

9   *Sir Thomas Wyatt. The Complete Poems*, edited by R.A. Rebholz (Penguin, 1978),
     116-117.

10   The terms 'formal' and 'dramatic' are here used in the distinctive sense suggested
     by Stephen Manning, 'Game and Earnest in the Middle English and Provençal
     Love Lyrics', *Comparative Literature* (1966): 225-241 (230), an article that pro-
     vides a useful survey of earlier twentieth-century attempts to move away from
     author-centred interpretations of medieval literature (reprinted in Maxwell S. Luria
     and Richard L. Hoffman (eds), *Middle English Lyrics* (New York and London,
     1974), 266-280.

11   *Poems of Alexander Montgomerie and Other Pieces from Laing MS. No 447*,
     edited by George Stevenson (STS, First Series 59, 1910), 218.

12   This notion of the lover who has to stay awake ('brek one's sleep') in the service
     of Venus had been present in Scottish poetry for some time already; see *Robert
     Henryson. The Testament of Cresseid*, edited by Denton Fox (London, 1968), 91
     (note to line 61).

13   A penchant for parody can also be traced in the large number of Scottish *contra-
     facta*, sacred parodies of secular tunes or instances of the reverse process, which is
     in fact the topic of the other contribution on Scottish literature to the present vol-
     ume, '*Contrafacta* and the *Gude and Godlie Ballatis*', by A.A. MacDonald. More-
     over, in comparison with English verse, in the days of Tottel's *Songs and Sonets*
     and the Bannatyne Manuscript, the Scottish literary tradition seems to have clung
     more tenaciously to other (semi)-parodic modes of poetry such as flytings, mock-
     heroic tournament poems, 'ballatis of vmpossibiliteis' or lying poems (for which
     see Fox and Ringler, *The Bannatyne Manuscript*, notes to items 221, 320, 341 and
     355-357), punctuation poems (for an example from the Maitland Foilio Manuscript
     [*c.* 1580], see Katharine M. Rogers, *The Troublesome Helpmate. A History of Mis-
     ogyny in Literature* (Seattle and London, 1966), 62-63, mock testaments, cata-

logues of ugliness and other travesties of courtly genres. Fox and Ringler's note on the Scottish poet William Stewart (p. xlii), illustrates in a nutshell how late medieval Scottish poetry enjoyed a remarkable continuity and uniformity in contents as well as form, which made it more resistant against change.

14   Fox and Ringler, *The Bannatyne Manuscript*, items 165, 197 and 230.

15   F.W. Brownlow, '*Speke, Parrot*: Skelton's Allegorical Denunciation of Cardinal Wolsey', *Studies in Philology* 65 (April 1968): 124-139 (137, 139).

5

'TO WEAVE A NEW WEBBE IN THEIR OWNE LOOME':
ROBERT SOUTHWELL AND
COUNTER-REFORMATION POETICS

JOHN R. ROBERTS and LORRAINE ROBERTS

In recent years, critics of early modern religious poetry have given such preponderant attention to 'Protestant poetics' and 'Reformation poetics' that the central importance of Robert Southwell and 'Counter-Reformation poetics' in the development of the English religious lyric of the late sixteenth and the earlier seventeenth centuries has been rather obscured and de-emphasised. The number of editions of Southwell's verse testifies in support of the conclusion that he was the most popular English religious poet of his age, much more so than were John Donne or George Herbert a few decades later. He led the way for the religious poets that followed him, his most significant contributions being not only the introduction of the meditative mode into English religious poetry but also the use of sacred parody—by whose example religious lyricists were encouraged to convert secular themes, images, forms, diction, and genres to the service of sacred verse.

A review of certain pertinent facts of Southwell's life sheds light on what his intentions were in using poetry as part of his ministry, an apostolate that ended in martyrdom on the morning of 21 February 1595 (O.S.), when he was hanged, disembowelled, and quartered at Tyburn—having been charged with treason.[1] His only crimes, however, were that he was a Jesuit priest, trained and ordained on the Continent, and for six years had secretly preached and administered the sacraments to Catholics in England.

His last hours were carefully recorded by his friends and co-religionists, and all of the accounts stress his joyfulness, contentment, and gentleness as he was carted through the streets of London and finally stood on the scaffold at Tyburn. Moments before his execution he professed that he was a Catholic priest and a Jesuit, prayed for the Queen and his country, and asked God to be merciful to him. He prayed,

> And this I humbly desire almightie God that it would please his goodnes, to take and except this my death, the laste farewell to this miserable and infortunate lyfe (although in this moste happy and fortunate) in full satisfaction for all my sinnes and offences, and for the Comfort

of many others; which albeit that it seeme here disgracefull, yet I hope that in tyme to come it will be to my eternal glory.[2]

This was the hour Southwell had hoped for and prayed for during his years of preparation for the priesthood in Rome and during his nine years as a missionary priest in the Catholic underground of England. A little more than a year before his departure from Rome for England in July 1586, when he was sorely disappointed that at that time he had not been chosen for the English Mission, he wrote the following to Claudius Aquaviva, then General of the Jesuits:

> It is Your Paternity's decision that I devote my self to the English here at Rome. May it also be your decision, by God's inspiration, that I do the same for England herself, with the supreme goal of martyrdom in view. I will not cease to strive with God in prayer that he may grant me this in his mercy ...[3]

When he was finally sent to England, Southwell regarded his mission as twofold: to minister to, encourage, and console those who remained committed to the Catholic faith and to win back, if possible, those who, because of their indifference, weakness, greed, or fear had abandoned that faith in the hope of gaining worldly goods, social status, and political correctness and power. In addition to dispensing the sacraments, preaching, and performing the other offices of his priesthood, Southwell committed himself fully to what Pierre Janelle calls 'an apostolate of letters', that is, to the writing of religious prose tracts and devotional poetry. Denied a pulpit from which to exhort and instruct his countrymen, Southwell turned to poetry as a major means of disseminating the Catholic position on important matters of faith, especially those doctrines that had been recently clarified and defined by the Council of Trent, and also as a powerful instrument for encouraging his countrymen to live lives of greater moral integrity and, above all, to seek repentance for their sins and gladly accept 'the cleansing properties of suffering undertaken in the name of faith'.[4]

At the same time, Southwell hoped that, through example, he would be redeeming poetry from paganism, old and new, and would show how it could be, in fact, the handmaiden of religion.[5]

All of Southwell's poetry in English was written during his active years as a missionary—from July 1586, the date of his return to England, until his imprisonment in June 1592.[6] Grosart and others have suggested that perhaps some of the poems were composed while Southwell was actually in prison, first in the Gatehouse, then later on in the Tower, and finally in Newgate; but we now know that during his imprisonment he was not allowed ink or writing materials, except once, when he was permitted to compose a letter to Sir Robert Cecil, dated 6 April 1593, asking to be brought to trial swiftly or to be released. In the letter Southwell specifically mentions that he has not been allowed writing privileges during his captivity and that he was only allowed to write his appeal as a special favour granted by Sir Michael Blount, the Lieutenant of the Tower. There is no evidence to indicate that the restrictions placed on Southwell in the early days of his imprisonment were lifted during the last twenty-three months of his life.[7] As far as we know, he had only a Bible, a breviary, and the works of St. Bernard to console him during his nearly three years of imprisonment, torture, and deprivation.[8]

Although Southwell's poems circulated in manuscript before his death, soon after his execution, they were published and became enormously popular among both Catholic and Anglican readers. Southwell, in fact, became the most widely read religious poet of his age. Scallon argues that Southwell's poems 'won popular acceptance because they manifested the kind of verbal wit which appealed to the Englishmen who patronised Shakespeare and Jonson and because they dealt with subjects which were of great interest to people in an age of tremendous religious upheaval'.[9] The first edition of *St. Peter's Complaint, with other Poems* probably appeared less than one month after Southwell's execution, and it was followed by a second edition later that year. In the same year, 1595, another volume, entitled *Moeoniae*, appeared in three separate editions. Nancy Pollard Brown, Southwell's modern editor, points out that the initials R.S. on the title page of *Moeoniae* and references to *St. Peter's Complaint* in John Busby's prefatory letter to the volume clearly show that the identity of the author for both volumes was known to the publishers as well as their London customers.[10] Although the earliest editions were probably limited to no more than 1250 to 1500 copies, the rapid succession of later editions highlights Southwell's popularity.[11] Between 1595 and 1636, eighteen editions of his poems were published, including two Scottish and two continental editions.[12] By way of contrast, between 1633 and 1695 thirteen editions of Herbert's *The Temple* appeared, and between 1633 amd 1669 only six editions of Donne's poems were published.

Southwell's earliest editors, all of whom were Anglicans, were very careful, however, to omit poems or parts of poems that express too directly specifically Catholic doctrines and traditional beliefs, such as the Assumption of the Virgin and transubstantiation. In addition to the omission of certain poems or parts of poems, the major difference between the editions and the surviving manuscripts is the ordering of the poems, an ordering that suggests that the manuscripts were intended for a Catholic audience while the printed editions were meant to appeal to a general English audience, both Catholic and Anglican.[13] The fact that both groups responded so enthusiastically to Southwell's poems suggests that perhaps the differences in doctrine and in religious sensibility between Catholics and many Anglicans in the later sixteenth and early seventeenth centuries were not nearly as great as some modern scholars have claimed. In the late 1590s Southwell stood as a John the Baptist in the wilderness of contemporary religious poetry, the precursor of much greater religious poets who followed his initiatives in the next few decades.

The single most important influence on Southwell was undoubtedly Ignatian meditation; it perhaps more than anything else accounts for the effects of immediacy and emotional appeal in his poetry. However, since Louis Martz and others have discussed extensively the influence of various kinds of discursive meditation on the religious poetry of the period, no comment further on this aspect of Southwell's art is needed.[14] Less well-known is how Southwell's poetics was informed by Ignatian spirituality in general and, in particular, by the Jesuit theorists at the Roman College while he was a student there.

Southwell's policy of using poetry to teach the Catholic faith grew directly out of the encouragement, both of the Council of Trent and Jesuit spirituality, to use the arts to involve the faithful affectively in the sacramental life of the Church and to instruct them in theological tenets. In the opening words of *The Spiritual Exercises*, St. Ignatius Loyola writes:

> Man is created to praise, reverence, and serve God our Lord and by this means to save his soul. The other things on the face of the earth are created for man to help him in attaining the end for which he is created. Hence man is to make use of them in as far as they help him in the attainment of his end, and he must rid himself of them in so far as they prove a hindrance to him.[15]

Inherent in this statement is the basic attitude of the Jesuits, and therefore Southwell, toward poetry. For them and for him, poetry is a 'created thing' that can be helpful in bringing human beings to salvation or a hindrance to their spiritual advancement. In so far as it contributes to their good, it is valuable; if it does not, then it has no inherent value at all.

This theory of poetry is clearly stated by Jacobus Pontanus (Spanmuller), an eminent and influential German Jesuit, in a treatise entitled *Poeticae Institutiones*. Although the work was not published until 1594, Pontanus had begun it as early as 1573 and his ideas were well-known among Jesuits.[16] Even if Southwell did not know this particular treatise, as a Jesuit he was clearly imbued with the ideas and spirit that this document embodies.

Pontanus's fundamental point is that poetry, like the other arts, must not be regarded as an end in itself. Whatever pleasure it gives, he maintains, must not be enjoyed or cultivated for its own sake but only in so far as it serves the cause of religion, virtue, and wisdom. Poetry, he says, is meant 'to teach while it delights', but, he adds, 'to teach more than it delights'.[17] Pontanus severely condemns all those who write on matters that are 'removed from virtue, some of them filling up whole books with amatory lewdness'.[18] For him, what is most important about art is the end for which the work is created; thus the nature of poetry for Pontanus is not artistry but moral wisdom. Although Pontanus's view of art is not exclusive to the Jesuits, it was clearly an idea that Southwell adopted because of his association with the Society of Jesus.

Another contemporary Jesuit theorist, Antonius Possevinus, more or less echoes Pontanus when he says, 'The first purpose of the poet must be, to make his reader better; his second only, to delight him'.[19] Here as elsewhere in Jesuit theory, there is a firm rejection of art for art's sake. Helen White reminds us that the late sixteenth century 'is the Post-Tridentine age when abuse of art is heavy on the minds of those concerned with the redemption of the Christian world'.[20] The Jesuits, fully aware of their intellectual leadership in this field, hoped to correct both in theory and in practice what to them seemed the degeneration of literature and of the arts in general. Rather than shun poetry and other forms of art, they were convinced that it was better to use for moral persuasion and doctrinal instruction that which was already attractive to their intended audience, and they believed that those attached to the things of this world must be enticed to religious conviction and devotional fervour by making palatable that which they are not easily attracted to.[21] In other words, they wholeheartedly endorsed the notion of 'sugar-coating' the didactic pill. If readers were indeed attracted to poetry and to its rhetorical, metaphorical, and imagistic 'ornaments', then all that needed doing was to dress up religion in a new and more fashionable garb. Pontanus, in an attack on those who aim to please more than instruct and improve, scornfully says that secular poets aim 'to gratify the vulgar, who are always fonder of pleasant than of useful things, and easily spurn wholesome doctrine unless', as he puts it, 'it is besprinkled with charms and delights of many kinds'.[22]

The Jesuits, in their attempt to attract the 'vulgar', recommended poetry of imitation, not poetry of inspiration. They chose to imitate classical as well as established vernacular literature that they deemed morally harmless and spiritually uplifting, or, in other words, to dress Christian ideas in established forms. It was in this context of Christian humanism that Possevinus in 1593 composed a general review of Christian poetry, extending the meaning of that classification to include also some classical writers. His aim was to justify the mingling of Christian doctrine and ideas with classical forms of poetry written in Latin.[23]

Critics such as Pontanus and Possevinus were very distrustful of 'inspiration' and 'imagination' and distinguish between 'ingenium' (roughly equivalent to inspiration or originality) and 'judicium' (judgment), extolling the latter, of course, as superior. Pontanus maintains that, instead of looking into one's self for poetic material, it is better to imitate classical forms that are suitable for religious themes. Endorsing derivativeness, Pontanus concludes his treatise by saying, 'We must strive with all our labour, so that those things we spoke of, appear not theirs, but ours; though where we took them from, learned men cannot be unaware'.[24] Particularly important in understanding Southwell's poetry is the idea of Jesuit theorists that the self must not be the focus in religious poetry; nothing idiosyncratic in the spiritual life of the individual poet was to serve as the material of poetry. As Nancy Pollard Brown quite rightly points out, Southwell's purpose in writing 'was one of service, not self-expression'.[25] Thus, Southwell's poetry, like that of Richard Crashaw—and to an extent like that of Herbert—was not intended to explore his own spirituality but rather to effect a change in his readers.

Of course, not all Jesuit theorists of the sixteenth century agreed wholeheartedly with Pontanus and Possevinus. One very notable exception is Francesco Benci or Bencius, a professor of rhetoric at the Roman College while Southwell was a student there, who, in his treatise entitled *Orationes de laudibus poeticae,* published in 1592, defends poetry against those who distrust it or look upon it as simply an attractive disguise for moral and doctrinal teaching. Bencius, while agreeing with Pontanus and others that poetry is indeed a vehicle for the teaching of virtue, rejects the notion that poetry should not be enjoyed for itself. To him, poetry is religion's sister, not its servant. His main argument is that poetry naturally leads men to virtue because it calms and soothes the passions and appeals to man's noblest aspirations, especially his love of beauty and his appreciation of genuine emotion. Thus, for Bencius, the moral effectiveness of poetry is not so much a justification for its existence as a confirmation of its inherent value. Because he believed poetry to be divine in origin, Bencius held that it must be Christian; and he, like Possevinus, argued that even classical poetry is 'Christian', in spite of appearances to the contrary. He claims that the first poets, in fact, were those of the Old Testament, that metre was invented by the Hebrews, and that Moses wrote in hexameters.[26]

It is precisely the Jesuit spirit and the influence of Jesuit theorists that account for Southwell's reason and purpose for writing poetry as well as his choice of subject matter and poetic models. No poet has ever stated more clearly his intention in writing poetry than did Southwell in a prose dedicatory letter addressed to his unidentified 'loving Cosen', a letter that is preserved in two manuscripts as well as in the early printed versions of *St. Peter's Complaint, with other Poems*. It reads in part:

> Poets by abusing their talent, and making the follies and fayninges of love, the customary subject of their base endevours, have so discredited this facultie, that a Poet, a Lover, and a Liar, are by many reckoned but three wordes of one signification. But the vanity of men, cannot counterpoyse the authority of God, who in delivering many partes of Scripture in verse, and by his Apostle willing us to exercise our devotion in Himnes and Spirituall Sonnets, warrenteth the Arte to bee good, and the use allowable. And therefore not onely among the Heathens, whose Gods were chiefely canonized by their Poets, and their Painim Divinitie Oracled in verse: But even in the Old and New Testament it hath bene used by men of greatest Pietie, in matters of most devotion. Christ himselfe by making a Himne, the conclusion of his last Supper, and the Prologue to the first Pageant of his Passion, gave his Spouse a methode to immitate, as in the office of the Church it appeareth, and all men a paterne to know the true use of this measured and footed stile. But the Divell as hee affecteth Deitie, and seeketh to have all the complements of Divine honor applied to his service, so hath he among the rest possessed also most Poets with his idle fansies. For in lieu of solemne and devout matter, to which in duety they owe their abilities, they now busy themselves in expressing such passions, as onely serve for testimonies to how unwoorthy affections they have wedded their wils. And because the best course to let them see the errour of their workes, is to weave a new webbe in their owne loome; I have heere layd a few course threds together, to invite some skillfuller wits to goe forward in the same, or to begin some finer peece, wherein it may be seene, how well verse and vertue sute together.[27]

These convictions and sentiments remind one of Herbert's two New Year's Day sonnets to his mother and of his defence of religious verse in 'Jordan (I)' and 'Jordan (II)'. In his statement, we immediately recognise the influence of Ignatian spirituality in Southwell's recommendation that all created things—including poetry—be employed in such a way as to lead men to God, not away from Him. We also see the influence of Possevinus and Bencius in Southwell's defence of poetry, in which he enumerates biblical occasions when poetry was used, even by Christ Himself. And we recognise the influence of Pontanus in Southwell's recommendation that the poet should use secular forms for religious subject matter. Southwell suggests in his dedicatory letter that the most effective way of redeeming and reforming poetry is to use the very artifices, techniques, and forms employed by secular poets—but to convert them to the service of God—as he says, 'To weave a new webbe in their owne loome'. As Martz points out, 'Looking about him, he might well have lamented the poor estate of English religious poetry, which hobbled along in worn-out garb, mumbling the same old tune, while on every side one might see the results of experiment in the poetry of profane love'.[28] The love poems of Breton, Lodge, Oxford, and many others were being read, admired, and imitated by that very class of people that Southwell was most eager to reach—the aristocracy; thus he chose to capitalise on this popularity by using the metrical forms and sometimes the diction and imagery of these poets in his sacred poetry[29]—a process that we now call 'sacred parody', a term given its fullest definition many years ago by Rosemond Tuve to describe Herbert's conversion of secular literary themes, figurative language, techniques, and forms for religious purposes.[30]

There are numerous instances of Southwell's use of sacred parody in his English poems, and his example was a shaping factor in the future of devotional poetry. Perhaps the most well-known, and obvious, is his 'A Phansie turned to a sinners complaint', which is a line-by-line parody of Sir Edward Dyer's poem, 'A Fancy'.[31] Using the manner, language, and metrical form of Dyer's poem, Southwell converts this love lyric into a meditative analysis of sin and its cure. He eliminates, of course, all pagan references; for example, when Dyer says, 'With Sisiphus and all his pheres,' Southwell substitutes, 'Judas and his cursed crue.' These kinds of substitutions are to be expected, but what is most intriguing about the poem is Southwell's ability to convert very convincingly a lover's complaint into a sinner's complaint by altering the subject yet keeping most of Dyer's original poem.

A second example of sacred parody in Southwell's poetry, again from Sir Edward Dyer, this time his 'My mynde to me a Kyngdome is', shows the wide range of Southwell's adaptations. Unlike the line-by-line parody (and, in fact, reply to 'A Fancy'), Southwell's 'Content and rich' completely restates the idea of Dyer's poem and adapts the phraseology in a much less direct manner, although there are several places in the poem that echo

Dyer's diction. Instead of Dyer's six-line stanza of iambic tetrameter, Southwell chooses the old poulter's measure, a form used by Lord Vaux in his poem 'Of a contented mynde' found in the most popular miscellany of the day, *The Paradise of Dainty Devices* (1576-1606). Perhaps Southwell had this poem also in mind when he composed 'Content and rich'. In fact, he is culling from a long-established tradition, the so-called poetry of the 'mean estate', not merely from a single poem. Martz points out that Horace's well-known poem on this subject had been adapted or translated in at least three poems that appear in *Tottel's Miscellany* (1557), most notably by Surrey in his 'Praise mean and constant estate', and that Southwell draws some of his ideas and specific images from Horace's poem, either directly or indirectly.[32] In contrast, then, to the rather mechanical adaptations found in some of Southwell's poems, 'Content and rich' shows his ability to use whole traditions and multiple sources in his attempt to effect a change in the direction of English devotional poetry.

Southwell's methodology of sacred parody is a pioneering effort that the major devotional poets of the seventeenth century, especially Herbert and Crashaw, will bring to perfection. One might cite, for example, the conclusion of Herbert's 'Jordan (II)', a parody of Sidney's ending of the first sonnet in *Astrophil and Stella*, and especially 'A Parody', a parody of 'Song: Soules joy, now I am Gone' attributed to William Herbert, third earl of Pembroke. From Crashaw one might recall his masterful Nativity Ode, in which he parodies several traditions, such as the Petrarchan and the classical pastoral.

One of Southwell's most successful efforts at converting profane poetry to sacred verse is his 'Marie Magdalens complaint at Christs death', in which he adapts the theme of the bereaved lover, which is so pervasive in Elizabethan poetry that it is impossible to suggest any one source. Thomas Morley, recognising the superiority of Southwell's poem, set three stanzas of it to music in his *First Booke of Ayres* (1600)—five years after Southwell's martyrdom and the first publication of his poems. Martz claims that in this poem, which he called Southwell's 'best example of sacred parody', 'we have the strongest possible evidence for Southwell's position as a precursor of the meditative line, and especially of Herbert'. He adds, 'Even in those poems in which he is only partially successful, we should not underestimate the role that his example and experimentation played in the shaping of later English poetry'.[33] Martz is right in suggesting that often the inferiority of some of Southwell's sacred parodies must be attributable to the weak models that he chose to imitate. Time after time, he turned to the kind of poetry best represented by *The Paradise of Dainty Devices*—primarily because it was the most popular, modish verse of the day. Since such poetry appealed to the very people Southwell wished to reach, he adapted it to the service of religion rather than better, but less popular, poetry.

Southwell turned not only to English and contemporary sources to parody. In his poem, 'What joy to live', he imitates the popular sonnet by Petrarch, 'Pace no trovo e no ho da far guerra' (*Rime* 134). Southwell's phrasing and his use of the six-line stanza suggest that he may have had in mind Thomas Watson's rendering of the poem that appears in *Hekatompathia, or the Passionate Centurie of Love* (1582).[34] Southwell, using the same basic ideas and stanzaic pattern employed by Watson, transfers them to describe the sense of exile experienced by the Christian who seeks spiritual fulfilment. In his best-known poem, 'The Burning Babe', Southwell cleverly parodies Petrarchan images of freezing and burning, tear-floods and flames, and in 'Joseph's Amazement', he draws upon the rhetoric of Petrarch by which Joseph is portrayed as a lover trapped between trust and suspicion—all of which is described in conventional Petrarchan paradoxes.[35]

The list of profane or secular genres that Southwell 're-wove' and converted to sacred purposes is indeed long and would include the epigram, the medieval complaint poem, plain-style wisdom poem, the consolatory poem, the fortune poem, and poems of moral admonition, to name only a few.

When Southwell returned to England as an underground priest, the Council of Trent (1545-1563) had been over for twenty-three years; but because English Catholics had been cut off, for the most part, from the major theological developments on the Continent, their Catholicism often was not fully informed by the doctrines and spirit of the Post-Tridentine Church. Thus, Southwell took it upon himself to deal with a number of issues in his poetry that the Council had addressed. An analysis of the subject matter of his poems shows how Southwell chose those themes and subjects that reflect major Counter-Reformation issues. In general terms, his major concerns were repentance for sin, episodes from the lives of the Virgin and Christ that emphasise specifically Catholic doctrinal matter, suffering endured for the sake of faith, and moral exhortations to live lives of exemplary integrity, humility, and Christian love. These subjects are obviously appropriate for a Church that was fighting for its very survival in England.

Perhaps a few examples will suffice to illustrate how the subjects and themes that Southwell explores in his poetry fit very purposefully into his specific ministry of consoling, encouraging, and instructing his countrymen

and how these subjects and themes are specifically Tridentine and Jesuit in
their emphasis.

In his sequence of fourteen poems on the lives of Mary and Christ,
Southwell most likely was influenced by Bencius and Pontanus, both of
whom had recommended that poets compose hymns on the liturgical feasts
of the Virgin. Bencius, in fact, wrote a number of poems on the life of
Christ and included poems on the Virgin and her Assumption.[36] It is important to remember that in pre-Reformation England devotion to Mary had
been particularly fervent; in fact, England was piously called 'Our Lady's
Dowry'. The Archbishop of Canterbury, Thomas Arundel, in 1399 noted,
'The contemplation of the great mystery of the Incarnation has drawn all
Christian people to revere [Mary], from whom came the first beginnings of
our redemption. But we [the English], being servants of her own inheritance and liegemen of her especial dowry, as we are commonly called,
ought to surpass all others in the warmth of our praise and devotion'.[37]
Thus, Southwell may simply be re-enforcing devotion to Mary that
remained strong among English Catholics and that perhaps still held some
appeal for those who no longer identified themselves with the Old Faith.
One has only to think of Donne's startling lines in 'Goodfriday, 1613. Riding Westward', written two years before his entry into the Anglican priesthood, 'durst I / Upon his miserable mother cast mine eye, / Who was God's
partner here, and furnish'd thus / Halfe of that Sacrifice, which ransomed
us'—a line that Barbara Lewalski rather conveniently overlooks in her discussion of the poem in *Protestant Poetics*. Or one recalls Herbert's wish in
'To All Angels and Saints' to address his vows 'most gladly' to the
'Blessed Maid', who was 'the cabinet where the jewel lay,' but adds, 'But
now, alas, I dare not; for our King / Whom we do all jointly adore and
praise, / Bids no such thing'.

Following this sequence on Mary and Christ come four meditative
poems on the nativity of Christ—'A childe my Choyce', 'New heaven, new
warre', 'The burning Babe', and 'New Prince, new pompe', all of which
make abundant use of paradox to teach that power resides in faith, not in
political strength, a lesson that would both encourage and console those
who were politically powerless and increasingly marginalised in English
society.

In three poems on Christ's agony in Gethsemane—'Sinnes heavie
loade', 'Christs Bloody sweat', and 'Christs sleeping friends', Southwell
places the suffering of his co-religionists in a larger context than the immediate one and offers them indirectly the consolation of joining their
agony to that of Christ.

In eight complaint poems on various figures of remorse—such as St. Peter, Mary Magdalen, and David—in which those who have grievously sinned regret their ways and, through tears of remorse, seek God's forgiveness—Southwell presents exemplary models of Christian repentance to his readers. Perhaps these poems also were intended as warnings to Englishmen who had given up or who were thinking of giving up their faith that conscience will have the last say. In these poems Southwell imports into English poetry the literature of tears that was so popular on the Continent, a tradition that culminates in Crashaw's 'The Weeper'.

The longest poem in Southwell's canon, 'St. Peters Complaint', is a dramatic monologue in which Peter offers a pattern of repentance for those Englishmen who were denied the opportunity to confess their sins to a priest or who rejected the practice of auricular confession. All of the elements for what is known as a 'perfect act of contrition' are set out—contrition, confession, the desire to make satisfaction, and absolution. Southwell finds Peter a particularly attractive choice of sinner because his sin was not simply one of betrayal (as Judas's was), but one of denial. Southwell seems to say that the Church can always reclaim those who betray their faith but that those who deny it are in much greater danger of being lost forever. The steps he charts in the process of obtaining 'perfect contrition' are exactly those prescribed by the Council of Trent for persons unable to make an auricular confession.[38] Thus, this poem, like all the others, has a specific didactic purpose completely in harmony with the exhortations of the Council of Trent and the Society of Jesus about the importance of art in leading persons to God.

In conclusion, a brief comment is required on one other very important aspect of Southwell's poetry that perhaps had greater influence on some of the devotional poets who followed him than has been generally recognised, and that is the issue of voice in his poems. Southwell's poetic voice has a rather consistent range that encompasses the didactic and hortatory, both expressed, for the most part, impersonally and objectively. Martz, in his attempts to link Southwell with the seventeenth-century devotional poets, claims that in his poetry Southwell is given to self-analysis and introspection[39], but that is a questionable observation. While in his personal life, as reflected, for instance, in his *Exercitia et Devotiones*, Southwell as a Jesuit obviously did engage in a great deal of self-analysis; in his poetry, however, he does not focus on himself but rather on the subject that he considers important to his English audience. Nancy Pollard Brown is correct in insisting that Southwell's purpose in writing was fundamentally service, not self-expression.[40] Clearly he is following the insistence of the Jesuit theorists that intimate, personal expression of the self ought to be avoided. For instance, in the sequence on the life of Christ and the Virgin, *Southwell's* response to these mysteries is *not* recorded; instead the reader is taught the doctrinal significance of these events by a didactic, objective voice that resorts to paradox and other types of wit to move the emotions. The sequence is not, strictly speaking, meditative; it is rather a collection of epigrams that move historically from poem to poem and doctrinally from stanza to stanza. We learn—but we do not actually see, hear, feel, or directly experience the events presented. These poems do not have that kind of dramatic unfolding that one expects to find in a meditative poem.

Although didactic, Southwell's voice is seldom polemical or argumentative. One reason, of course, is that most of his poems are on subjects that most Englishmen, both Catholics and Anglicans, endorsed and supported. But even in those poems that could have been seen as controversial by sixteenth and seventeenth century readers, such as 'The death of our Ladie', 'Of the Blessed sacrament of the Aulter', and two poems on contemporary events, 'Decease, release' on the execution of Mary Queen of Scots and the consolatary poem 'I dye without desert' concerning the imprisoned Earl of Arundel, Philip Howard, Southwell's voice is not argumentative.

On the other hand, many of Southwell's poems do not lack emotion or passion. When speaking of Christ and the saints, for example, his voice is one of familiarity, as seen in 'New heaven, new warre', 'New Prince, new pompe', and 'The Burning Babe', all of which are highly dramatic and meditative poems. But the important point to remember is that Southwell is not recording *his* own idiosyncratic responses to these biblical events and Christian themes; rather he stages them in such a way they will produce *in his reader* an affective and devotional response that is quite similar to the one achieved in many of Crashaw's poems. Even in 'The Burning Babe', which begins, 'As I in hoarie Winters night / Stoode shivering in the snow', the 'I' is not an individualized 'I', but rather a representational 'I', a generalised Christian witness, one not unlike the voice in many of Herbert's poems.

Considering Southwell's popularity, it is hard to believe that most, if not all, the devotional poets that followed him were *not* aware of his poetry. Several modern editors have pointed out numerous examples of echoes of Southwell's poetry in the major devotional poets of the seventeenth century, especially in Herbert's *The Temple*. But more much important than direct allusions are Southwell's example and practice of sacred parody and his introduction of meditative verse into English poetry.

Southwell's poetry, written under the most difficult of circumstances, with little time to re-write or revise, remains as an example of Counter-Reformation theory and practice and as a testament to an age that believed that both religion and poetry were of immense consequence. As one reads through these uneven poems, one is struck by how consistently Southwell held to his intention of converting secular poetry and baptising it into a new service. In his dedicatory letter to his 'loving Cosen', he wrote, 'I have heere layd a few course threds together, to invite some skillfuller wits to goe forward in the same, or to begin some finer peece, wherein it may be seene, how well verse and vertue sute together'. Had he not been executed at the age of thirty-three, Southwell would have witnessed how fully his invitation was accepted by some of the greatest religious poets in the English language.

Notes

1   For modern biographical accounts, see Pierre Janelle, *Robert Southwell the Writer: A Study in Religious Inspiration* (London, 1935); Christopher Devlin, *The Life of Robert Southwell: Poet and Martyr* (New York, 1956); and Nancy Pollard Brown's introduction to *The Poems of Robert Southwell, S. J.*, eds. James H. McDonald and Nancy Pollard Brown (Oxford, 1967), [xv]-xxxiv. All quotations from the poems are from this edition. Introductory material will be referred to as Brown.
2   As quoted by Brown from an account preserved at Stonyhurst College entitled *A Brefe Discourse of the condemnation and execution of Mr Robert Southwell*, p. xxxiv.
3   Devlin, p. 88.
4   Brown, p. xxix.
5   Helen C. White, 'The Contemplative Element in Robert Southwell', *Catholic Historical Review*, 48 (1962): 2.
6   Brown, p. xxii.
7   Ibid., pp. xxxi-xxxii.
8   Devlin, p. 290.
9   Joseph D. Scallon, S.J., *The Poetry of Robert Southwell* (Elizabethan & Renaissance Studies, edited by James Hogg, No. 11) (Salzburg, 1975), iv.
10 Brown, pp. lv-lvi.
11 Claire Grece Dabrowska, 'Robert Southwell, 1561(?)-1595: A Revaluation', *Roczniki Humanistyczne*, 6 (1957): 24.
12 For details concerning editions, see Brown, pp. lv-lxxvi.
13 Brown, pp. xcix-c.
14 Louis L. Martz, *The Poetry of Meditation: A Study in English Religious Literature of the Seventeenth Century*, rev. ed. (New Haven and London, 1962); see also John R. Roberts, 'The Influence of *The Spiritual Exercises* of St. Ignatius on the Nativity Poems of Robert Southwell', *Journal of English and Germanic Philology*, 59 (1960): 450-456.
15 St. Ignatius of Loyola, *The Spiritual Exercises of St. Ignatius*, translated by Louis J. Puhl, S.J. (Westminster, Maryland, 1951), 12.

16   Janelle, *Robert Southwell the Writer*, p. 118.
17   Pierre Janelle, *The Catholic Reformation* (Milwaukee, 1963), 138.
18   Ibid., p. 137.
19   As quoted by Janelle, *Robert Southwell the Writer*, p. 119.
20   White, p. 7.
21   Janelle, *Robert Southwell the Writer*, pp. 119-20.
22   Ibid., p. 120.
23   Janelle, *The Catholic Reformation*, pp. 170-171.
24   As quoted by Janelle, *Robert Southwell the Writer*, p. 122.
25   Brown, p. xviii.
26   Janelle, *Robert Southwell the Writer*, pp. 123-126.
27   *Poems*, p. 1.
28   Martz, p. 180.
29   A. Lytton Sells, *The Italian Influence in English Poetry: From Chaucer to South-well* (Bloomington, 1955), 320.
30   Rosemond Tuve, '"Sacred Parody" of Love Poetry, and Herbert', *Studies in the Renaissance,* 8 (1961): 249-290.
31   Brown, p. xcvi.
32   Martz, p. 199.
33   Ibid., pp. 191-193.
34   Brown, p. 145.
35   A.D. Cousins, *Catholic Religious Poets from Southwell to Crashaw: A Critical History* (London, 1991), 56.
36   Sells, p. 315.
37   As quoted in *A Dictionary of Mary*, edited by Donald Attwater (New York, 1956), 70.
38   L.J. Sundaram, 'Robert Southwell's *St. Peters Complaint*—An Interpretation' in *Studies in Elizabethan Literature*, edited by P.S. Sostri (Nagor, New Delhi, 1972), 9.
39   Martz, pp. 183-187.
40   Brown, p. xviii.

6

POISON AND HONEY:
THE POLITICS OF THE SACRED AND THE PROFANE IN
SPENSER'S *FOWRE HYMNES* (1596)

JONATHAN SAWDAY

The 'problem' of Edmund Spenser's *Fowre Hymnes* (1596) begins with the
dedication of the hymns and the ambiguous retraction contained within that
dedication—a retraction which is repeated in the body of the verses themselves. As Enid Welsford, over a quarter of a century ago, observed:

> Why should Spenser recant hymns which, whether reformed or unre-
> formed, express a lofty and spiritual ideal of love between the sexes?
> What was he recanting, and why? Are the first hymns Petrarchan or
> Platonic? Are the last hymns Platonic or Protestant? Are all four hymns
> Platonic and intended to depict various stages of the Ladder of Love,
> or were they all from the start written from a strictly orthodox point of
> view and planned to emphasize the contrast between Christianity and
> Neo-Platonism?[1]

Welsford's assumption, of course, was that the *Fowre Hymnes* presented a
paradox which was primarily intellectual. This may well be the case. But,
rather than attempting to re-trace the various philosophical schemes which
might locate the hymns in the opposition between platonic, Petrarchan, or
protestant discursive modes, I shall try and situate them in an altogether
more local political context. That context is determined by the very conditions of writing and reading which came to prevail amongst 'public'
writers, in England, in the last years of the sixteenth century.[2] My subject,
then, is the politics of Spenser's manipulation of the *codes* of the sacred
and the profane in the *Fowre Hymnes* of 1596. The autumn of that year was
a moment when, for reasons which I hope this essay will make clear, Spenser's own position had become suddenly, and dangerously, exposed. I shall
argue that the *Fowre Hymnes* were part of a concerted response to rapidly
shifting political circumstances—the uneasy realignment of faction which
swirled around the ageing Queen Elizabeth I in the mid 1590s.

I

The hymns were first published (together with the second edition of *Daph-naida*), in 1596 by William Ponsonby.[3] Spenser dedicated the *Fowre Hymnes* to the sisters Margaret Countess of Cumberland, and Anne (printed as Marie) Countess of Warwick, and dated the dedication 'Greenwich this first of September 1596'.[4] The two profane hymns ('Of Love' and 'Of Beautie'), the puritan Countesses are told in the dedication, were 'written in the greener times of my youth' (*SP* 690).[5] For all their supposed juvene-scent quality—a juvenescence which is unlikely given the relationship of *Amoretti* (1595) to the hymns—the effect of the verses (Spenser claimed) was uncomfortable.[6] The poems 'too much pleased those of like age and disposition, which being too vehemently carried with that kind of affection, do rather sucke out poyson to their strong passion than hony to their honest delight' (*SP* 690). And so, as though anxious not to appear to be encourag-ing profane love, Spenser embarked on a coda or supplement—the two 'sacred' hymns. Responsibility for embarking on the supplement, therefore, did not lie with the poet, but with his readers—specifically the two count-esses of the dedication—since Spenser claimed to be moved 'by the one of you two most excellent Ladies, to call in the same.' But, such a course of action proved to be impossible, due to the poems' wide dissemination. Unable to gather in the manuscripts, Spenser claimed that he had made the best of a bad job:

> ... I resolved at least to amend, and by way of retraction to reforme thcm, making in stead of those two Hymnes of earthly or naturall love and beautie, two others of heavenlly and celestiall. The which I doe dedicate joyntly unto you two honourable sisters, as to the most excel-lent and rare ornaments of all true love and beautie, both in the one and the other kinde ... (*SP*, 690)

What, exactly, is Spenser now dedicating to the two countesses? Ambigu-ously, the countesses would now appear to be the public recipients of a collection of verse, at least a large part of which has been expressly cat-egorised as, in some measure, corrupting. And what status, therefore, does a supplement possess? Does it cancel the precedent text? Or does it, rather, work in the reverse fashion: underlining the dangerously profane content of the text which has been supplemented? The point, however, is that both the sacred and the profane, the honey and the poison, are urged on to the pub-lic, and publicly urged on to the sisters who have thereby become not only ornaments of all true love and beautie, but *exempla* of that 'other kind' of love: the love which Spenser had set out to supplement.

This, then, is the elaborate fictional disguise with which Spenser had cloaked his verses. That it *is* a disguise, of course, depends upon the reader's belief that the first pair of hymns, with their exalted view of human love, could hardly have given offence even to the most resolutely puritan reader. Equally, it is difficult to read the second pair of hymns as an 'afterword', appended to the earlier hymns in an attempt to negate their supposedly corrupting effects. As Elizabeth Bieman has written: '... the interconnections that pervade the poems indicate that they were parts of one whole to the creator' though that wholeness need not preclude the possibility that the hymns were written 'through revisions to the first pair in the light of the second'.[7] Moreover, as any reader of the 'Mutablitie Cantos' can testify, the question of 'retraction' in Spenser's poetry is a complex issue over which we will need to pause for a moment.

II

In the Proem to Book IV of *The Faerie Queene*, first published in the same year as the *Fowre Hymnes*, we find Spenser embarking on (but not sustaining) an apology and retraction for 'praising loue, as I have done of late' (*FQ* IV. i Proem 1), which appears to be not dissimilar to the retraction to be found in the dedication to the hymns.[8] The necessity of retraction in *The Faerie Queene*, A.C. Hamilton suggests (*FQ* 426 note, 709 note), would appear to have been occasioned by the offence taken by William Cecil, Lord Burghley, at Spenser's authorship of certain earlier 'looser rimes'. It has been supposed that these 'looser rimes' were Spenser's coded attacks on Cecil to be found in 'The Ruines of Time' and 'Mother Hubberds Tale', published in the *Complaints* of 1591, but circulating in manuscript form at an earlier date. Yet, as the Proem makes clear, what was objected to was not so much satirical attack as 'profanity'—the poetic treatment of human sexual love. A more likely object of Cecil's displeasure, therefore, was the treatment of love to be found in *Amoretti and Epithalamion* published in 1595, or, indeed, in the earlier books of *The Faerie Queene* itself. In the retraction, having evoked Cecil's statesmanlike *gravitas*—'The rugged forhead that with graue forsight / Welds kingdoms causes, and affaires of state' (*FQ* IV. i Proem 1)—Spenser proceeds, unambiguously, to defend his poetry from the charge of wantonness:

> Such ones ill judge of loue, that cannot loue,
> Ne in their frozen hearts feele kindly flame:
> For thy they ought not thing unknowne reproue,
> Ne naturall affection faultlesse blame,
> For fault of few that have abusd the same.   (*FQ* IV. i Proem 2)

Far from this being (as Bieman seems to suggest) an attempt on Spenser's part to 'assuage' Cecil's displeasure, the Proem acts as a self-confident reprimand aimed at the 'rugged forhead'. Equally, the Proem as a whole amounts to a tutorial in the relationship between earthly and heavenly passion which (the implication is clear) those such as Cecil could not hope either to feel or to understand. 'To such therefore I do not sing at all' (*FQ* IV. i Proem 4), Spenser, testily, writes. Instead, he seeks shelter in the one who *will* understand: 'that sacred saint my soueraigne Queene'. Elizabeth, rather than Cecil and his kind, the Proem insinuates, is the true recipient of the text, so that Cecil's 'displeasure' at any 'looser rimes' is not merely a manifestation of inattentive and uninformed criticism, or even prurient misapprehension, but a solecism of the most grotesque kind.

Such a robust defence of the grammar and interrelationship of the sacred and profane sits uneasily besides the circuitous evasions of the dedication to the *Fowre Hymnes*. In the January of 1596 (when the second edition of *The Faerie Queene* containing Spenser's reproof of Cecil was entered on the Stationers' Register), Spenser felt entirely self-confident about that interrelationship. Yet, by September of that year (the date of the dedication to *Fowre Hymnes*), we find Spenser embarking on a complex, even agonisedly embarrassed, retraction and defence of verses which hardly deserve the level of auto-critique the author offers in the dedicatory material. A further complication becomes evident if we follow the Cecil connection, and turn to another example of a Spenserian 'apology' and 'retraction' for framing 'looser rimes'. This 'apology', a careful inspection soon reveals, is no apology whatsoever, but a careful, ingenious, and calculated insult aimed directly at Cecil, but couched in the dialectic of sacred and profane love.

In 1590, when the first edition of *The Faerie Queene* was published, the poem (Bks I-III) appeared with an appendix of dedicatory sonnets, one of which is addressed to 'the right honourable the Lo. Burleigh Lo. High Threasurer [sic] of England'. The sonnet runs as follows:

To you right noble Lord, whose carefull brest
    To menage of most grave affaires is bent,
    And on whose mightie shoulders most doth rest
    The burdein of this kingdomes gouernement,
As the wide compasse of the firmament,
    On *Atlas* mighty shoulders is vpstayd;
    Vnfitly I these ydle rimes present,
    The labor of lost time, and wit vnstayd:
Yet if their deeper sence be inly wayd,
    And the dim vele, with which from comune vew
    Their fairer parts are hid, aside be layd.
    Perhaps not vaine they may appeare to you.
Such as they be, vouchsafe them to receaue,
    And wipe their faults out of your censure graue.   (*FQ* Appendix 3)

Once more, we catch Spenser offering the Lord Treasurer a public tutorial in literary criticism. But this was a tutorial with a sting. The sonnet, which begins gracefully enough by invoking respect for both Cecil and his high office, and which characterises both the poem and the poet in such humble terms, soon reveals itself as something more when we catch the echo of the 'Bowre of Blisse' episode of *The Faerie Queene* (*FQ* II. xii). For Cecil is urged to lay aside 'the dim vele' which hides 'from comune view' the poem's 'fairer parts', in just the same way that Guyon had discovered within the richly over-wrought fountain the female figures who 'ne car'd to hyde, / Their dainty parts from vew of any, which them eyde' (*FQ* II. xii. 63). 'The dim vele' which Cecil must pierce, in order to come to the 'deeper sence' of the poem, echoes both the 'vele' of 'Christall waues' to be found in the erotoscopia which is the fountain, and the 'vele of silk and siluer thin' that (just) fails to conceal the body of Acrasia in her post-coital languor in the Bowre itself (*FQ* II. xii. 77). In other words, what Spenser appears to have set out to achieve in his dedicatory sonnet is not so much a careful retraction, as an artfully concealed joke at Cecil's expense. Deploying the language of 'profane' love, which reaches its apogee in the 'Bowre of Blisse', Spenser has publicly admonished the Lord Treasurer. The careful reader of *The Faerie Queene* (particularly the careful reader of the 1590s, possessed of some knowledge of the rivalry between the Leicester and Cecil factions at court) would have appreciated the joke.[9] For, in effect, the 'rugged forhead' is urged to peer more closely at the erotic element of the poetry. Cecil, the sonnet confidently predicts, will find himself in exactly the predicament of Guyon in the Bowre, embracing 'secret plesaunce' at the sights which protestant morality should eschew. But his gaze will go no further than that superficial (and profane) surface. The 'deeper sence' of the mystery will continue to evade the Lord Treasurer. It is as if Spenser has anticipated Cecil's ability to miss the point that the Proem to Book IV will later (in 1596) make, namely that from the classical tradition of the veneration of earthly love 'full many lessons did apply, / The which these stoicke censors cannot well denie' (*FQ* IV. Proem 3).[10]

Re-positioning the *Fowre Hymnes* within this rhetorical *and* political game of apology and retraction, we can begin to sense how they are participating in the political culture of the moment. If we accept that the hymns attempt to resolve the irresolvable tension between Spenser the puritan ideologue and Spenser the court artist by attempting to maintain a contradictory position of appearing to be *both* puritan ideologue *and* court poet simultaneously, then a further detail in the dedication becomes relevant.[11] Spenser did not, invariably, note the place and date of composition of his many dedications to patrons. When he does, however, 'place' his compositions—as in the case of *The Shepheardes Calendar* (1579), *Daphnaida* (1591), and *Colin Clouts Come Home Againe* (1595)—he tends to note his own residence: 'from my lodging at London thys 10. of Aprill. 1579' or 'From my house of Kilcolman, the 27. of December. 1591'.[12] The *Fowre Hymnes*, as we have seen, are carefully dated 'Greenwich this first of September 1596'. In other words, despite the affiliation of the poems with the puritanism of the dedicatees, they are also clearly labelled as emerging from the court.

But it was not as a court poet that Spenser was in the public eye in 1596. Rather, the puritan ideologue was foremost in the public mind. In the January of that year, as we have already seen, Spenser had supervised the first appearance of the second half of *The Faerie Queene* into the world, with its terrible vision in Book V of violence unleashed on Ireland, and its defence, as David Norbrook has noted, of the Leicester-Essex foreign policy. In the same year he was working on the *View of the Present State of Ireland* (1633)—a text which, of course, advocated, if necessary, the wholesale eradication of native (catholic) culture.[13] Moreover, the autumn of 1596 was also the period during which the *Prothalamion* was published, with its nostalgic evocation of the Leicester circle, and its hopeful anticipation of a resurgent and militant protestantism invested in Essex.[14] But, in the autumn of 1596 the political landscape had begun to shift. In October, Essex (at the advice of Bacon) had begun the cultivation of the Cecil faction—a realignment of political alliances which Spenser could hardly have welcomed, given his public and published opposition to Cecil.[15] Moreover, although the *Prothalamion* celebrated the betrothal of the two daughters of the Earl of Somerset which had taken place some time before 8

November 1596, and though the dedication to the *Fowre Hymnes* was (carefully) dated 1 September, there is no actual evidence as to which text was published first.[16] Indeed, one might surmise that, in the late autumn of 1596, the publication of the *Fowre Hymnes*, and with it the judicious re-traction of *exactly* the position which Spenser had maintained at Cecil's expense in the earlier part of that year, would have been all the more politic if the text had appeared *before* Essex began his October overtures to the Cecil faction. In short, September 1596 might well have been the earliest convincing date with which Spenser could signal *his* change of heart which is, after all, the true subject of the *Fowre Hymnes*. Whether it represents the actual date of completion, however, is another matter.

III

In other words, the dialectic between the sacred and profane can be under-stood not only as part of a wider cultural struggle between puritanism and humanism, where (as Alan Sinfield has remarked of Spenser's *Fowre Hymnes*), 'the humanist will not submit to the puritan', but also as a *vehicle* within which the courtier / poet can manoeuvre.[17] The sacred and the pro-fane, then, stand in uneasy counterpoint to one another, not only in an intel-lectual but in a directly political sense. An analysis conducted along these lines leads us to reflect on the condition and status of both writing and reading within the culture inhabited by a work such as the *Fowre Hymnes*. And here, a further level of tension, beyond that inherent within the dialec-tic form, or the debates of the allegorists, is suggested in Spenser's dedica-tion. That tension resides in the *fiction*—a fiction carefully crafted by Spen-ser—of the uncontrollable nature of both manuscript and print circulation. Once out of the writer's hands, Spenser implies, even within the more re-stricted sphere of manuscript circulation, what possible control does the author have over the text? More to the point, what control can be exercised over the hermeneutic skills residing in any possible community of readers? Here, we are negotiating that doubling, or shifting, inter-relationship of semi-public manuscript culture and public printed culture. Joseph Lowen-stein has written of the ways in which Spenser came to find print an 'im-periled' medium, and yet one which provided a 'sphere of complex self-defense'.[18] And the printed self-defence of the *Fowre Hymnes* is undoubt-edly complex, since it is involved with the related political and poetic prob-lems associated with the ideas of 'authorship' and 'repudiation'.

Disavowal and ownership—the process by which a text or an action could be both acknowledged and unacknowledged at one and the same time

—was part of the psychological fabric of Elizabethan political and literary culture. Perhaps it is equivalent to our modern, scandalous, idea of 'deniability'. What every poet-courtier, or courtier-poet, needed was a modicum of 'deniability' so that in the event of words or actions being 'misread', a strategic retreat could begin. Conversely, where actions or words were marked by the approval of those inhabiting the courtly milieu in which the poet moved, then the careful orchestration of 'deniability' could give way to its opposite—the assumption of ownership. Authorship, in other words, was a fraught condition. To be the author of actions or texts which gained approval was to see a return on the investment in time, patronage-seeking, and effort. But to be accused of the authorship of a text or event which gave rise to displeasure required a retreat into the subtle word-play of disavowal, or repudiation, once more. The game was made more complex since interpretation and judgment were themselves entirely contingent on the passage of time. Who could know whether or not today's approved text might become tomorrow's source of displeasure? Sir Thomas Hoby, in his 1561 translation of Castiglione's *Libro del Cortegiano* (1528) (*The Book of the Courtier*), expressed this anxiety in the following way:

> Let him [the courtier] consider well what the thing is he doth or speaketh, the place where it is done, in presence of whom, in what time, the cause why he doth it, his age, his profession, the end whereto it tendeth, and the meanes that may bring him to it: and so let him apply him selfe discreetly with these advertisements to what soever hee mindeth to doe or speake.[19]

Continually policing his speech, manner, and gestures, the inhabitant of the court world agonized over every utterance. And it is within this vista of continual, courtly, self-scrutiny that we should read the complex dedication of the *Fowre Hymnes*, where we can sense the factional world of court interests slipping over into the literary sphere inhabited by the hymns.

The Queen herself, of course, was an adept at the game of simultaneous authorship and distance. Elizabeth's famous 'answer answerless' which she gave in response to those pressing her to sign Mary Stuart's death warrant in 1587, for example, might have sprung from the pages of *The Faerie Queene* itself:

> If I should say, I would not do what you request, it might peradventure be more than I thought; and to say I would do it, might perhaps breed peril of what you labour to preserve.[20]

Having signed the warrant, another round of denial began, since Elizabeth ordered that the warrant be sealed, and then she countermanded the order. A crisis meeting of eleven councillors was called, and it was determined that the warrant be sent without any further consultation with the Queen. A text, then, had been authored but where was its authority? When Elizabeth heard of the execution, her rage was 'uncontrollable'. She went so far, according to the historian John Guy, as to investigate the possibility of having the secretary—William Davison—executed by royal prerogative for allowing the signed warrant to leave his possession. The hapless Davison was sent to the Tower, fined 10,000 marks, and imprisoned. Eighteen months later he was free and his salary had been restored to him.

This story is often recounted as an example of the Queen's command of 'masterful vacillation'. This may well be true, but it is also a story of authorship and ownership which runs like an invisible thread through the public and private discourses of Elizabethan culture. Assuming or refusing authorship, then, are two sides of a single coin. A text (or action) should contain its own principle of opposition. It should, ideally, deny itself even while it affirmed itself. The warrant should be signed and unsigned, sealed and unsealed, dispatched and undispatched at the same moment. This principle of simultaneous denial and affirmation structured the theoretical account of writing which Elizabethan literary culture generated. The clearest expression of the gesture was to be found in George Puttenham's account of figurative language in his *The Arte of English Poesie* of 1589. Figures and tropes, Puttenham wrote, create a 'certaine doubleness, whereby our talk is the more guileful and abusing'. Such 'doubleness' is part of an aesthetic which is a 'kind of dissimulation' in Puttenham's words, where 'the words bear contrary countenance to the intent'.[21] Discourse which is 'dark' is the mark to be aimed at—a mark that Spenser (famously) hit when he described *The Faerie Queene* as a 'darke conceit' in his 1589 letter to Raleigh (*FQ* 737). For all the discussion in the letter to Raleigh of 'gathering the whole intention of the conceit', intentionality is exactly what the letter was designed to fence or hedge.

The problem with which we are dealing, then, is the familiar difficulty in establishing what constitutes a truthful or false proposition—a debate which can be summarised in one word: equivocation. Equivocation, an art for which the Jesuits were peculiarly famous, was the facility, as Phineas Fletcher later expressed it in his violently anti-Jesuit poem *The Locusts* (1627), of 'mentall reservation' where a virtual falsehood in the form of a proposition is verbally true.[22] To Elizabeth's divines (as much as to her gaolers, her courtiers, and her poets) the art of equivocation was both a necessary skill and a constant object of attention and anxiety. Equivocation robbed the speaking subject of authority—and hence responsibility—since intention could no longer be inferred on the basis of the words which were spoken. For Sir Philip Sidney, whose *An Apology for Poetrie* was published (posthumously) the year before the *Fowre Hymnes*, poetry was a uniquely equivocal art:

> ... for the poet, he never affirms, and therefore never lieth. For, as I take it, to lie is to affirm that to be true which is false ... And therefore, though he [the poet] recounteth things not true, yet because he telleth not for true, he lieth not ...[23]

In other words, the degree of intention which is invested in the poetic statement has to be understood as minimal since poetry, by Sidney's definition, is incapable of affirmation. Here we have embarked upon a road which would lead, ultimately, to the twentieth-century proposition of Wittgenstein, that 'Language disguises thought'.[24] But for an Elizabethan courtier-poet it was not so much language in general, but poetic language in particular, wherein disguised thought could, paradoxically, be displayed.

IV

Spenser's *Fowre Hymnes* are, of course, profoundly equivocal. Understood as a system of mirrored parallels, the two sets of hymns seem to trace one another through a binary system of equivalence. Cupid and Venus in the first pair of hymns give way to Christ and Sapience in the second. The pagan is thus contrasted to the christian. The hymns of love (both sacred and profane) are presided over by male deities, those of beauty are presided over by female. Within such a structure of equivalence, we tend to assume that a species of progression is at work. The poems, then, appear to lead the reader upwards through a chain of ascent (informed by neoplatonic perspectives) by which earthly or transitory beauty and love is supplanted by the superior claims of heavenly rapture. Thus, in neoplatonic form, the sacred hymns require the existence of the profane to initiate the progressive ascent from outward to inward understanding.

To read the *Fowre Hymnes* in this way is to read them as exercises in spiritual development of a personal kind which accords entirely with the elaborate biographical fiction which Spenser had crafted into the fabric of the text, and which is displayed in the elaborate account (in the dedication) of the genesis of the hymns. That fiction structures the progression through the hymns as analogous to the passage between youth and age. Youth, then,

is the period of erotic poetry—the period of the first two hymns—while the
more sombre tones of maturity and age order the creation of the two later
hymns. The earlier text is cancelled by the later, and the wrong done to
morality rectified by the counter balance of sacred devotion. But we should
remember the example of Elizabeth's own careful manipulation of authorship and disavowal at this point. And we should remember, too, how Spenser had already manipulated the dialectic between the 'sacred' and the 'profane' in order to signal his own political allegiance within the shifting structures of court politics in the 1590s. What Spenser offers in the *Fowre
Hymnes* is a text which repudiates itself, denies responsibility, evades any
charge of adopting a position. The hymns have, in other words, their own
inbuilt principle of deniability, expressed in the opening stanzas of the
'Hymne of Heavenly Love' in the following way:

> Many lewd layes (ah woe is me the more)
> In praise of that mad fit, which fooles call love,
> I have in th'heat of youth made heretofore,
> That in light wits did loose affection move.
> But all those follies now I do reprove,
> And turned have the tenor of my string,
> The heavenly prayses of true love to sing.
>
> And ye that wont with greedy vaine desire
> To read my fault, and wondering at my flame,
> To warme your selves at my wide sparckling fire,
> Sith now that heat is quenched, quench my blame,
> And in her ashes shrowd my dying shame:
> For who my passed follies now pursewes,
> Beginnes his owne, and my old fault renewes.   (*SP*, 722)

If the Petrarchan convention of retraction is at work here, then whatever is
being retracted is not just a literary text or texts. Rather, it is any notion of
authorial responsibility. Just as Elizabeth signed, but did not seal, Mary's
execution warrant, so the poetic persona of the *Fowre Hymnes* has attempted to remove itself from the text by the device of (paradoxically)
insisting on its presence as a *former* authority reconstructed by the passage
of time. More importantly, the text is careful to implicate the reader, riven
by guilty desire, as a likely creator of profane (rather than sacred) meaning.
Guilt, or at any rate responsibility, is turned away from the crafted biographical persona—the creator of youthful and erotically charged libidinous
verse. All blame now lies with the reader: 'For who my passed follies now

pursewes, / Beginnes his owne, and my old fault renewes.' That is to say, 'My passed fault will now become your present folly'.

Within this ambience, what the *Fowre Hymnes* are setting out to achieve is a classic example of Puttenham's 'doubleness' or 'dissimulation'. It was as if Spenser had published the *Fowre Hymnes* as an insurance policy. To the courtly reader, the hymns will appear as an exercise in the fashionable courtly aesthetic of neoplatonism, with its poised negotiation of ascent between the profane and the sacred. To the puritan reader, they will appear as repudiations of exactly that philosophy, and thus be of a piece with the destruction of the Bower, and the consequent triumph of the values of Talus. And hence it follows that we need to be particularly careful in taking at face value a set of contraries such as the 'sacred' and the 'profane' when those contraries are discovered within the mirror-like world of court poetics and politics in the mid 1590s. The categories 'sacred' and 'profane' are not self-evident, particularly in the hands of a poet as alert to the nuances of the ebb and flow of political allegiance as Spenser undoubtedly was. We might even speculate that, in the autumn of 1596, the appearance of such a delicately contrived work as the *Fowre Hymnes* was not merely predictable, but necessary. Without questioning, for one moment, the intellectual and philosophical rationale which underpins the poetry of the hymns, we should also acknowledge that, in political terms, they might appear as extraordinary fortuitous performances. And that, perhaps, was the point.

Notes

1   Enid Welsford (ed.), *Spenser: Fowre Hymns, Epithalamion. A Study of Edmund Spenser's Doctrine of Love* (Oxford, 1967), 37. See also: Josephine Waters Bennett, 'The Theme of Spenser's *Fowre Hymnes*', *Studies in Philology* 28 (1931): 18-57; Mary I. Oates, '*Fowre Hymnes*: Spenser's Retractions of Paradise', *Spenser Studies: A Renaissance Poetry Annual* 4 (1983): 143-169.
2   For an account of the rise of the 'public' writer, see Richard Helgerson, 'The New Poet Presents Himself: Spenser and the Idea of a Literary Career', *PMLA* 95 (1978): 893-911; and Richard Helgerson, *Self-Crowned Laureates: Spenser, Jonson, Milton and the Literary System* (Berkeley, 1983).
3   For bibliographical details of the *Fowre Hymnes* see Francis R. Johnson, *A Critical Bibliography of the Works of Edmund Spenser printed before 1700* (London, 1966), 31-32.
4   Lady Margaret (d. 1616) was the daughter of Francis Russell, Earl of Bedford, and wife of George Clifford, Earl of Cumberland. Her sister, Anne (d. 1604), was the wife of Ambrose Dudley, Earl of Warwick, brother to the Earl of Leicester (see Welsford, p. 143). The confusion over the christian name of the Countess of War-

wick, Prof. Proudfoot has suggested to me, may be explained by the fact that 'Marie' was often understood as a contraction of the name 'Marianne'. On the patrons of the *Fowre Hymnes* see: Jon A. Quitslund, 'Spenser and the Patronesses of the *Fowre Hymnes*: "Ornaments of All True Love and Beautie"', in: Margaret Hannay (ed.), *Silent but for the Word: Tudor Women as Patrons, Translators, and Writers of Religious Works* (Kent, 1985), 184-202.

5 Edmund Spenser, *Shorter Poems* [*SP*] edited by William A. Oram *et al.* (New Haven, 1989). References to poems other than *The Faerie Queene* are to this edition.

6 See Einer Bjorvand and Richard Schell, 'Introduction' to *Fowre Hymnes*, in: *SP*, p. 684. On similarities between *Amoretti* and the *Fowre Hymnes* see: William C. Johnson, 'Spenser's "Greener" *Hymnes* and *Amoretti*: "Retraction" and "Reform"' *English Studies* 73 (1992): 431-443.

7 See Elizabeth Bieman, *Plato Baptized: Towards the Interpretation of Spenser's Mimetic Fictions* (Toronto, 1988), 154-155; and see Welsford, pp. 36-37.

8 Edmund Spenser, *The Faerie Queene,* edited by A.C. Hamilton (London and New York, 1977). All references to *The Faerie Queene* (*FQ*) are to this edition.

9 The Earl of Leicester, of course, had died in 1588 - an event which, as David Norbrook has remarked: 'was to mark a decisive setback for the puritan movement'. See David Norbrook, *Poetry and Politics in the English Renaissance* (London, 1984), 82.

10 Spenser's dedicatory sonnet to Cecil, just like his dedication to the *Fowre Hymnes*, has occasioned considerable critical puzzlement. Richard Rambuss, for example, in his subtle reading of the relationship of Spenser's poetry and his career, is unsure as to whether the sonnet is 'fulsome' (p. 93) or 'defensive' (p. 105). See Richard Rambuss, *Spenser's Secret Career* (Cambridge, 1993).

11 Spenser, though he may have been no puritan himself, was firmly associated with the more militant wing of Protestantism, and the 1590s, as Diarmaid MacCulloch has observed, was a period of retreat for upholders of puritan ideology. See Diarmaid MacCulloch, *The Later Reformation in England 1547-1603* (Basingstoke, 1990), 56-61. On Spenser's own religious views see Virgil K. Whittaker, *The Religious Basis of Spenser's Thought* (Stanford, 1950), *passim*.

12 Dedications to *The Shepheardes Calendar* (*SP* 21) and *Colin Clouts Come Home Againe* (*SP* 526). *Daphnaida* is simply dated 'London this first of January. 1591' (*SP* 493).

13 On Ireland and Spenser see the essays in Patricia Coughlan (ed.), *Spenser and Ireland: An Interdisciplinary Perspective* (Cork, 1989).

14 See, Norbrook, pp. 131-132. On court politics and competing factional interests see Simon Adams, 'Eliza Enthroned? The Court and its Politics' in Christopher Haigh (ed.), *The Reign of Elizabeth I* (Basingstoke, 1984), 55-77.

15 See John Guy, *Tudor England* (Oxford and New York, 1990), 445. On the competing Essex - Cecil factions see Conrad Russell, *The Crisis of Parliaments: English History 1509-1660* (Oxford, 1971), 251-255.

16 Neither the *Fowre Hymnes*, nor *Prothalamion* were entered on the Stationers' Register. The *Prothalamion* must have been composed after 7 August 1596 (following the return of Essex from the Spanish expedition, referred to in Stanza 9 of the poem), and before 1 October 1596 when the Court moved from Greenwich. Bjor-

vand (*SP*, 755) suggests September 1596 as the period of both the betrothal of the Somerset women (the marriage took place on 8 November), and the period of the poem's composition.

17   Alan Sinfield, *Literature in Protestant England 1560-1660* (London and Canberra, 1983), 28.

18   Joseph Lowenstein, 'The Script in the Marketplace' in Stephen Greenblatt (ed.), *Representing the English Renaissance* (Berkeley and Los Angeles, 1988), 273.

19   Baldassare Castiglione, *The Book of the Courtier*, translated by Hoby (London and Toronto, n.d.), 95.

20   Quoted in Guy, *Tudor England*, p. 335.

21   George Puttenham, *The Arte of English Poesie* (London, 1589) Bk. III, Ch. vii, Ch. xviii.

22   Giles and Phineas Fletcher, *Poetical Works,* edited by F.S. Boas (Cambridge, 1908), I, 141.

23   Sir Philip Sidney, *An Apology for Poetry,* edited by Geoffrey Shepherd (Manchester, 1973), 123-124.

24   Ludwig Wittgenstein, *Tractatus Logico-Philosophicus,* translated by D.F. Pears and B.F. McGuinness (1961, rpt. London, 1981), 19.

7

RE-HISTORICISING MACBETH

ARTHUR F. KINNEY

The year 1576 was an important cross-roads in the history of English theatre. In that year James Burbage signed the lease for a plot of land in Shoreditch in the Liberty of Holywell north of the city London. There in what
Steven Mullaney has called 'a transitional zone between the city and the
country', Burbage proceeded to build the Theatre 'alongside gaming houses, marketplaces, taverns, bear-baiting arenas, and brothels' where '(before
the dissolution) monasteries (had stood)'.[1] This bold move for secular entertainment involved a structure of considerable size. Herbert Berry reckons
it cost approximately £683 to build (plus or minus 2.5 per cent)[2] and was
constructed of timber, wainscoting, tile, brick, sand lime, lead and iron
erected mainly by carpenters and plasterers as well as, according to the sole
extant document describing the process, 'workmen of all sor*tes* for that
purpose' (30): the best guess now is that it was a black-and-white timbered
building with brick foundations and a tile—not a thatch—roof, with its
sides held together not by the usual joints and mortices but with iron fasten-
ings in sections that could easily be unscrewed and unbolted so that, in
1598, men could disassemble and deconstruct it and take it across the old
city and the river to rebuild it as the new Globe Theatre in Southwark on
the banks of the Thames.

But 1576 was also the year when, in May, the Diocesan Court of High
Commission in York sent a directive to the mayor and corporation of
Wakefield effectively banning the Corpus Christi play which had been
planned according to custom for June of the year.[3] 'The Wakefield letter',
according to Peter Womack, was

> part of the government offensive which brought the religious drama of
> the provincial towns to an end. The pageants were played for the last
> time at Norwich in 1569, at Chester in 1575, and at Coventry in 1579,
> and in most of these cases there was official pressure to close, whether
> from the ecclesiastical authorities, the Council of the North, or the
> Privy Council. All the major organs of state power were working
> against the plays, sometimes despite the apparent wishes of the urban
> authorities themselves. Burbage, on the other hand, seems to have
> made his risky investment *despite* the hostility of the city authorities,
> and because he was reasonably confident that he had the *support* of the

> Privy Council. Government policy on theatre, then—whether or not
> there was anybody actually thinking it through in such terms—was to
> promote a particular kind of drama in the capital while suppressing
> another kind in the provinces (96-97).

Thus by the time the first Globe was built for Shakespeare's company, the
Lord Chamberlain's Men had completed this fundamental shift from sacred
to secular entertainment, with a tetralogy of chronicle history plays from
the relatively recent reigns of Richard II to Henry V displacing the sacred
history of man staged in the Corpus Christi plays concerned with the dawn
of the Christian era.

This massive shift in the concept of human history preserved and promulgated in popular culture in the mid-Tudor years ought not to be unde-
restimated. On the political level, it has its ready analogies: not only the
imperialism of Henry VIII which stretched from London to Rome but also
in what E.H. Kantorowicz long ago studied as the theory of the duplex
royal body, merging the political with the metaphysical, whereby the mortal
body of the body of the King was merged with the immortal body of Kingship itself—the King's two bodies, distinct because of their opposition in
character yet identical in the singular identity they joined. This sense of the
political monarch embodying the divine position of right rule, initially
medieval in English origin, is another displacement—or perhaps invasion
—of the sacred by the secular, the profane. But we can measure how deeply this action runs when we recall that this entire sense of a duplex body is,
at its conceptual roots, a legal and political fiction drawn out of and thus
replacing the ecclesiastical doctrines about the duplex body of Christ. Just
as the immortal body of Christ was also embodied mortally in the son of a
Nazarene carpenter, so the King's two bodies permitted the English to
claim that the King was dead and that he also had long life—eternal life;
like Christ, the earthly King, not the Heavenly King, was he 'Who never
dies'. Mervyn James puts it succinctly, even 'epigrammatically': 'under
Protestantism, the Corpus Christi becomes the Body of the Realm'.[4]
Indeed, the Catholic calendar of saints' days gave way to an equally
crowded calendar of profane national celebrations and commemorations,
while the newly rising theatre was 'seeking to draw its miscellaneous audience into a new kind of unity by rehearsing the fall and redemption of England'.[5] Thus from the beginning, the preacher John Stockwood had perhaps
far more on his mind than we have credited him with when he remarked, in
1578, that the Theatre was one of the 'houses of purpose built ... without
the *Liberties*, as who woulde say "There, let them saye what they will say,
we wil play"'.[6]

This sweeping conquest of Corpus Christi by Corpus Regnum which in retrospect characterises English history from the advent of the Tudors to the Interregnum, did not come easily, did not proceed evenly across the island kingdom, and was forever being challenged, both by Puritans and by Catholics. In at least one play of Shakespeare, all of these forces of the sacred and the profane are at the centre of his attention. In *Macbeth*, a play which uses Stuart history to examine an historical past, Shakespeare pits the secular and the demonic against the spiritual and the sacred, Lady Macbeth, the 'fiend-like Queen' (5.9.35) and the witches and the 'dead butcher' Macbeth (5.9.35) against King Duncan of Scotland who 'Hath borne his faculties so meek, hath been / So clear in his great office, that his virtues / Will plead like angels, trumpet-tongu'd, against / The deep damnation of his taking-off' (1.7.17-20) and King Edward the Confessor of England with his royal touch against scrofula:

> A most miraculous work in this good King,
> Which often, since my here-remain in England,
> I have seen him do. How he solicits Heaven,
> Himself best knows; but strangely-visited people,
> All swoln and ulcerous, pitiful to the eye,
> The mere despair of surgery, he cures;
> Hanging a golden stamp about their necks,
> Put on with holy prayers: and 'tis spoken,
> To the succeeding royalty he leaves
> The healing benediction. With this strange virtue,
> He hath a heavenly gift of prophecy;
> And sundry blessings hang about his throne,
> That speak him full of grace.   (4.3.147-49)[7]

If J.R. de J. Jackson is helpful in teaching us to understand the forces of history in *Historical Criticism and the Meaning of Texts*, when he proposes that historical criticism aids understanding of history by being 'criticism that tries to read past works of literature in the way in which they were read when were new', *Macbeth* may help us to put into relief some contemporary attitudes towards the ideas of the sacred and the profane.[8]

But still the task of discerning these is not an especially easy one despite what might seem a morality play of Macbeth's rise and fall as a brief and abstract chronicle of the time. Take the witches in the opening scene, for instance. There the oxymoronic idea that 'When the hurlyburly's done' is 'When the battle's lost and won' (1.1.1-2) collapses into the more gnomic 'Fair is foul, and foul is fair' at the end (1.1.10), equally oxymoronic. But it is also essentially deconstructive, for these are observations that divide and polarise, that disrupt action before it occurs, just as their later prophecies in 1.3 will do. 'The Weird Sister', Duncan Salkeld comments, 'whose femininity has long been in doubt, happen to be versed in the mysteries of deconstruction and speak in aporias and double-binds ... The effect of their discourse is to unsettle the narrative of the play'.[9] Yet at the same time, this metaphysical language, this mystical mumbo-jumbo that fragments experience, also becomes incantatory—who of us did not know those lines, at least, by heart?—and so increasingly authoritative, a premise that sheds light on experience and event and so, in its own way, earns the role of a kind of truth-telling. Janet Adelman has seen this, too: 'When Macbeth's first words echo those we have already heard the witches speak—"So foul and fair a day I have not seen" (1.3.38), ... we are in a realm that questions the very possibility of autonomous identity'. In the play's 'last moments', she continues,

> as Macbeth feels himself increasingly hemmed in by enemies, the stage resonates with variants of his repeated question, 'What's he / That was not born of woman?' (5.7.2-3; for variants, see 5.3.4,6; 5.7.11,13; 5.8. 13,31) Repeated seven times, Macbeth's allusion to the witches' prophecy—'none of woman born / Shall harm Macbeth' after he has begun to doubt the equivocation of the fiend (5.5.43), mere repetition of the phrase seems to Macbeth to guarantee his invulnerability. And as he repeats himself, his assurance seems to turn itself inside out, becoming dependent not on the fact that all men are, after all, born of woman, but on the fantasy of escape from this universal condition.[10]

It is talismanic—temporarily life-giving as well as death-dealing.

In fact, we know, the witches, or weird sisters, only made oracular pronouncements; it is Macbeth whose political ambitions turn these into political prophecies that give him warrant to regicide, partly through a sense of historical forces, partly through a perceived supernatural sanction. Macbeth 'does not (here) pretend that evil is good', James L. Calderwood has noted, 'but takes it for what it is and finds a kind of exalted rightness in aligning himself with maleficent powers'. He goes on:

> To break open 'the Lord's anointed temple' (2.3.68), he imagines a counter-religion of violence, a cult of darkness whose goddess is Hecate and whose executive agents are withered murder, the wolf, and ravishing Tarquin. The regicidal act thus takes on the aspect of a murderous 'black mass' in which Lady Macbeth plays acolyte arranging

beforehand the poisoned chalices, and Macbeth himself takes the role of murdering priest advancing upon Duncan with Crosslike dagger upraised before him as the sleeping guards cry out 'God bless us' and 'Amen'. The black mass aspect of Duncan's murder is a radical extension of the sacralizing of violence on the battlefield, where Macbeth was supposed to bathe in reeking wounds and memorize another Golgotha. He now literalizes the symbolism of the Mass, which does memorize Golgotha, by killing the Christ-figure in fact.[11]

The acts are both earned and demonised by the further black Communion—the misbegotten banquet of 3.4 where sharing food and wine with his thanes, Macbeth alone sees a vision—the ghost of Banquo who cannot be, yet is, conveying, moreover, a certain insight and truth that Macbeth promptly realises:

> Blood hath been shed ere now, i'th'olden time,
> Ere humane statute purg'd the gentle weal;
> Ay, and since too, murthers have been perform'd
> Too terrible for the ear: the time has been,
> That, when the brains were out, the man would die,
> And there an end; but now, they rise again,
> With twenty mortal murthers on their crowns,
> And push us from our stools. This is more strange
> Than such a murther is.   (3.4.84-92)

Thus the deconstructing pronouncements of the sisters—their aporias—actually construct the play, so that what is foul is made fair—that is, true—in all its foulness.

Nor are such ugly prospects Macbeth's alone. They belong—at least in the language of this play—to Malcolm too. 'There grows' in him, he says,

> In my most ill-compos'd affection such
> A staunchless avarice, that, were I King,
> I should cut off the nobles for their lands;
> Desire his jewels, and this other's house:
> And my more-having would be as a sauce
> To make me hunger more; that I should forge
> Quarrels unjust against the good and loyal,
> Destroying them for wealth.   (4.3.77-84)

Such a speech may be, as he tells Macduff, a test, only a test, but it is followed by a savagery that is unequalled except by Macbeth; and it is a speech given to a thane who has left his wife and children exposed and vulnerable. Even Macbeth did not do that. There is a way, then, in which the fair of the play share in its foulness; and this, in turn, recuperates the witches.

The sisters are recuperated another way, too: their pronouncements, gnomic and unnatural, are made in time political prophecies. But if we follow Jackson—that we understand old texts when we read them as if they were new—we will recall that prophecies in the Tudor period were regularly taken to be political, however baffling or recondite; it is another way in which, during the sixteenth century in England, the secular was invading the sacred. Thus 'The Sayings of the Prophets' which Sharon L. Jansen has recently discovered in Folger MS Loseley b.546 are unscrambled through such conundrums as 'the subject of the rose killed by his father in the belly of his mother'[12] which, given to Cromwell to help the government's cause, were equally seen as subversive, so that Thomas Gibson was employed by Cromwell to turn anti-Henrician prophecies into obscure language and thus darken and hide interpretation that in fact supported the regime. To take another instance, we have probably all met, at one place or another, Elizabeth Barton, a servant in a country house in Kent who acquired prophetic gifts during an extended illness in 1525. What seemed controversial if not demonic to her parish priest, Richard Master, was found sufficiently holy when examined by the Archbishop of Canterbury, so that Edward Bocking, a Benedictine monk from Christ Church, Canterbury, declared her to be wholly orthodox—a judgment apparently confirmed when she was miraculously healed before the Archbishop's Commission at the Chapel of Our Lady in Court-at-Street during the Lenten season of 1526. At that point she entered the convent of St. Sepulchre in Canterbury as the famed 'Holy Maid of Kent', renowned for her sanctity, esteemed by the nuns at Syon Abbey, the monks at the Charterhouses of Sheen and London, and the friars at Canterbury, Greenwich, and Richmond. She had audiences with Henry VIII, Cardinal Wolsey, Sir Thomas More, Archbishop Warham, and Bishop Fisher before a swiftly advancing political change caused her pronouncements to be seen as subversive. Investigated now by Cromwell and Cranmer, she was associated with some of the King's most vocal critics, and in 1533 she was attainted of treason for her political prophecies, as they were now called. In April 1534 she was 'hanged at Tyburn alongside her confessor and a number of her principal adherents.[13] Handy dandy, which is the justice and which is the thief? The imagination that sees an imperial dagger in the air also sees 'on thy blade, and dudgeon, gouts of blood,/ Which was not so before' (2.1.46-47); the imagination that can see ahead in time—'If it were done, when 'tis done, then 'twere well / It were done quickly' (1.7.1-2); sees backwards, too, to the dark abysm of time. Closer in time to Shakespeare than the holy maid of Kent was the notorious John Darrell who in 1598—the year the Globe was built—was astonishing the town of Nottingham with his exorcism of William Sommers, the object, along with his sister, of a later commission of inquiry convened by the Archbishop of York. For the Puritan William Perkins, in his *Discovrse of the Damned Art of Witchcraft; so farre forth as it is reuealed in the Scriptures, and manifest by true experience* (1608), such dispossession was itself a holy act: 'The first and last Remedie, is Exorcisme, which is an adjuring and commanding the Deuill in the name of God, to depart from the partie possessed, and cease to molest him any more' (sig. Q3v), yet Darrell's very success as an exorcist, curing witch-craft, caused him to be suspected of demonism himself by the Archbishop of Canterbury, who summoned him to trial in an ecclesiastical court in London. There Darrell was convicted when Harsnet took over and caused two boys to sign a confession of charges against Darrell, saying he had taught fraudulent tricks to Sommers and—without seeing the either deposi-tion or evidence—Darrell was convicted. Who is the justice, and who exor-cises here? The witches, in all their baffling ways, catch the very torn fabric of religion and state in Shakespeare—as hard to judge in the play as eccle-siastical, court, and Puritan behaviour in the days when Shakespeare wrote his *Macbeth*.

There is a way, then, in which the play of *Macbeth* seems much simpler than the society out of which it grew: 'oftentimes', says Macbeth, 'to win us to our harm, / The instruments of Darkness tell us truths' (1.3.123-24). At one hard-working level, this play is decidedly providential:

> Events arc timed to follow uncannily, as if by some unseen hand: Macbeth's foreknown entry to the witches, the entrance of Ross and Angus which follows the prophecy with news that is its partial fulfil-ment; then the entrance of Macbeth on talk of Cawdor, and the Mess-enger who announced 'The King comes here to-night' (I.iv.28) as Lady Macbeth speaks of the crown. These are (only) the beginning of a net of circumstances that extend throughout the tragedy. As soon as Lady Macbeth is left alone, the hoarse raven should probably be heard; as soon as Duncan is murdered the owl shrieks (II.ii.2-3 and 15). Knock-ing at the gate appals Macbeth immediately he is alone after his crime (II.ii.56); Lennox and Macduff then speak unknowingly to touch his secret nerve.[14]

The dagger, the bell, the ghost of Banquo all reprimand him; but his secret-est knowledge is always already our secret knowledge, too. Like Macbeth, we are unwilling participants, at once welcoming and fearful of providential warning. We become, like Macbeth, and in the Porter's telling prophecy-of-sorts, equivocators.

But this very term, linked with Father Garnet in the trial of the Gun-powder Plot conspirators which was occurring as Shakespeare conceived this play about another Scottish king, was not only a devilish plot—with its devil's vault of dangerous gunpowder; its demonic fire the torch to touch it off—but, in James's hand, cause for an miraculous discovery by, as Cecil told him, his Solomonic wisdom, so that this work of the devil became a cause for celebration with a legal and religious holiday the celebration of which extended from 1606 to 1859. As William Woodson reminds us,

> The crown capitalized on this extraordinary event with an alacrity which lends credence to those historians who believe that the govern-ment knew about the plot from the first. London glowed red with bon-fires on the first November 5. As soon the as plotters were all in the Tower, the Council directed the Archbishop to prepare an annual Thanksgiving service in the liturgy. Celebratory sermons and tracts proliferated. The Parliament declared November 5 a national holiday ... Almost overnight, James saw created an array of celebrations of his preservation. He could not have wished a greater triumph in establis-hing the ideology of his imperial dynasty ... In the Sunday following the discovery of the plot, William Barlow, the King's chaplain, found in the plot 'an hyperdiabolicall diuelishnes', that Guy Fawkes would 'make himself drunke with the blood of so many Worthies, and so in-nocent'. In his address to Parliament, James compared the potential effect to the biblical flood, yet also asserted that 'the like was never either heard or read in this great and horrible attempt'. In the arraign-ment of Garnet on 28 March, the Serjeant at Law 'sayd *Horreo dicere* his lips did tremble to speak' 'the manner how to performe these hor-rible treasons'. In a nearly poetic amplification of the motif or horror, Coke's speech of indictment called attention to the mental horror of such a conspiracy: 'God, as Job says, *terret per somnia,* affrights by dreames, and *per visiones horrorem concutit,* and by visions shakes the minde with horror'.[15]

Thus James and his government transform demonism into miracle, sacralise the secular.

Such sacralising transformation of the demonically secular enters the play of *Macbeth* through Malcolm who, after talking of his own 'most ill-compos'd affection' (4.3.77), refers to 'the king-becoming graces', having none, 'As Justice, Verity, Tem'rance, Stableness, / Bounty, Perseverance, Mercy, Lowliness, / Devotion, Patience, Courage, Fortitude' (4.3.92-94) and from there to King Edward I, whose royal touch cures scrofula, 'A most miraculous work in this good King' (4.3.147). In the play, though, Malcolm has not part of this royal act of curing and instead leaves it behind him when he returns to bloody battle in Scotland. But Shakespeare's audiences knew of the royal touch which, Keith Thomas reminds us, was used during Elizabeth I's reign to countermand the Papal Bull of Excommunication issued against her. (In 1634 the ritual of such royal healing entered the Book of Common Prayer.)[16] In fact, William Clowes, Elizabeth's surgeon and later Serjeant Surgeon to James I, issued a treatise on scrofula in 1602 in which he describes a patient he was unable to cure but who was cured by Elizabeth; 'I thank God and the Queen of England' the victim later confessed to Clowes, 'I am by her Majesty perfectly cured and healed: and after Her Grace had touched me, I never applyed any medicine at all, but kept it cleane, with sweete and fresh cleane cloathes, and now and then washed the sore with white Wine, and thus all my griefes did consume and waste cleane away'.[17] James, however, mocked the King's Touch, for he saw its significance as conflicting and as equivocating as prophetic actions in *Macbeth*; it at once sacralised the king and yet displayed in its very ritual the King's submission to God; at the same time it promoted royal ceremony it smacked of papist superstition, derived from Edward the Confessor who by 1606 had been dubbed 'the supersititous Prince' (Willis 148).

The moment when the sacred can return in an age of the secular, then it is questioned and perhaps denied. Deborah Willis writes of the three ways Jacobeans thought of the royal touch:

1. The magical. The monarch's cures are the product of a supernatural power mysteriously inhering in the king's person ... This is the popular view ...
2. The orthodox. The monarch's cures are the product of a mysterious combination of prayer and natural process ... This is the 'official' view of state and church authorities ...
3. The theatrical: The monarch's cures are the product of the power of the human imagination responding to a ruse ... This is the view of James and possibly of a sophisticated courtly elite; in its darker version, it is the view of Puritan critics.   (148)

In the conversation of Malcolm and Macduff in 4.3—the long scene once thought digressive and expendable, but actually the core of the tragedy—all three of these views are implicitly raised and laid aside. *Macbeth* is thus Shakespeare's attempt to test the possibility of a sacralised drama in the more secular Jacobean age and finding it no longer viable, smacking of both papist superstition and Puritan exorcism. The most forceful way to dramatise religious forces is through the demonic art of witchcraft; even religious oaths would be banned. As Janet Clare writes of *Macbeth*: 'Four years after the (first) performance ..., James issued his proclamation against Dr Cowell's *Interpreter*, castigating men who waded "in all the deepest mysteries that belong to the persons or State of Kings or Princes, that are gods upon Earth" and meddled "with things above their capacitie". Shakespeare's circumspect redaction of his sources and the play's silence on those ideological issues which were anathema to James may well have sprung from judicious self-censorship'.[18] Whether or not that explains *Macbeth*, it is nevertheless true that the tragedy that opens on reports of brutality with the treachery of Cawdor ends amidst the carnal devastation at Dunsinane. Scone Abbey, by contrast, is barely mentioned.

Notes

1   Steven Mullaney, 'Civic Rites, City Sites: The Place of the Stage's in David Scott Kastan and Peter Stallybrass (eds), *Staging the Renaissance: Reinterpretations of Elizabethan and Jacobean Drama* (London and New York, 1991), 21.
2   Herbert Berry, 'Aspects of the Design and Use of the First Public Playhouse' in *The First Public Playhouse: The Theatre in Shoreditch 1576-1598* (Montreal, 1979), 31.
3   Peter Womack, 'Imagining Communities: Theatres and the English Nation in the Sixteenth Century' in *Culture and History: 1350-1600: Essays on English Communities, Identities and Writing* (Detroit, 1992), 96.
4   Mervyn James, 'Ritual, drama and social body in the late medieval English town' in *Society, Politics and Culture: Studies in Early Modern England* (Cambridge, 1986), 41.
5   Womack, p. 137.
6   Quoted Mullaney, p. 18.
7   All quotations are from *Macbeth*, New Arden text, Kenneth Muir (ed.) (New York and London, 1951; 1953).
8   J.R. de J. Jackson, *Historical Criticism and the Meaning of Texts* (London and New York, 1989), 3.
9   Duncan Salkeld, *Madness and drama in the age of Shakespeare* (Manchester, 1993), 111.
10   Janet Adelman, *Suffocating Mothers: Fantasies of Maternal Origin in Shakespeare's Plays, 'Hamlet' to 'The Tempest'* (New York and London, 1992), 131.

11 James L. Calderwood, *If It were Done: 'Macbeth' and Tragic Action* (Amherst, 1986), 99-100.

12 Sharon L. Jansen, '"And he shall be called Edward": Sixteenth-Century Political Protest and Folger MS Loseley b. 546', *English Literary Renaissance* 23 (1993): 237.

13 Diane Watt, 'Reconstructing the Word: the Political Prophecies of Elizabeth Barton (1506-1534)', unpublished essay.

14 John Russell Brown, *Shakespeare: The Tragedy of Macbeth* (London, 1963), 20-21.

15 William Woodson, 'Synchronic Structure in *Macbeth,'* unpublished paper for English 14, Shakespeare Society of America meeting in Philadelphia, 12-14 April 1990.

16 Keith Thomas, *Religion and the Decline of Magic: Studies in Popular Beliefs in Sixteenth- and Seventeenth-Century England* (Harmondsworth, 1971), 231, 228.

17 Deborah Willis, 'The Monarch and the Sacred: Shakespeare and the Ceremony for the Healing of the King's Evil' in Linda Woodbridge and Edward Berry (eds), *True Rites and Maimed Rites: Ritual and Anti-Ritual in Shakespeare and His Age* (Urbana, 1992), 148.

18 Janet Clare, *'Art made tongue-tied by authority': Elizabethan and Jacobean Dramatic Censorship* (Manchester, 1990), 138.

8

THE GOSPEL ACCORDING TO AEMILIA: WOMEN AND THE SACRED IN AEMILIA LANYER'S SALVE DEUS REX JUDAEORUM

ACHSAH GUIBBORY

In the history of Western religion, women have had a far more ambiguous relation to the sacred than men. Although women were celebrated in the Old Testament for their heroism and devotion to God, it was men that we are told were the priests and prophets chosen for God's service. With the destruction of the temple in 70 AD, the study of the sacred Torah became exclusively the province of males, and the rabbis replaced the priests, while women engaged in practical, domestic roles supporting the spirituality of the male scholars. In some ways, the advent of Christianity might have marked a change in women's relation to the sacred, for Christ's teachings could be seen as giving women equal access to the divine—'there is neither male nor female: for ye are all one in Christ Jesus' (Galatians 3: 28); the fact that all believers, male and female, are 'sonnes' of Christ (*e.g.* Galatians 4: 6-7) and strive to be his 'spouse' (*e.g.* Matth. 25: 1-13) might minimise gender as well as class differences.[1] But there were other passages in the New Testament that implicitly placed women at a farther remove from the sacred than men. Paul in I Corinthians 11: 4-8 insists that women in church must be 'covered' as a sign of their inferiority and subjection.[2] Whereas men can freely 'prophesy' in the church, Paul orders women to 'keepe silence' there, instead asking their husbands 'at home' about spiritual matters, over which men are presumed to have more authority (I Cor. 14: 34-35).

As the work of Elaine Pagels, Peter Brown and Caroline Bynum has shown, the growth of the Church as an institution reveals both the importance of women's devotion and the ways in which women were distanced from authoritative, direct contact with the divine. The early centuries of the church saw women martyrs, patrons of the church and ascetics, though the Church Fathers encouraged a sense of women's remove from the sacred by associating woman and the feminine with the body or 'flesh', and by presenting marriage as a model of Christian order in which women's 'subjection' to their husbands mirrors both the hierarchical order of society and the body's proper subjection to the rule of the soul.[3] From the late twelfth through to the fourteenth century, women saints and mystics cultivated and displayed their spirituality, insisting on women's special, intimate connec-

tion with God.[4] But as the Church grew, so did the power of the priests
and bishops, and restrictions were placed on women's activities within the
sacred Church.[5]

In some ways, the Protestant Reformation actually deepened the distance between women and the sacred. In getting rid of monastic orders and
religious houses, it deprived women of a special form of sacred experience.
In rejecting the adoration of the Virgin Mary and the female saints, it elim-
inated important models as well as objects for women's devotion. Moreover, Protestantism associated the 'feminine' with the supposed 'carnal
idolatry' of Roman Catholicism.[6] But Protestantism also had the potential
to give women equal access with men to the sacred.[7] All were 'brethren' in
God, all people could know God through reading the Scriptures, and women as well as men could be touched by God's grace.

Aemilia Lanyer's own relation to the sacred has seemed particularly
ambiguous. In 1611, she published a single volume of poetry which presented itself as sacred verse, but our contemporary source of information
about Lanyer, Simon Forman, presents her in his diary entries as a woman
very much of the world—the mistress of Lord Hunsdon, who married Al-
phonso Lanyer to cover an illegitimate pregnancy, who at the time she first
consulted Forman was engaged in seeking a knighthood for her husband,
and who would later take her brothers-in-law to court to secure her late
husband's custom patent. Her reputation for holiness has not been helped
by A.L. Rowse's inference from Forman's diary that she was promiscuous,
or his speculation that she was Shakespeare's dark lady.[8] Even Barbara
Lewalski has questioned the appropriateness of calling her poetry religious,
for she finds the poems quite diverse and notably worldly in their concern
with patronage.[9] I would argue, however, that, for all its concern with patronage, *Salve Deus Rex Judaeorum* asks to be taken seriously as religious
poetry that adopts Christ's message to give a special place to women in
devotion. *Salve Deus Rex Judaeorum* has a claim to our interest, not only
as the first substantial volume of poetry published by a woman in England,
but also because it is a significant cultural document expanding our understanding of women's religious roles. The importance of *Salve Deus* becomes clear when read within the broad historical context of woman's
vexed relation with the sacred as well as within the specific historical context of the Protestant culture of early Jacobean England—a culture that
assumed women did not have as privileged a connection with God as men,
but that also sanctioned the individual reader's authority to interpret the
Bible.

With the accession of James I in 1603, the dominant structure of power
shaping English culture and society became more distinctly patriarchal than

it had been in Elizabeth's reign. As a female ruler, Queen Elizabeth had violated the traditional assumption that women were subject to men. Though it has been argued that Elizabeth's example was the exception that proved the rule of patriarchy, the very existence of a woman monarch destabilised the traditional gender hierarchy. Moreover, in constructing her monarchical authority, she appropriated the symbols and imagery of the Virgin Mary, attempting to give religious sanction to her political rule and also implicitly preserving a powerful role for female spirituality. During her long reign, she served as head of the English Church as well as the state, thus assuming a spiritual authority that had been presumed to belong only to Protestant kings. But with the death of Elizabeth, a male figure of monarchical power replaced that of the Virgin Queen, and James promoted a rigorously patriarchal authority in both church and state. Whereas the English Church had followed the Catholic practice of allowing women as well as lay men to baptise in an emergency, James insisted in 1604 that only ministers could baptise, thus effectively restricting women's role in the church as he reinforced the distance between clery and laity (Crawford, 56). Masculine authority was also emphasised in the king's writings and speeches, as James figured himself as husband and father of the realm. Clearly preferring the company and advice of men, he created a court with a strongly homosocial and patriarchal ethos.[10] However, as Leeds Barroll and Barbara Lewalski have shown, this patriarchal ethos did not go unchallenged. James's wife, Queen Anne, established a separate court, which (in Lewalski's words) 'provided a locus, unstable yet influential, of female resistance' to the ethos and policies of James' court (*Writing Women*, 18).[11] This sense of a female alternative to the male nexus of power—both secular and sacred—informs Lanyer's poem. In her prefatory poems, Lanyer looks back nostalgically to the reign of Elizabeth; but in dedicating the volume to Queen Anne and the powerful noble women associated with her, Lanyer attempts to attach herself to Anne's court as it provided a female-centered alternative to James's.

Salve Deus Rex Judaeorum appeared in 1611, the same year as the King James Bible, which was the work of Launcelot Andrewes and a group of distinguished divines commissioned by James to provide 'an exact Translation of the holy Scriptures into the *English Tongue*'.[12] In the very year that the Authorised Version of the Bible was published, founded on the Protestant belief that every Christian should be able to read the Bible in the vernacular and dedicated to King James as 'the principall moover and Author of the Worke' (sig. A2v), Aemelia Lanyer published her version of the Passion, proclaimed her authority as a woman to read and interpret the Bible, and asked for the Queen's patronage of her work. Might we not, then, see *Salve Deus* as in some sense constituting an oppositional alternative to the monumental biblical project of James?

Though, as Lewalski observes, religious poetry was considered more appropriate than secular verse for women ('Re-writing Patriarchy', 98), *Salve Deus Rex Judaeorum* is hardly a conventional, modestly pious poem for a woman. Whereas the institution of the church had increasingly restricted women's roles, *Salve Deus* places women at the heart of the sacred: it is introduced by ten dedicatory pieces to prospective or actual women patronesses and a prose address to her 'Virtuous Readers' (defined as exclusively female), which defends the special affection and distinction Christ showed to women. The principal poem *Salve Deus* itself is a narrative of Christ's Passion that also contains a lengthy panegyric frame praising Margaret Clifford, Countess of Cumberland, as a virtuous woman and spouse of Christ, a catalogue of good women in biblical and classical history and a description of the Queen of Sheba as exemplary of female spiritual devotion. As an epilogue, the country-house poem 'The Description of Cooke-ham' presents the estate where Margaret Clifford lived as a spiritual retreat where women had a special connection with the holy. Though, as Elaine Beilin recognises, women's relation with the sacred pervades the entire volume (*Redeeming Eve*, 177-207), it is particularly striking in Lanyer's bold version of Christ's Passion that literally forms the centre of *Salve Deus*. I shall argue that, defying powerful cultural restrictions, Lanyer presents her poem as a true Gospel, inspired and authorised by God, offering a distinctive version of the significance of Christ's Passion, bearing a message for social as well as spiritual change, and founded on a critical and independent reading of the Scriptures which recognises the New Testament as not simply the Word of God but a series of texts, written by men, in which all parts are not equally authoritative. In reading the Bible, she discovers a disturbing discontinuity between Christ's teachings and those of his disciples.

Paul's advice that women remain 'silent' in the church not only discouraged women's speaking publicly about religious matters but also suggested that men possessed greater authority about spiritual concerns—hence their freedom to prophesy and the subsequent selection of men as priests in the church. Paul's comments about women's 'place' would be radically challenged in the foment of the Civil War years, when radical women of the 1640s and '50s took it upon themselves to preach or prophesy, claiming special inspiration from God. But the conduct books of the early seventeenth century and the 'Homilie of the state of Matrimonie', read regularly in every church during Elizabeth's and James's reigns, encouraged the silence of women, not only in the church but even within the home. Women's silence was a mark of their subjection, a subjection which confirmed the order of society as founded on the obedience of people to their superiors.[13]

Aemilia Lanyer's 'preamble' before the Passion makes clear her awareness that she is violating the social codes sanctioned by these books and by Paul's foundational verses that women be 'covered' and 'silent' in the church:

> But my deare Muse, now whither wouldst thou flie,
> Above the pitch of thy appointed straine?
> With *Icarus* thou seekest now to trie,
> Not waxen wings, but thy poore barren Braine,
> Which farre too weake, these siely lines descrie ...[14]   (ll. 273-77)

Aware that in seeking to narrate and interpret Christ's passion she is transgressing the 'appointed' boundaries for a woman (her insistent consciousness of gender makes these lines more than the conventional humility topos), she prays for God's 'Grace':

> Therefore I humbly for his Grace will pray,
> That he will give me Power and Strength to Write,
> That what I have begun, so end I may,
> As his great Glory may appeare more bright;
> Yea in these Lines I may no further stray,
> Than his most holy Spirit shall give me Light:
>   That blindest Weakenesse be not over-bold,
>   The manner of his Passion to unfold.
>
> Yet if he please t'illuminate my Spirit,
> And give me Wisdom from his holy Hill,
> That I may Write part of his glorious Merit,
> If he vouchsafe to guide my Hand and Quill,
> To shew his Death, by which we doe inherit
> Those endlesse Joyes that all our hearts doe fill;
>   Then will I tell of that sad blacke fac'd Night,
>   Whose mourning Mantle covered Heavenly Light.
>
>   (ll. 297-304, 321-28)

Like the women prophets during the English Revolution and like Milton in *Paradise Lost* and *Paradise Regained*, Aemelia Lanyer invokes divine inspiration, hence insisting on divine authority for what she will speak. Her prayer recalls Matthew's and Mark's account in the New Testament that when Christ sent out his Apostles to preach the Gospel, he told them: 'take no thought how or what ye shall speake: for it shal be given you in that houre, what yee shall say. For it is not yee that speake, but the spirit of your father which speaketh in you' (Matth. 10: 19-20; cf. Mark 13: 11). She extends the argument still further, suggesting that her very 'Weakeness' makes God's glory shine more fully, as if she is simply a medium for transmitting God's truth. But by publishing her interpretation of the Passion and its significance for humanity—a version which, like Milton's versions of biblical truth in his epics, will include significant departures from tradition and original additions—she defies Paul's prohibition against women's speaking publicly about religion, suggesting, as she will do later in the poem, that women are more qualified than men since in their weakness and humility they are closer to God and more open to his grace:

> But yet the Weaker thou doest seeme to be
> In Sexe, or Sence, the more his Glory shines,
> That doth infuze such powerfull Grace in thee,
> To shew thy Love in these few humble Lines ...   (ll. 289-92)

Echoing Christ's privileging of the poor, humble and weak, Lanyer suggests that the traditionally masculine faculty of reason ('Sence'), like the masculine 'Sexe', in its supposed strength competes with and hence may exclude divine illumination. If she is led by God's spirit and his hand guides her 'Quill', then her poem will be 'true', even perhaps in the sense that the Gospels, written by men visited by the spirit of God, are 'true'.[15] Like Milton later, she implies that biblical truth is not 'fixed' but that God may grant later, additional revelations. Lanyer cites evidence of being favoured by divine illumination when she claims in a final note 'To the doubtfull Reader' that she received the title for the work 'in sleepe many yeares before' (139). In her prayer for divine inspiration, which introduces her narrative of Christ's Passion, she not only follows in the footsteps of those holy women of early Christianity and of the later middle ages who claimed to be filled by the spirit of God, but also raises the possibility that a woman could be chosen to be a true witness of God, a belated 'author' of the Gospel of Christ. As she says with a simplicity born of confidence: 'I was appointed to performe this Worke' (139)—not by men but by God. Like the Gospels the male disciples wrote after the death of Christ, Aemilia Lanyer's, as we shall see, bears revolutionary messages radically at odds with the dominant values of the contemporary society and the institution of the Church.[16] Using the gospel form, she revives the gospel tradition of subverting worldly authority.

Lanyer's version of the Passion of Christ is a mixture of the conventional and the original. All the 'facts' and incidents are taken from the New Testament; her language is often close to the Bible—both when she describes the key events and when she praises Christ in terms taken from the *Song of Songs*, which had for centuries of Christian exegesis been understood to describe the reciprocal love between Christ and the Church. She draws her narrative of the Passion from the accounts in the Gospels of Matthew, Mark, Luke and John, but she takes on herself the ability to *interpret* the Bible, guided by grace, and emphasises the distinctive roles that women and men played in their relations to Christ. Her confidence that she has interpreted the Bible correctly is evident in her challenge to Queene Anne: 'judge if it agree not with the Text' ('To the Queenes most Excellent Majestie,' l. 76).

The story she tells is one of men's betrayal and women's faith. Following Matthew and Mark closely, she recounts how on 'That very Night our Saviour was betrayed,' Christ 'told his deere Disciples that they all / Should be offended by him' and forsake him (ll. 329, 337-38; cf. Matth. 26: 31-33, Mark 14: 27-29), how Peter who 'thought his Faith could never fall' and protested his constancy would before morning 'deny' Christ three times (ll. 341, 345-46; cf. Matt. 26: 34-35, Mark 14: 30-31, Luke 22: 33-34, John 13: 37-38), and how Christ in Gethsemane told Peter and 'the sonnes of *Zebed'us*' (James and John) of his sorrows (ll. 369-76) only to have them fall asleep rather than watch through the night (Matth. 26: 40-45, Mark 14: 37-38, Luke 22: 45). While Matthew, Mark, and Luke (but not John) mention the sleeping Apostles, Lanyer gives far more attention to this detail, drawing out its symbolic and spiritual significance:

> But now returning to thy sleeping Friends,
> That could not watch one houre for love of thee,
> Even those three Friends, which on thy Grace depends,
> Yet shut those Eies that should their Maker see;
> What colour, what excuse, or what amends,
> From thy Displeasure now can set them free?
>> Yet thy pure Pietie bids them Watch and Pray,
>> Lest in Temptation they be led away.

> Although the Spirit was willing to obay,
> Yet what great weakenesse in the Flesh was found!
> They slept in Ease, whilst thou in Paine didst pray;
> Loe, they in Sleepe, and thou in Sorrow drown'd ...
>
> (ll. 417-428; cf. Mark 13: 38)

But the sleep of the apostles signifies not just the inescapable weakness of the body—it is a defect of the heart: 'Their eyes were heavie, and their hearts asleepe' (l. 465). The ominous sleeping, the fatal inattentiveness to Christ, anticipates their disloyalty when Christ's 'foes' come to seize him: 'all his deere Disciples do forsake him' (l. 624).

> Those deare Disciples that he most did love,
> And were attendant at his becke and call,
> When triall of affliction came to prove,
> They first left him, who now must leave them all:
> For they were earth, and he came from above,
> Which made them apt to flie, and fit to fall:
> > Though they protest they never will forsake him,
> > They do like men, when dangers overtake them.   (ll. 625-632)

If Christ's apostles, his closest friends, 'forsake' him, what can one expect of his enemies? Lanyer makes explicit what actually seems implicit in the biblical accounts, that those responsible for Christ's death were all men: the Jewish high priest Caiphas; the witnesses who make false charges; Judas, whose example shows that only 'faithlesse dealing' 'can be expected / From wicked Man' (ll. 737-39); Pontius Pilate, who consents to Christ's death and frees Barrabas; King Herod; the 'Crier' and the 'Hangman' (ll. 961, 963); and the 'spightfull men [who] with torments did oppresse / Th'afflicted body' of Christ (ll. 993-94).

In sharp contrast to these men—who are guilty of contributing to Christ's death through evil, cowardice or (in the case of Pilate) the desire to please Caesar (ll. 919-20)—are the women. Again relying closely on the New Testament Gospels for her evidence, but particularly on Luke, who distinctly emphasises the importance of women in Christ's life, Lanyer presents women as the only ones to recognise Christ's innocence, remain constant in their devotion and be moved by compassion.[17] The tears of the Jewish women of Jerusalem elicit Christ's 'grace' as he comforts them (Luke 23: 27), though they cannot touch the men whose 'hearts [are] more hard than flint, or marble stone' (ll. 975, 1002). Elaborating on John's remark that Mary 'stood by the cross of Jesus' (John 19: 25), the poem describes the sorrows of the Virgin Mary, presenting her as a model of devotion (ll. 1009-1104, 1129-1136). Lanyer's extended attention to this 'Blessed' 'Mother of our Lord' (ll. 1031-32) recalls and perhaps revives the devotion to the Virgin Mary that blossomed in medieval Catholicism but withered with Protestantism.[18] But it is Pontius Pilate's wife who drives home Lanyer's point that the women are the true believers and who articulates the significance of Christ's Passion, a significance Lanyer finds implicit in the New Testament accounts but either unobserved or suppressed by male writers who have interpreted the Passion.

The role of Pontius Pilate's wife is her most original and startling addition to the narrative of the Crucifixion. The Gospel according to Matthew mentions in passing, 'Also when hee [Pilate] was set downe upon the judgement seate, his wife sent to him, saying, Haue thou nothing to doe with that just man: for I haue suffered many things this day in a dreame by reason of him' (Matth. 27: 19). But Lanyer expands the episode, giving the wife a ten-stanza speech that defends Jesus, offers an 'Apologie' for Eve, and asserts women's rightful liberty. It is this speech that has struck her readers as most radical. Lanyer's earlier claim that she receives 'divine illumination' in writing her poem sanctions her invention of this speech, authorising her version, which adds to the known Gospels of the New Testament, much as Milton later in *Paradise Regained* will invoke God's special inspiration in order to write what had been 'unrecorded left through many an Age' (*PR*, I, 16) about the temptations of Christ.[19] The argument of Pilate's wife's speech deserves further attention for its centrality in Lanyer's interpretation of the Crucifixion's significance.

The section begins as Lanyer, addressing Pontius Pilate, who is about to judge 'faultlesse *Jesus*' (l. 746), tells him in close paraphrase of Matthew 27: 19 to 'heare the words of thy most worthy wife, / Who sends to thee, to beg her Saviours life' (ll. 751-52). It ends ten stanzas later as Lanyer paraphrases the last part of Matthew's verse:

> Witnesse thy wife (O *Pilate*) speakes for all;
> Who did but dreame, and yet a message sent,
> That thou should'st have nothing to doe at all
> With that just man ...   (ll. 834-837)

The stanzas in between are the 'message' or 'words' that Pilate's wife sent, though a certain indeterminacy of voice has led some critics to suggest this is Lanyer's speech rather than that of Pilate's wife (Hutson, 170; Lewalski, 'Re-writing Patriarchy', 103). The confusion of voice is significant, for the poet's identification with Pilate's wife—a woman who also had a dream, whose knowledge came from divine illumination—allows her to speak with and for her. The implication is that both women have not only interpretive power but the right and responsibility to speak publicly. The words of both women violate the codes of their respective societies that encourage the silence of women and their subordination to the authority of husbands. Far from yielding to her husband, Pilate's wife advises him, judges Jesus more justly and makes her 'words' public, sending them to him. Thus in her intervention, Pilate's wife provides Lanyer with an example for the role she herself assumes in publishing her devotional poem. That the wife's words went unrecorded in Matthew (and Matthew is the only apostle to mention her) may suggest the silencing of women's words by the men who wrote the gospels, or their blindness to their importance—an omission Lanyer is out to correct.

The warning to Pilate to 'open thine eyes' yields to a defence of Eve contrasting her small, innocent sin with the sin Pilate commits in condemning Jesus. In Lanyer's reading of the brief narrative of the Fall in Genesis— the text that, subjected to the exegesis of men throughout history, had been used to sanction the authority of men and the inferiority and submission of women to their husbands—Eve appears 'simply good' (l. 765), possessing an 'undiscerning Ignorance' that allowed her to be 'deceav'd' by the 'cunning' of the 'subtile Serpent' (ll. 769, 773, 767). Though Lanyer's indictment of Adam as 'most too blame' (l. 778) because he was stronger and 'Lord and King of all' (l. 783) may seem sophistical, her emphasis on Eve's simplicity and on her generous nature (her 'fault was onely too much love, / Which made her give this present to her Deare', ll. 801-802) could be considered a plausible interpretation of the biblical account (Gen. 3: 1-6). Even more important, however, in a single move that overturns centuries of exegesis, Lanyer turns Eve's credulity into a *virtue*, much as she had turned her own weakness of 'Sexe' and 'Sense' into a strength. For Eve's credulity is presented as an innate tendency to believe and trust, that is, a disposition to faith—and thus her simple credulity links her to the receptive, humble faith that the Virgin Mary shows in receiving the visitation from God (she 'could hardly apprehend' Gabriel's 'salutation' 'Nor couldst [she] judge, whereto those words did tend', ll. 1058-1060) and to the faith of all the women who believe in Christ and instinctively acknowledge his innocence and divinity. The credulity and gullibility of Eve is but the reverse side of the faith that sustains these women and distinguishes them from the men who, either weak in faith or moved by hate rather than love, are complicit in the Crucifixion.

Because Pilate's act is far worse than Eve's sin, it lessens her guilt: Eve's 'weakenesse did the Serpents words obay; / But you in malice Gods

deare Sonne betray' (ll. 815-816). While Lanyer follows Genesis in ac-
knowledging that men 'had power given to over-rule us all' (l. 760; cf.
Gen. 3: 16), she argues that Pilate's sin—and by extension men's role in
crucifying Christ—invalidates and revokes God's sentence subjecting Eve
and her female descendents to their husbands' authority. If Pilate condemns
Jesus to die,

> Her sinne was small, to what you doe commit;
> All mortall sinnes that doe for vengeance crie,
> Are not to be compared unto it ...
>> This sinne of yours, surmounts them all as farre
>> As doth the Sunne, another little starre.

> Then let us have our Libertie againe,
> And challendge to your selves no Sov'raigntie;
> You came not in the world without our paine,
> Make that a barre against your crueltie;
> Your fault beeing greater, why should you disdaine
> Our beeing your equals, free from tyranny?
>> If one weake woman simply did offend,
>> This sinne of yours, hath no excuse nor, end.

(ll. 818-820, 823-832)

Here in this crucial passage, Lanyer offers a new understanding of the significance of Christ's Crucifixion. Rather than simply following the tradition
from Paul and Augustine through Luther and Calvin that interprets the
Crucifixion as generally abrogating the human bondage to sin, to the flesh,
and to the Old Testament laws that are the mark of human bondage to sin,
Lanyer sees it as, in addition, specifically redeeming *women*, liberating
them from their subjection to men under the Law.[20] Just as the 'sleeping'
apostles and the otherwise treacherous men failed to see what the women
saw in Christ, so Lanyer implies that throughout the history of Christianity
the male apostles who interpreted the events of the Passion and, after them,
the male interpreters of the Bible have failed not only to recognise women's
devotion to the sacred but also to understand the full significance of the
events surrounding the Crucifixion. Though her version of the Passion is
closely based on the 'facts' and words of the New Testament, her interpretation is independent of Church tradition. Identifying with the women who
from the beginning accepted Jesus, and especially with Pilate's wife,
Lanyer claims the authority to interpret the Bible and the meaning of
Christ's Crucifixion for humankind. In her Gospel, Christ's Passion

reverses the order that gave men 'power ... to over-rule us all', undoing the punishment that God placed on Eve and cancelling the bondage of women. Speaking through and with Pilate's wife, as if she were present at Christ's passion, Lanyer insists that now—with Pilate's condemnation of Jesus— there is a new dispensation that should make women the 'equals' of men, 'free' from their 'tyranny'. But the fact that she is also writing in seven- teenth-century England and protesting the continued subjection of women suggests that Christ's redemption, which should have changed the social order, has yet to be enacted on earth.

For Lanyer, Christ's Passion and his teachings bear significance for transforming the secular order of society as well as humans' spiritual rela- tion with God. Recalling the early Christians described by Elaine Pagels and Peter Brown and anticipating the radical Protestants of the mid-seven- teenth-century English Civil War, Lanyer recognises the radical message of Christ's life and death for reordering society. Many of the teachings of Jesus were socially revolutionary. The pronouncements that the last shall be first, and that the meek shall inherit the earth, inverted the social and econ- omic orders of secular society and thus were considered dangerously sub- versive in the centuries before Christianity became the established religion of Rome. Similarly defiant of the contemporary social order were Christ's teachings suggesting that the true Christian should cast off the bonds of marriage and family to follow Christ: 'if any man come to me, and hate not his father, and mother, and wife, and children, and brethren, and sisters, yea, and his own life also, he cannot be my disciple' (Luke 14: 26); 'He that is unmarried careth for the things that belong to the Lord, how he may please the Lord: But he that is married careth for the things that are of the world, how he may please his wife' (I Cor. 7: 32-33). For all the seeming worldliness of Lanyer's concern for patronage, she recaptures something of the revolutionary spirit of Christianity in her interpretation of the Passion as calling for a radical reordering of society even in her own time. Properly understood, Lanyer suggests, Christianity undoes not only the power hier- archy where the strong dominate the weak, but also the socially constructed gender hierarchy in which men rule over women—an order that character- ised early seventeenth-century England much as it did Roman and Jewish societies in the time of Christ, and that was inscribed in the social codes of marriage that were understood to uphold the larger social order.

In early seventeenth-century England, marriage, far from circumscrib- ing a fully private sphere, was part of the public world. Like the homily on marriage, the numerous marriage conduct books, with their various pre- scriptions for woman's obedience, all assume the value of marriage in sus- taining the order of society. While it is often mentioned that the marital

conduct books of this period show the Puritan valuing of companionate
marriage (in contrast to the supposed Catholic privileging of celibacy and
virginity), it is perhaps less well recognised that in Protestant England in
the late sixteenth and early seventeenth-centuries, marriage was particularly
valued because it was understood to embody, encourage and preserve a
hierarchical social order. Domestic order mirrors and breeds order within
the church and state. As Robert Cleaver puts it in *A Godly Forme of Houshold Government*, 'a Household is as it were a little Common-wealth'.[21]
Given this close connection between marriage and the social order, it is far
from coincidental that Aemelia Lanyer's poem, with its socially radical
interpretation of the Passion as offering a new liberty to women, also implicitly rejects the institution of marriage.

Lanyer praises those women whose devotion to Christ has taken the
place of earthly, human marriages: the Virgin Mary, who is 'Farre from
desire of any man' (l. 1077; her marriage to Joseph is erased from Lanyer's
text), and Margaret Clifford, who as a widow refuses to entertain the
'desires / Of idle Lovers' (ll. 1550-51) and is completely faithful to Christ,
whom she has chosen to be her sole 'Lord' and 'Lover' (ll. 1705, 1398).
Her prefatory poems encourage women to take Christ as their bridegroom,
to put on 'wedding garments' ('To all vertuous Ladies in generall', l. 8)
and take him into 'your soules pure bed' ('To the Ladie *Susan*, Countesse
Dowager of Kent, and Daughter to the Duchesse of Suffolke', l. 42). In
Salve Deus, she tells Margaret Clifford that Christ is the 'Bridegroome'
from whom she 'shalt never be estrang'd' (ll. 77, 60)—a phrase that evokes
the Countess's former unhappy marriage, in which for a number of years
she lived apart from her philandering husband. Drawing on the familiar
biblical analogy between human marriage and the relation between the
individual believer (or the Church) and Christ, particularly as developed in
centuries of Christian interpretations of the *Song of Songs*, Lanyer presents
Christ as the only 'true' 'Lover' (l. 1267), the only husband a woman
needs.

> This is that Bridegroome that appeares so faire,
> So sweet, so lovely in his Spouses sight,
> That unto Snowe we may his face compare,
> His cheekes like skarlet, and his eyes so bright
> As purest Doves that in the rivers are,
> Washed with milke, to give the more delight;
> > His head is likened to the finest gold,
> > His curled lockes so beauteous to behold;

> Blacke as a Raven in her blackest hew;
> His lips like skarlet threeds, yet much more sweet
> Than is the sweetest hony dropping dew,
> Or hony combes, where all the Bees doe meete;
> Yea, he is constant, and his words are true,
> His cheekes are beds of spices, flowers sweet;
>> His lips, like Lillies, dropping downe pure mirrhe,
>> Whose love, before all worlds we doe preferre.   (ll. 1305-20)

In a sense, this appropriation of the *Song of Songs* is conventional, as is her eroticisation of the relationship between the Countess and Christ: the language of human, erotic love is the only language we have for apprehending divine, spiritual love. But rather than emphasising the congruence between secular and sacred love, Lanyer draws the analogy only to reject secular love, arguing that Christ is the only true object of our love and fulfils all our desires. Whereas the interpretations of the *Song of Songs* in the Middle Ages saw Solomon and Sheba's marriage not only as describing the relation between Christ and the church but as validating or sacramentalising human marriage and thus supporting the social order (Astell, 31, 63, 179), Lanyer's reading of the *Song of Songs* ultimately points to a rejection of earthly marriage. Although Lanyer's praise of the Queen of Sheba might initially seem to validate a reordered human marriage in emphasising the equality between Solomon and Sheba ('Here Majestie with Majestie did meete, / Wisdome to Wisdome yeelded true content', ll. 1585-86) and celebrating female agency (she fearlessly travels over 'sea and land' to pursue her 'Desire', ll. 1601-1604), the example of Solomon and Sheba actually yields to the greater example of Margaret's passion for Christ, which leaves actual, secular marriage behind as a something no longer necessary for the fulfilment of Christian women:

> Yet this rare Phoenix of that worne-out age,
> This great majesticke Queene comes short of thee,
> Who to an earthly Prince did then ingage
> Her hearts desires, her love, her libertie,
> Acting her glorious part upon a Stage
> Of weaknesse, frailtie, and infirmity:
>> Giving all honour to a Creature, due
>> To her Creator, whom shee never knew.

> But loe, a greater thou hast sought and found
> Than *Salomon* in all his royaltie;
> And unto him thy faith most firmly bound
> To serve and honour him continually ...   (ll. 1689-1700)

Ultimately, *Salve Deus* uses the language of love and marriage to reject marriage in favour of a celibacy that recalls not so much the Catholic privileging of virginity as the socially revolutionary stance of those women and men in the early centuries of Christianity who, following Christ's teachings, chose virginity, repudiating the institution of marriage that was the foundation of their society, and disdaining to perpetuate that society by producing offspring.[22] The rejection of secular marriage in *Salve Deus* may also recall Queen Elizabeth's refusal to marry so as not to compromise her authority by having a man 'over' her. Whatever one makes of Lanyer's position as mistress of Lord Hunsdon in the early 1590s, her 1611 poem, with its revolutionary gospel spirit, its sense of exclusive devotion to Christ, its sense that earthly loves and marriages conflict with marriage to God, aligns itself with those passages in the New Testament in which Christ teaches that 'The children of this world marrie and are married. But they which shalbe counted worthy to enjoy that world, and the resurrection from the dead, neither marrie wives, nor are married' (Luke 20: 34-35; cf. Matth. 22: 30). It is notable that many of the women she dedicated her poetry to were in some sense independent of, or in conflict with, the authority of husbands.[23] Moreover, while her inclusion of mothers and daughters seems to emphasise family and lineage, sons and husbands are conspicuously absent in her addresses to contemporary women—almost as if these women, as she says of Christ, exist 'without the assistance of man' ('To the Vertuous Reader', 49).

The rejection of marriage in *Salve Deus* is an integral part of Aemilia Lanyer's socially radical understanding of the meaning of Christ's Passion. To reject marriage is to undo the hierarchical social order in which men rule over women, thus freeing women from bondage to men and thus fulfilling the redemptive significance of Christ's Passion. If the goal of life is union with Christ in heaven at the end of the world, then marriage, with its commitment to reproduction, only delays that goal. Moreover, for a woman to choose Christ as her only Spouse, her true lover, is not just to be devoted to God but to reject the authority of any earthly husband, an authority understood in early seventeenth century England to be representative of the authority of all earthly magistrates, particularly the king. Hence her argument has strongly subversive implications. King James well expressed this notion of the symbolic authority of husbands when in his speech to his first

English Parliament (19 March 1603) he compared the union between the monarch and his subjects to marriage: 'I am the Husband, and all the whole Isle is my lawfull Wife; I am the Head, and it is my Body' (*Political Works*, 272).

James's comment here, which genders the notion of obedience as it insists on the interconnection between marital and political order, echoes Paul's comments in Ephesians comparing a well-ordered marriage to the relation between Christ and the Church:

> Wives, submit your selves unto your husbands, as unto the Lord. For the husband is the wives head, even as Christ is the head of the Church, and the same is the saviour of his body. Therefore as the Church is in subjection to Christ, even so let the wives bee to their husbands in every thing ... So ought men to love their wives, as their owne bodies: he that loveth his wife, loveth himselfe ... This is a great secret, but I speak concerning Christ, and concerning the Church. Therefore every one of you, doe yee so: let every one love his wife, even as himselfe, and let the wife see that shee feare her husband (Ephesians 5: 22-24, 28, 32-33).

Paul's analogy identifies the husband with Christ and the head, the wife with the Church and the body, defining a mutual dependence and 'love' based on woman's 'subjection' and 'submission', which is seen as necessary for a well-ordered society. These foundational verses from Ephesians, as well as other New Testament verses on marriage in which the Apostles gave prescriptions for women's behaviour, were enormously influential in Lanyer's time.[24] Cited in the 'Homilie on ... Matrimonie' and marital conduct treatises, they were used to give religious sanction to the established social and political order. Frances Dillingham's *Christian Oeconomy* opens with the passage from Colossians 3: 18, 'wives subject yourselves to your husbands, as it is meete in the Lord', and quotes Paul's advice in I Timothy 2: 12 ('I permit not a woman to teach, neither to usurpe authoritie over the man, but to be in silence'). Robert Cleaver's *A Godly Forme of Household Government*, the most popular of these books (it went through nine editions between 1598 and 1624), repeatedly cites Ephesians 5: 22-27 to encourage wives' obedience to their husband, sometimes invoking a number of biblical passages in powerful combination: 'wives [should] submit themselves, and be obedient to their owne husbands, as to the Lord, because the husband is by Gods ordinance, the wives head, ... and therefore she oweth her subjection to him, like as the Church doth to Christ; and because [of] the example of *Sarah*, the mother of the faithfull, which obeyed *Abraham* and called him Lord' (Ephes. 5: 22, I Cor. 11: 3, I Pet. 3: 6, Ephes. 5: 24 cited in margin).[25]

Perhaps these conduct books, with all their emphasis on women's sub-jection, described an ideal at odds with actual practice. The point I wish to make, however, is that in all these treatises the Apostles, particularly Paul and Peter, are understood to provide unshakeable biblical authority for prescriptions about domestic order, seen as the basis of all order in society. These apostolic verses are precisely the ones Lanyer so insistently defies in *Salve Deus*, as she gives women a public voice, insists on their equality or even superiority, and argues against the authority of men to rule them.[26] The argument of the entire poem, as well as of Eve's Apologie, constitutes a firm rejection of those New Testament verses in which the Apostles rigor-ously prescribed wives' submission to the authority of their husbands. The evidence of Lanyer's poem thus suggests her recognition of a fundamental contradiction or discontinuity between Christ's teachings, which subverted the social order of Roman and Jewish society and emphasized the equality of the sexes, and those interpretations of Christ's message by his disciples that perpetuated the subjection of women.

Salve Deus reveals a surprisingly sophisticated hermeneutics, touched by a scepticism about the Bible one would not expect to find in the seven-teenth century, for she clearly distinguishes between, on the one hand, Jesus's words and the 'facts' of the Gospels and, on the other, the moral, domestic, and social prescriptions concerning women made by the male disciples and authors of the books of the New Testament. A discriminating reader of the text of the Bible, she suggests that all words of the Bible are not equally inspired and authoritative. For Lanyer, the prescriptions of Paul and the other disciples for ordering/subjecting women and for silencing them in the church—principles which are at odds with the teachings and actions of Christ as recorded in the Bible—prove to be misinterpretations of Christ's message that, supported by centuries of Christian commentary, have perpetuated the very bondage the Crucifixion was to have abrogated.

Finally, it is not only confidence in divine inspiration that allows Lanyer to claim religious authority; it is also her identification with a uniquely privileged woman, the Virgin Mary. Her description of the 'blessed Virgin' (l. 1025)—of 'meane estate' and 'lowly mind', 'hardly [able to] apprehend' Gabriel's salutation, yet deserving that 'the Holy Ghost should ... overshadow thee' (ll. 1034-35, 1058-59, 1082-84)—mir-rors Lanyer's sense of herself as lowly ('To the Queenes most Excellent Majestie', ll. 109-14, 127-28), 'Weake' in 'Sexe' and 'Sense', and fully receptive to God's grace and illumination (ll. 289-302). Like the Virgin Mary, she has been 'chosen' to be a vessell for Christ ('To the doubtfull

Reader'; cf. *Salve*, l. 1030), and thus her poem contains Christ. She presents his 'picture' as something the Countess of Cumberland can keep in her 'heart' and draw spiritual nourishment from (ll. 1325-28). But her prose dedication to the Countess insists she is offering not simply an image or picture, but God himself: 'Right Honourable and Excellent Lady ... I present unto you even *our Lord Jesus himselfe* ... Therefore good Madame, to the most perfect eyes of your understanding, I deliver the inestimable treasure of all elected soules, to bee perused at convenient times' (34-35; italics mine). The language here suggests that she is like the priests of the church who in celebrating holy communion offer Christ to the congregation.[27] Finding in Mary a precedent for a female priesthood, for woman's worthiness to contain and offer up God for human salvation, Lanyer thus assumes for herself something like the public, priestly power denied to women within the institution of the Christian church. In this assumption of a priestly function, she turns to women's advantage the Protestant emphasis on the priesthood of all believers. But she is also a true descendant of the early Christian women who believed they had the right to preach and even baptise, and of the medieval holy women who, as Bynum says, 'saw themselves as authorised to teach, counsel, serve, and heal by mystical experience rather than by office' (*Holy Feast*, 235) and thus challenged the exclusive, intimate connection with God enjoyed by the priest.[28] Lanyer's presumption of this authority was certainly radical in 1611. But even today, the idea that women might bear priestly authority remains intensely controversial—witness the furore over the decision to allow the ordination of women in the Church of England, a decision prompting clergy as well as lay Anglicans to consider conversion to Roman Catholicism. Claiming the authority to reinterpret the Bible and the significance of the Crucifixion, joining the ranks of the (male) apostles and correcting their prescriptions for human behaviour where they diverge from what seems to her the message of Jesus, Aemilia Lanyer takes the next logical step and defies the assumption that the priesthood is an exclusively male privilege.

Notes

1   Peter Brown, *The Body and Society: Men, Women, and Sexual Renunciation in Early Christianity* (New York, 1988) esp. Ch. 1 (5-32), discusses Christianity within the cultural context not only of Rome but of the first-century Jews. See also Elaine Pagels, *Adam, Eve, and the Serpent* (New York, 1988). On women's roles in early Judaism and early Christianity, see also Elisabeth Schussler Fiorenza, *In Memory of Her: A Feminist Theological Reconstruction of Christian Origins* (New York, 1983). On the discontinuities about woman implicit in the two creation

stories in Genesis, and their complex development through centuries of Christian tradition, see James Grantham Turner, *One Flesh: Paradisal Marriage and Sexual Relations in the Age of Milton* (Oxford, 1987). New Testament references are to the Geneva Bible (1602 ed.); i/j and u/v have been modenized.

2   The marginal annotations on these passages in the 1607 printing of the third (1602) ed. of the 'Geneva' New Testament, based on Beza, point out that the 'covering' of women 'declareth that the woman is one degree beneath the man by the ordinance of God', and that 'having their heades covered ... was then [in Paul's time] a signe of subjection'. *The Geneva Bible (The Annotated New Testament, 1602 Edition)*, edited by Gerald T. Sheppard, Pilgrim Classic Commentaries, Vol. 1 (New York, 1989), 85r.

3   See Pagels's account of the heroism of Thecla and Perpetua (Ch. 1-2). Brown (145) notes the important role of women in the church by 200 AD, though Pagels implies that as early as the deutero-Pauline letters of the New Testament (particularly Timothy I and II, and Ephesians) an attempt to suppress the empowering of women was evident in the case of Thecla, who claimed that women could teach and baptise (Ch. 1, esp. 24-26). See Augustine, *The City of God*, translated by Marcus Dods, 2 Vols. (New York, 1948) Bk. 14, Ch. 7 (II, 10-12), Bk. 15, Ch. 20 and Bk. 15, Ch. 22-23 (II, 84-89, 91-97) on the association of woman with flesh, which tempts man from God. On subjection in marriage as the model of order, see Augustine *CG* Bk. 14, Ch. 7 (II, 10-12), Bk. 19, Ch. 14 and 16 (II, 322-323, 325-326) and Pagels's discussion of Augustine (114). On the assocation of woman with the flesh, see also Brown's discussion of Ambrose (348-349) and Jerome (375-377); Pagels's discussion of Augustine, esp. 113-114; and Ann W. Astell's discussion of Origen in *The Song of Songs in the Middle Ages* (Ithaca, 1990), esp. 2-5. Brown and Pagels emphasize the powerful influence of Augustine on Christianity and, indeed, Western values (Brown Ch. 19; Pagels Ch. 5).

4   Caroline Walker Bynum, *Holy Feast and Holy Fast: The Religious Significance of Food to Medieval Women* (Berkeley, 1987).

5   Caroline Walker Bynum, *Jesus as Mother: Studies in the Spirituality of the High Middle Ages* (Berkeley, 1982), esp. Introduction (1-21) and 'Women Mystics in the Thirteenth Century: The Case of the Nuns of Helfta' (170-262). Bynum (*Holy Feast*) argues that the increased power of the clergy was related to the late medieval proliferation of holy women, for these women claimed an immediate, unmediated, intimate experience of God that was similar to that enjoyed by the priest. Astell sees a distinctly positive valuing of the feminine in religious experience in medieval interpretations of *Canticles*.

6   On the Protestant suppression of the feminine aspect of Catholic spirituality, see Maureen Sabine, *Feminine Engendred Faith: The Poetry of John Donne and Richard Crashaw* (London, 1992), 1-42 and Patricia Crawford, *Women and Religion in England 1500-1720* (London, 1993), 21-37.

7   Elaine V. Beilin, *Redeeming Eve: Women Writers of the English Renaissance* (Princeton, 1987), discusses the Reformist women prose writers and poets, some of whom contributed to religious polemic (see esp. 48-150). On women's status as defined in English Protestant writings, particularly in relation to Roman Catholicism, see also Charles H. and Katherine George, *The Protestant Mind of the English Reformation 1570-1640* (Princeton, 1961), 258-265, 275-289.

8   A.L. Rowse, *Sex and Society in Shakespeare's Age: Simon Forman the Astrologer*
      (New York, 1974); Rowse, 'Introduction: Shakespeare's Dark Lady' in *The Poems*
      of Shakespeare's Dark Lady (New York, 1979), 1-37.
9   Barbara K. Lewalski observes: 'The title of Lanyer's volume promises, somewhat
      misleadingly, a collection of religious poetry' ('Re-writing Patriarchy and Patron-
      age: Margaret Clifford, Anne Clifford, and Aemelia Lanyer', *Yearbook of English*
      Studies 21 [1991]: 98). See also Lewalski, *Writing Women in Jacobean England*
      (Cambridge, 1993), 213-241. Lewalski stresses the secular aspect of the volume as
      a 'defense and celebration of the enduring community of good women' (*Writing*
      Women, p. 213).
10   On Elizabeth, see Sabine, p. 13; Roy Strong, *The Cult of Elizabeth* (London,
      1977), 117-128, esp. 126; and Phillippa Berry, *Of Chastity and Power: Elizabeth-*
      an Literature and the Unmarried Queen (London, 1989), who emphasises the
      importance of Elizabeth's spiritual authority, noting also that the Queen assumed
      the title 'supreme governor' of the Church rather than 'supreme head', the title of
      Henry VIII (65-66). On James, see Sabine (25) and Jonathan Goldberg, 'Fatherly
      Authority: The Politics of Stuart Family Images' in Margaret W. Ferguson,
      Maureen Quilligan and Nancy J. Vickers (ed.), *Rewriting the Renaissance: The*
      Discourses of Sexual Difference in Early Modern Europe (Chicago, 1986), 3-32.
      For James's writings, see *The Trew Law of Free Monarchies* and his first speech
      to the English Parliament, in *The Political Works of James I*, introduction by
      Charles Howard McIlwain (New York, 1965), 55, 273.
11   See also Leeds Barroll, 'The Court of the First Stuart Queen' in Linda Levy Peck
      (ed.), *The Mental World of the Jacobean Court* (Cambridge, 1991), 191-208.
12   *Holy Bible* [King James Authorised Version] (London, 1611) dedicatory epistle
      'To the Most High and Mightie Prince James', sig. A2v.
13   *An Homilie of the State of Matrimonie* insists that wives should suffer in silence
      and 'be quiet', for they will get their reward hereafter; in *Certaine Sermons or*
      Homilies Appointed to be Read in Churches in the Time of Queen Elizabeth I
      (1547-1571), Facsimile Reprod. of the Edition of 1623, introduction by Mary
      Ellen Rickey and Thomas B. Stroup, 2 Vols in one (Gainesville, 1968), II, 245.
      On women's silence, see William Whately, *A Bride-Bush. Or, A Direction for*
      Married Persons (London, 1623), 200-201; Robert Cleaver, *A Godly Forme of*
      Houshold Government (London, 1603), 230 ('The best meanes therefore that a
      wife can use to obtaine, and maintaine the love and good liking of her husband, is
      to be silent, obedient, peaceable').
14   *The Poems of Aemilia Lanyer: 'Salve Deus Rex Judaeorum'*, edited by Susanne
      Woods, Women Writers in English, 1350-1850 (Oxford, 1993), 63. Subsequent
      references are included parenthetically in the text by line numbers.
15   In her emphasis on the role of women, Lanyer is closest to Luke, the one gospel
      written by someone who did not claim to have witnessed the Crucifixion.
16   The question of whether a woman could have written one of the Gospels is in-
      triguing. Among the Gnostic Gospels purporting to be the secret teachings of Jesus
      condemned as heretical (most of which were discovered at Nag Hammadi in 1945)
      is a Gospel supposedly by Mary Magdalen. On the *Gospel of Mary*, see Pagels,
      Adam, Eve, and the Serpent, p. 61, and Pagels, *The Gnostic Gospels* (New York,

1979), 11-14, 64-65. Fiorenza, *In Memory of Her*, argues for the importance of recovering 'the women disciples and what they have done' (xiv).

17   Lorna Hutson, 'Why the Lady's eyes are nothing like the sun', in: Isobel Armstrong (ed.), *New Feminist Discourses: Critical Essays on Theories and Texts* (London, 1992), 154-175, aptly observes: 'Lanyer figures the climax of the narrative as a drama of interpretation, in which women elicit radiance and meaning from the event which had remained mute and indecipherable to masculine exegesis' (170).

18   Beilin, p. 198, observes Lanyer's emphasis on Mary but does not see the possible Catholic significance of this. Instead, she sees Lanyer's poetry as 'ardently Protestant' (182). Lewalski observes that many of the dedications are to women 'linked through kinship or marriage with the Sidney-Leicester faction', which was strongly Protestant (*Writing Women*, 221). However, two of Lanyer's dedicatees—Queen Anne and Lady Arabella Stuart—had Roman Catholic connections; Anne may even have converted. Certain aspects of her poem (particularly the attention to the Virgin Mary, who has thirteen stanzas devoted to her) make the label 'Protestant' problematic.

19   John Milton, *Paradise Lost,* in: Merritt Y. Hughes (ed.), *Complete Poems and Major Prose* (New York, 1957).

20   See Augustine, *CG* Bk. 15, Ch. 2-3 (II, 51-53); Luther, *A Treatise on Christian Liberty* in *Works of Martin Luther*, Vol. 2 (Philadelphia, 1916), 312-348, and John Calvin, *Institutes of the Christian Religion*, translated by John Allen, 2 Vols (Philadelphia, n.d.) Bk. 2, Ch. 11 (I, 405-19); Bk. 3, Ch. 19 (II, 62-76).

21   Cleaver, *A Godly Forme of Houshold Government,* p. 13. See also William Gouge, *Of Domesticall Duties* (London, 1623), 'the family is a seminary of the Church and common-wealth' (17); and *An Homilie of the State of Matrimonie*. On the analogy of family and politics, particularly in the Stuart period, see Gordon Schochet, *Patriarchalism in Political Thought* (New York, 1975), 54-84, and Lawrence Stone, *The Family, Sex and Marriage in England 1500-1800* (New York, 1977), 152-154.

22   Brown (esp. Ch. 1-4, 5-102) gives an eloquent and sympathetic explanation of the socially revolutionary significance of sexual renunciation for the early ascetic Christians. See also Pagels, *Adam, Eve, and the Serpent*, esp. Ch. 1, 2, 4. Brown points out the social usefulness of Augustine's later defence of marriage in a society where 'the security of the Catholic church depended on the authority of male heads of households' (404).

23   Queen Anne had a separate court as well as a relatively separate life from her husband, King James, who was known for his homoerotic attachments to male favorites. (See Lewalski, *Writing Women*, pp. 15-43, on Anne's 'oppositional politics'.) The Queen's daughter, Elizabeth, was as yet unmarried; the Dowager Countess of Kent and Margaret Clifford, Countess of Cumberland, were both widdows; Margaret's daughter, Ann Clifford, was to be in conflict for many years with her husband as she struggled to gain legal rights to her inheritance from her father.

24   As Pagels (*Adam, Eve, and the Serpent*, 23-26) and Brown (57) have shown, the deutero-Pauline writings, which include Ephesians, Colossians and I Timothy, endorse marriage and thus 'correct' the preference for celibacy and sexual renunci-

ation in Paul's first epistle to the Corinthians (I Cor. 7: 1, 7-8), though the sense of gender hierarchy remains generally consistent throughout the Pauline epistles.

25   *An Homilie of the State of Matrimonie*, esp. 242; Francis Dillingham, *Christian Oeconomy: or Houshold Government* (London, 1609), 1, 11; Cleaver, p. 224. For further examples of reliance on these biblical verses, see also Whately and Gouge. 1 Peter 3: 1, 5-6 ('let the wives bee subiect to their husbandes ... For euen after this maner in time past did the holy women, which trusted in God tire themselves, & were subiect to their husbands. As Sara obeyed Abraham, and called him Sir'), which Cleaver paraphrases, was regularly invoked to encourage women's proper 'reverence'. See *An Homilie ... of Matrimonie*, pp. 242-243; Whately, p. 203; Gouge, p. 283.

26   On the differences between the Pauline and deutero-Pauline texts on women and sexuality, see Pagels, *Adam, Eve, and the Serpent*, pp. 23-25; on the differences between these texts concerning marriage, see Brown, pp. 44-58; and on the contradictions in Paul concerning gender, see Daniel Boyarin, 'Paul and the Genealogy of Gender', *Representations* 41 (Winter 1993): 1-33.

27   Cf. I Peter 2: 5, 9 on the faithful as a holy priesthood. But Peter implies it is men who speak God's words and minister: 4: 10-11. In her claims for being able to 'present' Christ, Lanyer recalls the medieval holy women who Bynum has argued were assuming the power of priests to handle and enjoy God ('Women Mystics in the Thirteenth Century: The Case of the Nuns of Helfta,' in *Jesus as Mother*, 170-262).

28   See Pagels, *Adam, Eve, and the Serpent*, p. 24, on the early claim of women's right to preach and baptise.

PART II

'NOR EVER CHAST ...':
JOHN DONNE, AMOROUS AND DIVINE

9

'LET ME LOVE':
READING THE SACRED 'CURRANT' OF DONNE'S PROFANE LYRICS

M. THOMAS HESTER

'*Pravum est cor omnium, et inscrutabile: Quis cognoscet illud?*' Prophetia Ieremiae 17: 9

'*I am much of one sect in the Philosophy of love; which though it be directed upon the minde, doth inhere in the body, and find piety entertainment there*'. John Donne

'*If you would teach a scholar in the highest form to read, take Donne*'. S.T. Coleridge

'*something's going on here, but you don't know what it is, do you, Mr. Jones*'. Bob Dylan

The first two printed editions of John Donne's poems open with an explanatory *Epistle* most remarkable for its assertion that he 'will have no such Readers as [he] can teach'.[1] In the poem which this wry exordium prefaces, the speaker says he will trace the 'progress of a deathlesse Soule ... whose life you shall finde in the ende of this booke', but when the readers reach the last stanza of that poem what they find instead is another description of Donne's 'sullen Writ', which is once again defined in terms of its enigmatic denial of their authority: this 'Writ ... just so much courts [whomever] read'st it ... as thou dost it'. And this warning is then followed by another 'picture' of the defiant poet—'Let me arrest thy thoughts, wonder with me'—which is then underscored by his final sardonic assertion that 'Of every quality comparison, / The onely measure is, and judge, opinion' ('Metempsychosis' 511-20). Even the 'quality' response to this 'Writ', that is, is only the reader's 'opinion'.[2] Although replaced in subsequent printing of Donne's *Poems* by 'The Flea' as the initial assault on the expectations of the readers, this 1633/1635 arrangement does provide an apt introduction to the reading of his poems, even while it warns that the 'sullen'—that is, the ill-humoured or moodily *silent*—'Writ' of this idiosyncratic author is not inclined to suffer the opinions of readers gladly, regardless of the assurance with which they are espoused.

As an introductory self-appraisal of Donne's witty poems, this Epistle is instructive as to *how and why* they seem framed, as this 'new Author' termed it in another defence of his wit printed in the same year, to 'cozen [the] expectations'[3] of the readers—especially their 'expectations' as delineated by that seminal treatise on poetry to issue from the Elizabethan court,[4] Sir Philip Sidney's defence of poetry as an 'architektonike' instrument of 'service' to the Protestant mission.[5] Sidney's *Defence* urged that the entire poetic project depends on the 'right' response of the readers. The 'skill of the artificer' may 'stand in the *idea,* or fore-conceit', but the entire pedagogical superiority of the poetic enterprise 'worketh substantially' in its capacity 'not only to make a Cyrus ... but to bestow a Cyrus upon the world to make many Cyruses, *if they will learn aright why and how that maker made him'*.[6] There is indeed much virtue in that 'if', for it indicates that central to Sidney's oration on the poetry as 'the best teacher' of 'virtue' (similar to Calvin's defence of the sacraments as 'useful' above all) is the will of the reader; even though it is the reader's 'infected will', he insists, that prevents him from 'reaching unto [the] perfection' known to his 'erected wit'. Indeed, Sidney's Petrarchan sonnet sequence seems framed primarily to confirm such a Protestant poetic through its iteration of how Stella's 'right' reading of the 'idolatry' of Astrophil's wilful lust eventually 'Clips the wings [of the sensualist with] Most rude despair', 'wraps' the vain lover 'in night', and renders even those 'thoughts which breed [his] delight' into a hell in which 'joy' is only 'annoy'. Sexual desire, as the sonnets appended to the 1595 edition of the sequence submit, is but a 'blind man's *mark'.*[7] But 'virtue [i.e., Stella] hath this better lesson taught' Sidney's 'phantastike' poet-lover—'Within myself to seek my only hire, / Desiring nought but how to kill desire'. If the readers 'learn aright' from this 'look' into the wilful 'heart' of sexual desire, they might well follow Sidney's own example of 'heroic' national service (and death) in Zutphen and 'make war, not love'—*'Splendidis longum valedico nugis'.*[8]

It is John Donne (whom some readers judge to be *the* poet of sexual desire and the 'splendid trifles' of amateur love sonnets), even more than Sidney, I would suggest, who is *the poet of supposition. 'If'* appears 90 times, in 43 of the 57 lyrics; *'but'* 98 times; *'yet'* over 30; *'but yet'* over a dozen. The 'intense verbal activity'[9] of the Donne lyric most often seems to be a touchstone. in fact, of the provocative expressiveness of *if, but,* and *however* as synecdoches for the 'subtile sophistrie' ('Natures lay Ideot'), the thrusts, reversals, 'hesitations and urgencies of feeling' of desire. Donne learned much, that is, from the 'skill' of Sidney 'the English Petrarcke' which is so brilliantly conveyed by the 'speaking picture' of human desire 'feigned' by the legendary Elizabethan in *Astrophil and Stella.* But the

Donne lyric, unlike the Petrarchan songs and sonnets, often seems to be as much or more a 'speaking picture' of the speaker's attempt to read the desire of his beloved than a 'representing, counterfeiting, or figuring forth' of the speaker's own desire. By focusing attention on the role of the love-poet as a 'reader' of the desires of his beloved, these lyrics often seem framed to challenge or even to deny the readers' comprehension of even the specific event(s) to which they are responding or meditating. Not only do they frequently not 'teach ... the Readers', but seem more concerned to reject their auditors' attempts to comprehend their 'mystery' even as they figure the speaker himself as similarly confounded. It was likely more than metrical roughness that led one of his earliest readers to conclude that 'Done for not being understood would perish',[10] and more than a concern with courtly etiquette that led Donne to confide to his best friend that he would 'suffer from many interpretations' if he published his manuscript poems.[11] My own reading of these poems is that they are profitably viewed in part as a witty critique of the poetry, the poetics, and the Protestant polemic best represented by Sidney's works, as a sort of witty 'counter-reformation' endorsement of the recusant Donne's early motto— '*Antes muerto que mudado*' (*Better dead than changed*): that central to their strategies of wit, that is, is Donne's attempt to distance himself from the views of love, religion, and poetry represented by the example of Sidney.[12] The following essay offers a brief overview of *how and why* Donne invents this violation of the major English Protestant poesis in some of his best-known lyrics. Following his own directive in a 1623 sermon on the Penitential Psalms—that 'in all Metricall compositions ... the force of the whole piece is for the most part left to the shutting up, ... *the last clause is as the impression of the stamp, and that it is that makes it currant*'[13]— this essay aims to look at how those moments of readerly 'incomprehensiblenesse' (to cite 'The First Anniversary') rely on the lexicon of the 'currant' Reformation debate between Roman Catholic and Protestant readers. These poems, we should not forget, were composed by the great-grand-nephew of Sir Thomas More, the nephew of the Jesuit leader Jasper Heywood and his exiled brother Ellis, the son of a woman who was living in virtual religious exile during the time of her son's lyric compositions, the other brother of the recently martyred Henry Donne; these lyrics, that is, can be profitably read as *analogies* 'currant' to the Donne's situation as he himself defined it in the first work published under his own name: the works of someone 'ever kept awake in a meditation of Martyrdome, by being derived from such a stocke and race, as, I believe, no family ... hath endured more in their persons and fortunes, for obeying the Teachers of Romane Doctrine'.[14]

Just as his (third) *Satyre* on the *absence* of 'our Mistresse faire Religion' in Elizabethan England relies on incriminating analogies between men's choices of a bride and their choices of the Bride of Christ, so the imaginary, meditative *sermones* about profane love in the lyrics are often transcribed in terms of the 'currant' debate about the meaning of the Eucharist. But, at the same time, these poems challenge the readers to privilege either the profane dramatic situation or the sacred analogy the 'dialogue of one' posits. Even as they figure the incarnation of the speaker's love in the terms of the 'currant' debate about the Real Presence in the sacred Feast within the temple, they seem to privilege both tenor and vehicle, literal and spiritual meaning, body and soul, presence and absence —all while challenging any reader besides the speaker's 'divine' beloved to understand the 'nature, and name' of his love. It is not just a send-up or eroticising of Petrarchan commonplaces, that is, that Donne composes in these witty poems: by figuring his profane love as either a (blasphemous) form of erotic *idolatry* analogous to religious heresy, or as a form of devotion to his mistress that might seem analogous to political or religious treason to those unable to understand it, these poems (to recall the operative verb of *Satyre III*) 'dare' that nosy, voyeuristic, intruding reader to read any political or religious conclusions about the lover's declarations and analogies. Such a strategy might well have been best described, in fact, in Donne's defence of his prose paradoxes to Sir Henry Wotton, for the poems seem also to have been 'made rather to deceive tyme than her daughter truth, ... alarums to truth, ... prettily guilt ... I am desirous to hyde them withour any over rec[k]oning of them or the[ir] maker'.[15] How this strategy of reader-denial works (in an age in which the death of the author was a real possibility and not just a *trompe l'oeil* of fashionable literary critical self-authorisation) can be briefly scanned in *the last clause* of the lyrics, where the readers both within and without of what Donne's lover insists is the 'temple' of their 'inscription' become 'no such Reader as [he] would teach'.

What this appropriation of the current theological debate about how to read the sacred text of Christ's Body in the last clauses of these profane lyrics intimates is what Donne in his lyrics does not 'dare' teach because his is an interdicted subject—not only as an apology for sexual desire but as an apology which frames its defence in terms of the current Catholic opposition to the Protestant poetic and theological oligarchy. Unlike the Protestant project of verbal teaching and clarification, Donne's conceits subsume the sacred into the profane, confounding our understanding by positing analogies between sacred and profane love in which we 'cannot tell' whether to privilege the vehicle or the tenor. Like the polyphony of a Catholic Mass spoken in a foreign or 'secret' language—and unlike the edifying 'plain' clarifications of the sacred Book in the Protestant homiletic 'lesson'— Donne's profane lyrics do not 'teach' but instead *present* a blend of voices, connotations, and 'meanings' which confound our understanding. We as readers really are *pro-fanum*—'outside the temple' of love's mysteries in which they are spoken. That is one significant way that Donne's poetry is decidedly different from that of a Sidney or a Spenser; *why* 'that maker made' it so I shall surmise more broadly after looking at examples of how Donne frames the last clauses of these overheard epigrammatic conversations in terms of current theological analogies.

Perhaps the best (or best-known) example of the 'incomprehensible-nesse' of Donne's love poems is 'The Relic'—that 33-line appraisal of the possible significance of the 'bracelet of bright hair' given the speaker by his beloved. As Anne Ferry points out, in this 3-stanza poem Donne's 'eaves-dropping [readers are] ultimately made the butt of a joke ... at the end of the poem when our position is equated with that of false-believers hearing a mock-lecturer in a language [we] are too unsophisticated to understand, ... and finally excluded from the secret knowledge which the speaker refuses to "tell"'. My concern, however, is not just with what Ferry calls the 'game [being played] with the reader' (112) but with how the poet's analogies frame that hermeneutic challenge or readerly frustration in the terms of the current theological debate about the significance of Christ's words in His institution of the sacraments. The speaker imagines a situation that might well recall that of many English recusants (such as Donne's younger brother who was caught by Topcliffe's secret police while celebrating the Catholic Mass of 'misdevotion'): an outsider or 'spy' from beyond the private borders of the lover's amatory 'engraving' is allowed to 'break ope[n]' the devotional practice he does not understand but which he interprets as a carnal practice, about which he then informs 'the Bishops, and the King', which then results in that interpretative community's reading of the lovers as violators of the 'late law'. The lover then asserts that 'All measure, and all language, [he] should passe, / Should [he] tell what a miracle' 'those meales' the lovers shared when 'comming and going'—thus asserting the single point about which Catholics and Protestants agreed about the significance of the Eucharist—that it was, in the Greek word for *sacrament*, a 'mystery'. Indeed, such a current analogy for the poem could also be provided by the Catholic tradition of the 'progress' or 'translation' of the relics of saints from one sacred place to another for the adoration of the faithful,[16] a tradition that is 'translated' here into a sort of Protestant *reading* of such physical texts, in which the power of the sacred relics to effect 'miracles' has been displaced by a reading of texts by secular authorities. One of the consistent complaints by Catholic historians of the age attacked the 'plundering' Protestants for the 'secular', meretricious bases of their Reformation as a form of mere personal enrichment; Nicholas Sander, for instance, cites the king's (Henry VIII's) 'trial' of St. Thomas à Beckett, in which he was 'found guilty of treason' as an 'excuse for the pillage' of 'the wealth lavished upon his tomb'.[17] One does not have to accept Sander's appraisal of the 'secular' foundations of the Reformation in England—nor Hilaire Belloc's conclusion that it was primarily successful because of the profit it brought to the 'new men' whose power and position flowed from the plundering of what Donne called 'our ruin'd Abbeyes' (*Satyre II*, 60)— in order to hear in the wryly humorous situation of 'The Relic' a recollection of a topic of considerable significance to the family of the author who would preface his *Pseudo-Martyr* with a defence of the 'teachings [and] learning' of his family's Catholicism. But perhaps what 'The Relic' aims to 'teach' through its *translation* of the Petrarchan trope of the beloved as a goddess who alone knows the ultimate meaning of this 'device' into the arena of Counter-Reformation hermeneutical debate is the limitations of the 'Protestant' privileging of the power of the reader to comprehend the 'mysteries' of 'saintly' love. Our own attempts to translate the experience of the poem into either a profane or a sacred reading—our inability to determine whether the poem wryly comments on the precarious situation of Catholics in a Protestant state, as well as our attempt to determine the precise nature of the 'little stay' of the two characters' relationship—is mirrored by that of the speaker's attempt to determine the meaning of his beloved's suggestive gift of 'bright haire'. Donne, in other words, confounds the readers within and without the poem: neither is 'taught by this paper' or this 'device'. No reader within the poem derives the 'correct' meaning of her emblematic 'hair', according to the speaker; in fact, whether 'this device' if that emblem or the emblematic 33-line shape of 'this paper' is not clear; we are left out of the hermeneutic circle here finally, saucily told by our poet who would have 'that age taught' that he would have to 'passe ... All measure, and all language ... Should [he] tell' (31-33). 'The Relic', then, might incline us to read here the residue of Donne's own displaced and illegal boyhood Catholic devotion being subsumed into a witty defence of the presence of the body in profane love—but to enforce such a reading on the poem, especially given the manner in which it moves from an erotic to a 'platonic' reading of the bracelet—would be for us to 'passe' the 'measure' and 'language' of the poem itself.[18] In other words, from a literary perspective the poem works ingenious variations on the trope of the beloved as *divine*—she alone knows the ultimate meaning of this 'device' through which the lovers might plan to 'make a little stay' on Judgement Day; she

knows whether this suggestive emblem of her body (or her soul) figures
forth her similarity to Mary Magdalene the saint or Mary Magdalene the
prostitute, or even whether the 'miracle she *was*' and 'did' indicates, to cite
the terms of the current theological controversy, 'a reall presence and a
corporall absence' or a 'Real Presence' in their relationship.[19] In 'The
Relic', that is, Donne's fanciful speaker, interrogating seven levels of supposition that would have to eventuate for a clear reading of the emblematic
'device' of the 'bracelet' to transpire, imagines three contradictory interpretations (or 'translations') of the significance of her emblematic 'bracelet'.
These readings by him of the meaning of what is apparently her gift to him
finally do not 'teach' us or him just what her gracious action means: she
alone is author of this mystery, a mystery that is framed as analogous to the
differing interpretations of sacred mysteries during Donne's age. Only her
originary reason for this gift is 'substantial', that is, for the speaker's readings and our readings of his readings remain 'opinions' which indicate only
our own desires to authorise the meaning of her gift and his 'paper'.

As Maureen Sabine has suggested, like our readings of the 'desires' of
Mary Magdalene's commitment to the body of Christ—washing it with her
'bright' hair, going to His grave on Easter morning to cover His body with
oils—our readings (as framed by Donne's speaker) seem unable to separate
the physical from the spiritual.[20] But we yet remain outside the lovers' private *sermo*,[21] like those readers within the poem who have also arrived to
read (and to 'spy' upon and violate the privacy of) this 'loving couple' after
the initiation of their 'mysterious' exchange. Even as the 'relic' trope en-
couages us to read a 'carnal' meaning before it reforms that view with a
'symbolic' reading of their relationship, the substance of her gift to him
remains mysterious, perhaps to the speaker but certainly to us, regardless of
how deeply we 'dig' into their engraving or into the 'paper' which is left
covering without uncovering the specific nature of their devotional practice.[22] And *why* the poet chooses to 'keep this hid' ('The Undertaking')—
as suggested by the framing of that devotion in terms of the worship of
saints and relics of his own family tradition—*may* or *may not* intend to
teach us how literally we should take the central figure of the poem by
which love and religion are identified.[23]

In a 1611 private letter to Henry Goodyer, Donne did submit that he
was 'much of one sect in the Philosophy of love; which though it be
directed upon the minde, doth inhere in the body, and find piety entertainment there' (*Letters* 121). He approached the same view in 'Aire and Angels' by claiming that the platonic idealisation of 'thy haire ... Is much too
much ... ; / For, nor in nothing, nor in things / Extreme, and scattring
bright, can love inhere' (19-22). Indeed, the identification of 'piety' and

'entertainment' and the emphasis on the body ('dare' one say, 'the real presence' of the body) in love in this letter would certainly incline one to read 'The Relic' in the same terms. But that letter itself Donne defines as 'a confident and mutual communicating of those things which we know'—but the poetic 'paper' does not 'tell' us what the lovers 'know' about the meaning of their 'device'. We are excluded from that 'mutuall' knowledge of which 'sect' of devotion the poet's beloved found to be pious entertainment—or, to privilege the poem's vehicle instead of its tenor, we readers cannot 'confident[ly] know' whether their religious sect and its reading of 'relics' was analagous to or contrary to their sexual 'sect'. I would suggest that we are 'taught' only how 'mysterious' is the 'sacrament' of love.

One of the fullest glosses (or glasses) on Donne's textual strategies is 'A Valediction, of my name in the window'—like the majority of his lyrics a farewell poem, and a farewell that focuses attention on the decorum of the genre itself. A sort of witty testing of its own generic roots (from *valeo*, 'to have force, power, or influence; to be healthy'), this anatomy of the powers and influence of its own words of farewell fantasises about the 'treason[ous]' limitations in all 'names' in order to question the means by which a reader can 'impute' its 'magique' without denying its fatal historicity. Much like the *Phaedrus*, itself a silenus box of narrative mirrors about validating the rhetoric of love, Donne's facetiously hyperbolic bedroom address, spoken 'Neere death' in either the Petrarchan or Ovidian sense, is an overheard or written speech about a previously 'engrav'd' writing which was intended to serve as an antidote to future rival writings during the author's absence—or, in terms of the amatory cliché it puzzles, the 'powers' of his 'letter' after his 'death'. Indeed, the first ten stanzas plead the power of that inscribed 'deaths head' he has scratched into her bedroom window (and all such 'dying ... murmurs') to bespeak his presence during his absence. He hopes and even intimately threatens that this 'reflection' of his 'ruinous Anatomy' will 'superscribe' any rival's 'page' and 'letter'. In fact, he wistfully claims, the 'magique' of his referential signature will efface and erase the influence of his amatory *doppelgänger*—that rival who is described as a sort of satanic imitator (and the poet-lover's own archimago) who 'corrupts' all that is 'maid' with his 'wit and land [and] gold'. Unlike the speaking lover's writing, which was inscribed at a sort of originary, ecstatic moment of sexual and self consciousness—'cut when love and griefe their exaltation had'—the rival's letter is characterised by the anxious lover as *mere* imitation, a 'battry' that would 'frame' and 'offend' 'Genius' and its joyful genesis in the two lovers' original vows.

But the poem itself—a writing about the past writing of his 'trembling name' which considers its future influence *as* a past or mortal inscription (and therein another 'pledge' or amatory *sacrament*)—shows the power of his signature to be dependent on its own mortal inventiveness or imitative *energeia* and, literally, to be enabled only by *her* response. He fancies that his name *could* 'step in' and 'hide' or cover up rival writings, but concedes that only 'Thine eye will give it price to mock' the 'grav'd rules' of the inconstant mortal world. Even the 'diamond' that 'grav'd' his name—in its first syllable and even the possibility that we hear *die-a-man* in the name of that 'rock'—bespeaks his name's need for an originary 'charme' and 'magique' beyond mortal words if it is to enable him to 'come againe'. Indeed, in all this provocative talk of a 'firm' name 'in thy Glasse', a 'bony name' once 'hard' as a 'rock', now a 'ruinous ... bone ... still with you' that longs to 'come againe' we may hear the play with *post coitum tristitia* of 'A Farewell to Love' (itself a re-writing of Wyatt's poem on the power of signs to offend love in 'Whoso list to hunt', itself a re-writing of Petrarch's *Una candida cerva sopra l'erba*). But even so, this rival interpretative 'pattern' only evokes again the inadequacy of discourse and intercourse as amendments of the consequences of the Fall, a curse located here (as in the anatomy of man's 'shortness' in 'The First Anniversary') in the mortality of his *dis*course: 'So shall *all times* finde me [and it] the same'. The poem itself, that is, as a repetition and supplement (and therein another rival imitation) of the 'firm' signature that is supposed to re-present him in his absence, is limited in its ability to *cover up* the obvious limitations of his physical (and sexual and verbal) mortality. The *sheet* of linen paper on which the poem is being written may temporarily cover the obvious temporality of his physiological 'firm[ness]' and direct her attention to the 'name' that remains in her window even after his absence/death/coitus—but the substantiality of all these *pledges* of discourse and intercourse is to be determined by *her* willingness to read them in terms of his intentions and desires. 'Here', he fondly hopes, 'you see me, and I am you'; but only if *her* wishes mirror or continue to 'repair' their desires and intentions, to 'recompact' their amatory contracts, can he hope to 'return' to her: only if she reads his signature as a present, ever-present sign of their divine-like tautology of desire—*in imagine dei*—can 'His letter' overcome the death of his parting, their separation.

The substantial superiority of her re-creative powers is endorsed further by Donne's appropriation once again of the lexicon of (Counter-)Reformation controversy. For embedded in all this bedroom discourse about rival writings and readings and the 'confessional' power of 'charmed names' to 'Emparadise' lovers threatened by the 'battry' of 'treason' and the assault of 'Disputed ... letters' is another saucy play with Roman Catholic and Reformed views of the 'supremacie' of the divine Word. The lover's representational signature is characterised in the terms familiar to the Protestant figurations of Christ's pledge as a *covering* that will 'hide' man's mortality after his death—a view that is thus wryly denied by the emphasis on the inability of such verbal 'magique' to re-deem his 'name' and re-unite the lovers. On the other hand, the characterisation of the beloved's re-creative powers as analogous to the trans-substantial power of Christ's *present* absence in the Catholic feast of Love subtlely endorses that interpretation of the doctrinal dispute. Once again, that is, Donne infuses the Petrarchan beloved goddess trope with an oblique contemporary/political inscription in order to challenge us to read more (or less) than can be read into the equivoques with which the poem concludes its self-analysis, equivoques that once again re-write the lovers' discourse in terms of current religio-political debate about the imputation of Grace and the idolatry of 'confessions' about 'our Mistresse faire Religion'.[24]

But the challenge to (and subsequent frustration of) the readers' interpretative powers is most fully presented in the final eleventh stanza, a sort of postscript, palinode or 'enscribed' annotation appended to the decalogue that is the body of the poem. In this self-reflexive plea for a charitable reading of his previous writing(s) Donne's lover admits the impotence of his signature and its imputative power: 'But glasse, and lines must bee / No meanes our firme sustantiall love to keepe; / Neere death inflicts this lethargie, / And this I murmure in my sleep'. But, he urges, she can give presence to his absent words: 'Impute this idle talke, / ... to that I go, / For dying men talke often so'. The 'firm' signature in the window—whether sign of a sexual or a spiritual relationship, or even a pun on *firma*, the Italian word for 'signature'—is more than its accidentals of 'glass and lines', he pleads: just like those of the Eucharist, the accidentals of their union to which he would contribute (and in 'to pay') with his body or which he would signify with his metaphorical 'deaths death' of a sign-ature, has 'substance' beyond such necessary rites or writings. Donne thus inscribes or signs his equivocal text with *the* verb ('Impute') that was central to the Reformation debate about the means and meaning of divine hermeneutics. How it is read tells a great deal about how (and why) we read the 'influence' of the reader as well as the writer of the poem's concluding directive. In one sense—of 'Impute' as *consider*—this last (new) testament is merely a concession that, although emotionally and psychologically true, his words are merely verbal gymnastics, the mere 'murmur[ing]' wit of someone afraid to leave her, someone who shows a lack of faith in both his 'idle' words and their (idolatrous) love 'Neere death'. In this sense, it might also be a paradoxical and disarming feint by which he 'kills' or 'superscribes' any unflattering self-image created by the first ten stanzas, for by effacing those stanzas with this rival 'letter' he enacts a sort of verbal 'biathanatos' by which he kills off one of his major rivals—himself as doubting lover—and therein offers to die for her (or with her) once again.

But 'Impute' could also retain its Pauline sense of divine imputation here. For the 'pattern' of the poem—by which it moves from an assertion of the 'influence' of its own words and analogies to an admission to its own helplessness before the power of 'loves magique' to 'undoe' all 'rules'— and thus a submission to *her* willingness to 'remembre ... right' and 'write ... right' the substance of their love—'clear[ly] reflects' her divine power to determine the 'mean[ing]' of his words. In one sense, the address juxta- poses Protestant and Catholic terms for the Eucharist in order to endorse an 'idolatrous' significance to their love. The designation of his inscribed name as a 'pattern still with you' after his death/absence, as a name that will 'step in' and 'hide' her sin when she might 'thaw towards' the satanic rival—the Reformers' terms for the imputation of Christ's *aliena iustitia* to cover the sins of the elect—is countered by the designation of the power of his name to be actually *present*—the Catholic view of the Eucharist.[25] But, then, the final stanza chooses the Catholic or 'idolatrous' reading of Christ's body for the lover's final analogy. This *is* 'idol' talk, as the pun urges, for she does have the power to *substantiate* their love and his words —through her response. Her response alone, in fact, can determine whether 'impute' means *to consider* or *to transfigure*, whether his 'talke' is *idle* in its fears and doubts or is foolish *idol*atry of someone unworthy of his devo- tion and sacrifice. It is, of course, a bold stroke, perhaps even dangerous in its saucy critique of Protestant doctrine in its appropriation of St. Thomas' *per modum substantiae*; shameful perhaps in its suggestion that, unlike Petrarch's idolatrous worship of Laura, the speaker has found a woman worthy of 'all our Soules devotion' (*Satyre III*). For just as he hopes that she would forget to whom she writes if a rival chance to 'thaw' her—'in forgetting *thou remembrest right* [and] unaware to me shalt *write*'—so now (just as he asks God to 'forget' his sins, his poems, and his 'idle talke' in the Holy Sonnets) he asks his love to forget the 'idle talke' of the first ten stanzas, or to *change* it into the *idol talk* addressed to an earthly goddess. Remember me, he asks, re-member me literally and spiritually, by trans- forming the mortal accidents, the 'glasse' and 'lines' of our love, into a 'substantiall' testament to the eternal being of our love. Only her reading can impugn the corrupt rival writings which his absence cannot 'hide' or cover up. Her response alone can re-write, re-pair, and re-deem his fallen words; she alone has the author-ity to 'substantiate' them.

Thus, while the last clauses of the poem initially offer an analogy to the sacramental debate by focusing attention on what both parties agreed to

—'glass and lines must be', i.e., one must have this sacrament—, the final claim of the speaker returns to the Catholic insistence on Real Presence: in the sacrament of love the glass and lines of the speaker's worship of his divine mistress—like the cup and words of the priest in the rite—are merely the accidentals of the Feast, merely signs engraved in the mirror of language; but they are not the *firma*, the physical signature or Real Presence that makes the ceremony substantial and, as a sacrament, a pledge of future beatific bliss. Now, to say that only His Presence, or her body in this case, is what makes their love Real(ly) Present is to figure their love, Petrarch and Sidney would agree, as *idol* worship—just to worship the Presence in the Eucharist, according to Bale and Knox, for example, is to make 'an idol of the altar', to love the papist 'god of bread' or 'the cake idol' that is equal, said John Marbeck, to 'the setting up of images of the calves in the temple builded by Jeroboram'; 'the poor God of bread is the most miserable of all other idols', said Knox.[26] The point of Donne's speaker is that the presence of the body alone makes this *sermo* substantial—literally and physically firm, but equally a signature of divinity or love/Love, a sacramental eucharist of physical love which, now that he is *dying* or leaving her presence, will remain a pledge, a promise, an oath, a mysterious covenant promising either a second coming or (if the sexual act has not occurred yet) a sacramental promise of her bestowing the beatific vision of sexual ecstasy on him upon his return. Without such substantial significance—without meaning/Meaning—without the authority of her love—all poetry, all love, all signatures (as postmodern gospels endlessly 'murmur') are merely 'meanes', merely *idle talk*—beyond which lies only death, and absence. Once again, that is, as in 'The Relic', Donne allows us to overhear a lovers' appeal that might seem framed to illustrate the insufficiency of 'mere' signs to convey a love that is 'substantial'. Presence, not 'imputation', even if such a preference for Presence might be termed 'idolatry', even if it might prove 'idle' to ask such 'grace' from such a goddess to such a 'dying' mortal—Presence alone can overcome the speaker's murmuring doubts; or, as Donne wrote in another valediction, 'How great love is, presence best tryall makes' ('of the booke'). She must decide, that is, whether 'impute' can be translated into 'substance'—and what the erotically suggestive analogy of a firm diamond penetrating a glass actually 'means'. Her desire, her love, her reading determine the mode and operation of his signs and whether they will be incarnated or remain metonymies of his undying (or 'dying') love. For when we (once again) attempt to 'impute' this analogy by which Protestant and Catholic readings of the Eucharist are appropriated to encourage or pray for the promise or performance of a sexual 'communion', then we cannot be sure whether to privilege its tenor or vehicle. We might readily be termed por-faced readers indeed if we take the poem to be a commentary on the current doctrinal debate about the 'means' of Justification, but then to dismiss Donne's inventive translation of this current lexicon as merely a metaphorical game might just as easily suggest our unwillingness to figure human desire in any but sexual terms.

Indeed, after reading 52 lines of comparisons in 'The Comparison' only to be reminded that 'Comparisons are odious', or after reading 396 lines of micro-macrocosmic correspondences in 'The First Anniversary' only to be told that 'art is lost, and correspondence too', and especially after being told in 'Satyre III' that men 'Seek true religion' just 'like as' they choose a bride, it might be difficult for Donne readers to impute these sexually-charged analogies between bedroom discourse and theological exchange as merely 'idle talke' on the poet's part. And in what is perhaps the best-known of Donne's apologies for the 'miracles' by which 'harm-lesse lovers' through their sacramental sexuality *merit* the veneration of Christ-like saints—'The Canonization'—Donne returns again to a dramatic illustration of the dilemma of his readers. In one sense, this poem's aggress-ive response to a protesting (puritan?) interlocutor who would deny the sub-stance of his love is figured in terms of the *currant* debate about the inter-cession of saints. It seems to support dramatically the belief that saints, to cite the Council of Trent, 'should be honoured and invoked',[27] even while ite eroticises the same Catholic imagery which poets such as Crashaw used to venerate The Virgin and The Name of Christ; the poem seems posed to flout, that is, the Calvinist contention that we should 'not dream that [the saints] have any other way to petition God' and that to invoke them 'is but to wish (through a drunken dream of our brain) to penetrate and to break into God's hidden judgments' ...[28] In fact, as John A. Clair points out, Donne's indignant priest of sexual love borrows the frame and rhetoric of the (5-stage) Catholic *processus* of canonisation in order to respond (in 5 stanzas) to the literalistic protester who would not 'allow' the speaker's form of devotion and its insistence on the presence of the body in the 'mys-terious' love rites in which he and his beloved engage.[29] That Donne here is not merely eroticising the commonplace of Neoplatonic poetry which fig-ures the beloved as a saint, however, is indicated again in *the last clause* when, having appropriated the liturgy, symbolism, and rites of Catholicism to 'prove' to the 'layetie' the nature of their love, he asserts that the intrud-ing auditor who was first told to 'Hold thy tongue' *'for God's sake'* will now 'Beg from above a pattern of [this] love'. In one sense the defensive lover's focus of attention on the aggressive interlocutor's obsession with worldly matters might well recall Father William Allen's typical recusant assertion that the Reformers 'care not what we believe, no further than toucheth their prince and temporal weal',[30] and the lover's defence could also offer an encoded response to Spenser's recent appropriation of the Catholic *Legenda aurea*[31] to 'canonise' the secular achievement of the Protestant Court (it is more than literary style, that is, that animates Donne's habitual rejection of Spenser). But what the words put into the mouth of his worldly intruder of 'The Canonization' by this priest of the sexual will 'prove', however, is that the central analogy that the poem asserts will remain 'mysterious' to this protesting worldly secularist; for, as translations of Calvin's *Institutes* affirm, 'pattern' is the Protestant term for the Eucharist and 'from above' an equally encoded hallmark of doctrine about the representational character of the Feast of Love.[32] Even *if* the intruder does 'invoke' them, that is, the precise terms of his invocation would denote his failure to understand the significance of 'Presence' to their miraculous love—no more than the Protestant evocation of a 'real presence and corporeall absence' of the Protestant rite, in Father Wright's wry terms, is the same as the Catholic 'locall' Presence. Whether this encoded lexical fissure undercuts the speaker's hyperbole or 'proves' his claims about the inability of the secular world of the Protestant Court to understand the 'mysteries' of both erotic *and* Catholic devotion is not clear. But however equivocally framed, the overall 'pattern' of 'The Canonization' is clear enough. It is that of 'The Relic': even the reader 'taught' by the speaker's defence misunderstands its significance.[33]

The central sacred conceit of the profane lyrics can also be 'spyed' in the last clauses of 'The Dream'. Generically kin to Sir Thomas Wyatt's erotic recollection of his absent mistresses ('It was no dream; I lay broad waking') and Sidney's Neoplatonic meditation on how Astrophil mischievously 'steals ... Stella's image' (and much more) while she sleeps—both of which are versions of Petrarch's naughty and 'idolatrous' wet dreams about Laura, Donne's 'Dream' shifts attention away from the Petrarchan lover's own sexual frustration, or his impish delight with the possession of an *image* of his desire, to offer another dramatic plea for her to reveal the 'reason' for her *real physical presence*—actually for her Gracious realisation of his 'hope'. Playing with the root senses of *prevenient* Grace (*pre-venire,* 'to come before') by which the speaker figures this propitious lady as having the divine wisdom to pre-vent his premature ejaculation (she came before he came), Donne again literalises/incarnates the major trope of popular Petrarchan poetry, by which the beloved *donna angelicata* seems *like* God, in the precise terms of the Counter-Reformation debate about the sacraments. The composition, analysis, and colloquy of the meditative address figure his 'Deare love' as an erotic incarnation of the creative Wisdom (stanza 1), the omniscient Knowledge (stanza 2), and the revelatory

Will (stanza 3) of someone whom it would be 'Prophane, to thinke ... any thing but thee'. She 'broke' his 'happy dreame ... wisely', proving herself 'so truth', capable 'To make dreames truth; and fables histories'. And even though he first thought 'thee' to be 'an Angell', he now 'knows' and 'confess[es]' her to be 'beyond an Angells art', even though her subsequent action of 'rising' instead of 'Comming and staying' makes him 'doubt, that now, Thou art now thou'. His outrageous characterisation of her coming and of then starting to leave his bedroom as a 'spirit[ual], pure, and brave' sexual embodiment of the Hypostatic Union—phrased so that *she* must decide whether he is deploying the conventional blazon of the beloved as divine or he is inviting her to share with him a send-up of the foolishness of such metonymies in the temple of the bedroom—seems poised 'twixt earnest and jest', in fact, when we recall the theological and political current of his 'profane' lexicon.

Two instances stand out. The first occurs as the last clause of the composition of the beloved as divine-like, prevenient wisdom who seems to arrive to substantiate his erotic dream of her: 'It was a theame / For reason', he recalls, but 'thou thoughtst it best' to '*act* the rest' of his dream. So reads the 1633 first edition of Donne's poems. But manuscripts from different major groupings read 'Lets *do* the rest' (*C57, Dobell, O'Flaherty* mss.). Both versions render the pun on 'rest' as the Beatific Vision and as sexual ecstasy, and thus agree on the central trope of the poem. The interpretative dilemma of this textual crux—whether the lovers are to 'act' or to 'do' that which will grant them such a sacramentally profane or profanely sacred experience—evokes another *currant* lexical debate: whether the sacrament of the Eucharist was an *act*, as in a play or representation or metaphorical pretence, or a *doing* in which something physically and really occurs. She 'broke' his dream, he surmises, in order to make it 'truth', that is, his reading of her coming is that it signifies a physical incarnation of his 'hope' for Grace. So his response, 'lets *do* the rest', merely conforms to her 'divine' will, by which she would, through her divine wisdom, substantiate his dream—just, in other words, as the Catholics confess of their 'deified sacrifice', the body of Christ is 'really present' and 'resident' in the Feast of Love or Mass. When the 'body' is 'broke' for Protestants, on the other hand, what occurs is merely a 'marke [or] signe of our profession ... , a Metonymy, a trope, wherby the name of the thing signified is attributed to the signe' (*Aphorismes* 135f)—Father Wright's sarcastic 'reall presence and corporeall absence'. Henry Holland's popular 1596 translation of the *Institutes* offers a useful gloss on one of the lexical game Donne is playing here. 'The arguments which the Papists use for the defence of the Masse', he urges, are of no waight, as the following: Christ sayd in the institution of the Supper, *Do this*: therefore he commaunded his Apostles and their successours to offer up or sacrifice his bodie unto God. For so this word *facere, to do it* (say they) is used everie where in holy Scripture, and so it is found also with prophane writers. But I say it is no good consequent, that because that word is elsewhere so taken, that therefore it is also so used in this place ... That the Supper be to represent Christes *sacrifice* and oblation ... we utterly deny. The holy Supper of the Lord (which the Papistes have transformed into the monster of the Masse) ... was instituted to be otherwise represented. (176)

Similar to the variants on *assume* and *assure* at the conclusion of Holy Sonnet 9, this *do/act* variant is remarkable not only as an instance of another submerged bawdy pun on Latin—*facit*, 'just do it'—but for how it forces an emendation *on us* that is analogous to the situation of the beloved in the poem. But, given the analogy of the woman as a divine presence in the temple of the speaker's bedroom, the choice here remains hers *to do*, not ours to re-present. The playful speaker aims to clarify, that is, the reasons for her mysterious, divine-like presence in his room, interrupting another of his dreams of paradise. Here, after identifying her as divine (either sexually or sacramentally) he invites her to engage in a physical act with him. Now this is figured once again as a sacramental moment—but which sacramental moment *we* cannot *say*. If it is only a Catholic mass, from a Protestant point of view, it would be merely an 'act'—an imitation of what Christ did when He died for His Bride. And to call it a Mass, Protestants urged would be to engage in a 'play', an act, a parody of the means for which the sacrament of the Eucharist was instituted. However, if the word is *do* the rest, then the point is that they are to engage in a substantial act of physical incarnation of the mystery of the sacrament. Which is it? *She* must decide. Apparently, however, she is just *acting* and is only sending him a signal, for at the end of the poem, when she 'goes' he offers this reading: 'Thou goest to come'. He does hold hard to that metaphor of her mysteriously divine appearance as a sacramental moment, however—for he now says he will have faith in the promise of her incarnation—his 'hope' is for a 'second coming' in which he will be ecstatically doing (or 'acting') the beatific joys of paradise. But then even the suggestion that 'Comming and going' means that she has denied his sexual reading of her presence may not be a 'firm' reading of this mysterious version of their exchange— for the potential for the sexual pun on *coming* might just as well signify she left only after his 'death'—and even his final request to 'die' could just as easily be a post-coital admission of his fallen condition and his 'hope' to 'stand' forever in her presence in her second coming. After all, in its evocation of yet another *currant* theological skirmish—the debate over Mark 5:39-40 about whether death is but a *sleep* and *dream* until Judgement as asserted by the Catholics or that one went directly to eternal 'rest' upon 'the sleepe of death' as asserted by the Protestants—the poem does not tell us exactly what she told him about how to read her presence—whether, that is, his dream of heaven is now over with her beatific arrival or he has to die to 'do the rest'. Did she, in other words, like the lover's instructive at the end of 'The Apparition', just tell him to *do the rest*—to go back to sleep—or did she enact his profanely divine 'dream'. *'Twere profanation to tell* the *layetie*'—that's us.

* * *

Why Donne's profane lyrics are framed in current sacred terms depends in some part on whom we choose to be his 'right readers'. *If* we wish to 'preserve the image of a young, clever university poet, whose aim, in part, was to impress the intellectuals',[34] then we return to the agenda of the 'universal monarch ... of wit' countering the current line of Neoplatonic court poetry with outrageously blasphemous conceits aimed in part to please, tease, and appease a coterie audience. (Wits just want to have fun.) But wit, of course, is an 'unruly instrument', which in Donne's case 'yokes' a critique of the Neoplatonic ideology of those court poets to a severe interrogation of the Protestant tenets underpinning that Sidneyan poetic: *if*, that is (which I find unlikely), the blasphemy aims merely to underscore Petrarch's and Sidney's appraisals of the anarchistic character of sexual desire.

Such a perspective yet remains feasible even *if* we turn the poems over to Anne More or to the meditative poet-lover himself: for it remains possible that Donne himself, in either a playful or intimate tone, either in poetic dialogues given to Anne or introspective/analogical evaluations of their own predicament, could not say whether he was attempting to *seduce* or to *convert* his beloved, the daughter of the robustly Protestant Sir George More. *If*, that is, the poems do figure forth in any way Donne's addresses to Anne More/Donne.[35] But yet, the *currancy* of the sacred analogies in his profane lyrics does seem to accentuate the purposeful blasphemy that animates their wit even while it uncovers a level of potentially dangerous play or 'art of Equivocation'[36] reflecting more Donne's own devotional predicament than his amatory situation at the time. It could be, that is, that the poems either ironically or seriously consider endorsing the contention of

Father Wright that 'he who is thoroughly grounded in the Catholique religion ... may well make it with protestancie, wel he may varie his affection;
but his judgement, *his conceit* ... hardly will he change or never' (A4v). As
such, we might best read in these poems Donne's 'conforming' of his religious confession to his socio-political situation—by which Anne substitutes
for Lady Holicherche[37]—itself a movement from the priority of the sacred
to an embrace of the profane of our own 'age of mis-devotion'—we might
well offset that vision with recognition of the crypto-Catholic *Arminianism*
central to *Doctor* Donne's assault on the politically correct Puritans in his
sermons.

But that is another 'land, and time', and one could not deny that Dean
Donne aims *to teach his readers*. If we keep in mind, on the other hand,
that Donne's framing of both sacred and profane loves as inevitably secret,
private, and mysterious, then we would recall that we 'stray' in reading
them merely literally or symbolically. Perhaps the ultimate or substantial
effect of the lyrics, on the other hand, is their refusal to 'privilege' the
reader outside the 'window' of their inscription—even when that reader is
the speaker himself. Readers remain the profane *layetie* literally and
hermeneutically *pro-fanum*, outside the temple of these private sermonic
meditations addressed by a sort of outlaw, politically incorrect amatory
priest to a 'miraculously' inexpressible mistress whose presence physically
and whose response personally are all that matter substantially to their sacramental 'dialogue of one'. It might just be, that is, that the most 'Catholic'
feature of these poems is how they *deny* the major *invention* of the Protestant Reformation—the *authority* and *assurance* of the reader to determine
the meaning of signs sacred and profane.. They 'prove' to remain 'mysterious by this love'.

It is worth recalling in conclusion, then, Donne's first published
description of readers, in his 1610 'Advertisement to the Reader' of
Pseudo-Martyr, where he asks to be 'defended' from 'those men, who ...
can spy out falsifyings in every citation: as in a jealous and obnoxious state,
a Decipherer who can pick out Plots, and Treason, in any familiar letter
which is intercepted'.[38] Perhaps that is what Donne had in mind when he
told Wotton that his works were 'brave nothings ... prettily guilt, ... made
rather to deceive time then her daughter truth', for Wotton himself had
reminded Donne in the same year (1599) that 'whatsoever we have done or
mean to do, we know what will become of it when it comes amongst our
worst enemies—which are Interpreters' (*Burley ms.*).[39] Such *anathemas*
might well underlie all Donne's lyrics about the dangerous fate of 'Loves
martyrs'.[40] In defiance of patriarchal, Protestant, Neoplatonic, and political
authority—speaking in an age when 'love ... is rage' and when his family

still did 'at [their] own cost die'—Donne would boldly plead (to Anne, to Sir George More, to the Protestant oligarchy, and, perhaps most of all, to himself): 'For God's sake ... let me love'.

Notes

1   All citations of Donne's poems are to the edition of John T. Shawcross, *The Complete Poetry of John Donne* (New York, 1967), which uses as its copy-text the 1633 edition of *Poems*.

2   This is Donne's term for what today would be called *ideology*, as distinguished from what he asserted to be the only 'worthy' subject of 'the mindes indeavours'- —'our Mistress Truth' ('Satyres' III, IV).

3   *Juvenilia* (1633) sig/ A1r.

4   Significant to Donne's poems is not the veracity of the legend of Sidney after his death but its prominence and influence at the court—and the uses to which it was made in promoting and supporting the Protestant cause. That Sidney, as Katherine Duncan-Jones (*Sir Philip Sidney: Courtier Poet* [New Haven, 1991]) has recently suggested, might have himself inclined towards Roman Catholicism in his late years seems not to have been known at the time, and certainly was not part of the propaganda of the Protestant polemicists. On the myth of Sidney in the age, see especially Richard Lanham, 'Sidney: The ornament of his age', *Southern Review (Australia)* 2 (1967): 319-40; and Alan Hager, 'The Exemplary Image: fabrication of Sir Philip Sidney's Biographical Image and the Sidney Reader', in *Sir Philip Sidney: An Anthology of Modern Criticism*, edited by Dennis Kay (Oxford, 1987), who calls for 'the deconstruction of a biographical image that Sidney's "friends" could not have shared' (59).

5   I cite the edition of J.A. van Dorsten (Oxford, 1966); composed around 1580, the *Defence* was first printed in 1595, the period when the majority of Donne's poems were composed according to Ben Jonson.

6   Italics are mine. On Cyrus as the prototypical *Protestant hero*, see M.J. Doherty, *The Mistress-Knowledge* (Nashville, 1991). Given the status and reputation of Sidney (or 'the Sidney myth') in the 1590s, Donne might recall this particular version on the traditional poet-as-maker trope in the mocking conclusion of his wry Ovidian *recusatio,* where his lover asserts that he can provide 'More glorious service' in the wars against religious rebels being conducted in Europe by his resolution to 'make at home,' not to 'kill men [but] make one by and by', 'staying to make men' ('Loves Warre', 40-46). On Donne's elegies as saucy critiques of the English Protestant projects in Europe and America, see R.V. Young, '"O my America": Pornography and Propaganda in Donne's Elegies', *South Carolina Review* 4 (1986): 35-48; and M. Thomas Hester, 'Donne's (Re)Annunciation of the Virgin(ia Colony) in *Elegy XIX*', *SCR* 4 (1986): 49-64, and '"over reconing" the "undertones" of "some elegies" by Donne', forthcoming.

7   Sidney invokes here one current Protestant term for the Eucharist ('mark'), thus adding the association of Astrophil's 'idolatrous' worship of Stella to the 'adulterous' idolatry of Roman Catholic Mass with its similar focus of attention on the

presence of the body/Body in the feast of love/Love. Citations of Sidney's poems are to the edition of David Kalstone, Sir Philip Sidney, *Selected Poetry and Prose* (New York, 1970).

8 It is not likely that Sidney inscribed this final epitaph for his sonnet sequence; but that does not mean that it was not read as his comment on his sequence by his 1595 readers. I place 'heroic' in marks here in order to recall that Donne never allows his readers to forget the (supposed) origins of the word, as playfully suggested by Plato's *Cratylus*, as deriving from the generation of heroes as the offspring of the pagan gods' eros. The relation of the sacred and the profane as 'heroism'—especially from the perspective of an 'outlaw' Catholic whose spiritual 'heroism' could be called 'treason' by the Protestants—is not irrelevant to Donne's constant juxtapositions of the secular and the spiritual shapes of love in Elizabethan England.

9 This is Kalstone's apt description of how Sidney 'doth draw the mind' in his sonnet sequence. As Anne Ferry shows in *The Inward Language* (Chicago, 1983), Donne was quite influenced by the portraits/voices of human desire by Sidney; it is not this skill at such portraits that Donne attacks, but the attitude towards love and Love that is the 'idea, or foreconceit' of Sidney's project.

10 Ben Jonson, cited in *John Donne: The Critical Heritage* (London, 1975), 70.

11 *Letters to severall Persons of Honour* (London, 1651), 197. See Annabel Patterson, 'Misinterpretable Donne: The Testimony of the Letters', *John Donne Journal* 1 (1982): 39-53; and M. Thomas Hester, '"this cannot be said": A Preface to the Reader of Donne's Lyrics', *Christianity and Literature* 39 (1990): 365-385.

12 Donne's unusual attitude towards his readers is also treated by Judith Herz, '"An Excellent Exercise of Wit that Speaks So Well of Ill": Donne and the Poetics of Concealment', in: *The Eagle and the Dove: Reassessing John Donne*, edited by Claude Summers and Ted-Larry Pebworth (Columbia Mo., 1986), 3-14; and William Schullenberger, 'Love as a Spectator Sport in John Donne's Poetry', in: *Renaissance Discourses of Desire*, edited by Summers and Pebworth (Columbia, Mo., 1993), 46-62; a different interpretatin of some of the same mixture of profane and sacred images in Donne's love poems is offered by Theresa M. DiPasquale, 'Donne's Catholic Petrarchans: The Babylonian Captivity of Desire', in *Discourses of Desire*, pp. 77-93.

13 *Sermons*, edited by Evelyn M. Simpson and George R. Potter (Los Angeles, 1953-1962), vi, 41. Emphasis added.

14 *Pseudo-Martyr* (London, 1610), sig. 11r. See especially Dennis Flynn, *Donne and the Ancient Catholic Nobility* (Bloomington, 1995) for the fullest appraisal of the Recusant conditions of Donne's situation.

15 'Burley manuscript', f. 308v.

16 See Patrick J. Geary, *Furta Sacra: Thefts of Relics in the Central Middle Ages* (Princeton, 1978).

17 *The Rise and Growth of the Anglican Schism* (1585), translated by David Lewis (Rockford, Ill., 1988), 142-143. For a fuller appraisal of the importance of this topic in Donne's poems, see M. Thomas Hester, '"Ask thy father": Rereading Donne's *Satyre III*', *Ben Jonson Journal* 1 (1994): 201-218.

18 On the difficulties of a 'platonic' reading of the poem, see Marvin Morillo, 'Donne's "The Relic" as Satire', *Tulane Studies in English* 21 (1974): 47-55.

19   Thomas Wright, *A Treatise, Shewing the Possibilitie, and Convenience of the Reall Presence* (London, 1591), 122v.

20   'No Marriage in Heaven: John, Anne and the Kingdom Come,' in: *'Desire of more': The Subject of Anne Donne in John Donne's Poetry*, edited by M. Thomas Hester (Newark, Del., forthcoming).

21   See John T. Shawcross, 'The Concept of *Sermo* in Donne and Herbert', *John Donne Journal* 6 (1987): 203-212.

22   The Greek for 'sacrament', *mysterium,* can also be translated 'secret' or 'hidden', as Protestants insisted in their citation of Eph. 5: 32 ('Sacramentum hoc magnum est') to support their view of marriage as 'a great secret' but not 'a great sacrament'. (See, for instance, the debate between William Fulke and Martin Gregory as recounted in Fulke's *A Defence of the Sincere and True Translation of the Holy Scriptures into the English Tongue*, The Parker Society [Cambridge, 1853].) Donne comically recalls this reading in his seven-stanza mock-ballad, 'The Undertaking', where he claims that one has 'done a braver thing', if, having loved 'Virtue attired in a woman' and 'from profance men' having 'hidden ...', you 'keepe that hid'. That poem, in fact, might well offer a revealing analogue for Donne's own relationship to Anne More before their relationship was discovered: see, for instance, the essays of Ilona Bell and Dennis Flynn on Donne's 'The Curse' in *'Desire of more'*.

23   R.C. Bald recounts this excerpt from Cresacre's 1726 *Life of More:* 'It was also credibly reported, that two of *John Heywood*'s sons, *Jasper* and *Ellis*, having one of the teeth of SIR THOMAS MORE between them, and either of them desirous to have it to himselfe, it suddenly, to the admiration of both, parted in two': *John Donne: A Life* (Oxford, 1970), 25.

24   On Donne's treatment of the same debate in his Holy Sonnets, see R.V. Young, 'Donne's Holy Sonnets and the Theology of Grace', in *'Bright Shootes of Everlastingnesse': The Seventeenth-Century Religious Lyric*, edited by Claude Summers and Ted-Larry Pebworth (Columbia, Mo., 1987), 20-39.

25   See, for instance, the important *Reformation of Church and Dogma 1300-1700* (London, 1984), 150ff, Vol. 4 of Jaroslav Pelikan's *The Christian Tradition.*

26   Cited in Margaret Aston, *England's Iconoclasts* (Oxford, 1988), 8.

27   *The Church Teaches: Documents of the Church* (Rockford, Ill., 1955), 214-215.

28   *Institutes of the Christian Religion,* 3.20.21ff, translated by F.L. Battles (Grand Rapids, MI, 1975), 71-72.

29   'John Donne's "The Canonization"', *PMLA* 80 (1965): 300-302.

30   *A True, Sincere, and Modest Defence of English Catholics*, edited by Robert M. Kingdon (Ithaca, 1965), 119. On the view of the Eucharist as 'a pattern in the peson of Christ' and 'above the elements of this world' (*Corpus Reformatorum*, 1834), see Pelikan, *Reformation of Church,* and Hollans's *Aphormses*, note 32 below.

31   Pointed our by Thomas Roche in a paper for the John Donne Society annual meeting, 1989.

32   An especially helpful contemporary example is the popular 'epitome' of Calvinism by Henry Holland, *Aphorismes of Christian Religion: or, A Verie Compendium of M.I. Calvins Institutions* (London, 1596).

33   As I menttioned in 'this cannot be said', an outstandingly puzzling example of the misunderstanding reader occurs in 'The Extasie', where Donne's saucy speaker submits that 'if some lover, such as we / Have heard this dialogue of one, / Let him still make us, he shall see / Small change when we ae to bodies gone' (73-76). Following his assertion that 'lovers soules [must] descend/ T'affections', imitating the Incarnation by which 'Love [is] reveal'd', this stanza contains most of the central terms of the theological controversy over the tenor and substance of the Eucharist, notably in its recollection of Trent's insistence that the 'unique mark of distinction' of the sacrament is that 'a change takes place in which the whole substance of bread is changed into the substance of the body of Christ our Lord' (*The Church Teaches,* 283). And 'small change' is, in fact, the English translation of the precise terms that Cardinal Bellarmine (whom Donne called 'the best defender of the *Roman cause*') uses in his *Disputationes* (1586-1593). The rich ambiguity of Donne's use of the current controversial terms here serves again to question to ability of the readers to understand the mystery of the lovers' 'dialogue of one' that is both the poem and their relationship. If the poem traces a wittily outrageous attempt at seduction, then once again it is left to the beloved to impute its meaning; and if it is a lecture on love's nature, then the dubious terms of surmise with which it concludes ('if ... as we ... shall see ... when') render problematic just what kind of 'change' the voyeur will see (in addition to raising some provocative questions about his motives). But, then, perhaps the questions raised about the motives and intentions of this fellow lover are intended to record another feature of the theological debate on which the wit of the poem borrows—the controversy as to just how and why the believer would *hear, mark* or *see* the Eucharist: both sides accused the other of engaging in idolatrous voyeurism, the Protestants claiming the Catholics' Mass was celebrated only by the priest, the Catholics claiming that the Protestants engaged in 'no act of devotion' since Christ's body was 'gone' from their table of 'memorial' (Wright, sig. R3r).
34   Raman Seldon, review essay, *MLR* 82 (1987): 165-166.
35   For reference to a volume of essays on the subject of Anne Donne/More as the 'subject' of Donne's poems, see note 20 above.
36   *Ignatius his conclave,* p. 33.
37   See Anthony Low, *The Reinvention of Love: Poetry, politics and culture from Sidney to Milton* (Cambridge, 1988), Ch. 2, for a similar view of Donne's poetry.
38   *Pseudo-martyr,* sig. 2v.
39   On the importance of this concern in the letters exchanged by Donne and Wotton, see Claude Summers and Ted-Larry Pebworth, 'Donne's Correspondence with Wotton', *John Donne Journal* 10 (1991): 1-36.
40   See Robert A. Bryan, 'John Donne's Use of the Anathema', *Journal of English and Germanic Philology* 41 (1962): 305-12, for a study of the poet's 'witty' use of this Catholic 'instrument' in his elegies.

10

DONNE'S JEALOUS GOD AND THE CONCEPT OF SACRED PARODY[1]

PAUL J.C.M. FRANSSEN

George Herbert is well known for what Louis Martz has called 'sacred par-odies': the use of profane forms and materials as vehicles for sacred subject matter.[2] Famous examples are the sonnets Herbert wrote to his mother when he was only seventeen. In these, the speaker deplores the fact that other sonneteers usually devote to profane mistresses the kind of praise that should be reserved for God; Herbert, of course, enacts his own advice in these very sonnets. Many years later, in 'The Forerunners', Herbert once more commented on this practice, comparing his programme of christian-ising profane metaphors to the rehabilitation of fallen women.

In a sacred parody, the relationship between form and content is hier-archical or even antagonistic: the sacred love that is the subject is seen as infinitely superior to the profane love that is used to express it. Metaphors must either be strumpets or good (celibate) Christians; there is no in-between.

The importance of 'sacred parodies' in Herbert's works should not blind us to the fact, however, that other forms of interplay between the sacred and the profane are possible. Form and content may be reversed, so that sacred language is made subservient to a profane view of life;[3] alterna-tively, sacred and profane love may coexist peacefully, each ruling in its own sphere, yet each capable of expression in terms of the other. It is in the latter terms that Michael Schoenfeldt has suggested that we read Herbert's 'Love (III)': in this poem, Schoenfeldt argues, the relationship between human and divine is allegorised as an erotic encounter between a feminised Christ and an impotent speaker.[4] In this case, the relationship between the sacred and the profane, Schoenfeldt asserts, goes beyond sacred parody (257):

> Rather than apprehending the awful discrimination of heavenly and earthly love, Herbert's reader is forced to grasp their equally awe-in-spiring similarity (263).

In this respect, Schoenfeldt sees Donne as Herbert's opposite: in Donne, we are never allowed to forget the differences between the all-important tenor and the humble vehicle (262-263).

Schoenfeldt's contrast between Donne and Herbert neatly reverses that in *Poetry of Contemplation* by Arthur L. Clements, who argues that Donne's serious love poetry is suffused by a kind of mystic spirituality that is more advanced than the meditative tone of his religious poetry: for Donne, the erotic and the religious are far from incompatible. Herbert, by contrast, 'fully enjoys only the Vision of God, not at all the Vision of Eros'.[5] From a different perspective, an earlier study by Murray Roston had argued that the interplay between the sacred and the profane in the works of John Donne manifests the 'recognition of the ultimate unity of mortal and divine love, the awareness that the two forms should be imaginatively merged and interchanged in order to achieve a mutual enrichment through the contact'. This is the 'Counter-Reformation tradition, with its encouragement to cultivate the bodily senses imaginatively, as a means of glimpsing the celestial'; and it 'stands ... at the opposite pole to what Louis Martz has called "sacred parody"'.[6] Martz had in fact ranged Donne with Southwell and Herbert as a sacred parodist; Roston argues that Donne does not parody or protest against earthly love, but regards the sacred and the profane as complementary sides of human experience. Recently Anne Ferry, too, has stressed the continuity between sacred and profane in Donne's 'Holy Sonnets', though not in his other works; Ferry argues that for Donne the sonnet form was associated with the then new concept of an inner self that cannot be captured in language; and it is only on that level, not on the linguistic plane, that the divine really differs from the erotic.[7]

There is, then, considerable disagreement about the adequacy of profane, particularly erotic, language to express the contact between the human and the divine in the works of Donne. Yet an understanding of the relationship between tenor and vehicle can be vital to our grasp of the tone of the poetry. In particular, this is the case when not the sweet raptures of lovemaking, but the less pleasant aspects of human relationships such as jealousy, fickleness and lovers' quarrels are the vehicles for man's relationship to God. It is beyond the scope of this essay to investigate the whole of Donne's poetic corpus in the light of this question. The present focus will be on the interplay between the sacred and the profane in Donne's poetic production of the period following the death of his wife Anne in 1617. In some of these poems, God appears as a jealous lover. In that period, at least, Donne definitely stresses the unlikeness rather than the likeness between the profane and the sacred.

As the above delimitation suggests, facts from Donne's life will here be taken into account in the reading of his poetry. It is not without trepidation that one embarks on such an expedition into this territory, especially in view of the frequent warnings against the resurgence of the biographical fallacy. However, recent work by many critics specialising in this period has been characterised by a noticeable Resurrection of the Author. Michael Schoenfeldt's book on Herbert could not have been written without an awareness of the frustrated political ambitions of Herbert's youth. As far as Donne is concerned, John Stachniewski and Richard Strier have both felt that the 'Holy Sonnets' can and should be read against the background of their author's life and times;[8] Strier has even volunteered the heretical opinion that 'sometimes the poetic speaker is the historical author, or is a direct projection of him (or her)' (358). If this is an acceptable procedure with all of the 'Holy Sonnets', then the two poems discussed here in some detail may also be regarded in the light of Donne's life; if they have little else to recommend them, at least they are among the few texts in the Donne canon that can be linked to specific biographical events. 'Holy Sonnet 17' ('Since she whome I lovd, hath payd her last debt') is generally assumed to have been occasioned by Anne's death in August 1617.[9] Even Anne Ferry, who notes a resemblance between the triangular situation in this poem and that in Shakespeare's sonnet 144 ('Two loves I have, of comfort and despair'), admits that Donne's sonnet is 'probably about his late wife' (220). The 'Hymne to Christ, at the Authors last going into Germany' was written on the occasion of Donne's leaving England on an embassy which took place in early 1619.

* * *

In shoring up his argument that the mystical imagery in some of Donne's serious love poetry is not just rhetoric, let alone a mere seduction ploy, Clements cites two lines from 'Holy Sonnet 17' in which Donne seems to affirm the reality of his wife's influence in leading him to God:

> Here the admyring her my mind did whett
> To seeke thee God; so streames do shew the head.

There can be no doubting Donne's seriousness here, as this is, in Anne Ferry's words, an 'elegiac love poem, probably about his late wife, to whom he was well known to have been devoted'.[10]

When we read these lines in context, however, we are struck by the speaker's strangely ambiguous attitude towards his deceased wife: on the one hand she is identified as the 'streames' that have led him to the 'head', to God Himself, in the best tradition of Neoplatonism; but on the other, once she had led him so far, her task was fulfilled, and she was dispensable;

God, after all, is ready to substitute His love for hers. There is even a rather unelegiac suggestion that she might have formed a threat to the speaker, so that God, in His 'tender jealosy', had to take her away:

> And dost not only feare least I allow
> My love to saints and Angels, things divine,
> But in thy tender jealosy dost doubt
> Least the World, fleshe, yea Devill putt thee out.

As Louis Martz has noted, these lines are profoundly ambiguous, as it is not clear whether Anne is seen as one of the 'saints and angels', in the tradition of Petrarchan hyperbole, or whether that line refers to the Roman Catholic reverence for angels and saints that Donne had been forced to renounce on his becoming an Anglican;[11] as John Carey has realised, the latter reading opens up the possibility that the lure of the infernal triad of the World, the Flesh, and the Devil corresponds to the speaker's idolatrous love for his wife.[12] Perhaps a choice between these alternatives is not even necessary, as Anne might qualify as a saint or angel now that she is in heaven, thus belonging to the category of pure beings that nevertheless should not be worshipped, whereas before she had 'payd her last debt to Nature' she might have been the embodiment of fleshly temptation, and thus definitely not to be worshipped.

Surely, if Donne had actually shared mystical experiences, 'Visions of Eros', with Anne, as Clements suggests, it is surprising to find him so unceremoniously dismissing 'the streames' once he has found the 'head'. In hindsight, erotic and sacred love are not so compatible as Clements might suppose. But incompatible does not mean incomparable: perhaps God, to Donne, really *is* like a jealous lover who will not brook a rival? In the latter case, can we take the speaker's resignation to God's will at face value? John Carey's discussion of Donne's works as expressions of the poet's personal obsessions with being loved suggests not; he sees the tone of the poem as one of 'affectionate reproach' (58-59). John Stachniewski goes even further, and sees the entire sonnet as a profoundly ironic indictment of an unreasonably jealous God rather than an acceptance of His divine authority (687). In such readings, Donne's metaphor of God as a jealous lover is taken literally, not as a sacred parody: divine and secular love differ only in degree, not in essence.

On the other hand, it is possible to take the speaker's words more or less at face value, and to argue that Donne is resigned to the fact that Anne's love has been replaced by the greater love of a God whose very jealousy proves His affection. This is the traditional reading offered by

Helen Gardner. She quotes from a letter Donne sent to his mother to console her after the death of her daughter, in which he uses similar metaphors
of divine jealousy.[13] Obviously, in a letter meant to comfort the bereaved,
bitter irony at an unjust God would be out of place. Neither Carey nor
Stachniewski explains how this letter fits into their ironic interpretations.

Louis Martz's reading is closer to that of Stachniewski and Carey than
to that of Gardner, without, however, being wholly ironic. The 'serenity' of
the opening lines is deceptive, the speaker really is dissatisfied and craves
for more love from God. Then he gains the insight that God's worries about
the temptations of 'the World, fleshe, yea Devill' are justified after all.
Nevertheless, this resolution 'is ... most precarious ... and leaves the reader
with no sense that the ever-recurrent instability of this speaker's mind has
really been overcome' (*Metaph.* 107-108). In his earlier book, *The Poetry
of Meditation*, Martz had listed 'Holy Sonnet 17' among the 'love-sonnets
of sacred parody' (216), which suggests that jealousy can no more express
God's motivation than secular love can be compared to the immeasurable
love of God. Martz does not explain the discrepancy, perhaps because he
feels there is none: after all, the speaker's dilemma could be seen from the
same perspective as that in other sonnets analysed by Martz—as a conflict
between the speaker's spontaneous impulses and his theologically informed
better knowledge (*Metaph.* 106). The image of the jealous God is the site
where this conflict seems to come to a head; taken literally, it contains the
seeds of an accusation, but in the final analysis the speaker is aware of the
inadequacy of his language, and softens it to an oxymoronic '*tender* jealosy', which is evidence of love rather than mere possessiveness. In such a
reading, the speaker is resigned to his loss in the end, but his images betray
the kind of residual aggression that Schoenfeldt has detected in Herbert's
ostensible courtesy towards his Lord. It may be significant that the first line
reads 'Since she whom I *loved* ...', in the past tense: the love of Anne is
already something of the past.

* * *

A later poem by Donne offers a useful gloss on the 'Holy Sonnet', and
makes the straightforward reading, in terms of an uneasy acceptance of the
primacy of divine love, more plausible. Helen Gardner has pointed out that
the theme of divine jealousy introduced in the 'Holy Sonnet' is 'more
powerfully expressed' in Donne's 'A Hymne to Christ, at the Authors last
going into Germany', and finds the resemblance close enough to influence
her dating of the 'Holy Sonnet' (78). There is indeed a strong kinship

throughout between 'Holy Sonnet 17' and the 'Hymne', which may justify the use of the one to elucidate the other. Both use similar metaphors for God, 'th'Eternall root of true love' in the 'Hymne' and the 'head' of the spring that can be approached through the 'streames' of earthly love in the 'Holy Sonnet'. In both images, Donne's speaker acknowledges the related-ness between both kinds of love, but stresses the primacy of divine love. Moreover, in both poems this is followed by a negative valuation of pro-fane love.

It is true that the 'Hymne' seems to speak of love in rather abstract terms, without specifying that those 'whom [Donne] lov'd there, and who lov'd [him]' included not just friends and children, but also (one presumes) sweethearts and his late wife; the only mistresses explicitly mentioned in this poem turn out to be metaphors for 'Fame, Wit, Hopes'. Yet the ele-ment of erotic love is present in the sacred parody that runs throughout the poem. Modern critics seem to have overlooked part of the parody: typical-ly, Milton A. Rugoff points out that the 'approach to God as a kind of holy mistress is evident *throughout the second half* of this poem.[14] The first half, however, is usually read as a straightforward typological argument. D.C. Allen, for instance, connects the first four lines with the tradition of religious ship imagery derived from Saint Augustine and other patristic sources:

> In what torne ship soever I embarke,
> That ship shall be my embleme of thy Arke;
> What sea soever swallow mee, that flood
> Shall be to mee an embleme of thy blood;

As Allen points out, Donne alludes to the concept of the Ship of the Church which will bring Salvation to those who are in it, thanks to the blood of Christ.[15]

What Allen overlooks, however, is that in the following lines the ship image is transformed into a sacred parody of a Petrarchan commonplace. Envisaging his voyage on board the ship, Donne's speaker prepares for rough weather, which he sees as analogous to God's displeasure:

> Though thou with clouds of anger do disguise
> Thy face; yet through that maske I know those eyes,
> Which, though they turne away sometimes, they never will despise.

What we have here is a man on a ship, who looks up at the sky hoping to see the loving eyes of Christ, but finds to his disappointment that they are

hidden behind 'clouds of anger'. To Donne's readers, this would have been
a familiar situation, for it is in exactly these terms that Petrarch's speaker
had described his predicament with respect to Laura. In one of Petrarch's
most famous sonnets, 'Passa la nave', the persona compares himself to a
ship lost at sea because his mistress's eyes (the stars by which he navigates)
are invisible:

> Hidden are my two sweet trusted signs;
> > Dead beneath the waves is reason and skill:
> > So that I begin to despair of the port.

> Celansi i duo miei dolci usati segni;
> > Morta fra l'onde è la ragion e l'arte:
> > Tal ch' i' incomincio a disperar del porto.[16]

The sonnet in question had been translated and imitated by a host of English sonneteers, including Wyatt, Drayton, and Spenser. In his well-known
adaptation entitled 'My Galley', Wyatt characteristically blames the lady
for his predicament; as d'Amico has noted, Petrarch's line 'Hidden are my
two sweet trusted signs' is rendered as 'The starres be hid that led me to
this pain'. In this way, Wyatt 'adds *pain*, changes the sense by making the
cause of his sorry condition her eyes; the woman is thus responsible for his
error' (137-138).

Spenser, on the other hand, downplays the element of criticism: his
speaker even remains hopeful that all will be well, that eventually the stars
(that is, the lady's eyes) will break through the clouds again:

> Yet hope I well, that when this storme is past
> > my *Helice* the lodestar of my lyfe
> > will shine again, and looke on me at last,
> > with lovely light to cleare my cloudy grief.

Donne's conceit, then, is a sacred parody. Like a profane mistress, Christ is
occasionally fickle and 'turns away sometimes', but He 'never will despise'. This conceit in the opening stanza of the 'Hymne to Christ' informs
the later images of divorce, mistresses, sexual jealousy and marriage. Christ
is indeed seen 'as a kind of holy mistress' throughout the poem, with the
same tantrums and jealous fits that are so often regarded as characteristic of
profane mistresses. Yet there is also a difference, as befits a sacred parody:
the sacred tenor cannot really be expressed by the profane vehicle. Whereas
most Petrarchan lovers are in despair when the mistress's eyes are hidden

behind the clouds, Donne's speaker is confident that Christ will show His face again: He 'never will despise'. Also, the divine jealousy is actually a virtue rather than a vice, and the speaker proudly asserts his own jealousy:

> Nor thou nor thy religion dost controule,
> The amorousnesse of an harmonious Soule,
> But thou would'st have that love thy selfe: As thou
> Art jealous, Lord, so I am jealous now,
> Thou lov'st not, till from loving more, thou free
> My soule: Who ever gives, takes libertie:
> O, if thou car'st not whom I love, alas, thou lov'st not mee.

Divine jealousy alone guarantees God's love for the speaker. It is the speaker himself who voluntarily asks Christ:

> Seale then this bill of my Divorce to All,
> On whom those fainter beames of love did fall;
> Marry those loves, which in youth scatter'd bee
> On Fame, Wit, Hopes (false mistresses) to thee.

So the speaker is quite prepared to renounce all his profane mistresses, who turn out to be not women of flesh and blood, but personifications such as 'Fame, Wit, Hopes', the 'false mistresses' we chase in our youth. On these, after all, only his 'fainter beams of love did fall', which now should be concentrated on the one object that is really worthy of that love: God, who is 'th'Eternal root of true love'. Divine love, then, is seen not as coexisting with but as transcending by far the love of this world.

In addition to the Petrarchan sonnet, there is one other profane context that may be relevant here. In some ways, the 'Hymne', being a poem of leave-taking, is also a parody of Donne's earlier valediction poems. These, too, had often begun with the theme of fear of death, to end as celebrations of the enduring strength of love. The 'Valediction: Forbidding Mourning' is a case in point: the image of the parting of body and soul in the opening lines may be taken to suggest that the love between the speaker and his mistress/wife is strong enough to endure even death, until the two of them are joined together again at the Resurrection. The theme of the power of love over death connects the valediction poems with Petrarch's worship of Laura after her death, no matter how much the kinds of love described may differ in other respects.

Though the 'Hymne' shares some of the concerns of the 'Valedictions', it is addressed to Christ, not to a mistress, and it seriously qualifies the premises of the earlier poems. Fear of death is unreal, since for the believer death is the way to Redemption; and the strength of profane love is denied, nullified in the face of the superior love of God. As in the 'Holy Sonnet', the speaker suggests that he has already given up all kinds of profane love by speaking about them in the past tense:

> I sacrifice this Iland unto thee,
> And all whom I lov'd there, and who lov'd mee;

In relation to the earlier valediction poems, then, the 'Hymne to Christ' can be read as a palinode, or poem of retraction: unlike divine love, profane love does not last forever. In this admission, Donne gives up one of the few Petrarchan elements that had characterised his earlier poetry.

* * *

As the 'Hymne' was written only about a year and a half after Anne's death, Donne's implicit criticism of earthly love and mistresses, taken at face value, may sound less than reverent with respect to his wife's memory. Again, as with the 'Holy Sonnet', we may ask how literally we should take Donne's resignation: could this poem, too, be read as a bitter indictment of God rather than of profane love? Did Donne really see God as jealous and fickle? Here I would plead for wariness. The tone seems to be not just resigned, but even positively ardent about God's love; when he asks God to divorce him from all that binds him to England, it is not a mere rationalization of a preexisting fact, but a colloquy, a prayer.

More fundamentally, we are faced with a choice between two literal readings that cancel each other out: either we take literally what the speaker says about women and his desire to be free from earthly ties; or we take seriously what he says about God's jealousy and fickleness. Whereas every poet's art lies in his power to transmute his experience, which will often involve the use of figurative language, about God we have no other choice but to speak in approximations. Donne made that very point in a sermon preached in 1619 during a stopover in The Hague, on this very same embassy to Germany. There are limits to the accuracy of metaphorical language in expressing the nature of God:

> God in the Scriptures is often by the Holy Ghost invested, and repre-
> sented in the qualities and affections of man; and to constitute a com-
> merce and familiarity between God and man, God is not only said to

have bodily lineaments, eyes and eares, and hands, and feet, and to
have some of the naturall affections of man, as Joy, in particular ...
And so, pity too ... But some of those inordinate and irregular passions
and perturbations, excesses and defects of man, are imputed to God, by
the holy Ghost in the Scriptures.[17]

So God is seen as endowed with human weaknesses and passions, including
'lazinesse, drowsinesse', 'sudden and hasty choler', 'scorn and contempt',
'Drunkennesse', and being 'jealous of his glory'. These, however, Donne
suggests, are mere accommodations to man's weakness, 'to constitute a
commerce and familiarity between God and man', and should not be taken
literally.[18] The same applies to Donne's poetic images involving God's
jealousy and fickleness. Donne knows very well that these images from
profane love are not adequate, but yet they capture something of man's
subjective view of his relationship with God. Donne's speaker (who may or
may not be a projection of Donne himself) seems to be torn between two
attitudes: on the one hand, there is the limited human perspective from
which God's actions are mysterious to man, which might seem like fickleness; and when God takes away beloved people, this might seem like jealousy. This level of direct emotional response is controlled, however, by the
theological reassurance that these are only man's distorted impressions of
God's love: bereavements are God's way of bringing man closer to salvation, by forcing him to concentrate his love wholly on God. In particular in
the 'Hymne' the importance of controlling primitive human urges by an
awareness of the deeper meaning of experience is stressed from the beginning:

> In what torne ship soever I embarke,
> That ship shall be my embleme of thy Arke;
> What sea soever swallow mee, that flood
> Shall be to mee an embleme of thy blood;

If fear of death can be overcome by keeping in mind the promise of Salvation in the afterlife, then also the 'clouds of anger' that follow are no more
than superficial signs, behind we should seek the deeper meaning of divine
love.

    Those who wish to take Donne's display of anger at an unreasonable
and jealous God too seriously might consider that the speaker also seems to
blame Anne. In the suggestion that, unlike the divine lover, earthly mistresses really are fickle and really do turn away forever, we might discover

a veiled criticism of Anne for having deserted the poet by her death, a sentiment that Donne's speaker in 'A Feaver' had voiced many years earlier:

> Oh doe not die, for I shall hate
>   All women so, when thou art gone,
> That thee I shall not celebrate
>   When I remember thou wast one.[19]

About Anne's death, Donne's biographer R.C. Bald has remarked:

> The death of his wife marked a turning-point in Donne's life; it deepened his sense of religious vocation, and produced something much closer to a conversion than the feelings which had prompted him to enter the Church. Until her death all Donne's deepest emotional experiences seem to have been associated with her; after her loss, his emotions concentrated themselves on the divine image and the activities connected with his sacred calling.[20]

The balance between sacred and profane love postulated by Clements and Roston has been upset; God's love is seen as infinitely superior to any mortal kind of love, including Anne's. The resignation of the 'Hymne' can only be read at face value, and this makes it likely that a similar attitude of uneasy resignation also underlies 'Holy Sonnet 17'.

Notes

1   I am grateful to Dr. Dayton Haskin for his perceptive comments and recommendations after reading an earlier version of this paper, and to my colleague Dr. A.J. Hoenselaars for his suggestions for improvements.

2   See Louis L. Martz, *The Poetry of Meditation: A Study in English Religious Literature of the Seventeenth Century* (New Haven, 1954), 184-193 and *passim*.

3   Cf. Donne's blatantly irreverent and cynical use of religious categories to describe profane love, e.g. the defence of promiscuity with the help of the religious concepts of 'things indifferent' and the 'kernell' and 'shell' of patristic exegesis in 'Communitie'. For the 'things indifferent', see Lindsay A. Mann, 'Radical Inconsistency: A Reading of Donne's "Communitie"', *University of Toronto Quarterly* 50, 3 (1981): 286.

4   Michael C. Schoenfeldt, *Prayer and Power: George Herbert and Renaissance Courtship* (Chicago and London, 1991), in particular 255-267.

5   Arthur L. Clements, *Poetry of Contemplation: John Donne, George Herbert, Henry Vaughan, and the Modern Period* (Albany, 1990), 81.

6   Murray Roston, *The Soul of Wit: A Study of John Donne* (Oxford, 1974), 180-182.

7   Anne Ferry, *The 'Inward' Language: Sonnets of Wyatt, Sidney, Shakespeare, Donne* (Chicago, 1983).

8   John Stachniewski, 'John Donne: The Despair of the "Holy Sonnets"', *ELH* 48 (1981): 677-705; Richard Strier, 'John Donne Awry and Squint: The "Holy Sonnets", 1608-1610', *Modern Philology* 86 (1989): 357-385.

9   E.g. *John Donne: The Divine Poems*, edited by Helen Gardner, second edition (Oxford, 1978), xxxviii; Stachniewski, p. 686; Strier, p. 358, n. 7. References to Donne's religious poetry throughout are to Gardner's edition, although I have adopted Grierson's numbering of 'Holy Sonnet 17' for ease of reference.

10   Ferry, p. 220. Donne's devotion to his wife has recently been questioned by Janet E. Halley, 'Textual Intercourse: Anne Donne, John Donne, and the Sexual Poetics of Textual Exchange', in Sheila Fisher, ed., *Seeking the Woman in Late Medieval and Renaissance Writings: Essays in Feminist Contextual Criticism* (Knoxville, 1989), 186-206.

11   Louis L. Martz, 'The Action of the Self: Devotional Poetry in the Seventeenth Century', in *Metaphysical Poetry*, edited by Malcolm Bradbury and David Palmer (London, 1970), 107.

12   John Carey, *John Donne: Life, Mind and Art* (London, 1981), 59. Cf. Stachniewski, p. 687.

13   Gardner, p. 78; cf. her 'Another Note on Donne: "Since she whome I lov'd"', *MLR* 52 (1957): 564-565.

14   Milton Allan Rugoff, *Donne's Imagery: A Study in Creative Sources* (New York, 1962), 87. Mine italics.

15   Don Cameron Allen, 'Donne and the Ship Metaphor', *Modern Language Notes* 76 (4) (April 1961): 308-312.

16   Both original and modern translation quoted from Jack d'Amico, *Petrarch in England: An Anthology of Parallel Texts from Wyatt to Milton* (Ravenna, 1979), 136.

17   John Donne, *Sermons*, edited by Evelyn M. Simpson and George R. Potter (Berkeley and Los Angeles, 1953-62) II, 288-291.

18   For Donne's attitude to the concept of accommodations and its theological background, see William Kerrigan, 'The Fearful Accommodations of John Donne', *English Literary Renaissance*, 4 (1974): 337-363.

19   *John Donne: The Elegies and The Songs and Sonnets*, edited by Helen Gardner (Oxford, 1965), 61-62; II. 1-4.

20   R.C. Bald, *John Donne: A Life* (Oxford, 1970), 328.

11

THE MIMETIC POETRY OF JACK AND JOHN DONNE:
A FIELD THEORY FOR THE AMOROUS AND THE DIVINE

PAUL R. SELLIN

When combined with classic predestinarian thinking, whether derived directly from St. Augustine's anti-Pelagian tracts or sixteenth-century intermediaries, mimetic critical theory offers intriguing possibilities for bridging the troublesome cleft between the profane verse of Jack the rake and the sacred vein of John the divine that has haunted Donne studies from the days of Walton to the present. Accordingly, I propose to take the Articles of the Synod of Dort of 1619 and apply them to the divine and secular lyrics as forms of poetic mimesis rather than pseudo-romantic self-expression in fashionable disguise. I do so not merely because the Dort formulas constitute one of the finest epitomes of Augustinian predestinarianism ever or because the synod that generated them was the most important ecclesiastical event in Donne's lifetime. Rather, the relevance of Calvinism to the poet's life that many biographical studies by myself and others have by now established, I think, invites application of the Dort findings to his works in a way that would not be feasible in the case of Crashaw, say, or Southwell.[1] After all, both the genesis of the synod in the clash between Perkins and Arminius and its aftermath that after 1619 led in England to the rise of Laud ran exactly parallel with Donne's life from his young manhood in the early 1590s to his full maturity as a divine, and he commented on the synodal process and findings both repeatedly and positively. Of course, one is free to apply any dialectic one wishes to a given author or *oeuvre*, but we must not entertain the illusion that all such applications are thereby of equal power or validity. As for the pertinence of mimetic analysis, critical propositions depend on historical assumptions, and as the ensuing argument will reveal, Donne's very verse itself in at least one clear instance betrays his awareness of Renaissance thinking about mimesis and pleasure that hearkens back directly to Aristotle's *Poetics*.[2] The aim is simply to develop a 'field' theory based on Renaissance Augustinianism that enables one to bring Donne's sacred and profane verse together under a single umbrella. The endeavour may also help against some current resuscitation of biographical fallacy in Donne Studies.[3]

According to Article I, Section 16, of the Dort *Judgement,* there are three classes of fallen man subject to the divine decree of predestination. The first consists of the elect. Although fallen underserving creatures, they enjoy the grace 'effectually' to 'perceive in themselves a lively faith', 'sure confidence of heart in Christ, the peace of conscience, and endeavour of filial obedience', and 'a glorying in God through Christ'. Accordingly, they are assured of the 'good houre of more plentifull grace', and they are blessed with joys attendant on certainty of salvation.[4]

The second involves Christians 'seriously converted unto God' who, as they are desperately aware of their need to stand in grace, suffer great Angst at the thought of reprobation because they do not feel assurance of election. They fall into two groups. The one consists of worshippers who are 'cast down' because, even though they 'use the means by which God hath promised, that he wil work' the 'signs of grace in them', they are nevertheless unable '*effectually*' to feel the the 'lively' faith that characterises minds sure of election (emphasis mine). The predicament of the others is even more dramatic. Although they 'hartily desire to turne unto God, to please him onely, and bee delivered from this body of death', they are unable to 'make such progresse in the way of godlinesse, and faith as they wish'. Understandably they are anything but comfortable 'with the doctrine of reprobation'.[5]

The third class comprises irreligious transgressors, people who 'have wholly enthralled themselves to the cares of the world, and pleasures of the flesh'. For them, the doctrine of reprobation 'is not without cause terrible' because they, and they alone, stand in danger of eternal damnation 'so long as they are not seriously converted unto God'.[6]

The moment one begins to think in terms not of poetic biography but of poets exploiting categories like these as objects of imitation, the Holy Sonnets divide into two sharply distinct distinct kinds of dramatic representation. However worthwhile the subject-matter orderings urged by Helen Gardner and others, it seems to me of much greater importance to realise that mimetically these poems divide into sonnets of Assurance and sonnets of Angst.[7] The sonnets of Assurance present fictional actions, characters, thought and emotions entirely different from those populating the others. Consider the trimphant braving that informs 'Death be not proud', for example.[8] Surely a better, more assertively dramatic realisation of assurance—that is, an effectual 'lively faith' caught in an instant of 'glorying in God through Christ'—is hard to imagine. Or if one seeks a telling profile of 'a sure confidence of heart', not to speak of the 'peace of conscience' or the 'practice of childlike obedience', one need go no further than the wonderer in 'Why are wee by all creatures waited on?', presented in the act of marveling before our eyes at a loving Christ who 'For us, his Creatures, and his foes, hath dyed' (14). Indeed, even when the contemplation of a gory image of the crucifixion of that Christ in 'What if this present were the worlds last night?' seems to begin in trepidation, the paradoxical confidence of the resolving sestet capitalises on Aristotle's observation regarding pleasure in mimesis of painful objects to thrust the poem explicitly into the very category I propose: 'No, No; ... Beauty, of pitty, foulnesse onely is / A sign of rigour: ... This beauteous form *assures* a piteous minde' (emphasis mine).[9] So too with the confidence in the incarnation expressed in 'Spit in my face yee Jewes', the 'lively faith' brought to life in 'Wilt thou love God, as he thee!' and even the touching expression of fleshly sorrow in 'Since she whome I lovd, hath payd her last debt / To Nature'—sorrow swept aside by the vision of an infinitely generous God who offers all His love in lieu of the lost beloved's (9-14). These six sonnets (plus 'The Annuntiation and the Passion', the 'Hymne to God my God, in my sicknesse', not to speak of 'The Crosse' and the 'imperfect' 'Resurrection') then, constitute a distinct kind of plot situation. The creatures inhabiting them differ markedly from those in the rest of the sonnets and the divine poems, and they are characterised by feelings of comfort attendant on secure faith.

All the other Holy Sonnets are poems of religious Angst, soliloquies portraying a person in a closed moment of venting intense feelings occasioned by anxieties past or present about the state of his soul and the availability of grace. Consider the situation which Donne constructs in 'As due by many titles I resign / My selfe to thee, O God'. Anything but a monument ot freedom of the will in matters of salvation, it rings instead with the cry of a man who knows that the Lord not only works mercy but also hands men over to Satan to do evil and seal their damnation. His predicament is not simply that he has resisted or insufficiently loves God or fails passionately to desire salvation. Rather, knowing himself a divine creature purposely created to share in the glorious destiny that Scripture promises, he is extremely agitated at finding himself still in the power of Satan and fears mightily what he suspects may be reprobation. The being who laments, 'Oh, I shall soone despaire, when I doe see / That thou lovest mankind well, yet will'nt chuse me' (12-13) is plainly one who, though he longs for nothing more, is made to state overtly his awareness that he is not yet 'chosen'—or 'elect'—, knows that grace cannot be commanded or earned, and that the strange ways of God carry the real possibility that for him, as an individual, grace may not be forthcoming. So too with 'If poysonous mineralls, and if that tree / Whose fruit threw death on else immortall us'. If an artist wished to dramatise a murmurer against the doctrines of original sin, election and reprobation, can a better monologue presenting a troubled soul in the act of indicting providence on these issues be imagined than that offered in the octave of this sonnet? The telling point, though, is the thought that causes the impassioned accuser to reverse his course, swallow his indignation at divine arbitrariness and bow to the inscrutable will and free pleasure of God. For the first line of the sestet puts on his tongue the text of Romans 9: 20: 'Who art thou that repliest against God?'—the very passage in Scripture that, right in tune with Luther, Section 18 of the same Dort Article uses to stop the mouth of just such railers.[10]

Diffident believers like these are anything but elect saints in a state of assurance, and the words they utter constitute vivid, affecting, essentially serious, indeed tragic portrayals of trembling, 'cast down' Christians who are, to say the least, 'terrified' at the thought of 'Reprobation'. Inasmuch as no less than nine of the sonnets of Angst—specifically 'O my blacke Soule!', 'This is my playes last scene', 'At the round earth's', 'Batter my heart', 'Father, part of his double interest', 'Thou hast made me', 'I am a little world', besides the two quoted above—conform to the line of action just described, it seems clear that the patterns that most attracted Donne essentially resemble the second group the Dort Articles envision, namely those 'who, albeit they hartily desire to turne unto God, to please him one-ly, and bee delivered from this body of death', yet 'cannot make such prog-resse in the way of godlinesse, and faith as they wish'.[11] As this predica-ment very well accounts for the emotions and thought animating 'Good-friday, 1613. Riding Westward' too, the mimetric pedigree of the poem is obvious.

However, Donne did not neglect another category of Augustinian inse-curity reflected in the Dort articles: that is, people who do not feel assur-ance, even though they are blessed with the power to 'use the meanes, by which God hath promised that he wil work' the signs of grace 'in us'.[12] The distinction is helpful in isolating the qualities and tone of five special sonnets of Angst that display dissatisfaction with efforts at worship. These are 'O Might those sighes and tears return again', which presents a devout melancholic whose mourning in 'holy discontent' yields insufficient 'fruit' (3-4); 'If faithfull soules be alike glorified', which displays a 'pensive soule' (13) that, knowing the hypocrisy of its own devotions, grieves because of awareness that 'circumstances' and 'signs' that would make the 'white truth' of his 'minde' 'descryable' are *not* 'immediately' 'apparent' (5-8); 'Show me deare Christ, thy spouse, so bright and clear', in which the prosperity of Papism 'on the other shore' and the eradication of Protestant churches in 'Germany' (204) raises troubling doubts about which is the true church and how God treats it;[13] and 'O, to vex me, contraryes meete in one', in which a practitioner of 'vowes', 'devotion', 'praying' and 'flatter-ing speaches ... court[ing] God' despairs before the 'humorous' inconstancy of his 'contritione' (3-13). While similar laments also appear in the hymns to God the Father and to Christ, the finest example occurs in 'La Corona'.

Although the fictive weaver of garlands, who in 'low devout melancholie' is here portrayed in the act of plaiting a wreath of 'prayer' and 'praise' as an offering to the Lord, begins by emphatically rehearsing the Scriptural promise that 'Salvation to all that will is nigh' (1), yet, as the poems unfold, we learn that this *vates* is himself anything but certain of his power so to will, and at the close of the sequence Donne causes him fervently to pray that God 'with thine owne blood quench thine owne just wrath' (94) and accept the proffered verse tribute, not as something meritorious in itself, but only 'if'—'if', that is—'thy holy Spirit, my muse did raise' (95). For this brooding artist is keenly aware that the Spirit may *not* have raised him, that the gift acquires merit *only* if it be the fruit of grace, and that he cannot even tell whether it is. The final utterance, 'Deign at my hands this crown of prayer and praise' (96), implies an ache that deftly touches the roots of human sympathy.[14]

Clearly then, the sonnets of Angst set forth personae radically different from those in the sonnets of Assurance, in that we see them suffering terror and near despair because they cannot command grace, seem to deserve better, and therefore thrill us with, as Sidney might say, 'just causes' of lamentation that cannot but move empathy in a 'kind' heart.[15] Yet at the same time, predestinarian expectations invest these 'speaking' pictures with a saving irony that softens the excessive psychological affliction informing them.[16] Were such pain as that which these characters undergo to be endless, the spectacle would be overwhelming, if not repulsive. However, unlike some students of the horrors of Calvinism, the well-tempered Augustinian is expected to understand that 'our mercifull God hath promised that he will not quench the smoaking flaxe, nor breake the shaken reede'; that as such affliction is itself a sign of grace, there is hope even if the speakers themselves show no sign of seeing it; and that 'such as these ought not to ... reckon themselves amongst the reprobate, but must diligently go forward, ... and ardently desire, and humbly and reverently expect the good howre of more plentifull grace'.[17]

What, then, happens to the Songs and Sonets if we go on and apply synodal dialectic as well to the 'Wanton Story' that Thomas Browne found in the 'Strange Fire' of what he saw as Donne's version of Augustine's 'Confessions'?[18] In such light, the profane elegies and the Songs and Sonets turn into dramatic portrayals of voluptuous worldlings who, 'unheeding of God and Christ the Saviour, have wholly enthralled themselves to the cares of the world, and pleasures of the flesh'—the very class of creatures, in short, to whom the doctrine of Predestination is, according to the Dort articles, 'not without cause terrible, so long as they are not seriously converted unto God'.[19]

The secular love lyrics feature at least three distinct sorts of transgressors. Characters 'who have wholly enthralled themselves' to the 'pleasures of the flesh' are the easiest to deal with. Their range stretches from coarse dialogues 'of one' ('The Extasie', 73) such as 'The Comparison' or 'The Anagram' to comic displays of amusing wit such as occur in the elegy 'His parting from her' or the love lyrics 'Change', 'The Perfume', 'Jealousie', 'Nature's lay Ideot', 'Communitie', 'The Indifferent', 'Breake of Day', 'Woman's constancy', 'The Flea', 'Love's Alchymie', 'Self Love', 'The Apparition' and many more. Such flagrant adulterers and fornicators —for that is what they either are or would be—typically vent high passions for absurd reasons, and their speech, which much resembles that of the 'Problems and Paradoxes', turns on tortured logic and perverse values that make them the obvious butts of their own discourse—e.g., 'Good is not good, unlesse / A thousand it possess' ('Confined Love', 19-20), 'Full nakedness! *All* joyes are due to thee' ('Elegy: Going to Bed', 33; emphasis mine), 'Change is the nursery / of music, joy, life, and eternity' ('Elegy: Change', 36), 'hope not for minde in women' ('Loves Alchymie', 23). The dramatic irony their discourse radiates, however, is clearly of a piece with that underlying the sonnets of Angst in that it too reflects on the limitations of the speakers. Whereas they themselves, like the revellers in Milton's *Comus*, lack the grace even to perceive their plight, the author expects his readers to see them for what they are, and out of a sense of moral superiority to disapprove—hence the fun. Amusing as these poems may seem, though, the undertone is serious, for such grossly sensual lovers stand in fact under a shadow they cannot avoid, however blind to it they may be. St. Paul put it thus in Romans 8: 5-8:

> For those who live according to the flesh set their minds on the things of the flesh, but those who live according to the Spirit set their minds on the things of the Spirit. To set the mind on the flesh is death, but to set the mind on the Spirit is life and peace. For this reason the mind that is set on the flesh is hostile to God; it does not submit to God's law—indeed it cannot, and those who are in the flesh cannot please God.

Other lovers—they occur in elegies like 'Going to Bed' or 'Loves Warre', or lyrics such as 'Lecture upon the Shadow', 'The good-morrow', 'The Sunne Rising', 'The Canonization', 'The Anniversarie', 'The Autumnall', 'The Dreame', 'The Extasie', perhaps even 'Sapho to Philaenis'—are more problematic. Although such dramatic speeches as these speakers utter equally imply Pauline voluptuaries whose devotion to the flesh manifests values as fully askew as those of thier simpler *confrères*, the words Donne imputes to them often paint such fine illusions of genuine passion that, by distracting us from closely examining the contents of what these voices actually say, the very credibility of the mimesis tempts us to agree with the point of view uttered and to respond with sympathy rather than chuckles. The technique is to soft pedal invalid proposition and flagant situation: no silly adulterer here furiously berating the virtuous wife he corrupted because she has taken up with another ('Natures lay Ideot'), no ridiculous lady deciding on masturbation because she finds no 'kind of' male through whom she can 'vent' her 'humour' 'freely' to 'prove' sex ('Selfe Love', 21-24). Instead Donne substitutes all sorts of misplaced allusions to religious, political and moralistic lore, often of a Catholic bent, such as specious distinctions between good and evil, true doctrine and false, priesthood and laity, canonisation and recusancy, saints and mystics, good and bad angels, spheres and intelligences, golden mean and excess, body and soul, Platonic love, free will and election, kingship and empire, scripture and revelation, orthodoxy and heresy, death and immortality—mostly false analogies misused to justify fleshly misbehaviour. This tactic has a double edge. It betrays, on the one hand, that as such lovers have in an undefined past had considerable, albeit unprofitable, exposure to Christian doctrine and ethics, so they should know better and cannot reasonably plead ignorance should the day of judgement come. On the other hand, it forces the audience unawares to call to mind the very doctrinal and moral criteria by which unwittingly these creatures show themselves wanting. Should readers fail to see this, the doubled irony begins to seem Swiftian.

There are, finally, a group of personae that populate what I like to think of as *humaniora*, the 'kinder' or 'more humane' Songs and Sonets. Unlike their brethren, these lovers do not indulge in outbursts of relatively trivial sensual passion. Rather, such lyrics feign lovers threatened with serious loss that we tend to accept as truly painful, and we therefore find their complaints justified. Here is where most of the valedictions belong— 'Forbidding mourning', 'Of the booke', 'Of weeping', 'The Expiraton' as well as perhaps 'Sweetest love, I do not goe' (are we really to take this lover seriously?) and the kindred elegies 'On his Mistris' and 'Here take my Picture'—as well as certain affirmations of transcendent love—'Image of her whom I love', 'Loves Infinitenesse', 'The Anniversarie', 'The Relique', perhaps 'Sonnet. The Token'. They also include a remarkable set of three *conquestiones* occasioned by the actual or threatened death of the beloved: 'A Feaver', 'The Dissolution' and 'A nocturnall upon *S. Lucies* day', the latter two of which, by virtue of matter shared with the Holy Sonnet 'Since she whome I lovd, hath payd her last debt / to Nature', serve as transitional poems linking the Songs and Sonets and the Holy Sonnets. Although these graver fictions indulge in highly complex thought and involuted figures sometimes reminiscent of the 'Obsequies and Exequies', they eschew overt absurdity, and the figurative language, even the exaggeration, is not necessarily inharmonious with the tone and seriousness of the occasion. As a result, the words have power to touch, and we are prone to respond with respect and pity.

Yet it is precisely here that Donne turns the very kind of irony inherent in the sonnets of Angst sharply back on the reader. For however strongly the fleshly ties in us may empathise with the expressions of human loss these poems contain, the melancholy fact remains that from a Pauline point of view such feelings ultimately but reflect 'cares of the world'. They derive from the inevitable incommodities such as separation or death that flow from mortal attachments, even if such love succeeds in transcending mere sensual pleasure. Never does Donne allow even the most sympathetic of lovers in the Songs and Sonets to put the Kingdom of Heaven first. In complete conformity with St. Paul, he restricts speakers like these to sad utterances bespeaking bitter emotional dislocation that before our very eyes crowds out the divine at the exact moment such thought should be entering their minds. The striking difference between the unreconciled misery exhibited in 'The Dissolution' or 'A nocturnall' and the transcendent assurance that their equally pained fellow-in-sorrow manifests in 'Since she whome I lovd' makes authorial presumption clear regarding the carnality of love fuelling such passion. Whereas even the grieving mourners in the Songs and Sonets display themselves as anything but as yet 'seriously converted unto God' (although they are both in the process of resolving to follow the beloved in death) the speech of the bereft lover in the sestet of 'Since she whome I lovd' shows explicitly that in terms of theological imperatives, carnal 'Love to Saints and Angels' is not, alas, ever to be mistaken as something 'divine', regardless of human need to maintain such illusion. God suffers 'tender jealosy' lest, in the emotions of such love, 'the World, fleshe, yea Devill putt' Him—Donne goes out of his way to have the lamenter state overtly—'out'.

Again the presestinarian stoicism of such Pauline thinking is replete with paradoxical irony. For if the reader believes it a matter of grace beyond the power of the lovers in 'A Feaver', 'A nocturnall' or 'The Dissolution' to attain the assurance expressed in 'Since she whome I lovd', the three poems in the Songs and Sonets take on quasi-tragic dimensions that generate emotional effects rather like those informing the sonnets of Angst, albeit located on a lower step on the stairway to heaven. Despite the power of their claim to human sympathy, all of these weepers remain imprisoned in precisely the 'vaine' 'Idolatry' that the sufferer in 'O Might those sighes and teares returne againe' (4-5) (not to mention 'If faithfull soules' [9]) is presented as explicitly regretting—and that under threat of a reprobation they do not see at all.

The virtue, then, of blending mimetic theory with late Augustinian predestinarianism is that the method obviates the customary dichotomy between Donne's sacred poetry and profane. According to such a line of reasoning, all the mimetic works appear essentially cut of one cloth, the Holy Sonnets, La Corona, and the divine poems capitalising on the problematics of election and assurance; the Songs and Sonets, reprobation; and the *Devotions on Emergent Occasions*, perseverance of the saints.[20] Such dialectics are valuable not because they are necessarily 'true' or biographically and historically valid, but because they forestall vain searches for sequence and discursive consistency among the divine poems that may not be so appropriate as some critics too readily assume, and they keep dubious, if not irresponsible, biography at bay. They also promote: 1) sharp discrimination among the dramatic postures and predicaments in which Donne places his speakers; 2) vivid awareness of the broad range of ironies that he employs, variously involving speaker, reader, and author in rich patterns that constantly shift, particularly between speaker and reader; 3) clear perception of the subtle entelechy behind his mocking, paradoxical use of theology and of religious allusions and imagery pervading even the most indecent of the elegies or Songs and Sonets; and 4) a firm grasp of the deft psychology informing some of the most involuted tricks of syntax and diction whereby he manipulates emotional responses. Most important of all, a mimetic approach enables one to mount a defence more compelling than hitherto against the little heeded but very telling charge that C.S. Lewis levelled against Donne's love poetry long ago, to the effect that, especially in light of the erotic literature of classical antiquity, it is but trifling and not very original if all it offers is clever Ovidian wit.[21] When profiled as Aristotelian mimesis against a backdrop of profound Christian existentialism, however, both the sacred poetry and the profane take on an elevating nobility and emotional power that far transcend the more superficial pleasures to which Lewis evidently thought the amorous fictions devoted.

Notes

1   E.g., E. Randolph Daniel, 'Reconciliation, Covenant, and Election: A Study in the Theology of John Donne', *Anglican Theological Review* 48 (1966): 14-30; Barbara K. Lewalski, *Protestant Poetics and the Seventeenth-Century Religious Lyric* (Princeton, 1979); Paul R. Sellin, *John Donne and 'Calvinist' Views of Grace*

(Amsterdam, 1983) and *'So Doth, So is Religion: John Donne and Diplomatic Contexts in the Reformed Netherlands, 1619-1620* (Columbia, Mo., 1988); Mary Arshagouni Papazian, 'Donne, Election, and the *Devotions upon Emergent Occasions*', *The Huntington Library Quarterly* 55 (1992): 603-619.

2   See note 9 below.

3   E.g., A.L. French, 'The Psychopathology of the "Holy Sonnets"', *Critical Review Melbourne* 13 (1970): 11-124; John Stachniewski, 'John Donne: The Despair of the "Holy Sonnets"', *ELH* 48 (1981): 677-705; Richard Strier, 'John Donne Awry and Squint: The "Holy Sonnets", 1608-1610', *Modern Philology* 86 (1989): 357-3874; Theresa DiPasquale, 'Ambivalent Mourning: Sacramentality, Idolatry, and Gender in "Since she whome I lovd hath payd her last debt"', *John Donne Journal* 10 (1991): 44-56.

4   *The Judgement of the Nationall Synode of the Reformed Belgique Churches Assembled at Dort, Anno 1618 and 1619 ... Concerning the Five Articles Controverted in the Belgique Churches: Englished out of the Latine Copie* (London: Printed for John Bill, 1619).

5   *Ibid.*

6   *Ibid.*

7   E.g., *John Donne: The Divine Poems*, edited by Helen Gardner, second edition (Oxford, 1978), xxxvii-lv; Don M. Ricks, 'The Westmoreland Manuscript and the Order of Donne's "Holy Sonnets"', *Studies in Philology* 63 (1966): 187-195; Stachniewski, *op. cit.*

8   Line references are to *The Complete Poetry of John Donne*, edited by John T. Shawcross (New York/London, 1968), whence titles, spelling and capitalisation.

9   *Aristotle: Poetics*, translated by Gerard F. Else (Ann Arbor, 1967), 20.

10   *Martin Luther: Selections from His Writings*, edited by John Dillenberger (New York, 1961), 191-192. Cf. Paul R. Sellin, 'The Hidden God: Reformation Awe in Renaissance English Literature', in R.S. Kinsman, ed., *The Darker Vision of the Renaissance* (UCLA Center for Medieval and Renaissance Studies, Contributions: VI) (Los Angeles, 1974), 147-196.

11   *Judgement, loc. cit.*

12   *Ibid.*

13   Concerns that also provided the point of departure for Constantijn Huygens's remarkable pastoral 'd'Utylandighe Herder' of late 1622.

14   Sellin, p. 194 and n. 27.

15   *Sir Philip Sidney: A Critical Edition of the Major Works*, edited by Katherine Duncan-Jones (Oxford/New York, 1989), 229.

16   *Ibid*, p. 217.

17   *Judgement* I, xii.

18   *John Donne: The Critical Heritage*, edited by A.J. Smith (London, 1975), 88.

19   *Judgement* I, 16.

20   Cf. Arshagouni Papazian, pp. 607-615.

21   C.S. Lewis, 'Donne and Love Poetry in the Seventeenth Century' and Joan Bennett, 'The Love Poetry of John Donne: A Reply to Mr. C.S. Lewis', in *Seventeenth-Century English Poetry: Modern Essays in Criticism*, edited by W.R. Keast (London/New York, 1962), 105-109 and 111-131, respectively.

12

SOME SACRED AND PROFANE CON-TEXTS OF JOHN DONNE'S 'BATTER MY HART'

GARY A. STRINGER

In this essay I am concerned to examine the interplay of John Donne's sonnet 'Batter my hart' with three distinct (though interlinked) Renaissance bodies and codes of discourse: (1) the theory and practice of Renaissance sonnet making—both generally and specifically with respect to two of Donne's major poetic competitors (Sidney and Shakespeare); (2) the Biblical background; (3) the evolving canon of Donne's own poetry.

As Rosalie Colie reminds us, Renaissance poets, both those who ventured critical statements and those who merely implied a poetic in their verses, could scarcely conceive of their art, perhaps even of life, apart from the notion of genre.[1] Generic theory provides, in Colie's words, 'a means of accounting for connections between topic and treatment within the literary system' and also of seeing 'the connections of the literary kinds with kinds of knowledge and experience' (29). In other words, a genre-system provides 'a set of interpretations, of "frames" or "fixes" on the world' and thus affords a 'ready code of communication both among professionals and to their audiences' (8). Indeed, Colie finds the idea of genre in the Renaissance so powerful that 'literary invention—both "finding" and "making"' was 'largely generic' (17), further asserting that the organisation of literature into kinds 'naturally encouraged the idea of competition, of overgoing' (11), just as it had when Cicero and Horace ordained prizes for the winners of literary contests. In sum, Colie argues that genre not only determined style and content in individual poems, but also made the poems communicable to audiences and established the bounds within which poets strove to meet the competition. And though Donne is vexingly reticent on questions of aesthetic theory, the evidence of his poetry indicates that he, no less than other writers, perceived and responded to the various generic pressures of the age.[2]

A significant strain among these generic pressures has to do with the relationship between topic and type, particular poetic kinds being linked in the literary system with particular kinds of experience. What the sonnet in Donne's time was primarily linked with, of course, was the theme of romantic love. It is true that Donne's predecessors had sometimes put the sonnet to other uses—there are, for instance, scattered dedicatory and topographical sonnets and numerous spiritual sonnets such as those of Constable

and Henry Lok—but these are exceptional. By Donne's time, if indeed not
by Petrarch's, the sonnet was so closely identified with the central theme of
love that the form had become a virtual metaphor for the subject. To write
a sonnet was to write of love, or—which is quite as significant—to have
one's effort measured against the expectation that it should be so. This
expectation perhaps explains why in 1598 Meres (in *Palladis Tamia*) cat-
egorically characterises as 'sugred'[3] the same Shakespearean sonnets in
which Colie finds many 'caustic' and 'vile' elements (69-73); and it
explains why Herbert, in a sonnet addressed to God in 1610, could ask
without appearing oblivious of the poetic environment, 'Doth Poetry / Wear
Venus Livery? only serve her turn? / Why are not *Sonnets* made of thee?'[4]

The simple fact of Donne's choice of the conventional fourteen-line
verse form for his Holy Sonnets locates these poems unmistakably in the
realm of Petrarchan love poetry, but we need not rely solely on inferences
from generic theory to perceive this connection. In the actual language of
the sonnets, Donne's intermingling of the Petrarchan code with the language of Scripture is clearly evident, and this amalgamation is nowhere more
obvious than in 'Batter my hart'. In the early textual artifacts always immediately preceded by the Holy Sonnet 'What yf this present were the
worlds last night?', in which Donne's speaker characterises his past as a
period of 'idolatree' spent in the service of 'profane Mistressis', 'Batter my
hart' figures the persona as the unwillingly conquered female object of
desire, betrayed by her designated guardian and powerless of herself to
regain her original relationship with her one true love. The persona's only
hope lies in the Lord's willingness to retake by force that which Satan has
unlawfully possessed:

> 16
> Batter my hart, three-persond God, for you
> > As yet but knock, breathe, shine, and seeke to mend;
> > That I may rise, and stand, orethrow me; and bend
> Your force to breake, blow, burne, and make me new.
> I like an vsurp'd towne to'another dew
> > Labour to'admit you, but Oh to no end.
> > Reason your viceroy in me, me should defend,
> But is captiv'd and proves weake or vntrew.
> Yet dearly I love you, and would be loved faine:
> > But ame betroth'd vnto your enemy:
> Diuorce me vnty or breake that knott agayne,
> > Take me to you, emprison me, for I
> Except you enthrall me neuer shalbe free,
> Nor euer chast except you rauishe mee.[5]

Obviously drawn from several areas of human experience, the imagery of this poem ramifies in a number of different directions, only a few of which will be traced here. The dominant imagery of the sestet is clearly sexual, and the second quatrain describes a siege, but the vocabulary of the first quatrain seems to imply several other kinds of activity. To complicate matters, the final couplet, where we expect a summing up, uses both love imagery and the language of conquest, as though the poem had developed only two conceits. Not only does this language entail various areas of human experience, but it is mediated to us through multiple codes of discourse; and many of the words and phrases resonate within more than one frame of reference.

This may be seen, first of all, by examining the Biblical elements in the sonnet's verbal structure. In language that is primarily Scriptural, if not imaginally consistent, the opening quatrain implores the Lord to act violently in the speaker's life:

> Batter my hart, three-person God, for you
>> As yet but knock, breathe, shine, and seeke to mend;
>> That I may rise, and stand, orethrow me; and bend
> Your force to breake, blow, burne, and make me new.

The speaker's reference to God as 'three-person', of course, accords with Scriptural teaching, and these lines urge the Lord to strengthen the speaker by the paradoxical method defined in such New Testament passages as Luke 14: 11—'... whosoeuer exalteth him self, shalbe broght low, and he that humbleth him self shalbe exalted'—and such Old Testament texts as Job 22: 29: 'When *others* are cast downe, then shalt thou say, I am lifted vp; and *God* shal saue the humble persone'.[6] The word 'stand', of course, which defines the position to which the speaker aspires, refers to a New Testament concept of virtually mantric power, recalling Paul's reminders in II Corinthians 1: 24 ('by faith ye stande') and Romans 11: 20 ('thou standest by faith') and especially his admonitions to the Ephesians—'Put on the whole armour of God, that ye may be able to stand against the assauts of the deuil. ... take vnto you the whole armour of God, that ye may be able to resist in the euil day, & hauing finished all things, stand fast. Stand therefore, and your loines girde about with veritie ...' (6: 11, 13-14).[7] The four sets of opposing verbs in lines 2 and 4, moreover—which define, respectively, God's present gentle dealings with the speaker and the harsher measures necessary if the latter is to 'rise, and stand'—all echo Scriptural descriptions of God's treatment of His human children. The word 'knock' recalls the Son's invitation in Revelation 3: 20: 'Beholde, I stand at the

dore, and knocke. If anie man ... opñ the dore, I wil come in ...'.
'[B]reathe' reminds us that '[t]he Lord God also made the mā of the dust of
the grounde, and breathed in his face breath of life ...' (Gen. 2: 7), that He
gives life to all (in John 20: 22, Christ breathes on the disciples and says,
'Receiue the holie Gost'). God's 'shin[ing]' refers to his sending Christ,
characterised in John 1: 9-10 as 'the true light, which lighteth euerie man
that cometh into the worlde', a light that the 'worlde knewe ... not'. And
that God seeks 'to mend' recalls Jesus' reply to the Pharisees' question why
His followers did not observe the established Jewish custom of fasting: '...
no man pieceth an olde garment with a piece of newe cloth: for that that
shulde fil it vp, taketh away from the garment, and the breache is worse'
(Mat. 9: 16).

Line four records the alternatives that the speaker begs to have replace
his former treatment—'breake, blow, burne, and make me new'. These,
too, derive from Scripture. The word 'breake' recalls David's similar supplication for God's favour, after he had sinned with Bathsheba: Psalm 51: 8
refers to the 'bones, *which* thou [God] hast broken' in bringing David to
repentance, and in verse 17 the contrite Psalmist declares, 'The sacrifices of
God *are* a contrite spirit: a contrite & broken heart ...' (cf. Ps. 2: 9).
'[B]low', intensifying the 'breathe' of line 2, requests a violent visitation of
God's spirit that echoes Isaiah 40: 7: 'The grasse withereth, the floure
fadeth, because the Spirit of the Lord bloweth vpon it ...'. '[B]urne'
reminds us that the Lord is 'like a purging fyre' who shall 'fine the sonnes
of Leui ...' (Mal. 3: 2-3), and the speaker's request to be made 'new'
accords with Paul''s statement that '... if anie man *be* in Christ, *let him be* a
new creature' (II Cor. 5: 17).

Though the initial phrase 'Batter my hart' is—or can be read to
be—metaphorically consistent with the conceit of the besieged city developed later, I do not find the language of this quatrain figuratively uniform
in every detail and therefore do not read a single, imaginally consistent conceit in the octave of this poem (what would it mean to 'mend' a town, for
example?).[8] The octave is thematically unified, however, since Donne has
relied on various Biblical descriptions of God's dealings with humans to
establish four sets of alternative terms, each set of which makes a metaphorically consistent unit in the poem, even where the individual parts
would not so harmonise if quoted in their original Scriptural contexts.[9]
Furthermore, Donne has carefully selected and disposed the verbs of lines 2
and 4 to indicate just what kind of experience he is asking God for. The
Scriptural passages alluded to in line 2 all portray God and man in potential
or formal relationship, not in real union: God seeks admittance to the
human heart, sustains the creature with breath, proffers spiritual illumina-

tion, makes reform possible. But line 4 calls for something more radical and real: God must break through the door, send a blast of His spirit, scorch out impurities, recreate the inner man. This line clearly describes a religious conversion, an overpowering manifestation of God's spirit that breaks down all barriers between Him and His estranged child. In other Holy Sonnets, we see the persona quail in a terrible sense of sinfulness, contemplate the crucifixion, even envision his own future glorification, but none of these poems seems so urgent, so essential to the speaker's actual spiritual life as this in which he utterly prostrates himself before the will of his Maker.

The second quatrain supports this reading of the first with a conceit depicting the speaker as 'an vsurp'd towne' ineptly defended by the 'weake or vntrew' viceroy, Reason, a description that accords with Paul's assertion in Romans 1: 20 that human understanding should be adequate to keep one on the Godly path (the conceit of these lines may derive something from Paul's image in II Timothy 2: 26 of the devil as a spiritual bandit who sets 'snare[s]' for the unsuspecting). Then the sestet introduces a metaphor of Christ and the soul as lovers and records the speaker's final, desperate plea for divine intervention:

> Yet dearly I love you, and would be loved faine:
> But ame betroth'd vnto your enemy:
> Diuorce me vnty or breake that knott agayne,
> Take me to you, emprison me, for I
> Except you enthrall me neuer shalbe free,
> Nor euer chast except you rauishe mee.   (9-14)

Looming largely in the background here is what the Geneva Bible entitles *'AN EXCELLENT SONG which was Salomons'*, and the 'Argument' affixed by the Genevan editors is worth quoting: 'In this Song, Salomón by moste swete and comfortable allegories and parables describeth the perfite loue of Iesus Christ, the true Salomón and King of peace, and the faithful soule or his Church, which he hathe sanctified and appointed to be his spouse, holy, chast, and without reprehension'. Of course, New Testament precedents for Donne's sexual imagery are not uncommon (cf. Rev. 21: 9 and Eph. 5: 22-25, e.g.), and one of the most apposite in the present case is II Corinthians 11: 2: '... I haue prepared you for one housband, to present you *as* a pure virgine to Christ ...'. From this metaphor derives much of the substance of the sonnet's sestet: the 'betroth[al]' to Satan (called Christ's 'enemie' in Matthew 13: 39), which reflects the speaker's as-yet-unregenerate nature; the request for divorce, elaborated in still other Biblical language (cf. Lk. 16: 13 or Isa. 58: 6: 'Is not this yᵉ fasting, that I [the Lord] haue chosen, to loose the bands of wickednes ... and that ye breake euery yoke?'); the desire to be ravished. The image of siege in the second quatrain finally culminates in lines 12-13, lines which echo such scriptural verses as Romans 6: 18—'Being then made fre from sinne, ye are made the seruants of righteousnes'—and John 8: 36—'If the Sōne therefore shal make you free, ye shalbe fre in dede'. The last four lines complete the sonnet in a masterly way, both harmonising the sexual and military imagery of the middle lines and, in using paradox, relating that synthesis to the first quatrain rhetorically. Perhaps such an intricately fashioned poem is the necessary vehicle for such a crucial and complex theme.[10]

* * *

In the foregoing discussion I have attempted to locate this poem generally within the Petrarchan sphere of discourse and to demonstrate some of its specific linguistic debts to Scripture. But the language of the sonnet obviously connects with that of a number of Donne's other poems—some quite secular/profane indeed—and I should like further to suggest a couple of specific interconnections between this poem and poems by Shakespeare and Sidney.

Perhaps because we have in recent years come to understand the intertextuality of poems in more sophisticated (and, I think, more accurate) ways, current readers are likely to see in this poem intra-canonical echoes that a previous generation would have missed. As has been recalled above, Scripture itself provides warrant for sexual language in describing the relationship of God and the soul, and once we begin to think in those terms, 'Batter my hart' begins to reverberate with echoes from Donne's Ovidian love elegies. Exulting over the body of his mistress, the audacious speaker of 'Elegie: Loves Warre' exclaims 'Here let me parle, *batter*, bleede, and dy [emphasis added]' (this is Donne's only other poetic use of the word 'batter'); and the impatient lover of 'Elegie: Going to Bed' importunes

Come, Madam, come, all rest my powers defie,
Until I *labour*, I in *labour* lie.
The foe oft-times, having the foe in sight,
Is tir'd with *standing* though he never fight ... [emphases added]

and does not scruple to develop his invitation in explicitly religious terms. I am not prepared to argue that every iteration of a word within a poet's canon necessarily forges a meaningful link with every other, but I would suggest that these repetitions of 'batter', 'labour', and 'stand' are significant and intentional, and in what follows I shall explain what I think they mean.[11]

The clue to understanding this matter lies in the aforementioned 'What yf this present were the worlds last night?', which characterises a former period of waywardness in the speaker-poet's life as an 'idolatree' spent in the pursuit of 'prophane Mistressis'. By alluding in 'Batter my heart' to his previous licentious uses of such words as 'stand' and 'labour' in the love elegies, I would argue, Donne first of all precisely specifies the kinds of guilt and corruption (the sins) of which he prays to be absolved and chastened. But this is not all: in defining his confession of sin and prayer for conversion against the priapic *insouciance* of the earlier love elegies, Donne greatly increases the credibility and power of his current spiritual posture, for we see that this speaker is not simply someone who happens to know that Scripture sanctions a description of the relationship of God and the soul in marital/sexual terms, but an experienced wooer who in the past has impudently flaunted his sexual successes and dominant maleness. For such a speaker verbally to relinquish his masculinity and cast himself in a subservient female part—to decline to the exact opposite of all that he has gloried in being before—is to dramatise his abjectness and verify the sincerity of his motives in the strongest possible terms. Finally, I would suggest that in alluding to the love elegies in the specific vocabulary of this sonnet, Donne consciously intends to rehabilitate the language of his former carnality and make it fit for a higher purpose. He seeks to redeem the language of Petrarchism, in other words, to cleanse it of the 'caustic' and the 'vile' and to devote it to sacred employments.

Even as we hear the language of this speaker's former eroticism in the words of the sonnet, we ought also, I think, to detect explicit echoes of 'Satyre III' in the sonnet's word 'stand': '[God] made thee to *stand* / Sentinell in his worlds garrison' (30-31); 'to *stand* inquiring right, is not to stray' (78); 'on a huge hill, / Cragged, and steep, Truth *stands*' (79-80); 'men do not *stand* / In so ill case, that God hath with his hand / Sign'd Kings blanck-charters to kill whom they hate ... [emphases added]' (89-91). Though there is insufficient space here fully to trace the implications of this link, in general terms I think the connection signals an intention to return to the essential subject matter of the satire, but to rewrite what the poet had formerly cast as a medieval quest-for-truth narrative in the more modern form of the Petrarchan sonnet cycle. Indeed, the sonnet does show Donne more movingly and personally (and, perhaps, more Calvinistically) engaged than he had been a dozen years before.[12] In contrast to the confident, public, hortatory declamation of the satire, the language of the sonnet is anxious, private, and supplicatory; and in the sonnet the speaker seems more experienced and sympathetic—and, finally, more credible—than he had been in the satire.

* * *

Though the fact has not much affected the practice of critics, we have known since at least the appearance of Helen Gardner's *John Donne: The Divine Poems* in 1952 that 'Batter my hart' was not among the first group of Holy Sonnets Donne wrote and circulated.[13] Along with 'Spitt in my face ye Iewes', 'Why ame I by all Creatures wayted on?', and 'What yf this present were the worlds last night?', 'Batter my hart' was in fact one of four sonnets Donne wrote after he had already composed and circulated an original group of twelve; and—as Theodore Sherman has recently shown— the final version of the work we call the Holy Sonnets, a twelve-poem sequence that includes these four new poems, is the end-product of at least three authorial revisions.[14] The major instance of revision entails Donne's composition of four new sonnets, corollary abandonment of four of the originals, and rearrangement of the new twelve-poem group; and we might wonder what lay behind this move. Or, to approach this issue from a some-what different direction, we might wonder *when* he decided to effect this revision. Though not all parts of her argument on the dating of the Holy Sonnets are equally plausible, Gardner's suggestion that at least the first version of the Holy Sonnets must have existed by late summer 1609 (when Cecelia Bulstrode died and Donne penned the elegy beginning 'Death I recant') is persuasive; and this postulation, along with the fact that Donne did revise the sequence and that 'Batter my hart' emerged as part of that revision prompts the brief mention of two final instances of intertextuality between this sonnet and other poems.

Anyone alerted to look for it by Donne's choice of the Sidneyan sonnet form can find a great deal of what used to be called the 'influence' of *Astrophil and Stella* on Donne's Holy Sonnets. And no sonnet in Donne's group interconnects with this ancestral text so extensively as 'Batter my hart'. In Donne's poem, for example, we might hear echoes of Sidney's 36th sonnet:

> *Stella*, whence doth this new assault arise,
> A conquerd, yelden, ransackt heart to winne?
> Whereto long since, through my long battred eyes,
> Whole armies of thy beauties entred in.

> And there long since, *Love* thy Lieutenant lies,
> My forces razde, thy banners raisd within ...[15]

but the language of Sidney's 'Fourth song' forges the most direct and telling connection between the two works. Set at night when the old folks have already gone to bed, the 'Fourth song' explicitly records Astrophil's attempt to seduce a reluctant Stella, whose resistance is denoted in the demurring refrain 'No, no, no, no, my Deare, let be'. After the speaker has gone to great lengths to demonstrate that time and place both do then adhere, the last stanza comes across as highly ambiguous—we simply cannot be certain whether Astrophil gets his way or not because of the possible inversion/*double entendre* of the final line. Most significant for the present discussion, however, is the refrain reiterated throughout Astrophil's importunity—'Take me to thee, and thee to me'— which carries a specific and insistent sexual meaning. This is, of course, the phrase Donne quotes in line 12 in 'Batter my hart', though Donne uses the plural form 'you' rather than Sidney's 'thee', and this quotation, taken together with other closely parallel language and Donne's use of the older poet's sonnet form, seems to link Donne's sonnet—indeed, his whole revised cycle—with Sidney's in an unmistakable way.

Some might see in this link a retaliatory gesture, as though Donne were saying to the ghost of Sidney, 'Here is how you should have written your cycle!' Indeed, there is a certain theory of influence that would require this interpretation.[16] I should like to make a somewhat different point, however —that when Donne decided to write sonnets in the Sidneyan mode, he necessarily rejected the option of writing them in other forms. And the form most conspicuously *not* imitated in these sonnets is that of Shakespeare, whose sonnets were first published in 1609, the year in which Donne's sonnets were perhaps written or perhaps finally revised. Indeed, it is tempting to wonder whether the imminent or recent publication of Shakespeare's sonnets did not play at least some part in stimulating Donne to issue the short-but-splendid, rhyme-linked sequence of sonnets within which 'Batter my hart' consists, a sequence that has come to be regarded as a major achievement in the genre.

Notes

1   Rosalie Colie, *The Resources of Kind: Genre-Theory in the Renaissance*, edited by Barbara K. Lewalski (Berkeley, 1973). See especially Chapter 1, 'Genre-Systems and the Functions of Literature'.

2   Leah Jonas, 'John Donne', in *The Divine Science: The Aesthetic of Some Repre-sentative Seventeenth-Century English Poets*. Columbia University Studies in Eng-lish and Comparative Literature (New York, 1940), 151: 273-279, brings together Donne's few scattered remarks on the art of poetry.

3   Quoted in F.E. Halliday, *A Shakespeare Companion* (Baltimore, 1964), 312.

4   Quoted from F.E. Hutchinson, *The Works of George Herbert* (Oxford, 1941), 206.

5   I quote Donne's Holy Sonnets from the text in the Westmoreland ms. as edited in Theodore J. Sherman, 'A Critical Edition of the Holy Sonnets of John Donne'. Dissertation University of Southern Mississippi, 1993. Other quotations of Donne's poetry are from *The Complete Poetry of John Donne*, edited by John T. Shawcross (New York, 1967).

6   I quote Scripture throughout this essay from *The Geneva Bible: A Facsimile of the 1560 Edition*, edited by Lloyd C. Berry (Madison and London, 1969).

7   See J.L. Jackson and W. E. Weese, '... "Who Only Stand and Wait": Milton's Sonnet "On His Blindness"', *Modern Language Notes* 72 (1957), 91-93, who cite Paul's words in Ephesians on the concept of 'standing' as an active Christian pos-ture. The concept is also important in *Paradise Regained*, of course.

8   Between 1953 and 1963 a still-useful critical exchange on this sonnet, including extended analysis of its imagery, was carried out in the pages of the *Explicator*, *Modern Language Notes*, and *College English*. Contributors included J.C. Leven-son (*Explicator* 11, Item 31, and 12, Item 36), George Herman (*Explicator* 12, Item 18), George Knox (*Explicator* 15, Item 2), A.L. Clements (*Modern Language Notes* 76, 484-489), and John E. Parish (*College English* 24, 299-302).

9   This is essentially a New Critical understanding of the function of poetic language, one aptly summarised in Wendy Steiner, 'The Case for Unclear Thinking: The New Critics versus Charles Morris', *Critical Inquiry* 6 1979): 259: 'Rather than simplifying things by eliminating troublesome asystemic factors, as science does in formulating its rules and concepts, art is all-inclusive and hence "ironic". It con-tains its own contradictions within it and manages to endow all elements with validity in a structure reinforced, paradoxically, by the otherwise incompatible nature of its components'. Such points in a poem as this, of course, are precisely where the deconstructionist first inserts the crowbar.

10   Grammatically the poem is structured as a dramatic opening plea based on impera-tive verbs (II. 1-4), a narrative account written in the indicative mood (II. 5-10), and a concluding dramatic plea that again employs the imperative (II. 11-14). The structure of the poem thus enacts its theme, as the sestet 'batters' the octave, breaking it into the opening and concluding quatrains.

11   In reviewing Stephen Booth's *Shakespeare's Sonnets* 2(New Haven, 1977), Philip Brockbank, 'The Semantics of the Sonnets', *TLS* 23 June 1978: 686, cautions that in sorting through a poet's canon in quest of possible and potential resonances amongst words, critics should take care to ascertain that any such linkages are actually validated by the verbal 'order of the poem'.

12   Dennis Flynn, '"Awry and Squint": the Dating of Donne's Holy Sonnets', *John Donne Journal* 7 (1988): 43, suggests that the Holy Sonnets 'may ... have been written in the 1590s'. I have here accepted a later date of composition for the Holy Sonnets, but even if they and the Satyres were both composed in the 1590s, my point about the relationship of 'Batter my hart' and 'Satyre III' would still hold.

13   (Oxford, 1952). See especially pp. xxxvii-lv.
14   Sherman's work on the Holy Sonnets will be substantially incorporated in volume 7, part 1, of The Variorum Edition of the Poetry of John Donne, forthcoming from Indiana University Press.
15   Quoted from *The Poems of Sir Philip Sidney*, edited by William A. Ringler, Jr. (Oxford, 1962) 182-183.
16   See Harold Bloom, *The Anxiety of Influence* (New York, 1973).

13

JOHN DONNE AS MEDIEVALIST

DOMINIC BAKER-SMITH

Coleridge remarks in his *Table-Talk* that a defining feature of Donne's religion is its emphasis on the cross, and any survey of his writings will confirm the accuracy of this observation. Not the cross as a banner or rallying cry, or as a focus for subjective emotion, but the cross as the ultimate paradox, a *coincidentia oppositorum* in the manner that Augustine describes it in the *Confessions*:

> for us was he unto you both the Victor and the Victim, and therefore the Victor because the Victim; for us was he unto you both the Priest and the Sacrifice, and therefore the Priest because the Sacrifice: born your Son, he changes us from slaves into your sons by becoming a slave.[1]

The act of meditation abbreviates the distinct stages of a process into the instantaneous recognition of Christ's power, a recognition which underlies the charged conceit of Donne's 'Upon the Annunciation and Passion falling upon one day. 1608', a fusion of events conveyed in medieval iconography by a cross of lilies:

> All this, and all betweene, this day hath showne,
> Th'abridgement of Christ's story, which makes one
> (As in plain Maps, the furthest West is East)
> Of the Angel's *Ave*, and *Consummatum est*.[2]

The abridgement here offers its own variation on the turn of the ninth-century hymn 'Ave Maris Stella' which uses the reversal of *Eva* into *Ave* to bond the fatal apple with Gabriel's salutation, the very moment that initiates redemption. The common feature of this particular kind of wit is the collapse of temporal process to provoke an instantaneous perception or epiphany of the whole economy of redemption; hence the centrality of the cross, not only as the fulfilment of the types of Old Testament history but as an awesome illustration of the paradox of the Incarnation by which a 'Sun' can by 'rising set, and by that setting endlesse day beget'.[3] The victim is again the victor, the meeting point for contrary modes of being.

Donne's thoroughly Augustinian interest in the faculty of memory has been noticed often enough. At bottom it is a way of reading events and allotting them their place in the ordained scheme of things: for him typology is more than an historical device since it reinforces the individual's sense that there is a narrative order behind events, one that extends even to the humdrum frustrations of a scholar refused preferment. In fact memory—*stomachus animae* in the phrase Donne adopts from Augustine— is the mental space or gallery where the drama of our salvation is displayed, 'Thou hast a good and perfect memory, if it remembers all the Holy Ghost proposes in the Bible ... This is the true contracting, and the true extending of the memory, to *Remember the Creator*'.[4] Put this way its function may sound impersonal, but Donne is always anxious to stress *applicatio*, the projection of the subject into the sacred space of memory; in the Whitsunday sermon of 1628 he recalls how,

> They had wont to call Pictures in the Church, the lay-man's book, because in them, he that coulde not reade at all, might read much. The ignorantest man that is, even he that cannot reade a Picture, even a blinde man, hath a better book in himself; in his owne memory he may reade many a history of God's goodnesse to him (*Sermons*, VIII, 216).

The memory is, quite literally, the Holy Ghost's pulpit. Not only do Donne's words provide an apt commentary on Protestant interiorisation of received iconography but they also illuminate the manner in which the Bible can be read as a repertory of roles, a wardrobe (to adopt Donne's own comparison) which can offer something for our wearing (*Sermons*, III, 367). The pattern of individual testing and grace points to the events of sacred history and these in their turn find their true scope in the falling and rising of the true Sun, Christ. The capacity of such a reference system to offer consolation and strength is evident enough (Archbishop Laud's typological comparison of his own plight on the scaffold with that of the Israelites crossing the Red Sea is one compelling example), and Donne found relief from his own uncertainties in just such a sense of religion as a mode of relating to the scheme of things. It also provided him with the basis for his religious use of wit, understood as nothing other than a system for conveying relationships. In this, as Walter Ong pointed out many years ago, he displays a marked affinity to the liturgical poetry of the Middle Ages.[5]

Humanism invented the Middle Ages, those dreary, gothic centuries which divided classical culture from its renaissance. Purists like Roger Ascham cast medieval literature on the dunghill; or, at least, that is what he would have liked to have done—in reality medieval Latin literature survived in some form in the law, the church and the universities. The Elizabethan revival of interest in things medieval was substantially political in its origins. Chivalry took on new life to allow the political role of a female monarch, and when the Society of Antiquaries was founded in 1588 through the initiative of William Camden, Clarenceux King-at-Arms, much of its energy went into investigating feudal tenures and service. So it is not surprising to find one member of the Society, the herald Francis Thynne, who also happened to be a member of Lincoln's Inn and a friend of Donne's employer Sir Thomas Egerton, preparing a paper on the duties and rights of the office of Earl Marshall for its new incumbent, the Earl of Essex. Sir Robert Cotton, that assiduous collector of medieval manuscripts, drew up a comparable report on the office of High Steward, probably for Henry Howard, later Earl of Northampton. Given the constitutional blackhole that threatened on the death of the ageing queen, a partnership of aristocrats and antiquarians made good sense.[6]

Something of this can be detected in the heightened projection of the Order of the Garter as an instrument of aristocratic participation in national life. The poetic celebration of these concerns by George Peele praises two knights or knights-to-be of the order, Henry Percy, ninth Earl of Northumberland (the 'wizard' Earl), to whom 'The Honour of the Garter' (1593) is dedicated, and Henry Wriothesley, third Earl of Southampton, who is compared in 'Anglorum Feriae' (1595) to the romance hero Bevis of Southampton. The medieval conventions adopted by Peele are reinforced in his Garter poem by an intimacy with the history of the Order which can only have come from access to its archives. These two peers, both of whom were to have some degree of familiarity with Donne, were of course important patrons and collectors (and, incidentally, concerned about toleration of Catholics); the collection of books and manuscripts which Southampton presented to St John's College, Cambridge, in the 1630s—valued at £360— was almost entirely made up of medieval religious writings, with Gower as the only secular author.[7] The importance of such developments in promoting an interest in pre-humanistic culture cannot be doubted; the 1590s are the decade of *The Faerie Queene*, as well as the full-flowering of the history play. They also cover Donne's period as a student at the Inns of Court.

This hasty sketch may serve to suggest some of the forces at work to encourage a positive interest in medieval studies at the very period when Donne was attaining intellectual maturity. But in his case there is a more narrowly defined interest to be considered, that is his attention to medieval religious writing. While the Society of Antiquaries, substantially made up of lawyers or those with legal training, was concerned with political and national issues, Reformation disputes had already generated a religious antiquarianism. Matthias Flacius, whose martyrology of reform influenced John Foxe, initiated with his collaborators on the Magdeburg 'Centuries' (*Historia Ecclesiae Christi*, Magdeburg 1561-74) the classic Protestant formulation of history as a conflict of the true and the false churches. History was of the essence, and the Anglican claims to have restored authentic observance could only further stimulate the investigation of old records. For a person like John Donne, haunted by questions of religious affiliation from his days at Lincoln's Inn at least until his ordination in 1615, reading in these materials must have been compulsive.

There is only space in this essay to touch briefly on the significance of medieval materials for Donne's poetry, but one can start by asserting their special relevance to his occasional religious verse—meaning for practical purposes those poems which extend beyond the limits of the meditative sonnet. Indeed, one important feature of these occasional poems (and for reasons that will become evident I include among them 'A Litanie') is the way they attempt to mediate between personal situation and public forms. 'Goodfriday' is the most obvious example. So it is not surprising if they seem to take on an almost liturgical character derived from Donne's familiarity with early Christian and medieval hymnography. Some of the greatest examples, the hymns on the cross by Venantius Fortunatus for instance, might still be found in the harshly reduced range of the Tridentine missal, but a large body of relevant material was in any case available by means of collections of antiquities. Humanistic strictures were most severely directed at scholastic authors; pre-scholastic Latin was tolerated and its hymns approved. This was partly because such writers still reflected a patristic glow and their style was intensely biblical; just as significantly, they predated many of the abuses that had given rise to the Reformation. The Catholic George Cassander, whose irenical theological writings captured Donne's interest, also published a collection *Hymni Ecclesiastici* at Cologne in 1556 and this was reprinted at Paris in 1616. An energetic early editor was George Fabricius who produced several volumes 'ex poetis veteribus Christianis' during the 1560s. But, as has already been suggested, it is after the *Historia Ecclesiae Christi* of the Magdeburg Centuriators and the Catholic response led by Cardinal Baronius that antiquities receive intense scrutiny and whole archives begin to appear in print, frequently—as with the English antiquarians—with some political motive in the background. Melchior Goldast, councillor to the Emperor Rudolph II, produced in 1606 his massive collection *Alamannicorum rerum Scriptores* which includes the life of the monk-poet Notker Balbulus written by the monastic chronicler Ekkerhard. We shall return to Notker in a moment. The Jesuit Christoph Brouwer, born at Arnhem in 1561, edited writings of Venantius Fortunatus

and Rabanus Maurus as well as records of the ancient Christian centre of
Fulda and the lives of early German saints. He was also a correspondent of
Justus Lipsius and probably fed him material for his *De Cruce libri tres*, the
first edition of which appeared in 1592.

With this book we come on one that we can be sure Donne read attent-
ively, since the list of cruciform analogies given in his early poem 'The
Crosse' exactly matches the patristic conceits illustrated in one of Lipsius'
plates.[8] *De Cruce* appeared in numerous editions down to 1675, and one
cam imagine Donne's interest with the figure of Lipsius himself, a scholar
of international reputation who had hovered, ill-at-ease, on both sides of the
confessional divide. Lipsius' book was intended to mark his final return to
Catholicism (and his departure from Leiden), and he apparently received
help from a number of Jesuit correspondents.

Apart from a survey of classical references to the material details of
crucifixion, *De Cruce* also contains a vast anthology of patristic passages
on the mystery of the Cross. When Lipsius' plate of *inventiunculae* (that is
his own rather dismissive term) is set by Donne's poem the debt is clear,

> Who can deny mee power, and liberty
> To stretch mine armes, and mine owne Crosse to be?
> Swimme, and at every stroake, thou art thy Crosse,
> The Mast and yard make one, where seas do tosse.
> Looke downe, thou spiest out Crosses in small things;
> Looke up, thou seest birds rais'd on crossed wings;
> All the Globes frame, and spheares, is nothing else
> But the Meridians crossing Parallels.
> Materiall Crosses then, good physicke bee,
> And yet spirituall have chiefe dignity.

If the learned philologist finds this kind of thing mildly embarrassing,
Donne shows a more positive appreciation of

> Thine ancient *servants*, whose delight it was to write after thy *Copie*, to
> proceede the same way in their expositions of the *Scriptures*, and in
> their comprising both of *publike liturgies*, and of *private prayers* to
> thee, to make accesses to thee in such kind of language, as thou wast
> pleased to speake to them, in a *figurative*, in a *Metaphoricall language*
> [9]
> ...

Donne, we may conclude, was a better medievalist than Lipsius, better able
to enter the imaginative world of the Fathers than the learned interpreter of
Stoicism.

The passage I have just quoted comes, admittedly, from a mature work,
the *Devotions*, but it is in the spirit of his earlier reading. Take that reference to 'their composing both of *public liturgies*, and of *private prayers* to
thee': in an undated letter to Sir Henry Goodyer (it must date from 1608,
the year of *Biathanatos* when Donne was devastated by neuritis) he refers
to his own 'meditation in verse, which I call a Litany'.[10] It is interesting
that Donne is so alert to the discrepancy between the private nature of
meditation and the public character of a litany since he goes on to justify
his composition by appealing to two litanies he has encountered 'amongst
ancient annals, I mean some 800 years', in which private concerns and
public petitions are similarly linked. These are by two monks, Ratpertus
and Notker, about whom he then gives some details. Both of them had been
monks at the great Swiss abbey of St. Gall in the ninth century, Notker
playing a key role in the evolution of medieval hymnography through his
elaboration of the regular sequence.[11] Donne's information, which characteristically he quotes inaccurately, together with 'Epigrammata seu Hymni
sacri illustrium virorum antiquorum patrum monasterii S. Galli', can all be
found in another massive antiquarian collection, the *Lectiones Antiquae* by
a Nijmegen canonist Henricus Canisius, professor at Ingoldstadt, having
been copied for him 'ex membranis antiquis' by one of the monks, Dom
Jodocus Metzler. Volume V of this collection in which the St. Gall material
appears was only published at Ingolstadt in 1608, so one is faced with the
likelihood that Donne saw it so soon because he had already been involved
by Thomas Morton in vetting Jesuit controversial literature, Ingolstadt
being a particular important source. Canisius declares that these antiquities
merit publication 'so that ancient piety may be made available to our
times'.[12] It seems likely, then, that this is what Donne responded to, lock-
ing his own tribulations into the modes of a world that was innocent of late-
medieval or Reformation disputes.

Donne informs Goodyer that it had been Pope Nicholas V (Canisius
actually states Nicholas III) who so valued the devotion of the two monks
'that he canonized both their Poems, and commanded them for publike
service in their Churches [that is, in the dependencies of St. Gall]: mine is
for lesser Chappels, which are my friends ...'. It was with Goodyer in particular that, at this difficult period in his career, Donne exchanged letters
which are suggestive of a common attitude on issues of church allegiance,
rating personal motivation above formal adherence. He sees his own litany
as all the more acceptable since 'neither the Roman Church need call it

defective, because it abhors not the particular mention of the blessed
Triumphers in heaven; nor the Reformed can discreetly accuse it of attribut-
ing more than a rectified devotion ought to doe'. Apart from Mary, no individual saints are named in Donne's poem; instead, although we are taken
through the usual categories of holiness, the familiar pattern of intercession
is suppressed. Instead the poem offers thanks, for 'that faire blessed
Mother-maid', for the grace manifested in 'thine Angels', 'thy Patriarches',
'thy Eagle-sighted Prophets'; as the possessive pronoun makes clear, the
entire litany is addressed directly to God, the source of all holiness in the
Saints. In fact the originality of the conception is well illustrated in stanza
xiv, as the litany progresses from invocation to petition, 'O Lord deliver
us'; but the danger we pray to avoid is that of overconfidence in our own
prayers:

> Heare this prayer Lord, O Lord deliver us
> From trusting in those prayers, though pour'd out thus.

So the initiative is reserved to God, but the intervention of grace in time by
way of the saints is joyfully celebrated. The remarkable seizure and elaboration of received motifs by the private imagination which generates the
power of Donne's later hymns has its origins here in the personal modification of romanesque piety. This rectification of 'pietas antiqua' for the use
of his intimate friends was primarily an act of reassurance to himself, a
projection through literary means of the authentic Church he so anxiously
sought after.

The idea of the cross directs attention to the very ground of redemption, Christ's submission to death; but if the idea is not controversial, the
image of the cross might be. In 1592, the year that Lipsius published the *De
Cruce*, the learned Jesuit Jacobus Gretser published his polemical tract
Lutherus Staurophilus to show that while Luther had honoured the image of
the cross, his followers had rejected it (it is the argument which Herbert
presents in *De signaculo crucis*, 'Cur tanta sufflas probra in innocuam Cru-
cem?'). Gretser, whose name is inserted into *Ignatius his Conclave* presumably for writing a hostile commentary on James I's *Basilikon Doron*, was
another professor at Ingolstadt, and his extended researches on devotion to
the cross resulted in three substantial volumes *De Sancta Cruce,* which
appeared there between 1598 and 1608. In contrast to Lipsius whose aim is
to illuminate the historical evidence about crucifixion, Gretser seizes with
enthusiasm on anything that he can find relevant to the cult of the cross—
hymns, texts from the Greek fathers, numismatic inscriptions, even pilgrim
maps. The *De Sancta Cruce* offers a source book for the study of a *mental-*

ité rather than an historical event and in that lies its importance. Given his access to books from Ingolstadt and his proven interest in Lipsius' study, it would be surprising if Donne had not peered into Gretser's eclectic volumes. Certainly, he shared the spirit of Gretser's argument, 'that God always from the beginning wished to keep the figure of the cross in the eyes of man, and so ordered things that man can do almost nothing without encountering the image of the cross'.[13] If Donne's 'The Crosse' amounts to little more than the rehearsal of an ingenious mnemonic system, by 'Goodfriday' this has evolved into a mature theological perception, one which provides that almost casuistical balancing of private anxieties and public forms which Donne first achieved in 'A Litanie'.

'God loves not innovations' Donne observed, 'old doctrines, old disciplines, old words and formes of speech in his service, God loves best'. (*Sermons*, II, 305); provided of course that they are 'rectified'. Innovation in the sense that Donne implies here upsets the balance between the individual believer and the historical community, it ruptures the continuum of memory. It is interesting that Terence Cave, against the background of Gallicanism, has pointed to the period 1590 to 1610 as the highpoint for the assimilation of medieval Latin hymns into French devotional poetry, a time which exactly matches Donne's own anxious search for an acceptable relationship to tradition, and it is this engagement with 'old words and formes of speech' which nourishes the strikingly liturgical character of Donne's occasional religious writing from 'A Litanie' to the Hymnes of his maturity.[14]

Donne is particularly fond of the image of tuning or playing an instrument to convey the religious life: behind the distractions of business, travel or sickness, he clings to a vivid sense of the Church as a synchronic community presented as 'this universall Quire' ('A Litanie'), or 'thy Quire of Saints' ('Hymne to God my God'), or in the poem on the Sidney Psalms as the instrument played by Christ, 'The Organist is hee / Who hath tun'd God and Man, the Organ we'. In just this way liturgy is intended to tune, to assimilate personal circumstances to archetypal roles—to canonise them, in fact. That Donne could, as Walton reports, have 'A Hymne to God the Father' set to music and sung by the choristers of St Paul's indicates how far to him the poem transcended the merely private; as with the sermons, the subject self is made available to any who, in Herbert's words, 'would thrust his heart / Into these lines' ('Obedience'). In this respect, the plan of Henricus Canisius to make ancient hymns once more available had a richer harvest than even he might have expected.

Notes

1   '... pro nobis tibi victor et victima, et ideo victor, quia victima, pro nobis tibi sacerdos et sacrificium, et ideo sacerdos quia sacrificium, faciens tibi nos de servis filios de te nascendo, tibi serviendo', *Confessions*, X: 43.

2   All quotations of Donne's poetry are taken from Helen Gardner's edition of *The Divine Poems* (Oxford, 1952; rev. 1978). On the lily-cross see C.R. Pocknee, *Cross and Crucifix* (London, 1962), 65.

3   'Goodfriday, 1613'; the whole poem is a supreme example of the exploitation of Christian paradox.

4   *The Sermons of John Donne*, edited by E.M. Simpson and G.R. Potter, 10 vols (Berkeley, 1953-62) II, 246.

5   W.J. Ong, 'Wit and Mystery: A Revaluation in Medieval Latin Hymnody', *Speculum* XXII (1947): 310-341.

6   On the broad interplay of interests see for example Marie Axton, *The Queen's Two Bodies: Drama and the Elizabethan Succession* (London, 1977); Kevin Sharpe, *Sir Robert Cotton, 1586-1631: History and Politics in Early Modern England* (Oxford, 1979); Richard C. McCoy, *The Rites of Knighthood: The Literature and Politics of Elizabethan Chivalry* (Berkeley and Los Angeles, 1989).

7   G.R. Batho, 'The Library of the "Wizard" Earl', *The Library*, 5th series, XV (1960): 246-261; J.A.W. Bennett refers to Southampton's gift in *The Humane Medievalist and Other Essays* (Rome, 1982), 369, n. 12.

8   J.A.W. Bennett, *Review of English Studies*, n.s. V (1954): 168-169; see also F.P. Pickering, *Literature and Art in the Middle Ages* (London, 1970), 248-253.

9   *Devotions Upon Emergent Occasions*, 'Nineteenth Expostulation'; edited by A. Raspa (Montreal and London, 1975), 100.

10 The letter is printed in *John Donne: Selected Prose*, edited by E.M. Simpson (Oxford, 1967), 130-133.

11 See F.J.E. Raby, *Christian Latin Poetry* (Oxford, 1953), 211-215; W. von den Steinen, *Notker der Dichter und seine geistige Welt* (Berne, 1948).

12 *Lectiones Antiquae*, tomus V (Ingolstadt, 1605), 726.

13 Jacobus Gretser, *De Sancta Cruce*, tomus I (Ingolstadt, 1608), 167.

14 Terence Cave, *Devotional Poetry in France c. 1570-1613* (Cambridge, 1969), 184-186, 293.

DONNE'S REINVENTION OF THE FATHERS:
SACRED TRUTHS SUITABLY EXPRESSED

P.G. STANWOOD

> *'Wit in Divinity is nothing else, but Sacred Truths suitably expressed'*
> Robert South (1634-1716)[1]

In his *Life* of Donne, Izaak Walton describes the way in which the great preacher set to work: 'As he usually preached once a week, if not oftner, so after his Sermon he never gave his eyes rest, till he had chosen out a new Text, and that night cast his Sermon into a form, and his Text into divisions; and the next day betook himself to consult the Fathers, and so commit his meditations to his memory'.[2] Obviously, Donne makes use of the Fathers, of Augustine, Ambrose, Chrysostom, Basil, and others, both Latin and Greek. The many references to them in the sermons provide clear testimony; but *how* did he consult them—that is, in what text, or edition, or form? And *how* did he make use of them in the actual composition of the sermons? My answer to the first question must for now be brief and mainly undemonstrated or implied: I believe that Donne, when he came to compose his sermons from 1615 onwards—the date of his ordination—had already compiled a set of commonplace books filled with headings and *sententiae* extracted from patristic and later authors well suited to the exposition of scriptural texts and themes. My answer to the second question forms the subject of this essay. Since Donne seldom confers with his patristic sources directly, he often quotes inaccurately and out of context; for his aim is to recreate these sources in accordance with his immediate rhetorical purpose. In their edition of the *Sermons*, Potter and Simpson provide an extended discussion of Donne's sources, with appended lists that identify a number of passages from St. Augustine quoted or referred to by Donne and as well a list of later commentators that he also cites.[3] But these editors' interest is chiefly to enumerate and to give an inventory, pausing only to discuss in broad and somewhat misleading terms Donne's use of Augustine. So there is still an obvious need for a more detailed examination of the particular way in which Donne employs his sources.

I began this investigation by using the index of the Latin Fathers based on the Corpus Christianorum now available on CD-Rom, called CETEDOC, making my search on the dedicated terminal in the library of the Pontifical

Institute of Medieval Studies at St. Michael's College in the University of
Toronto. Since Donne usually cites his patristic authorities very generally,
at best with a marginal note, for example, to 'August.' or 'Gregor.' or
'Tertul.', one often has great difficulty in locating the exact reference, especially in so copious a writer as Augustine. Yet to identify these quotations
illuminates Donne's homiletic practice and his religious imagination. With
the assistance of the computer, and ready access to almost all of the works
of Augustine—and a number of other Latin Fathers—I located many of
Donne's elusive citations and could begin to understand more clearly his
compositional mode. For convenience in reporting the results of my initial
study, I shall look primarily at one, possibly early (though undated) sermon, on Psalm 32: 1, 2, the second of the penitential psalms—a group of
psalms that was a favourite with Donne, providing him with texts for twen-
ty-one sermons: 'Blessed is he whose transgression is forgiven, whose sinne
is covered; blessed is the man, unto whom the Lord imputeth not iniquitie,
and in whose spirit there is no guile' (9: 250-73).[4] The sermon is characteristic of Donne, with the usual introduction, division of the text into parts,
with exposition and proofs, and a peroration; it is also typical in the arrangement and handling of patristic authority. Let us see in a few examples
how Donne confers with the Fathers.

At the beginning of this sermon, Donne 'proposes' the text, expressing
concern that the title of the psalm should also be part of its first verse.
Donne gives a passage from Augustine's *De civitate dei* (18.38.7-9): *'Vt in
Authoritate apud nos non essent, nimia fecit eorum Antiquitas'*. Augustine
is referring to the canon of the scriptures, some writings of which on
account of their antiquity must be regarded with suspicion. 'The Church
suspected them', Donne says in paraphrase; 'but that reason alone, is so far
from being enough to exclude any thing from being part of the Scriptures,
as that we make it justly an argument, for the receiving the Titles of the
Psalmes into the Body of Canonicall Scriptures' (9: 250). Donne is quoting
Augustine not in support of his argument, but in opposition to it; he is jus-
tifying his present *invention* of the text not because of what Augustine has
said, but because of what he did not say. Augustine is not writing here
about the psalms at all, or even referring to them, but rather he is discussing
in large terms the authority of the canon. Donne's use of Augustine, while
apparently important and vivid, is curiously irrelevant; and Augustine's
comments appear so that they can be dismissed.[5]

A little later in the first 'division' of the sermon, in which title and first
verse have been declared parts of the text, Donne is examining David's
'catechism', gathered from diverse and rich sources: 'Blessed is the man'
and his liveliness in teaching, and in his finding of 'abundant impressions,

and testimonies of ... knowledge in all arts, and all kinds of learning' (9: 252). To illustrate his idea, Donne invokes classical, scriptural, and patristic authority. A close look at the references to Augustine again displays Donne's method of quotation, which is not interested so much in what the original says, but in the manner of the language and its ability for enhancing the argument. In one of his few citations in all the sermons from *De doctrina christiana* (2.40.28-35), Donne writes that 'Every man that comes from Egypt, must bring some of the Egyptians goods with him. *Quanto auro exivit suffarcinatus Cyprianus ...?*' (9: 253). Augustine is commenting on the Israelites who took away the ornaments of the Egyptians when they fled, putting such goods to better use; and similarly, the false teaching of the Egyptians unwittingly provided others, who were better informed, with knowledge that helped in the worship of one God 'through which the vain cult of idols is abolished'.[6] Donne has expanded Augustine's particularised observation to 'every man that comes from Egypt' who *must* bring some of the country's goods with him. The connection with the beginning of Psalm 32 is fragile, indeed, for Donne means only to urge that there is more in this text and in all of David's psalms than we can at first know. 'Catechisticall, and Fundamentall Doctrines' may begin in unexpected places, Donne is saying, and this is the point of his reference to Augustine's *Confessions* (3.4.7), which immediately follows the one from *De doctrina christiana*. Augustine's conversion from the world began with Cicero's *Hortensius*: '*Et surgere jam cœperam ut ad te redirem*, By that help I rose, and came towards thee' (9: 254). Donne has Augustine's general sense, though he has made him say something slightly different from what he actually wrote: '*Viluit mihi repente omnis uana spes et immortalitatem sapientiae concupiscebam aestu cordis incredibili et surgere coeperam, ut ad te redirem*' ('Suddenly, every hope became worthless to me and I yearned with unbelievable ardour of heart for the immortality of wisdom. I began to rise up, so that I might return to Thee').[7] The idea of 'help' is implicit, and the 'rising' is still expected, but not, as in Donne, already completed. Donne is writing of initial and unlikely openings to wisdom, and he dances through his illustrations—now to Justin Martyr, then to Basil, in order to declare his present theme: the usefulness of some special knowledge to a few persons, but the grandness of Christ's embracing all knowledge for the salvation of mankind. In such a process lies David's catechism.

Donne is evidently writing—or preaching—with the company of the Fathers, but not really with their exclusive support; for he reinvents them in the elaboration of his texts. This point may be well observed in the second part of the sermon on Psalm 32, that is, in the consideration of the nature of the blessedness that David praises. In defining this quality, and leading us into its further consideration, Donne says: 'And the end of knowing our selves, is to know how we are disposed for that which is our end, that is this Blessednesse; which, though it be well collected and summed by S. *Augustine, Beatus qui habet quicquid vult, & nihil mali vult,* He onely is blessed, that desires nothing but that which is good for him, and hath all that ... in those particulars, which here, in *Davids* Catechisme, constitute this Blessednesse' (9: 257). Donne here is remaking Augustine to fit into a new scheme. Borrowing from Augustine's earliest work, the dialogue *De beata vita* (AD 386), 'The Happy Life', he is rephrasing one of its statements to accord with his own present need and context. Augustine actually writes (3.21.107-8), 'Erit ... beatus, qui quod uult non habet' ('He is happy who does not have what he wishes').[8] There is more, but nothing that quite says what Donne is remembering Augustine to have said. Yet the allusion to Augustine has the sound of authenticity, though it is largely an imagined reconstruction. But these references all pass by quickly; and we must look further into the sermon for sustained development of a patristic allusion.

A third principal branch of the text deals with 'transgression', a theme to which Donne warms. The burden of sin in all its manifestations brings us down and sinks the whole world, as in the first flood, or consumes it, as in the last fire. Such a weight of so much oppression and misery recalls for Donne the memorable statement in the *Confessions* (1.13.21), *'Et quid miserius misero non miserante seipsum?* What misery can be greater, then when a miserable man hath not sense to commiserate his owne misery?' (9: 258). But Augustine is remembering his classical study, of learning to weep for the dead Dido, not for his own death in God's love: 'What is more wretched than the wretch who is not aware of his own wretchedness, who sheds tears, indeed, for the death of Dido, which occurred because of her love of Aeneas, but who does not weep over his own death which occurs because he does not love Thee, O God, Light of my heart and Bread of the inner mouth of my soul, the manly Power who espouses my mind and the bosom of my thought?'.[9] Donne omits most of Augustine's sentence with its poignant context. He has taken only the first part which is easiest to adapt to his immediate purpose; and one supposes he may have been attracted to it for its striking alliteration and inventive word play.

Yet Donne continues, in his depiction of the burdensomeness of sin, with a further reference to Augustine: 'Our first errors are out of Levity, and S. *Augustin* hath taught us a proper ballast and waight for that, *Amor Dei pondus animae,* The love of God would carry us evenly, and steadily, if we would embarke that' (9: 258). Now the word *pondus* or weight, occurs over 150 times in Augustine's works, the present instance (or one much like it) being repeated in two other sermons with the sense also of

'ballast' (1: 199, 5: 204; and cf. Augustine, *Epistola* 55, 2.10.18). Very
close to Donne's use in this sermon on Psalm 32 is the passage in the *Confessions* (13.9.10), where Augustine writes: 'Pondus meum amor meus; eo
feror, quocumque feror. Dono tuo accendimur et sursum ferimur; inardesci-
mus et imus' ('My weight is my love; by it I am carried wherever I am
carried. By Thy Gift, we are inflamed and are carried upward; we are set on
fire and we go').[10] Augustine wishes to convey the power of God's grace
against which he struggles, and yet by which he is sustained and buoyed up.
But Donne's idea is to see the weight of God's love as the steadying ballast
which one carries along with the freight of sin; Donne has turned the conceit into a navigational image, which is surely very far from Augustine's
intention. We see, then, that Donne cites Augustine very loosely but quite
imaginatively in order to achieve his own purpose. Here the citation serves
principally to excite our senses and encourage our approval of a new argument.

I have referred so far only to Donne's use of Augustine, partly because
he is the Latin Father that Donne most often cites and also because his
works are now so easily accessible—and recoverable—with computer tech-
nology. But Donne refashions not only Augustine to suit his own rhetorical
designs, but also he bends other Fathers to fit his style. The sermon on
Psalm 32 provides a good example of a passage from Tertullian (*c.* 160-
225), which Donne transforms. The instance is near the conclusion, where
Donne is celebrating God's mercy, the full antidote to sin and the source of
pardon for all iniquities. Donne is especially forceful in his acclamation by
building a series of parallel clauses whose crescendoing power leads to an
exaltation. The passage, from *De patientia* (15.1-4), begins in Tertullian,
but it ends in Donne: '*Si apud Deum deponas injuriam, ipse ultor erit*, Lay
all the injuries that thou sufferest, at Gods feet, and hee will revenge them;
Si damnum, ipse restituet; Lay all thy losses there, and he will repair them;
Si dolorem, ipse medicus; Lay downe all thy diseases there, and he shall
heale thee; *Si mortem, ipse resuscitator*, Dye in his armes, and he shall
breath a new life into thee; Add wee to *Tertullian: Si peccata, ipse sepeliet*,
lay thy sins in his wounds, and he shall bury them so deepe, that onely they
shall never have resurrection' (9:272-73). Donne is not unfaithful to Tertullian's general sense: 'Si iniuriam deposueris penes eum, ultor est; si
damnum, restitutor est; si dolorem, medicus est; si mortem, resuscitator
est'.[11] But Donne has restructured Tertullian to gain greater vividness and
dramatic intensity, notably by introducing the intensive 'ipse' in the series
of clauses, and by replacing the present with the future tense; for it is
toward 'the laver of Regeneration' that Donne means to proceed and where
he will leave his auditors at the end of his sermon. In taking up Tertullian's

confident statement of God's mercy—and patience—Donne has also expanded it with his own language in an additional clause that is grammatically parallel with the previous ones, and also extends and complicates the imagery of 'si mortem, resuscitator' (death — revival) with 'si peccata, sepeliet' (sins — burying).

In a similar way, Donne adapts Tertullian's *De resurrectione mortuum*, passages of which he intersperses in his sermon preached at St. Paul's on Easter Day, 1623, on Acts 2: 36: 'Therefore let all the house of Israel know assuredly, that God hath made that same Jesus, whom ye have crucified, both Lord and Christ'. Near the end of the sermon, where he is leading his congregation to celebrate their own resurrection in Christ's rising, Tertullian's phrases form the thread running through Donne's discourse. But they are taken from three or more non-consecutive places in *De resurrectione mortuum* (especially chapters 15.8, 8.8, 63.15), and they occur in new forms. In expanding on a hint in Tertullian, Donne says that 'when our bodies are dissolved and liquefied in the Sea, putrified in the earth, resolv'd to ashes in the fire, macerated in the ayre, *Velut in vasa sua transfunditur caro nostra*, make account that all the world is Gods cabinet, and water, and earth, and fire, and ayre, are the proper boxes, in which God laies up our bodies, for the Resurrection' (4: 359). Donne's exuberant statement has loosely absorbed and expanded Tertullian's concluding remarks (especially in 63.15), but inserted 'transfunditur caro nostra' ('our body is transformed'), which is Donne's phrase, not Tertullian's, though imaginatively ascribed to him.

Perhaps students of Donne, influenced by the tendentious judgements of some earlier editors, have long supposed that the sermons reveal significant patristic influence simply because the Fathers so often appear in his texts. This may indeed be so; but I think we must look with care at a great many more quotations to see if Donne is not in fact wresting the Fathers out of their own texts. We should not be surprised to discover that 'influence' needs redefining and may even flow in two directions; for Donne's copious invention and powerful imagination create new terms in the midst of old works.

Notes

1   See South's sermon on Matt. 13: 52, 'The Scribe Instructed', preached at St. Mary's, Oxford, 29 July 1660, in *Three Restoration Divines*, edited by Irène Simon (Paris, 1976) II, i, 245-246.

2   *The Life of Dr. John Donne*, in *Lives*, edited by George Saintsbury (London, 1924), 67.

3   See *The Sermons of John Donne*, 10 vols (Berkeley, 1954-62) 10: 295-401. Refer-
      ences to the sermons are from this edition, given by volume and page number in
      the text.

4   On the dating of this sermon, see my 'Donne's Earliest Sermons and the Peniten-
      tial Tradition', in *John Donne's Religious Imagination: Essays in Honor of John
      T. Shawcross*, edited by Raymond-Jean Frontain and Frances M. Malpezzi (Con-
      way, AR, 1995), 360-373.

5   Augustine writes: 'Quorum scripta ut apud Iudaeos et apud nos in auctoritate non
      essent, nimia fecit antiquitas, propter quam uidebantur habenda esse suspecta, ne
      proferrentur falsa proueris' ('The writings of these [Jude and Enoch] have never
      been accepted as authoritative, either by the Jews or by us Christians, but that is
      because their extreme antiquity makes us afraid of handing out, as authentic,
      works that may be forgeries'. *De civitate dei* is in the Corpus Christianorum Series
      Latina 47-48 (Turnholt, 1955). The translation is by Gerald G. Walsh and Daniel
      J. Honan in the *Fathers of the Church: Writings of Saint Augustine* (New York,
      1954) 8: 145.

6   'Nam quid aliud fecerunt multi boni fideles nostri? Nonne aspicimus quanto auro
      et argento et ueste suffarcinatus exierit de Aegypto Cyprianus doctor suauissimus
      et martyr beatissimus? quanto Lactantius? quanto Victorinus, Optatus, Hilarius, ut
      de uiuis taceam? quanto innumerabiles Graeci? Quod prior ipse fidelissimus Dei
      famulus Moyses fecerat, de quo scriptum est quod *eruditus* fuerit *omni sapientia
      Aegyptiorum*' ('For, what else have many noble and loyal members of our faith
      done? Do we not perceive with what an abundance of gold, silver and clothing that
      very eloquent teacher and blessed martyr, Cyprian, was loaded when he left
      Egypt? with what an abundance Lactantius was enriched, and Victorinus, Optatus,
      Hilary, and innumerable Greeks, not to speak of men who are still living? That
      most obedient servant of God, Moses himself, was the first to do this, and it was
      written of him that he ["was instructed in all the wisdom of the Egyptians"]'). See
      De doctrina christiana, in Corpus Christianorum Series Latina 32 (Turnholt,
      1962), translated by John J. Gavigan in *Fathers of the Church*, 2nd ed. (New
      York, 1950), 113.

7   The *Confessionum* is in Corpus Christianorum Series Latina 27, edited by Lucas
      Verheijen (Turnholt, 1981), translated by Vernon J. Bourke in *Fathers of the
      Church* (New York, 1953), 55.

8   See Corpus Christianorum Series Latina 29 (Turnholt, 1970).

9   'Quid enim miserius misero non miserante se ipsum et flente Didonis mortem,
      quae fiebat amando Aenean, non flente autem mortem suam, quae fiebat non
      amando te, deus, lumen cordis mei et panis oris intus animae meae et uirtus mari-
      tans mentem meam et sinum cogitationis meae?' The translation is by Bourke (see
      note 5), 21.

10   Translated by Bourke, p. 416.

11   Tertullian is quoted from the Corpus Christianorum Series Latina, 2 vols (Turn-
      holt, 1954).

15

DONNE AND THE PAST

JEREMY MAULE

I

Of the many books Donne read and disciplines of knowledge that he found he needed, the subjects we might now group as history seem to have given him least satisfaction. They were not necessarily unappealing, as they gave him some good matter to tease and things that he learnt from reading in them helped him to win arguments or at least make points. Still, almost no historian emerges with credit from his writings, and when he was led to imagine history as a body of knowledge (though as often as not he seems to have thought of it as just a large fat book) it was usually as a body that got in the way of more important things, and arrogated powers that Donne was unwilling to grant. How this was so, and perhaps why, this essay will try to show.

Not all historians were objectionable, of course. Donne was a friend, for example, of the great antiquary Sir Robert Cotton, and helped him in the early 1600s by drafting legal opinions in what we would now call international law.[1] But Cotton's enthusiasm for the science of records or those projects of monuments (moniments/muniments) that fuel the poetry of Spenser and Drayton seems not to have excited Donne's imagination to more than a jolly despising: 'Stranger than seaven Antiquaries studies'.[2] The joke resurfaces hoarily (it was in any case a borrowed one) in his epigram 'Antiquary': 'If in his Studie Hammon hath such care / To'hang all old strange things, let his wife beware'.[3]

Antiquaries may shade off into mere collectors, gulls like the one in Earle's character of 'An antiquary' whom 'Beggars coozen ... with musty things which they have rak't from dunghills', or the re-appearing Hammon of Donne's 'Satyre V', whose sale of antiquities turns in a hefty loss.[4] But the case is hardly better, often worse, for those historians whose practice is not in relics, but in writing. Donne is not always ungenerous—quite. From time to time, he will *use* one of the early historians of the Christian Church, Bede or Eusebius, or Rufius Festus on the early Roman empire; but none of these authors emerge with character from his deployment of them, in the way that Augustine or Tertullian or Origen do for him. Most historians, though, fare far worse than Eusebius at his hands. Sir Walter Ralegh's great attempt to syncretise biblical and classical event in *The History of the*

World is treated with solvent irony in one of Donne's *Problems*[5]—an irony ill-deserved, perhaps, as Donne's later *Essays in Divinity* (1614-15) show considerable similarities to the first three chapters of Ralegh. The resemblance, in part at least, is due to a common source, the Spanish Jesuit Benedictus Pererius' *Commentaria et Disputationes in Genesim* (1589-98);[6] but Donne is no likelier to acknowledge one debt than the other, and when Pererius comes to be mentioned by Donne, it is only to be kicked, for his inadequate appreciation of '*Francis George*, that transcending Wit'.[7]

The popular Tudor historians hardly fare better. The inclusive chroniclers from whom Shakespeare drew his histories are models for Donne of a different kind: undiscriminating, unsubstantiated, compendious gossip-mongers. Their slow folio leaves of trivialities, Donne insinuates, are the natural texts to collocate with the unshakeable bore of 'Satyre IIII'. Holinshed, by a sort of half-pun, joins the hogshead as a capacious unit of measurement:

> He takes my hand, and as a Still, which staies
> A Sembriefe, 'twixt each drop, he nigardly,
> As lothe to enrich mee, so tells many a lye.
> More than ten Hollensheads, or Halls, or Stowes,
> Of triviall houshold trash he knowes; He knowes
> When the Queene frown'd, or smil'd, and he knowes what
> A subtle States-man may gather of that;
> He knowes who loves; whom; and who by poyson
> Hasts to an Offices reversion;
> He knowes who'hath sold his land, and now doth beg
> A licence, old iron, bootes, shooes, and egge-
> shels to transport; ...
>   ... And wiser then all us,
> He knowes what Ladie is not painted.   (ll. 94-105, 107-8)

We are close here to Sir Politic Would-Be of Jonson's *Volpone*. These tattling, domestic Tacitists are impaled on Donne's anaphora: 'He knowes / ... and he knowes what / ... / He knowes who ... whom; and who ... / He knowes who ... / ... And wiser than us all / He knowes'. And *we* know, from the breathless run-on in which the metre is made to mime this gossip, that this can hardly pass for history. 'Maw' is Donne's word (as it Spenser's, for Error's 'books and papers', and Earle's antiquary)[8] for this gobbling read-all: 'But hee is worst, who (beggarly) doth chaw / Other wits fruits, and in his ravenous maw / Rankly digested, doth these things out-spue'.[9] Donne shares, it seems, Nashe's contempt for these 'lay Chronigraphers, that write of nothing but of Mayors and Sheriefs, and the deare yeere, and the great Frost'.[10]

Soon the bore of 'Satyre IIII' 'thrusts on' to Continental gossip, and Donne scouts another form of printed history:

> ... as if he undertook
> To say Gallo-Belgicus without booke
> Speakes of all States, and deeds, that have been since
> The Spaniards came, to the losse of Amyens.

The new news-books are now the target. Donne is quick to notice that the *Mercurius Gallo-Belgicus* had begun its Annual Register in 1588, the year the Spaniards came; his terminus, 'the losse of Amyens', signifies what Faculty syllabuses call the present day—the town fell to the Spaniards on 11th March 1597, and the poem was evidently finished before its recapture later in September of that year. In mentioning both Gallo-Belgicus and 'Hollensheads' Donne is making what amounts to the same point about the bore—his remorseless, dial-an-encyclopaedia, voracious, up-to-the-minute unstoppableness. It's still much the same point in 1611, when Donne was quick to spot similar qualities, this time in print, in his mock-encomium 'Upon Mr Thomas Coryat's *Crudities*':

> When wilt thou be at full, great Lunatique? ...
> Goe then: and as to thee, when thou didst go,
> *Munster* did Townes, and Gesner Authors show,
> Mount now to Gallo-Belgicus; appear
> As deepe a States-man, as a Gazettier   (ll.17, 21-24)

But whereas Donne's distaste for the chroniclers, like Heylyn's later, is tilted against 'confusion, and commixture of unworthy relations',[11] his charge against *Mercurius Gallo-Belgicus*, as his epigram of the same title makes clear, is of a worse sin against intelligence: credulity. And appropriately, his language takes on a religious flavour to bring home the charge:

> ... I confesse
> I should have had more faith, if thou hadst lesse;
> Thy credit lost thy credit; 'Tis sinne to doe,
> In this case, as thou wouldst be done unto,
> To beleeve all.

Annabel Patterson has recently claimed, in *Reading Between the Lines*, that
these passages show Donne preferring elite to popular culture, and invites
us, in an essay ('The Small Cat Massacre') that wears all its project in its
title, to recover Holinshed and his fellows as Geertzian heroes, homely and
egalitarian ethnographers of Tudor culture.[12] But this sort of political cor-
rectiveness radically underestimates the scope of Donne's contempt for
historians of every wash. He is as suspicious of the grander as of the more
trivial attempts at 'politic' history; we hear no equivalent, counter-balanc-
ing praise of Camden or de Thou. Nor should we expect one, from the man
who undertook a sympathetic defence of the mysteries of state, and thought
it a braver thing to keep them hid.[13] If the collectaneous 'maw' is the antiquaries' mark, the word that signs for Donne the absurd knowingness of the
politic and explicative, the conspiracy historians who unmasked their times,
is 'Statesmen': 'Statesmen', a Donne letter explains, 'who can find matter
of state in any wrinkle in the King's socks'.[14] Donne seems always to
have associated such facile readings of motivation with the Court's per-
rasive secularism: a Whitehall sermon of 1628 warns against friends who
will misconstrue 'thy present application of thy self to God in prayer' as
'but an argument of thy Court-dispaire, and of thy falling from former
hopes there'.[15]

Religious history too, for Donne, has its voluminous Holinsheds, its
credulous Mercuries, its politic insinuaters. And here its appalling aggrega-
tion, its characteristic gatheringness, began to matter. Early in his career,
such 'intangl[ings] among bookes and papers' seemed but 'mischance', the
sort of heterogeneal dreamwork, flung 'abroad at all adventures', that he
teases in *The Character of Dunce*, whose

> ... compositions differ only *Terminorum positione* from dreames, noth-
> ing but rude heapes of immaterial, incoherent drossy rubbish stuff
> promiscuously thrust together.[16]

'Satire IIII', though, hints at a different plane of objection from the aesthetic. The bore's complimenting tongue, Donne complains, can cozen,
win, pay, flatter, make men speak treason. It can also (and it comes as a
climax, rather than a mere confirmation: all men are liars, but ecclesiastical
historians are the biggest) *lie*— 'outlie either / Jovius, or Surius, or both
together' (lines 47-48). Both Paulus Jovius and Laurentius Surius were
Roman Catholic historians, hostile chroniclers of the Reformation, and in
Surius' case a collector, in six volumes, of saints' lives. Both were traditional targets of Protestant suspicion.[17] Nothing could indicate more clearly the direction of Donne's developing thoughts on Church history than the

textual history of this line. The very earliest of Donne's poems to circulate as a textual unit were the five verse satires, together with *The Storme* and *The Calme*. Five examples of this small 'book' survive in manuscript, two imperfect.[18] The three others, though, all carry for 'Surius' the alternative reading and Protestant name of 'Sleydan', the first lay historian of the Reformation and the man to whom Surius' *Commentarius ... ab anno 1550* was written in animadversion and reply. Empson, broadbrushing: 'Donne spoiled one of his own jokes out of professional caution' (he picks up and entrenches Milgate's suggestion that the change was made for Egerton, Donne's employer).[19] Whatever Donne's motive for the change, 'Surius' —that is to say, the deliberately heavy pointing of an attack on Roman Catholic inscriptions of tradition and history—is the shape of the future for Donne's narrowing thoughts on the past.

Three works in particular from his middle years mark this renegotiated, but still satirical, perception of history as one increasingly dominated by the trajectory of religious belief: *The progress of the soul (Metemphychosis)* (1601), *Pseudo-martyr* (1610) and the Latin and English texts of *Ignatius his conclave* (1611). In each, and for the first time in Donne's writings, the shape and genre of the work require a form in some ways committed to the historiographical: a progress-poem, a piece of historical casuistry, and a modern satire that offers its own *Gallo-Belgicus* of the debates in Hell. Each depends, to some degree, on reading history 'straight'. In *Metempsychosis* the poet (for once the variation is apt: the speaker is an all-too-Poetical figure whose portentous, du Bartas-like weight Donne starts by obliging his readers to carry) is to track the 'deathlesse soule' of Eden's apple along the line of history and (apparently) up the scale of being. In *Pseudo-martyr* he must ground the subject's civil obedience, the Oath of Allegiance after the Gunpowder plot, in a reading of the whole history of Imperial-Papal relations. (An unrewarding task, but luckily for Donne, James I's *Triplici Nodo Triplex Cuneus* (1608) had already done much of his research for him.) *Ignatius his conclave* seems to have been more in the nature of a reward to himself for having written *Pseudo-martyr*: it is certainly more stable in tone, more self-contained in structure, more confident in its parodic gestures. All three end abruptly, but only *Ignatius his conclave* shows any sign of having meant to do so.

Many of the earlier topics of distrust survive into these early seventeenth-century engagements with history. The giant Danielic quaternion with which the *Progresse* kicks off looks suspiciously joky for a start, and when Donne also stuffs into the same first stanza morning, noon and night, the four metallic ages, two epical 'I sings' and Josephus' pillars, and dedicates the poem to Infinity, it is hard to have much confidence in de Quincey's discovery in it of the 'gloomy sublimity of Ezekiel or Aeschylus'.[20] A livelier conclusion might be that Donne is eclectically acute to potential structures for holding his history together: the poem has affinities with du Bartas, Ovid's *carmen perpetuum*, and the use of Cain and Seth as organisers in the spiritual explication of history in Augustine's *City of God*, for example.[21]

If the history-project of *Metempsychosis* can be said to proceed by parody, it is parody less of a particular author, perhaps, than of the huge and absurdly firm goals (*fines* is the usual word) that humanist historians were wont to propose. The poem drifts on, instead, and eventually out, with the amiable and learned shapelessness of Rabbinical commentary. It may be the nearest thing we have in English verse to Sir Thomas Browne. The historiographical assaults of the controversies, by contrast, are much more targetted if hardly less self-indulgent affairs. The superstitious credulity that cannot distinguish truth from falsehood and is not interested in doing so, for example, resurfaces in the vigorous third and fourth chapters of *Pseudo-martyr*, which attack in turn the more ludicrous and miracular extravagances of the saints' lives (Surius revisited) and the doctrines of merit and of purgatory that underpin such beliefs. But now, below what John Carey has called, with some justice, 'an uproarious saga of sanctified buffoonery', a second rhetorical strategy can be discerned, one which plays up every possible doctrinal or political disagreement within the Church of Rome. Even the quaintest of saints' lives, it seems, have their politics: Donne includes in *Pseudo-martyr* and *Ignatius his conclave* a reminder that 'incessant Sermons to the people, of the lives of *Saints* and other *Ecclesiastique Antiquities*' are Gregory XIII's specific brief to the new Oratorian congregation,

> ... that the world which in such a rage of devotion ran towards the Jesuits, might be arrested a little ['*Iesuitarum* torrens ... languidior paulo, tepidiorque redderetur', in the Latin] upon the contemplation of an Order which professed Church-knowledge as the other did State-knowledge.[22]

And that 'the Iesuits exceed all other, ... in all those points, which beget or cherish this corrupt desire of false-Martyrdome' is the main proposition of the fourth chapter. Elsewhere in the same work Donne plots the annals of 'Controuersies, after the *Dominicans* and the *Iesuites*, had with much earnestnesse prouoked, and with much biternes replied vpon one another'.[23] Though he carries some of his old historiographical targets, then, into new controversies (Almanacs, Ephemerides and Gazettiers crowd thickly into the closing pages of *Ignatius his conclave*, for example)[24] what he cannot take with him is the mocking detachment from historical method that had proved such a weapon of spirit in writing his own distance from the Court. Now he too must read Italian history like a Tacitus, run over the latest books of events, stuff his own chronicles, however mockingly, with the domestic tattle of the Legendaries (small *saint* massacre), epitomise or compendiously swell. Even Pope Joan, a piece of pseudo-history as Donne was later rather grudgingly to concede in the pulpit, is not spared an appearence in 1611: 'cum et aliquando Ecclesia nostra *Foeminae Pontifici* se crediderit'.[25] Jesuits, though, made Donne much angrier than Popes did.

Are there strategies of style that help Donne to fend off these more mundane engagements of the controversial historian, or is a muddying involvement implicit in the controversial tasks he has taken on? Something might be made, perhaps, of a feature of *Pseudo-martyr* that its enemies seem to have found genuinely disconcerting, its disproportion. The chapter-lengths vary wildly, and tone and topic veer unpredictably from farce to Counter-Reformation scholarship; neither quite carries the other, as they might in Erasmus, and it is hard to know whether to read Donne's contribution as missorted through the haste of a Royal command (Walton tells us it was written in six weeks flat)[26] or as a cheeky surprise-tactic of the sort Ramus recommends for victory in the pragmatic oration. Certainly, *Ignatius his conclave* has some very polished little pedantries which suggest that Donne was a controverialist experienced enough: his ability to throw in Tholosanus' *Syntagma Iuris Universi* (1599), a folio of over a thousand pages, merely to prove that 'the Cardinals, who were wont to meet oftner, meete now but once in a weeke',[27] looks unaccidental. The difficulty might be easier to reformulate if we had a better idea of the extent of Donne's research work for Bishop Morton.[28]

Some of Donne's scepticism, then, about the way in which histories were written, about the elements and mixed motives of their composition, can be fairly applied to his own writing, which is not free of the local aggressions and digressions he so sharply exposes in other authors. But the predominant impression remains that of a critical and independent, if not always a generous, reader. In some sense this historiographical temper in Donne can fairly be described as modern. First, it shares with the sharper humanist scholarship (the sharpness is by and large the sharpness of philology and law, further whetted by the Reformation) a lively sense of documentary suspicion. (What would a history be like that had been written in prison? '... like a Bird in a Cage, hee takes his tunes from every passenger that last whistled'. What was the point of writing a History of the World, another joke in *Problem II* runs, if you were an atheist and thought it had

always been there anyway?)[29] Sometimes the impossibility of getting it
right made such efforts comical, easily mocked. Sometimes Donne was
comforted by the reflection that God hides things deliberately: 'I remember
that it was God which hid *Moses*'s body, And the Divell which laboured to
reveal it'.)[30] Whether or not '*Abraham*'s booke *De formationibis* is yet
alive', (and if so whether it were 'suppositious') was another pleasing topic
in Donne's repertory of *hidden* history.[31]

Secondly, Donne's historiographical cynicism is often accompanied by
a particular verbal turn, in which, if the past is signed as impossible to
recover, the present is marked with a rhetoric of the degenerate. This is
particularly audible in *Problems*. 'Why dye none for love now?' 'Why did
the Devill reserve Jesuits for these latter times?'[32] Where now we write
late, later, latest, Donne speaks of the late age, these latter times. 'What if
this present were the world's last night?' One fear he sometimes entertained
was a fear that the world might be running down. Another was his intermit-
tent presentiment of the apocalypse: angels *need* wings, Donne explained in
1626, 'wings of great use', for 'the Divell is busie, he knows his time is
short'.[33]

Such double perspectives are helpful in reading Donne's vigorous
attacks on, and arguments with, the concept of the past as well as its local
inhabitants. Donne can look easily modern—sceptic, learnedly distrustful,
unpersuaded. But unpersuaded of what? Part of his distrust of human histories springs from the way in which he associates faith with submission to
reason. As Debra Shuger writes, Donne is frequently 'hostile to philosophy,
viewing it as a culpable attempt at self-sufficiency',[34] and he often challenges the favourite, self-assertive texts of Renaissance Stoicism:

> to come to be good men out of Plutarch or Seneca, without a Church
> or Sacraments ... this is pride, and the pride of the Angells;[35]

> the first breath of [God's] indignation blowes out thy candle, extin-
> guishes all thy Wisdome, all thy Counsells, all thy Philosophicall sen-
> tences, disorders thy *Seneca*, thy *Plutarch*, thy *Tacitus*, and all thy
> premeditations.[36]

To replace the disordered gossip of *histoire evenementielle* with the
ethically grounded contemplation of classical example offers Donne no
scope, then, for improving the way in which we read ourselves against the
world's transactions. His fine New Year's poem to Sir Henry Goodyere
measures stringently the cycles of repetition to which the ungrounded contemplation of the self is liable:

> Who makes the Past, a patterne for next yeare
> Turnes no new leafe, but still the same thing reads;
> Seene things, he sees again; heard things doth heare;
> And makes his life, but like a pair of beads.

The rosary's turning mimes the year's encirclement, but does nothing to rotivate the self inhibited by habit:

> Would you redeeme it? Then your selfe transplant
> A while from hence ...

Donne's advice to his friend is friendly in wanting to criticise, friendly (he compares its common round of virtues to the copybook mottoes found on the edge of plates) in deprecating the tinges of hostility such criticism might appear to voice. His language is spiritual ('redeeme ... soul ... heaven ... God ... father', the vocabulary continues) and also down-to-earth. Put yourself in a new place, it advises. Stop hawking; be more truthful. Defamiliarise. Abandon the failed rationalities of failed reforms. Aim at a 'livelier taste of God'. (In another poem that takes audit of age's advance, Herbert arrives at a similarly chastened reviving:

> Go birds of spring: let winter have his fee;
>   Let a bleak palenesse chalk the doore,
> So all within be livelier than before.)[37]

One way of reading the past, Donne's poem suggests, is as a form of human blockage to a simpler, more radical, God-given narrative. The idea was to prove both emotionally rewarding and theologically difficult in Donne's professional writings, that is, in his sermons.[38] To these I turn next.

II

Donne's responses, then, to attempts to inscribe the human past, to reify it in works of history, and to argue from these reifications, sound elegantly sceptical where they are not more mordantly suspicious. How such suspicions encountered the English law that was Donne's first profession we do not learn: what Alan Cromartie has characterised as the law's 'utter formlessness' in the years before Coke's *Reports* and *Institutes* took the work in hand seems at once to provide a model for rhetorical free play, and a necessity to fall back on some sort of argument derived from the authority of national custom.[39] But the Christian Church claimed to be 'historical' in a unique way, posing certain events to which its believers must always look back and a scripture in which to find them. It was not a system whose truth, if lost, could be recovered by rational argument in the way Pythagoras' theorem or English common law might.

When it fell to Donne to approach that version of the past that was the body and marrow of controversial divinity, his initial response seems to have been uncharacteristically cautious. Stanza XIII ('*The Doctors*') of Donne's litany, for example, starts boldly enough with a vision of 'Thy sacred Academie above' at prayer in Heaven that their own faults—'what they have misdone / Or mis-said'—do not undo their later readers. Yet the petition that closes the verse is more generous. Its formula ('Lord let us runne / Meane waies, and call them stars, but not the Sunne') appears to place Donne's relation to Tradition firmly within the most cautious version of fundamental theology available within the Protestant mainstream, what A.N.S. Lane and Richard J. Bauckham have termed the 'ancillary' tradition, one which saw the Fathers' witness to Scripture as relative and dependent, and thought of Christian tradition as offering assistance but constituting no norm in the interpretation of Scripture.[40] Donne's phrasing echoes neatly John Jewel's *A Treatise of the Holy Scriptures* (1570):

> They were witnesses unto the truth, they were worthy pillars and ornaments in the church of God. Yet they may not be compared with the word of God ... They are our fathers, but not fathers unto God; they are the stars, fair and beautiful, and bright; yet they are not the sun: they bear witness of the light, they are not the light.[41]

In the years after Trent, Protestant theologians developed this position into a flexible and sophisticated tool of polemic. Works like Daniel Tossanus' *Synopsis de Patribus* (Heidelberg, 1602) or the more concentrated posthumous patrology of William Perkins (*William Perkins His Probleme*, printed 1604)[42] synthesised vigorously and effectively the doctrinal acceptability, the textual canonicity and an historical-contextual understanding of Patristic writings: *quantum eis deferendum, quo tempore vixerint, quacum cautione legendi*, as Tossanus' subtitle neatly sums up the hermeneutic on offer. Under such pressures Jewel's 'Fair, and beautiful' starts to slide: 'The Fathers in many points of Divinitie have spoken very unfitly', starts Perkins in a paragraph of 'Preparatiues'.[43] And what follows is a crisp analysis of how controversies led people to adopt rhetorical counter-stances that bent doctrine to the heat of disputation, or to the paganism of an early audience/

readership, or of how mere 'Rehearsall' has been read as dogmatic assertion. Both Protestant patrologists see their work as a counter-poison to
Roman views that stress either the coinherence of Scripture and Tradition
or, more strongly, the material insuffficiency of Scripture[44]; these Tossanus likens to 'those flatterers of *Dionisius Siculus* who licking up the
Tyrants spittle affirmed it to be sweeter than Nectar'.[45] Tradition for the
ancillarists, rather, is at best evidential, or corroborative. For Perkins, admiration and exculpation go hand in hand; Tossanus offers to show 'in one
and the same Father what is authenticall, what erroneous, irreptitious, and
infected'. Donne himself never offers to attempt a systematic critique along
the lines of Perkins, but the outlines of a similar generosity, at best condi-
tional and always strictly controlled by a sense of evidential, and not dogmatic, function, can be detected in the Preface to *Biathanatos*, and perhaps
in the relaxed eclecticism of *Essays in Divinity*. It was not till Daillé that
the energy and confidence of such Protestant discriminations of traditions
began to unravel.[46]

In Donne's sermons, however, a very different note is heard. Much has
been made (much of it in a larger Anglo-Catholic tradition of interpretation
which has consistently sought to push Protestant positions on Tradition
back into a model of coincidence with Scripture) of Donne's imaginative
sympathies with the Fathers, with Augustine, Basil and Tertullian above all.
The lists of Donne's 'Sources' in volume 10 of the great *Sermons* edition
are a signal instance of such a tendency towards undiscriminated co-option
of the *testimonia patrum*. And it is true that in the cultic practice, if not the
systematic theology, of Elizabeth's and James I's England icons continued
to survive in glass and stone of the Four Fathers of the Church, much in the
way that the nineteenth-century church builder at Bicton, in East Devon,
worked to a scheme of corbels that offer a narrative of the Church of England Fathers, Hooker and Andrewes and Donne predictably in prominence.
Such narratives testify to the selective paradosis that any institution is apt to
lineate into its own history, of course; the reason they deserve suspicion
here is that Donne himself is so hostile to such hypostasising of human
authority. For Donne the Fathers (*as* the Fathers) are not a procession he
piously hopes to join, but a problem: a problem repetitively voiced, in each
of the ten volumes of Sermons, a problem that provides enormous scope for
the energies of his distrust. Here only a sketch of those incredulous energies
can be attempted.

They start with the words themselves, *Fathers, tradition*. 'The Religion
of our Fathers, the Church of our Fathers, the Worship of our Fathers',
Donne writes, 'is a pretext that colours a great deale of Superstition ... It is
a great and dangerous wickednesse, which is done upon pretext of Antiqui-

ty'.[47] Donne is sublimely uninterested in the *historical* projects of the post-Reformation English church: the grubbing up of early British Christianity, the whole attempt to loop back behind the Roman mission, excites him not a whit. Tradition for him is addition (again and again he collocates the words), and it is this addition that he attacks in metaphors of organic proliferation, lines and branches, 'incisions and concisions', 'collateral and subdivided', that turn out to be cuts and wounds through which Scripture drains.

Such betraying aggregations come under a double charge from Donne. At the same time as he feigns dogmatic indifference to the accumulating weight of ceremony, of 'mystic signification', of 'declaratory tradition' (all of which may be reasonable, or at least explicable within an understanding of national or ethnic custom) he resents furiously the Roman Church's raising them with penalties to the status of salvific requirement. 'In a days warning, and by the roaring of one Bull, it grows to be damnation to day to beleeve so as a man might have beleeved yesterday'. To his own unitive or prolocutorial theologies of voice (to speak in less generous terms, aggrandisements of preaching), Donne opposes images of Tradition which sign it as competitive and noisy overspeaking: 'the voyce of that part is louder', a voice that would 'pronounce upon every Invention and Tradition of your own a *Quicunque vult* ... and clogge every problematical proposition with an Anathema'.[48]

Traditional Protestant resistance to the idea of coercive Tradition often drew itself on the Fathers—Cyprian's 74th Letter, a favourite exhibit in Milton's early tracts as in many others, was the base-text for the Fatherly admission of error retorted upon the Fathers. This is the rhetorical strategy that Tossanus and Perkins raise to the power of system: both their works are explicitly intended as pedagogical handbooks of reading method, instructive controls on the exposition of Reformed orthodoxy. (The pressures on that orthodoxy from a *different* direction, from Anabaptists and Socinians, are the forces that make Protestant accounts of Tradition sound at times confusingly like the coinherent model that they aim to reject.) Donne's sermons, in the great majority, are sterner in tone, simpler in proposition on this point: his rhetorical energies are spent less in the discrimination or historical contextualisation of plural readings than in focussing such pluralities to a single word (often a single syllable: 'they', 'Men') ripe for the rigours of his emphatical exclusion and denunciation. 'They intend Destruction, a tearing, a renting, a wounding the Body and Frame and Peace of the Church'. Who are they? The answer is usually 'Tradition of Men': 'They put not on the garment of Christ conformably, but in a coarser Stuffe (Traditions of Men, in stead of his Word)'. Shirts of such stuff,

Donne reflects ruefully, are Nessus' wear: it 'takes away the honour of
having been witnesses for Christ, and the consolation and style of Martyrs'
merely to die for Tradition.[49] Tradition is not adoption in Christ, he urges,
preaching on Isaiah 2: 6, 'They please themselves in the children of strang-
ers'; or, more swellingly, on 1 Timothy 1: 11, 'A kingdome consists not of
slaves. We preach a kingdom. A kingdom is able to subsist of itself without
calling in Forrainers. The Gospel is so too, without calling in Traditions'.
Foundations, not Superedifications: Apostles not Samaritans; Christians not
Philippians, unable to hear Paul's preaching 'impermixt', but lusting after
'Traditionall and Additional Doctrines'.[50]

Occasionally Donne sounds a more eirenic and consciously adiapho-
ristic note ('why introduce Contrarieties in Fundamentall things indifferent', he asks in an early sermon), but the rhetorical attack on tradition
hardens, until it sounds like the table-talk of Luther (who could claim to
find more of worth in Aesop than Jerome, Chrysostom only a gossip, Basil
not worth a penny, *und so weiter*). Indeed, it is through Luther ('it is well
said by Luther') that Donne negotiates a desired re-emphasis:

> When ... traditions and additions of men are imposed upon us, as com-
> mandments of God, then *viriliter agendum* (we must quit ourselves like
> men), we must dispute like men (like learned men), preach like Men ...
> pray like Men ... resist like Men.[51]

The emphasis on preaching is important here. On those few occasions when
Donne imagines Scripture and Tradition in more generous coexistence, it is
the paradox of Christ in the Power of Concord that holds them together.
The word is no easier for Donne than for Spenser, whose Concord masters
Love and Hate: Donne's antinomy is even more striking, where Christ as
cornerstone is 'able to unite and reconcile (as it did in Abraham's house) a
Wife and a Concubine' in one bed, 'the bed of all ease, yet ... labour required'. The power is *Lux*, but as for the labour: '*Ecce VOX*'. Again and
again, Donne's reprehension of tradition, of the ossified unauthorised assertion of the doctrinal weight of merely human history, leads on into a differ-
entiated defence of the pulpit.[52]

What such a manoeuvre still left in question was the history of Scripture itself. Donne is sharply alive to what is variable in the translations of
the text, and often bounces Geneva against King James, as he does Rabbinical against Patristic and Reformed commentary. What are odder are the
moments where his fierce reprehensions of tradition and invention issue in
the imaginative recompense of an invention of his own. Again the contrast
with Perkins is instructive. Perkins' *A Treatise Concerning the Sacred and*

Only True Manner and Method of Preaching had developed, in the face of Lutheran and other worries about the Epistle of James, a subtly graded canon within the Scriptural canon. Donne will have none of it. For all his demonstrated learning in the troubled history of Scriptural canonicity, he preferred his Scriptures whole: Moses' one book, not five, in *Essays in Divinity*, and, still more strikingly, a big-bang theory of the New Testament that could match his own obsession with the moment of *Fiat* in Genesis:

> Ask of Christ speaking in his Word, there you shall know; produce the Record, the Scripture, and there is *Communis salus*; I wrote unto you of the common Salvation [he is quoting Jude 1: 3]: What's that? *Semel tradita fides*, sayes that Apostle there: the Faith which was once delivered to the Saints: where *semel* is not *aliquando*; once, is not once upon a time, I cannot tell when; but *semel* is *simul*, once is at once: The Gospel was delivered all together, and not by Postscripts.[53]

III

The arguments of this paper can be summarised briefly, as follows. Donne finds very little to admire in any work of history. Chroniclers were baggy monsters with no sense of decorum; up-to-the-minute newsbook histories would print anything, true or false; and secular, classicizing historians were no more to be trusted, whether they pretended to offer politic insights into hidden motives or served up the stodgy and deluded exemplarities of moral self-sufficiency. Human history-making would always be dogged by the pluralities of human opinion: 'there are marked an hundred differences in mens Writings concerning an *Ant*'.[54]

Religious history (Bible record and Church history) would always be controversial: 'Contemplative and bookish men, must of necessitie be more quarrelsome then others'.[55] But Donne struggled to keep the two components firmly, ontologically separate. Moses 'was principal Secretary to the Holy Ghost' and as such 'very credible, though he be his owne Historiographer'. But no reformed historian ever wins Donne's praise, and he shares few if any of their concerns to mount an historical argument for the primitive purity of the English Church. On the contrary, Luther's vigorous rejection of arguments from tradition and authority seems to have appealed to Donne. He was aware of, and sometimes gave voice to, the increasingly sophisticated patrology of Protestant scholars in the years after the Council of Trent. But his imaginative sympathies lay with rejection rather than qualification, and at times he seems ready to throw out the doctrinal baby with the Patristic bathwater. He increasingly came to think that Roman Catholic histories were particularly bad: some made credulous collections of superstitious taradiddles, others, worse-motivated, wrote lies designed to practise upon the credulous. The Roman habit of penally requiring belief in matters that should have been *adiaphora* is fiercely condemned, and Donne exhibits no sign of wishing to erect alternative historical shibboleths. Underlying these Roman errors, as he can be shown to have consistently believed from at least 1609, were fundamental assumptions about the Church's claims to historical authority: tradition was addition, and he wanted none of it, though a saving formulation about national custom must be thought to qualify the rigour of some of these pronouncements.

Genesis is the only history, in fact, that moves Donne to unqualified enthusiasm; he is famously fond of its opening. This sort of absolutist creation-narrative is bound to pose problems, however, when the canon of the New Testament comes to be considered. Donne's sermons show considerable awareness of early Church history (as of many other kinds, although the sharp end of documentary research by early modern antiquaries never seems to have moved him to more than mirth). But he came to prefer, when thinking about the history of Christian scriptures, to ignore what he can be shown to have known of their gradual and disputed canonicity. Instead he invents for them a mythical moment of powerful and instantaneous origin. To speak the Word from the pulpit, he claimed, was at once to perform the disassembly of tradition's aggregated clutter, and to re-enact this originary scriptural force.

The energies with which Donne enunciated these positions, in whatever genre of his writings they are found (and some at least profess to be eirenical), are predominantly satirical in mode. That Donne can be mordant, uncharitable and often very funny should not come as a surprise to anyone. It does suggest, though, that critics who read Donne's 'Anglicanism' as a time-serving piece of apostasy should think harder about the coherency of his attitudes towards the human past and the ways in which Christians miswrote it; and that Anglicans who claim Donne (as many have, from Walton onwards) to join with Hooker and Andrewes as a learned pillar of their middle way might pause to think what a strange beast he was.

'Though I yet', his longest satire had jokingly ended,

> With *Machabees* modestie, the knowne merit
> Of my worke lessen: yet some wise man shall,
> I hope, esteeme my writs Canonicall. (IIII, ll. 241-4)

Donne's lifelong scepticism about the projects of interpretation, about the possibilities of writing history justly; his comic apprehension of the whole lumbering weight of the business; his scholarly and substantiated sense of 'unsincere translations ... prejudices and forconceived opinions ... under-minings and batteries', of the 'curious vanities and excesses' that infiltrate and ornamentalise our study: all these made him feel that modern author-ship could of its nature only produce apocryphal work. It is an extraordi-nary strength in Donne that these verdicts *fund*, not sap, those moments of power and esteem when he felt otherwise, when he spoke and wrote 'Canonicall'. At such moments, he did not feel like God, or even like James I. He did feel like John the Baptist, like a Prolocutor, like an ambassador, an angel even. He felt powerful, and apprehended the dangers of doing so.

Notes

1   Donne's opinion on the precedency of ambassadors is bound in with Jacobus Val-desius, *De dignilitate regum regnorum Hispanae ... seu legatis eorum* (1602) in British Library Cotton MS. Cleop. F. vii; R.C. Bald, *John Donne: a life* (Oxford, 1970), 142 & Index.

2   'Satyre IIII', line 21: all Donne's poetry quoted in this essay is given in the text of Herbert J.C. Grierson: *The Poems of John Donne*, 2 vols (Oxford, 1912). The considerable problems in this and all other editions are well laid out by Ted-Larry Pebworth, 'Manuscript poems and print assumptions: Donne and his modern edi-tors', *John Donne Journal* 3 (1984), 12-17.

3   E.g. Henri Estienne, *L'introduction au traite de la conformite des merveilles an-ciennes et modernes* (Paris, 1566), 11. Nobody has succeeded in identifying Ham-mon, whom the manuscripts give also as 'Haman' and 'Hammond'.

4   John Earle, *Microcosmography*, edited by Alfred S. West (Cambridge, 1897), 57; 'Satyre V', lines 86-87.

5   *Paradoxes and problems*, edited by Helen Peters (Oxford, 1980), 24: '11: Why doth Sir Walter Ralegh write the Historie of these times?'

6   Discussion in *The sermons of John Donne*, 10 vols, edited by Evelyn M. Simpson and George R. Potter (Berkeley, 1953-62), 10: 367-370, developing Simpson's comments in *Essays in Divinity* (Oxford, 1952), 101-102. Sir Thomas Browne was another profiter by Pererius.

7   *Essays in divinity*, 10; at 11 Pererius 'seems peremtory'; at 15 Donne, 'because to me it seems reasonable and clear', is happy 'to leave Pererius'; at 19 finds him gravelled in the arithmetic of Scripture chronology ('Pererius confesses'), but useful in the margins at 27, 74, and to have 'not unusefully observed' at 52. Unac-knowledged borrowings from the Jesuit at 17, 18, 32, 60, 72, 83 and 89.

8   'Hee is a man strangely thrifty of Time past, and an enemy indeed to his Maw, whence he fetches out many things when they are now all rotten and stinking': *Microcosmography*, 56.

9   'Satyre II', lines 25-27, with special reference to plagiarists.

10   *Pierce Pennilesse, his supplication to the divell* (1592), sig. D4.

11   Peter Heylyn, *Microcosmus* (1639).

12   (Wisconsin, 1993), ch. 5; a fuller and more nuanced discussion of 'Satire IIII' appears in Patterson's next essay, pp. 173-175, where the poem's anxious sense of treason and Elizabethan intelligencing are well brought out.

13   Jonathan Goldberg, *James I and the politics of literature* (Baltimore, 1983), ch. 2: 'State secrets'.

14   To Sir Robert More, 28 July 1614: Washington, Folger MS. L.b.537. Edmund Gosse, *The life and letters of John Donne*, 2 vols (1899) is still the only useful printed source for a partial text of those Donne letters not published in the seventeenth century.

15   *Sermons* 8: 182.

16   I follow the text in *Paradoxes and problems*, 59-62. Its editor (acting to some degree under the direction, as it appears, of Dame Helen Gardner) demotes the piece to the Dubia, xlviii, as showing 'little of [Donne's] wit'. ('Elegy 14' and 'Sappho to Philaenis' are other works that did not suit Dame Helen's notion of what fitted Donne.) Peter Beal's *Index of English literary manuscripts*, I/i: DnJ 4091-4095, is less expurgatory. The piece certainly *circulated* as Donne's.

17   Wesiey Milgate's edition *The satires, epigrams and verse letters* (Oxford, 1967), collects the literature helpfully. Jean Bodin, *Methodus ad facilem historiarum cognitionem* (1566), which includes an attack on Jovius, was the main source for later sixteenth century attempts to unify a humanist model of historical writing: George Huppert, *The idea of perfect history* (Urbana, 1970).

18   Beal, *Index* I/i DnJ 31-34, 40; discussion at p. 246, col. 1.

19   William Empson, *Essays on Renaissance literature I: Donne and the new philosophy*, edited by John Haffenden (Cambridge, 1993), 160, reprinting with Empson's amendments an essay of 1972; Milgate, lvii.

20   *Blackwood's Magazine* 34 (1828), 892-893, cit. Milgate xxxi.

21   John Klause, 'The Montaigneity of Donne's Metempsychosis', in Barbara K. Lewalski, ed., *Renaissance Genres* (Cambridge, Mass., 1986), 418-443, writes very well about its ingredients.

22   *Pseudo-martyr* (1610),   261; *Ignatius his conclave*, edited by T.S. Healy, SJ (Oxford, 1969), 70-71.

23   *Pseudo-martyr*, p. 100; cf. *Sermons* 7: 123.

24   Clavius as a political astrologer, p. 87; the Jesuits' *Annuae Litterae ... anno 1609* as 'a certaine idle Gazettier', p. 95.

25   *Conclave Ignatii*, p. 82; the English muffles it rather, p. 83. Donne's concession ('Truely, there are some passages in the Legend of Pope *Joan*, which I am not very apt be believe') at *Sermons* 7: 153.

26   Izaak Walton, *The Lives of John Donne, Sir Henry Wotton, Richard Hooker, Gorge Herbert and Robert Sanderson*, edited by G. Saintsbury (Oxford, 1927), 44-45.

27   *Ignatius his conclave*, p. 57 and n.

28   Healy, Appendix C (169-173), reviews the evidence and declines to decide, though most of his own new findings point towards collaboration. Donne's own books, which continue to resurface at intervals, perhaps need reinspecting.

29   Edited by Peters, p. 24, reading the extended text in 'Group III' manuscripts.

30 *Essays in divinity*, p. 13.

31 *Essays in divinity*, p. 12. The answer to both questions was yes, as it happened: G. Postellus, *Liber Iezireh, sive formationis mundi* (Paris, 1552).

32 *Problems* V and XIX, respectively.

33 *Sermons* 7: 1, *passim*.

34 Debra Shuger, *Habits of thought in the English Renaissance* (Berkeley, 1990), 202: 'almost always hostile', in her account.

35 *Sermons*, 9: 379.

36 *Sermons* 2: 354. This and the last quotation are borrowed directly from Shuger's account.

37 'The Forerunners', lines 34-36.

38 The poems are, throughout Donne's career, the work of an amateur, though it is clear from the *Anniversaries* that Donne had a good idea of what professional poems should look like. Donne's rare printings and reluctant dissemination of his works in manuscript bespeak both a *general* attitude towards chamber-verses and a particular, personal anxiety. The general attitude is clear enough in *The table-talk of John Selden*, edited by Samuel Harvey Reynolds (Oxford, 1892), 135-136: 'If a man in a private chamber twirls his bandstring or plays with a rush to please himself, tis well enough; but if he should go into Fleet-street and sit upon a stall and twirl a bandstring or play with a rush, then all the boys in the street would laugh at him'. This under the topic-head *Poetry*. But Donne also betrays a massive 'recipient anxiety syndrome'; the considerable evidence is reviewed by Roy Booth in a witty essay, 'Ideating nothing', *English* 37 (1988), 203-215. A letter to Goodyer is typical—'let goe no copy of my Problems, till I review them. If it be too late, at least be able to tell me who hath them' (*Letters to Several Persons of Honour* (1651), 108. After some years of neglect, the topic of Donne in manuscript now verges on the fashionable: see e.g. Richard B. Wollman, 'The "press and the fire": print and manuscript culture in Donne's circle', *Studies in English Literature 1500-1900* 33 (1993), 85-98.

    The corollary of such a study should be a much sharper sense of how Donne came into print. But there is no modern edition of the major prose work printed in his lifetime, *Pseudo-martyr*, and the best material for studying Donne's considerable activity as self-editor, the changes between print and manuscript in the *Sermons*, remains almost wholly neglected since the pioneer studies of Sparrow, Potter and Simpson. As an admired professional preacher, Donne became newly enthusiastic about print, and came by 1621 to see it in altogether more generous terms as a means whereby 'the learning of the whole world is communicable to one another, and our minds and our inventions, our wits and compositions may trade and have commerce together, and we may participate of one anothers understandings'.

39 Alan Cranatic, *Sir Matthew Hale* (Cambridge, 1994), 11.

40 A.N.S. Lane, 'Scripture, tradition and church: an historical survey', *Vox Evangelica* 9 (1975), 37-55; Richard Bauckham, 'Tradition in relation to Scripture and reason', in Richard Bauckham and Benjamin Drewery (eds), *Scripture, Tradition and Reason* (Edinburgh, 1988), 117-145. I am grateful to Mr. Sean Hughes of Trinity College, Cambridge for these references and for the benefit of his wide learning in the topic of this section.

41 John Jewel, *Works*, ed. J. Ayre (4 vols, Cambridge, 1845-50), iv, 1173-4. For the clearest statement in contrast, see the 'decem veritates' of the 'Preface' to John Fisher, *Assertionis Lutheranae Confutatio* (1523).

42 *Gulielmi Perkinsi Problema* (1604); variant English translations in the second volume of Perkins' English *Workes* of 1609 and 1617.

43 (1617), 487; (1609) has the weaker 'Controuersies' for 'Divinitie', 556, col. 2D. *Problema* (1604), sig. A2ᵛ: 'Patres multa de rebus sacris incommode loquuti sunt'.

44 'Antidotum' ('Counter-Poison') in Perkins' longer title. He explores 'The difference' most succinctly in *A Reformed Catholike: A Golden Chaine* (1600), sigs. Qqqlᵛ-4; cf. William Cowper, *Workes* (1623), 648-52, for the difference in dialogue-form.

45 *A synopsis or compendium of the fathers* (1635), sig. A1ᵛ. For an example of spittle-licking, John Angel, *The agrement of the holye fathers* (?1555), 'of auctoriteis of the fathers', sigs 03-6ᵛ.

46 Yves Congar, *Tradition and traditions: an historical and a theological essay* (1966), surveys the shifting balances. For a sense of English *application* in these polemics, see e.g. Robert Dodaro OSA and Michael Questier, 'Strategies in Jacobean polemic: the use and abuse of St Augustine in English theological controversy', *Jnl. Ecclesiastical History* 44 (1993), 432-49; Peter Lake, 'The Laudians and the argument from authority' in B.Y. Kunze and D.D. Brautigam (eds) *Court, Country and Culture: Essays an Early Modern British History in honor of Perez Zagorin* (Rochester, NY, 1992), 149-75. For the unravelling, Brian Armstrong, *Calvinism and the Amyrout heresy* (1969).

47 *Sermons* 9, 6: 96-238, for a less hostile account; 10, 6, *passim* for unremitting aggression on 'Traditions'.

48 *Sermons* 6, 15: 357-8 and 7, 4: 122-6, where 'They will not say ... That a man could be saved without beleeving the Articles of the *Councell of Trent*, a week before that Councell shut up'.

49 On 'Tradition' and 'Traditions of Men' see, e.g., *Sermons* 2: 185; 3: 209; 4: 130, 141, 148, 193-4, 249; 5: 159, 259; 6: 98, 140, 187, 302; 7: 83, 120, 167-8, 172; 8: 162; 10: 103-4, 147-52. Jeanne Shami, 'Reading Donne's Sermons', *John Donne Journal* 11 (1992), 6-11, sounds a powerful warning against arguments raised from just such fragmentary lists. Here I believe Donne's emphasis to be consistent. For Cyprian as proof-text in the topos 'Tradition against Tradition', *Opera* (Paris, 1593), 229; John Milton, *Of Reformation Touching Church-Discipline in England* (1641), 33.

50 *Sermons* 3: 253; 4: 277; 8: 165; 10: 103.

51 *Sermons* 6, 9: 51-91.

52 *Sermons* 6, 6: 291-336.

53 *Sermons* 3, 9: 100-107.

54 *Essays in divinity*, p. 14.

55 *Biathanatos* (1650), 20.

PART III

RELIGION, RHETORIC AND REVOLUTION IN THE SEVENTEENTH CENTURY

16

HELICON AND HILLS OF SAND:
PAGAN GODS IN EARLY MODERN DUTCH AND
EUROPEAN POETRY

MARIJKE SPIES

In 1663, when Holland's greatest poet, Joost van den Vondel, published one of his few tragedies on mythological subject matter, *Faëton*, he added a preliminary justification:

> Nobody will think that I will reinstate paganism. My only purpose is the furtherance of morality by presenting this beautiful fable on the stage as a mirror of pride. For the old Egyptian and Greek mythological stories cover a threefold knowledge, of history, of nature and of human morals ... I remember the late professor Vossius saying, that if he should write a commentary on Ovid's *Metamorphoses*, it would prove to be the most learned book ever written.[1]

I will not enter into Vondel's exact sources for this opinion.[2] Suffice to say it might have sounded a bit old-fashioned. More important to my argument is that it was also an antagonistic opinion. Vondel's statement, introduced by historical reference to the Christianisation of the Low Countries and backed up not only by a reference to the learned Vossius but also by a quotation from the 4th century Christian apologist Lactantius, must be regarded as a rather militantly formulated choice of sides in a literary conflict that had already divided the Dutch literary world for over a hundred years. It was a conflict between classical and Christian humanism, and in that perspective it is most telling that Vondel, the most biblical of all Dutch playwrights, spoke up in support of mythology with all the authority of his —by then—unsurpassed prestige. But it was also a conflict between realism and idealism, nationalism and internationalism, universalism and historical thinking. All these aspects were interwoven, and changed positions with regard to each other in the course of time. If not an inter*play*, there certainly was an internal *struggle* going on in this regard between the sacred and the profane in Dutch literature.

    As far as I know, it started with Dirck Volkertsz. Coornhert.[3] Coornhert had formulated his objections to the mythological 'fabrications', as he called them, of the rhetoricians by around 1550. Because his objective was to teach, he had no use for them, only for truth as learned by biblical parables.[4] His opinion is reminiscent of Erasmus, who in *Ciceronianus* (1528) had underlined the inappropriateness of classical examples and images for modern, Christian, purposes:

> Wherever I turn I see everything changed, I stand on a different stage, I see a different theatre, a different world. What am I to do? I am a Christian and I must talk of the Christian religion before Christians. If I am going to do so in a manner befitting my subject, surely I am not to imagine that I am living in the age of Cicero, ... and scrounge a few poor words, figures and rhythms from speeches which he delivered in the senate?

And somewhat further on:

> What shall our meticulous Ciceronian do? ... Shall he for the Father of Christ say 'Jupiter Optimus Maximus', for the Son, 'Apollo' ...? Shall he for the Queen of Virgins say 'Diana' ...?

That would be most unlike Cicero. Instead, one should speak as Cicero would have done if he had lived today 'as a Christian among Christians'.[5] The comparison with Erasmus' dialogue is the more apt, because in his text Coornhert had mentioned Cicero as the master of all eloquence.

Many years later, in 1582, Coornhert broached the question once more. Referring to the words of Virgil:

> Me, too, the Pierian maids have made a poet; I, too, have songs; me also the shepherds call a bard, but I trust them not,[6]

he declares himself alien to the Pyeridian family of the Muses and his poetical work alien to the elevated language of Mount Parnassus. He will not use such pompous adornments as provided by the names of Ceres, Bacchus and Venus, but speak in his own Dutch language about real, truthful issues. True artfulness lies in an adequate verbal representation of reality, visualising things as they are.[7]

Coornhert's moralistic aim is as outspoken as ever. Nevertheless one has the impression that this time, the general purport of his remarks is secularised. It seems to be the Dutch language that, more than Christian belief, is incompatible with the use of pagan deities. Coornhert's younger friend Hendrick Laurensz. Spiegel is still more explicit on this point. In his extensive didactic poem 'Mirror of the heart' (*Hert-spiegel*), written around the turn of the century, he proclaims the 'Dutchness' of Dutch literature.

'Should a Dutch poet be acquainted with Greek and Latin, while it was here the first pastors lived?' he asks his readers, pastors being traditionally considered the inventors of poetry.[8] And he continues: 'Mount Parnassus is too far away. There is no Helicon over here, only dunes, woods and brooks'. In his choice of words explicitly referring to Coornhert, he too advocates writing in Dutch about truthful issues. He does not strive for exotic pomp either, nor after the favour of the Muses, living high up Mount Parnassus.[9]

Especially interesting is Spiegel's further explication in the 4th book of his work. There Apollo tells how he and the Muses have transported truth, originally hidden under the cover of fable stories, from Mount Ararat, via Brahmans, Egyptians, Jews, Greeks and Romans, to Italy and France. But these days, authors such as Coornhert have made them desire to settle in Holland, the conclusion being that everybody should write in their own language because the Muses have no preference on that point.[10] To Spiegel the time for mythology had gone, not so much because the relevance of the pagan gods had been surpassed by Christian truth, but first and foremost because of the rise of a national Dutch culture. In the centuries to come, these two arguments continued to alternate in the larger argument against mythology. But before we enter into that, we must first direct our attention to the defenders.

Dutch rhetoricians, especially those in the southern provinces, had derived their predilection for mythological examples, for 'poetry' as they called it, from the French 'grands rhétoriqueurs'. Soon afterwards, the new Renaissance mode, as realised in France by poets such as Sebillet, Ronsard and Du Bellay, had been introduced in Ghent and in Antwerp by Lucas D'Heere and Jan van der Noot respectively. Like their French forbears, they justified the use of classical mythology with a neo-platonic theory of inspiration and harmony in which the image of Mount Helicon, inhabited by Apollo and the Muses, played a central role.[11]

Antwerp had already been proclaimed as the seat of Parnassus in the 1562 edition of the plays that had been performed a year earlier at the famous festival of rhetoricians at that city.[12] Three years later D'Heere claimed the same honor for Ghent.[13] With the great emigration stream to the northern Netherlands from about 1580 on, these notions were introduced into Holland too. Their most important champion was D'Heere's former pupil, Karel van Mander.

Van Mander expanded the neo-platonic conception of mythology with a threefold—historical, natural and ethical—significance as formulated by the Italian mythographer Natalis Comes and the French translater of Ovid, Barthlémy Aneau.[14] In the introduction to his own explication of the

Metamorphoses of Ovid, published in his *Schilder-boeck* in 1604, Van Mander spoke of:

> Important knowledge, of natural as well as of heavenly things, and
> useful lessons, hidden under the cover of these inventions by learned
> and able poets, who, inspired by a secret force, as enraged and beyond
> themselves, write their verses and poems.[15]

So, in the chapter on Bacchus, he not only relates everything about the invention of wine and the moral effects of its consumption, but also supplies the information that Bacchus had been a king in Arabia, who commanded a great army of men and women, thanks to which he conquered all Asia and India.[16]

It is not astonishing that in the same text he rather bitterly speaks of those who 'despise all mythology, saying that it is all lies not worth reading'.[17] And there are good reasons to believe that in saying so he had Spiegel in mind.[18]

Karel van Mander's Ovid interpretations had great influence on painters as well as poets. A painter by profession himself, he was one of the leading figures of the so-called 'Haarlem mannerist school'.[19] As a poet his influence was at first limited to the group of poets, nearly all of them refugees from the south, who were united in the 'Helicon' project. In their collectively conceived anthology of poems, 'The Dutch Helicon' (*Den Nederduytschen Helicon*), Van Mander's explications are used over and over again.[20] But soon his influence reached further than this rather close-knit group he himself had organized. One of those who profited, almost from the beginning of his poetic career, was Joost van den Vondel, who, as we saw, in 1663 still adhered to the same threefold method of interpretation.[21]

In the meantime, other discussions had taken place. In March 1619 Constantijn Huygens wrote a sonnet adressed to Anna Roemers Visscher, whom he had met a month earlier. It was a reaction to a sonnet from her, in which she had asked him for news from the Helicon. He lets the Muses answer her: she had better come herself to see, because Constantijn is unknown over there and does not know anything about what is going on. At the other side of the autograph Huygens had scribbled the verses of Virgil: 'Me, too, the Pierian maids have made a poet, [etcetera], but I trust them not'.[22]

The incident would not have merited any attention if two years later Huygens had not entered into a sort of poetical discussion with Pieter Cornelisz Hooft. In January and February 1621 both poets exchanged sonnets on the occasion of Huygens' departure to England. Elsewhere I have argued that in these poems Hooft formulates a neoplatonic conception of poetry, illustrated this time by the mythical figures of Orpheus and Arion, and that Huygens rejects this conception as far as his own poetry is concerned, with an appeal to his 'Dutchness'.[23] Even if in this case there was no question of anything aside from playful irony, it seems sure that Huygens did not envisage a neoplatonic background for his own poetry, nor any of the mythological imagery that was connected to it. But there is more.

In 1603, one year before Karel van Mander published his Ovid interpretation, the newly appointed professor at Leyden University, Daniel Heinsius, had delivered his inaugural lecture *De poetis et eorum interpretatoribus* (Over poets and their interpreters). There, as well as in the dedication of his *Elegiae* published earlier that year, the neoplatonic conception of poetry as a heavenly inspired force that gave expression to cosmic harmony and sympathy in its images, was formulated in a much more learned and philosophical way than Van Mander had done. But above all, Heinsius' conception was much more poetical, laying full emphasis on the beauty of rhythm, sound and images, and rejecting all far-fetched allegorical interpretations. The same year, in his study of the *Erga kai Hemerai* (works and days) of Hesiod, Heinsius underlined once more the beauty and wisdom hidden in the images of gods, demigods, mythical poets and heroes of the ancient world.[24]

These same ideas lay behind the poetical correspondence carried on in 1615 between Heinsius, his cousin Jacob van Zevecote and Anna Roemers. Here the Helicon myth of Apollo and the Muses, about which Huygens was so ironic, played a central role. And a few years later, these same ideas once again inspired Hooft in his exchange of poems with Huygens.[25]

In the meantime Heinsius had seen his own Dutch poetry published by his friend Petrus Scriverius in 1616, including his famous 'Bacchus-hymn' (*Hymnus oft lof-sanck van Bacchus*).[26] This very extensive poem testifies to his great knowledge of classical mythology. Scriverius had added a still more extensive and learned commentary, in which all available knowledge was presented, sometimes even combined with traditional allegorical interpretations. More important to my argument, however, is Heinsius' own prologue to the poem, in which he explains why a Christian poet should use the pagan lies no one believes in any longer.

Referring to the Christian fathers and doctors of the church as well as to classical authors and philosophers, he argues that mythological fictions are nothing but names for natural entities and forces, like 'wine' and 'love', and their good and bad qualities. According to this philosophical view all Greek wisdom was contained in these stories. Therefore there was no question of adoration of pagan gods, and no reason for any Christian poet to avoid using their names.[27]

Heinsius, as was to be expected, does not speak of any allegorical meanings, but limits his commentaries on the story to the qualities and effects of wine. His verses on the newborn Bacchus for instance run like this:

> Why are you naked, o Evan, and pictured without any clothes? Because you hate lies and do not love double meanings. Truth lies hidden in your sweet drink. For when we are drunk our tongues are loosened and all that is buried in our hearts comes to life in our mouths.

The poem abounds with mythological stories and learned details, but the interpretations never exceed the physiological and, mostly, psychological level. It must have been this combination of erudition and very direct individual expression that made the poem so unique at the time:

> ... the tongue sticks to the mouth. Babacta, what is this? Give me your drink, and cure my illness. Chase away those water goddesses and pour me out abundantly, that I conquer my sorrows and cares. Why are you following me all the time, why do you make me roam about? What wrong did I do towards you? ... Where do you want me to go? In the water, as they say? Who should save me?[28]

The publication of Heinsius' collected Dutch poetry (*Nederduytsche poemata*) was something of an event, to be judged by the subsequent publication of six editions in the following six years.[29] It was perhaps no wonder that a reaction ensued. Dirck Rafaelsz Camphuysen, a dissident and as such dismissed parson, continued the tradition started by Coornhert and tackled the question.

Two factors may have augmented Camphuysen's indignation. First, in the 1618 edition of his poetry Heinsius had published after his Bacchus-hymn a parallel 'Hymn of Jesus Christ' (*Lof-sanck van Iesus Christus*). Secondly, Camphuysen's attack would have been fuelled by the fact that, since his marriage in 1617, Heinsius had become closely related to the so-called 'gomarist' faction of the public church and was even appointed secretary to the synod of Dordrecht.[30]

In a poem addressed to his friend and co-dissident Joannes Geesteranus, Camphuysen rebuked Heinsius for his hypocrisy, writing as he did of Bacchus as well as of Christ, of worldly love as well as of eternal bliss. In another poem, entitled 'Law of good poetry' (*Wel-rymens wet*), he launches a severe attack on all Greek and Latin learning and mythology. And given the literary situation of the moment it seems more than likely that here, too, he had Heinsius in mind.

It is striking how much this last poem makes one think of Coornhert, who was much admired in the dissident circles Camphuysen belonged to. Camphuysen uses the same arguments, sometimes almost the same words as Coornhert had done. For Camphuysen too, in a good poem the words should be adequate representations of the issues at stake, and nothing else. All pompous learning and pagan mythology, and everything that is not in accordance with the Dutch language, is to be avoided. The catchwords are nature and simplicity, the objectives are virtue and wisdom, which are beautiful enough in themselves and do not need any external adornments.[31]

Did his remarks reach Heinsius? We should not forget that Camphuysen and Heinsius wrote for different publics. Besides, since his marriage Heinsius had not written such poetry and even the publication of his juvenile verse had (at least formally) taken place without his consent.[32] In 1621 he had published his religious-didactic poem *De contemptu mortis*, but after that his poetical creativity seems to have dried up.[33] Nevertheless, he must have known about Camphuysen's views, being the most frequently read of all Dutch poets. So, when he came forward with a new publication eleven years later, it must have come as a shock to him that the discussion started again.

In 1632 Heinsius published his religious tragedy *Herodes infanticida* with a dedication to Constantijn Huygens. A few months later a young French man of letters, Jean Louis Guez de Balzac, to whom Huygens had sent a copy, entered into a correspondence with him on the subject, forwarding some critical notes. Elaborated into a full treatise, these were eventually published under the title *Discours sur une tragedie de Monsieur Heinsius intitulée Herodes Infanticida*. Heinsius, who was furious, reacted in the same year with a *Epistola qua dissertationi D.Balzaci ad Herodem Infanticidam respondetur*. As the question became linked to other quarrels in which Heinsius was involved, it developed into a 'cause célèbre' in the European literary world.[34]

Balzac's objections centre on two points: belief and appropriateness. He concedes that Herod, being a romanized Jew and a idolater at that, might have used the names of pagan gods. But introducing an Angel as well as a Roman Fury on the stage in a single play is not acceptable. The pagan gods and demons died with the coming of the Christian God. The intermingling of the two will not result in their restoration, but it will certainly undermine the truthfulness of Christianity. Besides, it is inappropriate —even blasphemous—for a Christian writing for a Christian public to adorn his language in this way.

This last argument is Erasmian, but the first, about the undermining of truth, is not, as far as I can see. Heinsius' defense, partly the same as that brought forward in 1616, does not impress him. Furies such as Tisiphone cannot be regarded as merely visualised passions, virtues and vices. They were gods to the Romans. Their functions—religious and not psychological —were those of gods, and Heinsius, too, had depicted them as gods.[35]

In my opinion here is the gist of the question, at least to the Dutch public. Until then all emphasis had been on stylistic qualities: using the names of pagan gods was considered pedantic and pompous. Instead, one should use one's own language, and in a simple and straightforward way. With an outspoken religious author such as Camphuysen this pompous antique imagery assumes an extra moral connotation of vicious sensuality, and, in a religious context, of blasphemy.[36]

But Balzac's objections go further. In my opinion they imply a fundamentally historical view of religious and cultural development. What makes the mythological gods really dangerous is not the exotic quality of their names, not even the sinfulness of the passions they are said to signify, but the fact that once they had indeed been considered gods. As such, and because they are no longer believed in, they represent a real threat to the credibility of the Christian God.

I do not think the import of Balzac's criticism was fully understood by most Dutch poets—if they knew about it at all. Opinions mainly continued to develop along the lines drawn by Coornhert and Camphuysen on one side and Heinsius on the other, albeit that both sides seemed to withdraw more and more into their own, respectively religious and profane, domain. Thus in the so-called 'urgent warning' preceding Willem Sluijter's collection of 'Psalms, spiritual hymns and songs' (*Psalmen, lof-sangen, ende geestelike liedekens*, 1661), we read that he had followed the style of the Bible, and avoided the 'alien and false adornments of the antique fables and the names of pagan gods, trying to speak with simple edifying words'.[37]

There was, however, at least some receptivity. Perhaps the intensive reworking by Daniel Mostaert of Heinsius' challenged tragedy is one example. Besides reorganising the whole structure, Mostaert removed all references to pagan deities and replaced the major objective of Balzac's scorn, Tisiphone, with the ghost of Herod's brother-in-law.[38] A clear echo of Balzac's opinions on a more abstract level can be found in the arguments against mythology advanced by Joachim Oudaan. At the same time Oudaan, a great admirer of Coornhert as well as of Camphuysen,[39] again extended his objections to the use of mythology to *all* poetry, secular and profane.

The first of Oudaan's anti-mythological writings was a wedding poem, written in 1662 and directed to his friend Joan Blasius, who had published a small mythological reference book. Here he wishes all pagan gods back to hell, which is generally reminiscent of Balzac's argument. In addition he sneers at those who applied such poetical ornaments, that they were beggars' finery, good for uninspired poets only.[40] Fifteen years later he elaborated these arguments in a long poem, especially dedicated to this issue. But there are reasons enough to assume that in the meanwhile he did not keep them to himself, one of them being the reaction of Vondel's pupil Joannes Antonides van der Goes.

In 1671 Antonides published his extensive epic-didactic poem on the river Y, *Ystroom*. Among the preliminaria figured a laudatory poem by Oudaan, full of such praise as such poems ought to give, but ending with some critical remarks: 'What a pity that a false varnish is splashed over such a beautiful piece of work' and 'I do not value adornments in need of justification'.[41] The justification was given in the same work, in a small treatise preceding the poem itself, reason enough, I think, to consider it the result of previous discussions.

Antonides begins by repeating Vondel's proposition, formulated in his defence of *Faëton*, and which we may now consider a reply to Balzac: nobody would think he was trying to reinstate paganism. Next he turns to Heinsius. He quotes Heinsius in the 1616 edition of his Dutch poetry, that mythological fictions were only names for natural phenomena and human passions. But then he continues with the argument Heinsius had advanced in his reply to Balzac[42]: that as such they constituted the major adornment of all poetic language.

As one of the famous instances to illustrate this second point, Antonides refers *inter alia* to Sannazzaro, who in a poem on the Virgin had attributed prophecy of the birth of the Saviour to Protheus.[43] If anything, this example makes clear how principled, and how antagonistic, was the stand he took: the same poem had been used by Erasmus in his *Ciceronianus* as a negative example, a passage that in its turn was quoted by Balzac.[44] But there is yet more to it. For the mere fact that he appeals to this poem to justify his own secular *Ystroom* implies that to him too the problem was not confined to religious poetry only.

Six years later, in 1677, Oudaan eventually came up with a fully-fledged argumentation of his position in a poem entitled 'Religion and idolatry disclosed: to present day poets' (*Godsdienst- en het godendom ontdekt: aan de hedendaagsche dichters*). Here, at last, he elaborates the two points already present in his epithalamium for Blasius. Firstly, that the mythological gods had indeed been gods to the Greeks and the Romans, and that therefore their poetical renaissance was a flirtation with devilish forces and as such an insult as well as a threat to the Christian creed. And secondly, that their so-called poetical beauty was nothing but idleness and lewdness.[45]

Before the Balzac-Heinsius discussion took place, nobody had ever taken pagan gods so seriously, nor judged Parnassian style so negatively. The difference is striking: no more allegorical interpretations à la van Mander, nor the more symbolic interpretations advocated by Heinsius. The time for neo-platonic conceptions of poetry had passed. Instead, an acute awareness of historical development had grown, in the light of which the pagan gods could only been conceived as idols. Idols that had been overcome: the use or non-use of mythology was not longer a question of genre or style, but one of time. As modern times were Christian, no poet should use pagan imagery anymore, whether in religious or in profane poetry.

It would be another hundred years before the consequences of these new conceptions were fully drawn, at least in the Netherlands. In 1765 the young Rijklof Michaël van Goens published a treatise on the 'use of fables in modern poetry' (*Uitweiding over het gebruik der oude fabel-historie in de dichtstukken der hedendaegschen*), in which he opposed the use of mythology on historical grounds.[46] His arguments were essentially the same as Oudaan's. The difference of period was mainly reflected by the fact that what in 1677 could be expressed in a seven-page poem was in 1765 given in a forty-three page scholarly essay (complete with quotations and references). The pagan gods had indeed been argued off the poetic stage.

Notes

1   Joost van den Vondel, *Werken*, edited by J.F.M. Sterck et al., Vol. 10 (Amsterdam, 1937), 33-34. All quotations are translated by M. Spies.
2   For a general survey of Ovid's influence on 17th century Dutch poetry and especially on Vondel, see: Mieke B. Smits-Veldt, 'Orpheus, dichter-leermeester, minnaar en martelaar', *Lampas* 21 (1988): 361-382, and the older literature mentioned there.
3   For the discussion between Coornhert, Spiegel and Van Mander see: Marijke Spies, '"Poeetsche fabrijcken" en andere allegorieën, eind 16de-begin 17de eeuw', *Oud Holland* 105.4 (1991): 228-243; esp. 228-233 and 238-241.

4   *Het Roerspel en de comedies van Coornhert*, edited by P. van der Meulen (Leiden, 1955), 18. As to the year 1550 see also 223.

5   Erasmus, *The Ciceronian: a dialogue on the ideal Latin style*, translated Betty I. Knott, in Erasmus, *Collected works*, edited by A.H.T. Levi, Vol. 28 (Toronto/Buffalo/London, 1986), 383, 388 and 392.

6   Virgil, *Eclogues, Georgics, Aeneid*, translated by H. Rushton Fairclough, rev. ed., Vol. 1 (London/Cambridge (Mass.), 1965), 66-69.

7   Coornhert 1955, pp. 156-158.

8   Cf. Julius Caesar Scaliger, *Poetices libri septem* I.4 (Lyon, 1561), facs. ed. A. Buck (Stuttgart-Bad Cannstatt, 1987), 6.

9   H.L. Spiegel, *Hert-spiegel*, I, 59-60, edited by F. Veenstra (Hilversum, 1992), 6, 9 and 11.

10 *Hert-spiegel* IV, 49-128, in Spiegel (1992): 93-98.

11 Cf. Graham Castor, *Pléiade poetics. A study in sixteenth-century thought and terminology* (Cambridge, 1964), 24-50.

12 *Spelen van sinne vol scoone moralisacien* [etc.] (Antwerpen, 1562), B 2 verso.

13 Lucas D'Heere, *Den hof en boomgaerd der poësien*, edited by W. Waterschoot (Zwolle, 1969), 24-29.

14 Eric Jan Sluijter, *De 'heydensche fabulen' in de Noordnederlandse schilderkunst, circa 1590-1670* [etc.] (Den Haag, 1986), 312-317; Karel van Mander, *Den grondt der edel vry schilder-const*, edited by H. Miedema, Vol. 2 (Utrecht, 1973), 307 and s.v. 'platonisme'.

15 Karel van Mander, *Wtlegghingh op den Metamorphosis Pub.Ouidij Nasonis* [etc.] (Haarlem, 1604), *3 recto.

16 Van Mander 1604, 23 verso-25 verso.

17 Van Mander 1604, * 4 recto.

18 Spies 1991, pp. 232 and 240-241.

19 Sluijter 1986, pp. 14-16.

20 Cf. for instance: Jacon van der Schuere, 'Choor, ofte versamelingghe der Muses' in *Den Nederduytschen Helicon* (Haarlem, 1610), 50-61.

21 Cf. Joost van den Vondel, *Twee zeevaart-gedichten* [etc.], edited by Marijke Spies, 2 vols (Amsterdam/Oxford/New York, 1987), passim.

22 Constantijn Huygens, *Gedichten*, edited by J.A.Worp, Vol. 1 (Arnhem, 1892), 134-135.

23 Marijke Spies, 'Arion - Amphion: Huygens en Hooft in de stormen van 1621-1622' in E.K. Grootes et al. (eds), *Uyt liefde geschreven. Studies over Hooft* (Groningen, 1981), 101-116; esp. 105-106.

24 J.H. Meter, *The literary theories of Daniel Heinsius.* [etc.] (Assen, 1984), 38-67.

25 Vondel 1987, Vol. 1, 216-221.

26 Daniel Heinsius, *Nederduytsche poemata* (1616), edited by Barbara Becker-Cantarino (Bern/Frankfurt am Main, 1983).

27 Daniel Heinsius, *Bacchus en Christus. Twee lofzangen*, edited by L.Ph. Rank, J.D.P. Warners and F.L. Zwaan (Zwolle, 1965), 24-35 and 99-104.

28 Heinsius 1965, resp. vs. 51-56 (114-116) and vs. 645-654 (184).

29 Heinsius 1983, 'Einleitung', pp. 26-35.

30 Baerbel Becker-Cantarino, *Daniel Heinsius* (Boston, 1978), 19-20.

31 D.R. Camphuysen, *Stichtelycke rymen*, Vol. 2 (s.l., 1624) resp. 179-180 and 170-175. Cf. also: M.A. Schenkeveld-van der Dussen, 'Camphuysen en het "genus humile"' in H. Duits et al. (eds), *Eer is het lof des deuchts* [etc.] (Amsterdam, 1986), 141-153.

32 Heinsius 1965, 'Introduction', p. 16.

33 Becker-Cantarino 1978, p. 66.

34 Gustave Cohen, *Écrivains Français en Hollande dans la première moitié du 17e siècle* (Paris, 1920), 275-291.

35 J.-L. de Guez de Balzac, *Oeuvres*, edited by L. Moreau, Vol. 1 (Paris, 1854), 'Discours huictiesme', 320-360.

36 Cf. Camphuysen 1624, Vol. 2, 179-180.

37 Wilhelm Sluiter, 'Noodige onderwijsinge en vermaninge aenden Christeliken sanger ende leser' in *Psalmen, lof-sangen, ende geestelike liedekens* [etc.] (Deventer, 1661), b 3 recto-verso.

38 Cf. for instance: Daniel Heinsius, *Herodes infanticida. Tragoedia* (Lugd. Bat., 1632), 39-40 and Th. Ag., *Treurspel. De moord der onnoozelen* (Amsterdam, 1639), B 3 verso. As to the author, cf. P.H. van Moerkerken, 'Wie is de schrijver van het treurspel "De moord der onnoozelen"?', *Tijdschrift voor Nederlandsche Taal- en Letterkunde* 13 (1894): 136-143.

39 J. Melles, *Joachim Oudaan. Heraut der verdraagzaamheid* (Utrecht, 1958), 57-59 and 177.

40 Cf: J. te Winkel, *Ontwikkelingsgang der Nederlandsche letterkunde*, 2nd ed., Vol. 4 (Haarlem, 1924), 109.

41 J. Antonides van der Goes, *De Ystroom* (Amsterdam, 1671), *** 4 recto.

42 Heinsius, *Epistola qua dissertationi D.Balzaci ad Herodem Infanticida respondetur*, edited by M. Zuerius Boxhorn (Leyden, 1636).

43 Antonides 1671, 'Voorreden', ** 1 recto - ** 3 recto.

44 Erasmus 1986, p. 437; Balzac 1854, Vol. 1, p. 328.

45 Joachim Oudaan, *Poëzy*, Vol. 1 (Amsterdam, 1712), 32-38.

46 [R.M. van Goens] *Uitweiding over het gebruik der oude fabel-historie in de dichtstukken der hedendaegschen* in *Een pleidooi voor de wetenschappelijke beoefening van de letterkunde* [etc.], edited by J.B. Brandt Corstius (Groningen, 1972), 69-112.

17

'LOVE THOU ART ABSOLUTE': RICHARD CRASHAW AND THE DISCOURSE OF HUMAN AND DIVINE LOVE

CLAIRE WARWICK

The quotation which forms part of the title of this essay comes from the 'Hymn to St Teresa'. The poem opens with the acclamation: 'Love thou art absolute, sole Lord / Of life and Death'. Such a statement can leave the reader in little doubt of the importance of love in Crashaw's devotional world. Crashaw is obsessed by love; it is omnipresent in his poems. It can be mild or terrifyingly powerful, the gentle child of the 'Epiphany Hymn', or the despot of 'Hymn to the Name', who compels converts to 'bow before [him]'. He says that from Teresa's works he 'learnt to know that love is eloquence', and Crashaw's development of an eloquent discourse in which to express his own adoration for this 'lord of love' is the focus of my discussion.

It seems appropriate to the theme of this volume that I should begin with Crashaw's poem of homage to *The Temple*, that leading seventeenth century exemplum of the interplay of sacred and profane in devotional verse. Herbert and Crashaw may seem to be about as different as religious poets could possibly be, and, indeed, critics have often found Herbert as congenial and rewarding to read as Crashaw is alien and off-putting. Yet Crashaw himself revered Herbert's poetry, and in naming his poems *Steps to the Temple* strove to associate his writing with the earlier poet's, although as humbler means of access to the greater work. The anonymous preface to the reader describes Crashaw as 'Herbert's second but equall',[1] and other seventeenth century writers like William Winstanley and David Lloyd agreed with this judgement.[2] Thus, though the style of the two poets differs, seventeenth-century readers, at least, perceived a strong connection between them. Helen Wilcox has shown that soon after *The Temple* was published it was already being recommended as a devotional text.[3] Crashaw recommends it to a woman as just such an aid to devotion.

Crashaw's 'On Mr. Herbert's Book', exemplifies the way in which he used the resources of secular love to develop a way to express his love for God.

> Know you fair on what you looke;
> Divinest love lyes in this booke,
> Expecting fire from your eyes
> To kindle this his sacrifice.   (ll, 1-4)

At first the book seems to be recommended to the woman as an engaging romance, as its religious nature is hidden by ambiguous language until line four. The vocabulary is erotically allusive throughout the poem. Phrases like 'morning sigh', 'balmy air', 'perfumed prayer', 'the shrine / Of your white hand' immediately call to mind secular, Petrarchan conventions. At the same time, these exist in tension with religious language, such as 'sacrifice', 'Angel', 'Prayer', 'devotion'. The new language emerges almost by competing with the discourse of love with which it coexists.

Crashaw has, however, suffered at the hands of critics who seem to judge him by some sort of Herbertian norm of decorum in religious writing. Crashaw's overt use of sensual images and sexual language has been greeted at best with suspicion, and at worst with allegations of bad taste.[4] However, I hope to demonstrate that his use of erotic language is much less perverse and febrile than his reputation would suggest. In order to do this, I believe that it is essential to look at his earliest published poems, the *Epigrammata Sacra.*[5]

Crashaw's seventeenth-century contemporaries clearly valued the epigrams highly; both Holdsworth and Barnes include them in lists or recommended reading for undergraduates at Cambridge University.[6] However, the collection as a whole is relatively neglected by modern critics. Although Laurens and Balavoine praise it as 'une réussite incontesible, où se réconclient la doctrine et le sentiment, l'ésprit et la poésie',[7] Patrides' opinion seems more typical: 'Crashaw's efforts are in fact mostly exercises laboriously bent after a pre-determined effect; and so far one would not have wished them to have been more numerous than they are'.[8] Yet they are extremely valuable to us, not only as accomplished works in themselves, but because the references Crashaw makes to the tropes of Latin erotic poetry can provide information about the way he intends to construct a discourse of religious love.

The opening poem, 'Lectori' or 'To the reader', is of vital importance to any understanding of Crashaw's religious writing. At first sight the layout suggests that readers are facing an erotic poem. This kind of elegiac couplet was the metre used by the Latin erotic elegists Tibullus, Propertius and Ovid. From the very opening of the poem, Crashaw associates himself with secular erotic writing. Yet he is at pains immediately to distance himself from it .

Salve. Jamque vale. Quid enim quis pergeret ultra?
    Qua jocus et lusus non vocat ire voles?
Scilicet hic lector cur nostra habere non est;
    Delitiis folio non faciente tuis.
Nam nec Acidalios halat mihi pagina rores;
    Nostra Cupidinae nec favet aura faci
Frustra hinc ille suis quicquam promiserit alis:
    Frustra hinc illa novo spetet abire sinu.   (Lectori, ll. 1-8)

Hail. And now farewell. For why would anyone go any further? Will
you go where playful joking does not call? Obviously reader this is not
the reason you will be ours; this book does not aim at your pleasure.
For neither does this page breath out Acidalian dews, nor does our
breath favour Cupid's torch. In vain will he [Cupid] have promised his
wings anything from this: in vain may she [Venus] hope to depart with
a new heart from here.[9]

He is playing with the expectations that a reader used to Classical Latin
poetry may have, alternately setting up then knocking down our preconceptions.

Like Herbert in 'Love I', Crashaw uses the vocabulary of the rejected
discourse while indicating his separation from it. The opening lines are full
of vocabulary redolent of the densely allusive language of the Classical
Latin Elegists, such as 'iocus', 'Lusus' and 'Delitiis' and the later reference
in line 26 to 'salax' or saltiness, meaning wit.[10] This is very much 'insiders' poetry; he expects the reader to know who 'he' and 'she' are in lines
7-8, and the full effect of what is to happen in the poem relies on the recognition of such language. However, it is obvious that he is specifically denying any erotic intent. From the outset, Crashaw plays with our expectations
by creating a tension between what we know of these words' usual signification in an erotic context, and the meaning which they must take on in this
instance.

Throughout the opening section of the poem he associates himself with
the classical past. The text is full of allusions to mythological figures associated with love, from Cupid, Venus and her lover Adonis, to Circe, the
enchantress who seduced Odysseus. Ovid's erotic poetry is suggested by
'nudae Veneres', and the succession of female exempla in lines 31ff. In
'The Thanksgiving', Herbert had alluded to Ovid, and stated his intention
to produce a new 'Book of Loves'. Here Crashaw attempts to discover how
this may be achieved.

Both Crashaw and Herbert would have been familiar with Ovid from their school-days, as his poetry was used as an example of Latin at its most elegant.[11] The erotic poems were considered too salacious to form part of the official curriculum. However, they were usually bound in the same volume as the *Heroides*, the most commonly studied of Ovid's elegiac poems. Thus they were easily available to any inquisitive pupil. An example of what appears to be a school copy in Cambridge University Library shows heavy annotations in several hands in the *Heroides*, which are not present in the *Amores* and *Ars Amatoria*.[12] However it seems highly likely that these would have been privately read, even if not part of the official curriculum. Despite the recall and burning of Marlowe's translation of the *Amores* in 1600,[13] the erotic poetry had already become a profound influence on thinking and writing on love.

Crashaw deliberately recalls Ovid's *Amores*, which open with the refusal of one type of poetry for another in I,1. The poet claims to have been trying to write epic, until side-tracked by Cupid. Crashaw portrays Cupid attempting a similar attack on him, but he, unlike Ovid, refuses.

> Saepe puer dubias circum me moverat alas;
>   Jecit et incertas nostra sub ora faces.
> Saepe vel ipsa sua calamum mihi blandus ab ala,
>   Vel matris cygno de meliore dedit.
> Saepe Dionaeae pactus mihi serta coronae;
>   Saepe, Meus vates tu, mihi dixit, eris.
> I procul, i cum, matre tua, puer improbe, dixi:
>   Non tibi cum numeris res erit ulla meis.   (ll. 43-50)

Often the boy moved his fluttering wings around me and hurled his unpredictable darts around my face. Often that flatterer gave me a quill from his own wing or a better one from his mother's swan. Often he promised me garlands from the Dionaean crown; often he said to me 'You will be my poet'. But I said, 'Go far off, go with your mother wicked boy, there's nothing for you in my verse'.

Line 48 obviously recalls Cupid's triumphant shout, as he snares Ovid:

> Lanavitque genu sinuosum fortiter arcum
>   'quod' que 'Canas, vates, accipe' dixit 'opus'.
>   (Amores I,1 ll. 25-26)

> And bent his sinewy bow upon his knee,
> Saying, 'Poet, here's a work beseeming thee'.[14]

However, Ovid gives in without much more than token resistance, whereas the repetition of 'Saepe', 'often', in Crashaw's text shows that his has been a protracted struggle to resist Cupid's advances. He is, then, placing himself in a position which is directly comparable to the most famous of erotic poets. He shows that his development as a religious poet stems from a refusal of such temptation. But by making the situation and language so close to that of Ovid's poem, he shows very clearly the origins of his new form of poetry.

Crashaw then turns a poem which has so far defined itself only by negatives to a positive aim. In line 57 he changes the direction of the poem so delicately that it may almost pass unnoticed.

> Gleba illa (ah tua quam tamen urit adultera messis)
>   Esset Idumaeo germine quanta parens
> Quantus ibi et quantae premeret puer ubera matris
>   Nec caelos vultu dissimulare suos
> Ejus in isto occuli satis essent sydera versu
>   Sydereo matris quam bene tua sinu   (ll. 57-62)

That soil (ah how your adulterous harvest still burns) would have been greatly productive with the seed of Idumaea! How great a boy would there press the breasts of how great a mother! And with a face not concealing his own heavens. In that verse his eyes would be stars enough; how very safe in his mother's starry embrace ...

Here both the vocabulary and the sense of the passage show how he is attempting to create a new form of writing by reaction to another. Christ and Mary appear in the text by growing out of what are seen to be their direct predecessors. As Kenneth Larsen notes,[15] they are direct analogues of Venus and Cupid. This development was not unique to Crashaw, and was in some ways another indication to the reader of the kind of poetry they were about to read. Stella Revard notes that in Neo-Latin hymns Venus and The Virgin share some of the same iconography.[16]

Religious subject matter now enters this text through erotic language. The word used to describe Mary's embrace of her son is the sexually charged 'sinu' already used in this way at line 8. Yet the threat of Cupid and his mother can only be banished by taking a further step of actually turning them into the Virgin and Child:

> Cede puer (dixi, et dico) cede improba mater:
> Altera Cupris habet nos; habet alter Amor.

Scilicet hic Amor est. Hic est quoque mater Amoris
Sed mater virgo. Sed neque caecus Amor.   (ll. 83-86)

Surrender boy, [Cupid] I said, and still say, surrender shameful mother;
another Venus holds me, and another love. It is obvious that this is
love, and that this is the love's mother. But the mother is a virgin, and
this Love is not blind.

The reader is challenged to suspend any preconceptions about sacred and
secular language, as the Blessed Virgin is equated with the goddess of sexual love. The same word, 'Puer' is used to mean both Cupid and Christ and
'Amor', as love signifies both the old love and the new. The transition
between the old and new is made so easily that the reader hardly notices the
slippage in signification. Crashaw describes representatives of another love,
but still uses the classical conventions of his model.

   The Christ child is a direct equivalent of Cupid; he even borrows his
darts, and is asked to use them on the poet:

O Amor, innocuae sunt pia iura pharetrae;
       Nec nisi de casto corde sagitta calens.
Me, puer, o certa, quem figis, fige sagitta.
       O tua de me sit facta pharetra levis

...
Fige, puer, corda haec. Seu spinis exiguus quis,
       Seu clavi aut hastae cuspide magnus ades;
Sue maior cruce cum tota; seu maximus ipso
       te corda haec figis denique. Fige puer.   (ll. 89-92, 95-98)

Oh love who possesses the sacred laws of a harmless quiver, and an
arrow that only ignites a chaste heart. Oh boy, [Christ], pierce me
whom you pierce with your well-aimed arrow. Oh may your quiver
become light because of me.

Pierce this heart, boy, you are present very little in those thorns, more
in the sharp point of a spear or nail, even more in the whole of the
cross, most of all you transfix this heart with your very presence,
pierce boy.

The image is initially modeled on Ovid's request to Cupid in Amores II, 9,
in which he casts himself as a victim of love.

Fige, puer: positis nudus tibi praebeor armis;
    hic tibi sunt vires, hic tua dextra facit,   (ll. 35-36)

Strike boy, I offer thee my naked breast,
Here thou hast strength, here thy right hand doth rest ...

The newly sacred boy in Crashaw's poem is asked to pierce the speaker
with weapons from Cupid's hitherto exclusive armoury. The violent images
of piercing are at first derived from the classical erotic convention of 'Militia Amoris', or 'the battle of love'.[17] However, by line 95, the weapons
have changed to 'spinis' and 'hasta', the thorns and spear which now con-
note the crucifixion. The boy is now the Christ-child, who is asked to inflict
the injuries on the poet which He had suffered on the cross. We are also
made aware that the images of ecstatic piercing, so prevalent in the later
poetry, may derive less from St. Teresa's vision than Cupid's dart.[18] By
using Cupid as the model from which Christ develops, Crashaw is attempting to do much more than merely produce a polar opposite. Though Crashaw rejects the carnal purpose of Cupid's arrows, he has created Christ in
his pagan image.

    The process by which a Christian discourse is created from a classical
model is illustrated in another of the epigrammes which uses the the convention of 'militia amoris', 'In Cicatrices Domini'. The shift from the classical certainty of Amor as Cupid with his erotic weaponry to the Christian
deity occurs in the gap between the first and second stanzas.

Arma vides; arcus, pharetramque, levesque saggitas,
    Et quocunque fuit nomine miles Amor.

His fuit usus Amor: sed & haec fuit ipse; suumque
    Et jaculum, & jaculis ipse pharetrae suis.   (ll. 1-4)

You see the weapons, the bow, quiver and the light arrows, and by
whatever name, this soldier was Love. Love used these things, but he
also was these things himself, he was both dart and the quiver for his
own darts.

It is left to the reader to assume that the second Amor connotes Christ.
Gradually we are made aware that the scene is that of the Crucifixion, not
through specific information but by the hints the text provides. Crashaw
relies on the reader's ability to decode the text using his/her knowledge of
the Bible. The change from the influence of the vestigial imprint of Ovid to

that of the gospels is achieved by a gradual slippage in the meaning of the words 'Love', 'soldier' and 'weapons'. *'Amor'* at first denotes Cupid, then, still by implication, Christ. *'Miles'* is at first the legendary Cupid with his bow. The weapons are then transformed into the armaments of a new, self-wounding love, whom we suspect to be the self-sacrificial Christ. The signification of *'Miles'* shifts to that of a human soldier who, we surmise, must be a Roman guard at Calvary. In stanza six the soldier could still be a Vergilian hero like Turnus, driven on to slaughter by Furor. The victim of the attack is Christ, but still a very Roman hero. The weapons are again changed into the biblical spear and thorns. However, the Crown of thorns is still described by, and perhaps united with, classical vocabulary.[19]

> Seu digito suadente tuo *mala Laurus* inibat
> Temporibus; sacrum seu bibit hasta latus: (ll. 13-14)

> Whether, with your finger's persuasion, the evil laurel Wreath entered his forehead, or the spear drank from his holy side.

Crashaw is able to emphasise the triumphal element in the Crucifixion, by using the vocabulary of a Roman victory. Christ is not conquered in death, but becomes the Triumphator, crowned with a laurel.

In his poem 'On Mr Herbert's Book' Crashaw emphasises that the co-operation of the reader is vital. The book is 'Expecting fire from your eyes / To kindle this his sacrifice'. It is the role of the reader to act as the arbitrator between the two types of language. If she is able to create a balance between the two discourses, then the interaction of the two will re-animate the love inherent in the waiting text. As both 'Lectori' and 'In cicatrices' show, Crashaw expects the reader to use his/her knowledge of both Classical erotic poetry and the Bible to de-code the text. If we are unable or unwilling to do so, we cannot appreciate how this new discourse of love is created, nor what type of love this Christian version may be. At the end of 'Lectori' he returns to address the reader directly:

> Ah durus! quicunque meos, nisi siccus, amores
> Nolit; et hic lacrymae rem neget esse suae   (ll. 119-120)

> Oh cruel, whoever rejects my love unless dry-eyed, let him deny there is a cause for his tears.

This complaint is directed at an unresponsive reader, and carries the force of the lament of rejected lover in Latin love poetry.[20] The object of the poet's entreaty has now shifted from Cupid, the instigator of love, to Christ, its object, to the reader, who is asked to participate in both love and worship through poetry.

'Lectori', then, provides an insight into the way Crashaw adapts erotic discourse to produce a new 'discourse centred in Heaven', as the preface to *Steps to the Temple* puts it (75). Crashaw does not attempt to break away from the Roman language and its discourse. Instead, 'Lectori' stresses how closely related the two types of love are. He uses erotic poetry as a linguistic resource for a new discourse, while still relating it to its origins.

In 'Non Nudus Amor' we are warned that this type of love is far more complex than its classical model. Several connotations of the word 'Nudus' are used to drive home the shift between classical erotic discourse and 'discourse centred in Heaven'.

> Falleris. & nudum male ponis (Pictor) Amorem:
>   Non nudum facis hanc, cum sine veste facis.

> Non hic est (dum sic digito patet ille fideli)
> Tunc, cum vestitus, tunc quoque nudus amor?

> You are mistaken painter, and you wrongly depict Love naked. You do not show him unadorned only by painting him without clothes.

> Surely when He [Christ] reveals himself at the fingertips of a faithful person, He is then, despite clothing, undisguised love.

The literal meaning of 'nudus', 'naked', facilitates a reference back to the image of the naked putto, Cupid, while the figurative sense of 'unadorned', and thus true, allows the shift into a religious discourse. Crashaw's mastery of the epigrammatic form[21] allows him to exploit the space between the stanzas as a way of inscribing in typographical layout the gap between the two types of love. The contrast between the upper case letter denoting love in the first stanza, and lower case in the second, though conceivably a compositorial error, is also important. Classical Amor is love and only love, and thus a deity with limited influence. Christ may exemplify love, but his power as a deity need not only be predicated on this one quality.

Having demonstrated how Crashaw uses the influences of classical erotic poetry to inform his writing on love, it is now possible to show how this affected his writing about love in the English poetry. In 'On A Prayer Book, Sent to Mrs M.R.', the tension of sacred and Classical is immediately apparent.

> Loe here a little volume, but large book,
>> (Feare it not, sweet,
>> It is no hipocrit)
> Much larger in itself then in its look   (ll. 1-4)

This is reminiscent of the opening of Catullus I, which stresses the poet's need to express his ideas within a small poetic space. Indeed the witticism of 'heaven and all / Heavens royall Hoasts incampt, thus small' is the seventeenth century poet's equivalent of:

> iam tum, cum ausus es unus Italorum
> omne aeuum tribus explicare cartis   (Carmen I, ll. 5-6)

> in the days when you alone in Italy were daring to compress the whole history of the world into three volumes of a single book.

This use of allusion allows Crashaw to make his point about the value of this book while still retaining the lightness of tone suggestive of a playful love lyric. Thus pre-Christian, classical aesthetics are applied to a the liturgy of a Christian church. He also alludes to contemporary politics. The particular resonance of 'royall hoasts incampt' would not have been lost on Crashaw's original readership.

   A shift of signification in which the poem's language moves from classical eroticism to Christian love begins in stanzas 3-5. The procedure by which this is achieved is strikingly simliar to the one which I have demonstrated in 'Lectori'. Initially, the language of *Militia Amoris* dominates, with the sauciness of the encampment of 'loves great Artillery ... in [her] white bosom'. Yet the language begins a subtle shift to effect the gradual change of tone. From the erotic 'white bosom', it moves to the more moral 'chast heart'. 'Militia Amoris' now does become the Church Militant with its 'Armory of light', which no longer mounts a playful attack, but becomes a powerful weapon of defence against the dangers of sin and hell. By stanza 5 the erotic vocabulary may still be present, 'Those of turtles chast and true', but it has been gradually subsumed into a religious discourse.

   As the poem develops, the discourses become even more inter-related. Just as Christ and Mary, in 'Lectori', developed directly from their classical models, Venus and Cupid, so in this poem Crashaw moves from classical to biblical eroticism as a model for his own language. He uses the parable of the wise virgins as a kind of Christian justification for his methodology.[22] The effect of Christ's teaching in parables was gained by the move from a familiar earthly example to the Christian lesson of the story. In order to make an abstract idea or value comprehensible a familiar analogue was used. Thus Christ warns his followers always to be ready for the coming of God's kingdom by the example of women who are ready to welcome a bridegroom.

This parable is particularly apt for Crashaw's use. He needs to examine and explicate a highly complex and abstract idea; that is the relationship of love between God and humanity. To do this he uses a familiar human analogue, that of earthly sexual love. Crashaw's own poetic methodology is thus 'sanctioned' by the similarity of his and Christ's mode of expression. Insted of adopting the poetic strategy of Ovid, the most celebrated writer of classical, profane love poetry, he now uses the methodology of Christ's teaching. The embodiment of Christian love now proves to be a poetic influence, as well as an object of worship.

He is also able to draw upon the erotic possibilities of the story itself, that of a visiting bridegroom. He was well aware that the bridegroom of the highly erotic *Song of Songs* was considered to be an allegory for Christ, and the love in the canticles was seen as the relationship between himself and humanity or the church. Indeed the vocabulary derived from the Song of Songs in the two final stanzas, for example the 'deare silver breasted dove', 'her morning spouse ... all fresh and fragrant as he rises',[23] shows that Crashaw is influenced by biblical as well as classical uses of erotic language.[24] Thus, through alluding to the story of the wise virgins, he has provided himself with a justification for the eroticism which is to follow.

The remainder of stanza 9 begins the build-up of meaning in an agglomeration of ecstatic language. He recognises the limits of spoken language to deal with the ecstatic in religious experience.

> Words which are not heard with eares,
> (Those tumultuous shops of noise)
> Effectuall whispers whose still voyce
> The soule it selfe more feeles than heares. (ll. 59-62)

In his attempt to produce a written language which will enter a spiritual dimension, the only linguistic register left is that of the sensual. Yvor Winters has objected that:

> the poet who insists on dealing with the mystical experience and who becomes involved emotionally in the sexual analogy runs the risk of corrupting his devotional poetry generally with sexual imagery. It is not that sexual experience is 'immoral'; but it is irrelevant ... [and] can result in nothing but confusion.[25]

Yet when Crashaw has made clear that no other form of language will do, the only resource left is the erotic. As Simone Weil protested:

> To reproach mystics with loving God by means of the faculty of sexual love, is as though one were to reproach a painter with making pictures by means of colours composed of material substances. We haven't anything else with which to love.[26]

Far from being irrelevant, the language of sexuality is the most apt to describe the rapturous 'ek-stasis', literally standing outside the self, felt in devotional meditation.[27] In stanza 10 he uses orgasmic language as the nearest he can manage to experiences 'for which it is no shame, / That dull mortality must not know a name'.

> Delicious deaths, soft exhalations
> Of soule: deare, and divine annihilations.
>   A thousand unknowne rites
>   Of joyes, and rarifyed delights.   (ll. 71-74)

He uses language which describes the most ecstatic human experience of love to form an analogy for the projected experience of heavenly love. St Francis De Sales placed human sexual ecstasy and that caused by the worship of God at opposite ends of a continuum of love stretching from human to divine. He explains that either experience may produce the same state: 'because an Ecstacie is no other thing then a going out of ones selfe, whether one goe upwards or downwards, he is truely in an Ecstacie'.[28] Going up refers to 'divine pleasures', and down refers to sex. Human love is not rejected, but seen as a much lowlier form of love for God. In the same way Crashaw uses familiar earthly experience to create an analogue for an imagined heavenly consummation.

Crashaw has been criticised for a lack of analytical and argumentative structure and for the overly emotional tone of his writing. Petersson comments, 'While Crashaw's interest in the life of the intellect is minimal, his attraction to the spiritual passion of Catholic baroque is limitless'.[29] It is true that his poetry presents ample evidence of his own 'spiritual passion', yet it seems unlikely that an unthinking hedonist would have been able to construct a discourse of love in the complex fashion which Crashaw did. The aim of this essay has been to demonstrate that Crashaw's erotic language is far from being a grutuitous or tasteless venture into an area unfitting for religious poets. His struggle to develop a discourse in which to express spiritual ecstasy indicates not only a personal obsession with his love of God, but a desire to communicate it to his readers in terms that they may understand. From the linguistically familiar vocabulary and conventions of erotic poetry, he works towards the unfamiliar territory of ecstatic contemplative worship. From classical eroticism he moves gradually towards his own language of Christian love. Such a language is justly called a 'discourse centred in Heaven' (75).

Notes

1   'The Preface to the Reader', *Crashaw's Poetical Works*, edited by L.C. Martin (Oxford, 1927), 75. All further references are to this edition.

2   David LLoyd, 'Richard Crashaw' in *Memoires of the Lives, Actions, Sufferings and Deaths of those Noble, and Excellent Personages, that Suffered by Death, Sequestration, Decimation, or Otherwise for the Protestant Religion* (London, 1688), 619; William Winstanley, 'The Life of *Launcelot Andrewes* Bishop of Winchester', in *England's Worthies. Select Lives of the Most Eminent Persons of the English Nation from Constantine the Great to the Death of Cromwell* (London, 1660), 295. See Hamish Swanston, 'The Second Temple', *Durham University Journal* 25 (1963): 14-22.

3   Helen Wilcox, '"Heaven's Lidger Here": Herbert's Temple and Seventeenth Century Devotion' in David Jasper (ed.), *Images of Belief in Literature* (London, 1984), 153-168 (153).

4   Those who criticise Crashaw include Robert M. Adams, 'Taste and bad-taste in Metaphysical poetry: Richard Crashaw and Dylan Thomas', *Hudson Review* 8 (1955): 61-77, William Empson, *Seven Types of Ambiguity* (London, 1930), 280; and Frank Warnke, *European Metaphysical Poetry* (New Haven, 1961), 15.

5   Richard Crashaw, *Epigrammata Sacrorum Liber* (Cambridge, 1634).

6   Richard Holdsworth, 'Directions for a Student in the Universitie', Emmanuel College Manuscript 1.2.27, (1), and Joshua Barnes, Emmanuel College Manuscript II-I.1.11. No 173. Cited in Thomas F. Healy, *Richard Crashaw* (Leyden, 1986), 58.

7   Pierre Laurens and Claudie Balavoine, *Musae Reduces: Anthologie de la Poesie Latin dans l'Europe de la Renaissance* (Leiden, 1975), Vol. II, 494.

8   C.A. Patrides, 'Richard Crashaw: The Merging of Contrarieties' in his *Figures in a Renaissance Context*, edited by Claude J. Summers and Ted-Larry Pebworth (Ann Arbor, Michigan, 1989), 141-160 (145).

9   Translation here and throughout is my own.

10 See R.O.A.M. Lyne, 'The Neoteric poets', *Classical Quarterly* 28 (1978): 167-187.

11 See J.W. Binns, *Intellectual Culture in Elizabethan and Jacobean England: The Latin Writings of the Age* (Leeds, 1990), 291-307, and T.W. Baldwin, *William Shakespeare's Small Latine and Lesse Greeke* (Urbana, 1944), esp. Vol. I, 285-436, and Vol. II, 380-455.

12   Publius Ovidius Nasonis, *Poemata Amatoria* (Antwerp, 1545), X.11.29. Baldwin seems to have found a 1566 reprint of the same edition, which must have been a standard textbook, in the British Library, 11355. aa. 26, showing the same sort of markings. Baldwin, Vol. II, 421.

13   See Edward Arber, *A Transcript of the Registers of the Company of Stationers of London, 1554-1640,* Vol. III (London, 1876), 316.

14   Translations are from Marlowe's version of the Amores, since this would have been available to seventeenth century readers.

15   Kenneth Larsen, 'Richard Crashaw's *Epigrammata Sacra*', in: J.W. Binns, ed., *The Latin Poetry of English Poets* (London and Boston, 1974), 93-121.

16   Stella P. Revard, 'Crashaw and the Diva: The tradition of the Neo-Latin Hymn to the Goddess' in John R. Roberts (ed.), *New perspectives on the Life and Art of Richard Crashaw* (Columbia, 1990), 80-99.

17   See E. Thomas, 'Variations on a Military Theme in Ovid's *Amores*' Greece and Rome, NS 2 (1974), 151-65, and P. Murgatroyd, '*Militia Amoris* and the Roman Elegists', *Latomus* 34 (1975): 59-69.

18   For an account of this, see *The Vida, The Flaming Hart, or the Life of the Glorious S. Teresa*, translated by Sir Toby Matthew (Antwerp, 1642), 419-420.

19   Vida employs very similar vocabulary in his description of Christ's torments before the Crucifixion. Marco Girolamo Vida, *The Christiad*, edited and translated by Gertrude C. Drake and Clarence A. Forbes (London and Amsterdam, 1978), Book 5, lines 372-379.

20   Julius Caesar Scaliger discusses elegy, and notes the trope of the excluded lover as a convention in *Poetices Libri Septem* (Lyons, 1561), 169, c. 2. For modern discussion of this idea, see Francis Cairns, *Generic Composition in Greek and Roman Poetry* (Edinburgh, 1972), 6 and 76, and Gordon Williams, *Tradition and Originality in Roman poetry* (Oxford, 1968), 546ff.

21   See Austin Warren, *Richard Crashaw* (Baton Rouge, 1939), 83, 89, and J.A.W. Bennett, 'Recusants and Hymnodists', in his *Poetry of the Passion: Studies in Twelve Centuries of English Verse* (Oxford, 1982), 168-198.

22   For discussion of the way in which Crashaw uses spiritual authority as a justification for his language, see Thomas F. Healy, 'Crashaw and the Sense of History' in Roberts, *New Perspectives* 49-66 (58).

23   See *Song of Songs*, ch. 5, ll, 2 and 12, ch. 4, ll, 14-16, and ch. 7, l, 13.

24   Stanley Stewart, *The Enclosed Garden* (London and Madison, 1967).

25   Yvor Winters, *Forms of Discovery* (Chicago, 1967), 91-92.

26   *The Notebooks of Simone Weil*, translated by Arthur Wills (London, 1956), Vol. II, 472.

27   See Anthony Low, *Love's Architecture: Devotional Modes in Seventeenth Century English Poetry* (New York, 1978), 128ff.

28   St. Francis De Sales, *A Treatise of the Love of God*, translated by Thomas Carre (Douay, 1630), 39.

29   Robert T. Petersson, *The Art of Ecstacy: Teresa, Bernini and Crashaw* (New York, 1974), 124.

18

'TIL WE MIX WOUNDS':
LITURGICAL PARADOX AND CRASHAW'S CLASSICISM

JEFFREY JOHNSON

During the summer of 1640, while serving as catechist at Little St. Mary's, Richard Crashaw found himself involved in controversy. It seems that John Shilburne, a parishoner living near the chapel, had filed an official complaint against him. In particular, Shilburne charged not only that Crashaw retained his young catechumens at evening prayer for an excessive length of time, but also that he 'did in his catechisinge saye that an angell hath winges & a bird hath winges & yf the bird fly upp to heavn will there be ever an Angell moore?'.[1] In his account of this incident, Hilton Kelliher defends Crashaw by noting both that 'Shilburne's complaint that Crashaw kept the children too long probably indicates Crashaw's real enthusiasm for his duties, in the performance of which one can readily believe that he might lose track of time', and that 'That the Prayer Book catechism makes no mention of angels merely shows that, like any thorough and conscientious teacher, Crashaw was not content simply to follow the outline laid down there' (196). There are, however, any number of critics who, finding nothing of delight in Crashaw's penchant for exceeding the bounds in both form and content (whether in his ministerial duties or in his verse), would agree with Shilburne's assessment that 'When Mʳ Crashaw was made a Scholler, there was a ploughman spoyled' (193).

Although it is true, as Thomas Healy notes, that 'Crashaw is not a theological poet' in the sense that for him 'Devotion over dispute is advocated',[2] it is everywhere apparent in Crashaw's religious verse that excess and expansion distinguish his habit of mind and, thereby, define him theologically. This habit reveals itself not only in the poems Crashaw published in more than one version (the later of which consistently exceed the length of the earlier) and in his verse translations (which invariably elaborate upon their sources), but, more importantly, in his use of the classical genres of epigram, hymn and ode, in which Crashaw celebrates and imitates the wit of God, conjoining in Christ human and divine, heaven and earth, profane and sacred.

The central action of Crashaw's religious verse is a liturgical one of mixing, which typologically reflects not only Christ's miracle at the wedding in Cana where he turned water to wine (John 2: 1-11), but especially the confluence of water and blood that issued from the side of the crucified

Son of God (John 19: 34). In this context, the veritable flood of liquids Crashaw blends together throughout his religious verse (especially water, blood, wine, tears and milk) recreates the liturgical action of the priest mixing water and wine during the Mass. The liquid imagery, as well as the instances of liquefaction, found throughout the Divine Epigrams, 'The Weeper', the Teresa poems and 'Sancta Maria Dolorum', for example, reflects Crashaw's Laudian perception, as Healy explains, 'that ritual and ceremony in a liturgical context becomes a means of constantly renewing history, making it everpresent through its sacramental reenactment' (100-101).

Beyond this mixing of liquids, however, Crashaw also combines, with similar liturgical effect, sight and sound in his epigram 'Marc. 10. The blind cured by the word of our Saviour',[3] as well as speech and silence in his epigram 'Matthew. 27. And he answered them nothing' (No. 40).[4] In other instances, the blood on the crucified body of Christ becomes his 'purple wardrobe' (No. 44); the bloody thorns worn by Christ bloom as roses (no. 43); the open wounds of the martyrs are 'purple Doores' and 'Ruby windowes' ('Hymn to the Name of Jesus', 217, 218); the tears of St. Teresa turn to gems and 'Wrongs repent to Diademms' ('A Hymn to St. Teresa', 150); and in his epigram 'On the wounds of our crucified Lord' (no. 45), Crashaw turns those wounds into mouths that bloom as roses and eyes that bring forth '*Ruby*-Teares'. In 'The Weeper' (1652), Crashaw finds that in the tears of Mary Magdalene the contests 'of woes / With loves, of teares and smiles', of 'rain and sunshine, Cheekes and Eyes' are brought together 'in kind contrarietyes' (st. xvi). In a similar manner, a choral interjection near the end of the 'Hymn in the Glorious Epiphanie' pleads for:

> A commerce of contrary powres,
> > A mutuall trade
> > 'Twixt sun and Shade,
> By confederate Black and White
> Borrowing day and lending night.   (ll. 214-218)

This persistent blending and confusing of substances is the expansive method by which Crashaw celebrates, liturgically, the paradoxes found in Immanuel (God with us). Two passages from 'Sospetto d'Herode' emphasise, by contrast, the theological necessity in Crashaw for mixing 'contrarietyes'. The first addresses the puzzlement of Satan concerning how 'a maid should prove a Mother', how 'Gods eternall Sonne should be mans Brother', how 'a pure Spirit should incarnate bee, / And life it selfe weare Death frail Livers' (st. 21). For four stanzas, Satan ponders these paradoxes until the poet concludes, 'These are the knotty Riddles, whose darke doubt / Intangles his lost Thoughts, past getting out' (st. 24). The second passage, at the end of the poem, questions the fear and jealousy of Herod toward the infant Christ: 'why should he wish to prey / Upon thy Crowne, who gives his owne away?' (st. 65) and 'What his steeds? alas / Poore Beasts! a slow Oxe, and a simple Asse' (st. 66). Both Satan and Herod reveal their conflict with God and their existence outside of His mercy because the paradoxes found in Christ remain for them 'unmixed'.

    This characteristic action of discovering 'a commerce of contrary powres' is, as Harold Skulsky has recently argued, 'a calculated, emphatically repeated act of speech', which he labels 'pseudometaphor'.[5] In particular, Skulsky explains that Crashaw consistently requires the reader to agree to misread the imagistic mixtures. After all, we cannot understand Crashaw literally when he writes of the crucified Christ, 'O these wakefull wounds of thine! / Are they Mouthes? or are they eyes?' (Divine Epigram, No. 45); we do not believe, in a physical way, that the world, awaiting the birth of God's Son, 'First turn'd to eyes; / And then, not knowing what to doe; / Turn'd Them to Teares, and spent Them too' ('Hymn to the Name of Jesus', 136-138); and, finally, Crashaw himself insists that the reader confuse reason and sight in those familiar lines from 'The Flaming Heart':

> Readers, be rul'd by me; and make
> Here a well-plac't and wise mistake,
> You must transpose the picture quite,
> And spell it wrong to read it right;
> Read HIM for her, and her for him;
> And call the saint the SERAPHIM.   (ll. 7-12)

From this use of metaphor, Skulsky concludes that Crashaw is involved in a sacred game in which 'to counterfeit *mis*understanding is to celebrate understanding' (65). Mixing, in this exaggerated manner, is Crashaw's method for realising that no response of faith is too expansive in its attempt to know the eternal God.

    What controls and holds in place these imagistic and metaphoric aspirations is Crashaw's fundamental assumption of faith; he writes for those who already believe that Jesus is the son of God and the saviour of humankind. As a result, the task for Crashaw is not to portray struggles between faith and doubt, but rather, to induce experiences of adoration and worship within particular biblical situations and contexts. This is precisely the idea that Eugene Cunnar espouses in the conclusion of his reading of 'Hymn to the Name of Jesus': 'The poem completes itself outside of itself through ritual action, specifically the act of bowing. If Crashaw's reader has followed him this far and bowed now [at the end of the poem], then that reader has become a living hymn fulfilling Crashaw's hymnic goal'.[6]

In her discussion of 'Crashaw's Sacred Voice', Lorraine Roberts articulates a similar expression of liturgical action and interaction between poet and reader:

> The impersonality of Crashaw's voice suits his intent of creating an everyman who can witness sacred events, be affected by their emotion and meaning, and engender that same response and significance in his reader ... It is the voice of a poet who chooses to adopt a persona that bridges the gap between past and present, heaven and earth, God and man.[7]

Because Crashaw's verse assumes and fervently asserts Christian faith, the impersonal nature of the voice he employs is entirely appropriate, for Crashaw fashions the odes and hymns, in particular, as ritualised acts of public enunciation. Considerations of voice, then, reveal Crashaw's emphasis, as Healy explains, upon Ciceronian eloquence, 'believing that formal and elegant oratory could move listeners towards the divine and create a bridge between the earthly and heavenly' (50). Oratory itself, therefore, is another means by which Crashaw seeks to achieve liturgical mixing.

A consideration of Crashaw's poetic voice, particularly when discussed in terms of his understanding of and desire for rhetorical eloquence, touches upon the classical aspects of his religious verse. In addition to the liturgical purposes and effects of voice in his poems, the verse forms Crashaw most often uses—epigram, hymn and ode—themselves require a more impersonal voice since they are formal and public genres that have moral and hortatory aims.

The particular goal of the epigram, beyond the characteristics of terseness and wit for which Crashaw demonstrates such aptitude, is for the poet to 'make his friend sport, and anger his foe, and give a prettie nip', as Puttenham describes.[8] Crashaw uses poetic voice to fulfill the moral and hortatory aims of the genre in his own epigrams by establishing a tone that permits teasing with one's friends (Jesus, Mary, the apostles) and chastising one's enemies (sinners of various kinds).[9] Of course, Crashaw never slavishly imitates in these early poems Martial or any other writer of the genre, including the Jesuit epigrammatists; instead, he creates from the form something new, something reflecting his theological bent for expansion.

In his discussion of Crashaw's epigrams, R.V. Young argues convincingly that Crashaw, in response to his impulse to create a sense of wonder, transforms the pagan finality of the classical epigram by employing 'the ambiguity and paradoxical resonance which lurk in the terseness and point of the epigram to suggest potential transformation—the radical *otherness* latent in the redeemed world'.[10] In other words, within this classical form, Crashaw refashions the defining characteristics of concision and wit 'not to close a subject', as Young explains, 'but to open it up' (145) through acts of liturgical paradox, specifically by reinforcing those acts of mixing which define the quality of expansion in Crashaw's verse. Young concludes his study by noting that in this context the epigram, as a genre, becomes for Crashaw 'insufficient in itself and, like "the witt of love", it "overflows" into other forms' (152).

Of course, the genres that Crashaw's art flowed into and combined with are the classical hymn and ode, between which there was no sharp distinction in antiquity or among Renaissance critics since, as Stella Revard demonstrates, 'the words *hymn* and *ode* both mean *song* and were used interchangeably'.[11] With these classical forms, which were ceremonial and choral poems intended for public worship, Crashaw found the vehicles best suited to combine with his distinctive use of imagery and metaphor. In particular, this formal classical poetry appeals to Crashaw because it is, as Revard describes, 'especially attentive to the occasion for which it is composed, designed to celebrate specifically that occasion and the persons and gods connected with it' (179), and its basic goal is, as Cunnar asserts of the Greek hymn, 'to praise the gods and thereby establish a relationship between the praiser and the praised, man and god' (103-104).

To begin with, Crashaw's own hymns and odes are occasional poetry; they celebrate sacred moments in Christian history (the exaltation of the name of Jesus, the Nativity, the Epiphany and the assumption of the Virgin), as well as particular women who model the attitudes of praise and adoration Crashaw seeks to instill in his reader (Mary Magdalene and her tears, St. Teresa and her ecstatic visions and Mary, the mother of sorrows). In addition, the choral effects utilized in classical hymns and odes in order to create a sense of reciprocity between praiser and praised is not lost on Crashaw. His hymns and odes not only, at times, incorporate the joining of voices into a designated chorus (most notably in 'Hymn in the Glorious Epiphanie', 'Hymn in the Holy Nativity' and 'Office of the Holy Cross'), but also, more typically, create choral effects as the poet, serving as choir director/priest, compels the reader to participate in public acts of adoration and praise (as evidenced, for example, in 'Hymn to the Name of Jesus', 'The Flaming Heart' and 'Sancta Maria Dolorum'). The common ground between the occasional nature of Crashaw's hymns and odes and the reciprocal relationship they seek to create exists, once again, in a liturgical act of mixing. The events and people Crashaw celebrates in these longer works, as well as the poetic form in which he celebrates them, consistently reiterate the central moment of Christianity—the manifest union of the divine and human in the Incarnation. Because God came to the world in the person of Jesus, there is for Crashaw no barrier between sacred and profane, for he seeks to bring all of the creation into harmony, both musically and theologically, in order to praise the Creator.

For this task, it is eloquence that Crashaw desires, and he uses all that is available to him to proclaim his devotion to and ardor for the one in whom he believes. In 'Hymn to the Name of Jesus', the persona invokes his soul, his heart, his voice, his whole being, as well as Nature and Art and, in fact, all things in heaven and earth, saying, 'Come; and come strong, / To the conspiracy of our Spatious song' (70-71). In a similar manner, the voices of the three Kings in 'Hymn in the Glorious Epiphanie' join in choral harmony, confessing, 'Nor was't our deafnes, but our sins, that thus / Long made th'Harmonious orbes all mute to us' (131-132). Finally, the individual songs of Tityrus and Thyrsis, along with the chorus of shepherds, culminate in the full chorus that concludes 'Hymn in the Holy Nativity':

> *Wellcome, all* WONDERS in one sight!
>   AEternity shutt in a span.
> Sommer in Winter. Day in Night.
>   Heaven in earth, and GOD in MAN.
> Great little one! whose all-embracing birth
> Lifts earth to heaven, stoopes heav'n to earth.   (ll. 79-84)

However, as Crashaw reiterates throughout his religious verse, the harmonising effects of this kind of liturgical mixing, as typological recreations of the Incarnation, do not come without a price; he is acutely aware that 'there is witt in wrath' ('Office of the Holy Cross' Third Hour), that harmony is not possible without suffering.

In addition to the Divine Epigrams, many of which address the infant martyrs and the various wounds on the crucified body of Christ, the hymns and odes also illustrate the 'witt of wrath'. For example, 'Hymn to the Name of Jesus' does not conclude before portraying the bloody wounds of the martyrs; the opening stanzas of 'Hymn for New Year's Day' are stained with allusions to the circumcision of the infant Jesus; 'The Weeper' examines and interprets the tears of Mary Magdalene specifically in relation to the suffering of her Lord; and Crashaw advises the Countess of Denbigh, in his verse letter (1652) by urging her, 'Meet his [Christ's] well-meaning

Wounds, wise heart! / And hast to drink the wholesome dart' (45-46). As these representative passages exemplify, Crashaw realises that redemptive harmony is only possible through sacrificial acts of emptying. Philippians 2: 5-11, which describes Christ's kenosis—the emptying of his divine nature into human form and subsequent humiliation of death on a cross— serves as scriptural text not only for 'Hymn to the Name of Jesus', but also for Crashaw's consistent theological emphasis that within this fallen world, there is no life without death, there is no healing without suffering.

In her reading of 'The Flaming Heart', Vera Camden explains that even though Crashaw insists that the reader 'transpose the picture quite, / And spell it wrong to read it right' (8-9), 'his insistence is ineffectual and so he proposes to himself, to the reader, and ultimately to the "wronged" Teresa a pattern of reconciliation and compensation'.[12] In particular, Camden argues that 'if the painting will not bend to be undone according to Crashaw's interpretation, then the poet will not only do with this proud wrong but will, through the conceit of the wound, turn it to advantage' (274), which is precisely what he accomplishes:

> For in love's feild was never found
> A nobler weapon than a WOUND.
> Love's passives are his activ'st part.
> The wounded is the wounding heart. (ll. 71-74)

Focusing upon the last two lines of this passage, Heather Asals makes a similar point in her discussion of 'Crashaw's Participles': 'Present active has been identified with the perfect passive participle in the grammar and logic of love which is *shared being* and the sharing of Being with being perfecting itself'.[13] In other words, love paradoxically manifests itself in suffering, in acts of wounded emptying that permit 'contrarietyes' to mix, for as Crashaw writes in 'Hymn to the Name of Jesus', 'It was the witt of love o'reflowed the Bounds / Of Wrath, and made thee way through All Those WOUNDS' (223-224). As a result, the Crucifixion touches the Incarnation; the wounds of Christ manifest the divine love that empties itself to mix with, and thereby redeem, the sin-filled need of humanity.

The impulse that calls Crashaw to use the images and metaphors he does is the same impulse that compels him to present them in classical forms, as he seeks to unify all of creation with the Creator. Crashaw's habitual pursuit of expansion in his verse typifies, therefore, the divine love that seeks to enfold humanity in its redeeming embrace. This is not, however, a one-sided action in which the profane is subsumed in the sacred. Instead, God himself shows the way of love in the Incarnation/Crucifixion

of Christ. Crashaw's poetic method reflects the wit of God in that through
sacrifice, through emptying by means of suffering, the expansive act of
mixing (that means love) can occur, as heaven and earth, profane and
sacred are joined in Christ:

> By all those stings
> Of love, sweet bitter things,
> Which these torn hands transcrib'd on thy true heart
> O teach mine too the art
> To study him so, till we mix
> Wounds; and become one crucifix.
>
> ('Sancta Maria Dolorum', st. X)

Notes

1   Hilton Kelliher, 'Crashaw at Cambridge', in John R. Roberts (ed.), *New Perspectives on the Life and Art of Richard Crashaw* (Columbia, 1990), 196.
2   Thomas F. Healy, *Richard Crashaw* (Leiden, 1986), 12, 13.
3   *The Complete Poetry of Richard Crashaw*, edited by George Walton Williams (New York, 1974), No. 30. All references to Crashaw's poems are from this edition.
4   See also No. 16 and No. 33.
5   Harold Skulsky, *Language Recreated: Seventeenth-Century Metaphorists and the Act of Metaphor* (Athens, 1992), 56.
6   Eugene R. Cunnar, 'Crashaw's Hymn "To the Name above Every Name": Background and Meaning', in Robert M. Cooper, ed., *Essays on Richard Crashaw* (Salzburg, 1979), 119.
7   Lorraine M. Roberts, 'Crashaw's Sacred Voice: "A Commerce of Contrary Powers"', in John R. Roberts, ed., *New Perspectives*, 78.
8   George Puttenham, *The Art of English Poesie* (1589) (Menston, 1968), 43.
9   Paul A. Parrish, *Richard Crashaw* (Boston, 1980), 50.
10   R.V. Young, Jr., 'Jonson, Crashaw, and the Development of the English Epigram', *Genre* 12 (1979): 148.
11   Stella Revard, 'The Seventeenth-Century Religious Ode and Its Classical Models', in Claude J. Summers and Ted-Larry Pebworth (eds.), *'Bright Shootes of Everlastingnesse': The Seventeenth-Century Religious Lyric* (Columbia, 1987), 176.
12   Vera J. Camden, 'Richard Crashaw's Poetry: The Imagery of Bleeding Wounds', *American Imago* 40 (1983), 274.
13   Heather Asals, 'Crashaw's Participles and the "Chiaroscuro" of Ontological Language', in Cooper (ed.), *Essays*, 39.

19

MILTON'S ORPHIC HARMONY:
OVIDIAN IMITATION AND CHRISTIAN REVELATION
IN *THE NATIVITY ODE* AND *THE PASSION*

MARK BERGE

The early English poetry of John Milton illustrates dramatically the uneasy interaction between the classical and Christian literary traditions in the 1600s. As a youthful poet brought up in a Protestant world, Milton had succeeded in reaching beyond the mechanical schoolroom exercises and the pervasive allegorical commentary to discover for himself an emotional kinship with the classical love poet. In 1642 he was able to reminisce on this bond in his *Apology for Smectymnuus*:

> others were the smooth elegiac poets, whereof the schools are not scarce, whom both for the pleasing sound of their numerous writing, which in imitation I found most easy and most agreeable to nature's part in me, and for their matter, which what it is there be few who know not, I was so allured to read that no recreation came to me better welcome.[1]

However, in spite of Milton's emotional recollection, Davis Harding concludes narrowly that the poet 'had been taught the mechanics of close imitation in verse, which involved being soaked through and through with the phraseology and imagery of Ovid'.[2] Imitation of Ovid had long been accepted as a proper activity for schoolboys but the enthusiasm Milton shows for Ovid in particular goes far beyond any mechanical imitation.

Linda Hutcheon's characterization of imitation places more value on the transcending qualities of emulation rather than its ability to teach poetic technique. She compares Renaissance imitation with present day parody in that it is 'a workable and effective stance toward the past in its paradoxical strategy of repetition as a source of freedom'.[3] Ovid, certainly one of the greatest of the 'smooth elegiac poets', was thoroughly assimilated by Milton in his thoughts and writing, providing the forms in which Milton began to write. *Poems 1645* displays in retrospect the many influences, chiefly among them Ovid's influence, which Milton eventually abandoned as limiting to his poetic experience. In Louis Martz's words 'the entire volume strives to create a tribute to a youthful era now past—not only the poet's own youth, but a state of mind, a point of view, ways of writing, ways of living, an old culture and outlook now shattered by the pressures of maturity'.[4] Milton's small volume is carefully planned to give the reader a sense of the poet's rising powers and no two poems so strikingly reveal the process itself of poetic identification and supersession of the poetic master as *The Nativity Ode* and *The Passion*. Through these two poems the Ovidian-trained youth is at one instance elated and the next deflated by the fundamental disparity between the classical and Christian.

That Milton's later poems portray such a strong Christian belief is a major stumbling block in appreciating the early attitudes of the poet. The essential problem regarding *The Nativity Ode* and *The Passion* grows out of the biographical misconception of Milton's religious dedication. As early as his Latin elegies, the young poet is assumed to have decided upon a Christian purpose for his poetry to reflect his Christian seriousness. Douglas Bush reflects that 'in Elegy 5 (Dec.-Jan. 1629-1630) the innocent neopagan gives way to the aspiring poet-priest'.[5] This assumption may be premature because the 'poet-priest' becomes difficult to find once the ambition of the poet/mage to re-create an Ovidian Age of Gold is discovered within both poems. Milton's skill allowed him successfully to combine classical and Christian inspiration well after his assumed 'conversion' to serious Christian poetry in *Elegia Sexta*. However, the jubilation on completing his celebration of the birth of an Orphic Christ left him unprepared for the failure that writing on the death of his poetic creation would bring.

On the surface, Milton's *Nativity Ode* seems to be written in the 'tradition of late-classical and Neo-Latin celebrations of the Nativity'.[6] As far as this 'tradition' is concerned, Louis Martz finds it short-lived: 'The dating, "Compos'd 1629", accords with the Nativity poem's relation to an age and mode of English poetry now outgrown both by nation and by the poet' (51). D.M. Rosenberg, on the other hand, stresses the pastoral tradition of Virgil and Spenser as Milton's models.[7] It is clear that *The Nativity Ode* relies on many subtexts and traditions to illuminate its subject; however, D.M. Rosenberg ignores his own observation of an Orphic tradition in poetry: 'The pastoral poet imitates Pan's pipes and sees himself in a pastoral succession descending from Orpheus' (19). John Warden's detailed volume on this Orphic tradition includes Patricia Vicari's observation that 'Orpheus has a highly personal, as well as emblematic, significance for Milton'.[8] In this light, Ovid's rendering of Orpheus in his *Metamorphoses* should be carefully considered, especially in view of Louis Martz's observation that *Elegia Sexta*, taken in its chosen context between the playfully Ovidian *Elegia Quinta* and the erotic *Elegia Septima*, does 'not wholly lay aside the tone of "Ovidian banter"' (52). What, then, can we make of *The Nativity Ode* when in the midst of the 'Ovidian banter' of *Elegia Sexta*

Milton asserts that he is going to write gifts for the birthday of Christ?:
'Dona quidem dedimus Christi natalibus illa; / Illa sub auroram lux mihi
prima tulit' (*Elegia Sexta*, 87-88).[9] The answer lies in the nature of Milton's 'gift' and the significance of Orpheus as a poetic model. Ovid's
Orpheus in *The Metamorphoses* focuses on the singer's control of sexuality
and the nature of poetry. This, I believe, is a better model suited to answer
the questions about *The Nativity Ode*'s emphasis on sexuality in a world
controlled by poetic music.

In *The Metamorphoses*, Ganymede, Cyparissus, Hyacinth, and even
Love herself, Venus, all figure in Orpheus' song of incest, lust, narcissistic
idol worship, and guilt. Orpheus exposes the dangerous side of love due to
his grief and shame at losing Eurydice a second time:

> cecini plectro graviore Gigantas
> sparsaque Phlegraeis victricia fulmina campis.
> nunc opus est leviore lyra, puerosque canamus
> dilectos superis inconcessisque puellas
> ignibus attonitas meruisse libidine poenam.
>
> (*Metamorphoses* X, 148-155)[10]

Orpheus seeks to control nature, (as he does by gathering trees around himself before he sings [*Metamorphoses* X, 85-108]), his intent being to
replace the 'bestial' side of nature with human control. Ovid's parody of
Orpheus' 'solution' to sexual ruthlessness culminates in the singer's death
at the hands of crazed, beast-like women, the Maenads. Orpheus' failure
provides Milton with an Ovidian model to imitate and improve. Restoration
of the Orphic music that can charm the 'bestial' side of nature, sexual licentiousness in particular, remains a primary theme throughout *The Nativity
Ode*. Milton's attempt at following the Orphic tradition with a truncated
version of the myth, ending in success rather than death, accords with *Elegia Septima*'s pledge supporting the poetry of love:

> Ian tuus O certe est mihi formidablis areus,
> Nate dea, iaculus nec minus igne potens
> Et tua fumabunt nostris altaria donis
> Solus et in superius tu mihi summus eris.   (95-98)[11]

The image of an offering, a sacrifice, occurs prominently in *The Nativity Ode* and highlights the ill-masked ambition of the poet:

> The star-led Wizards haste with odors sweet
> O run, prevent them with thy humble Ode,
> And lay it lowly at his blessed feet,
> Have thou the honour first, thy Lord to greet.   (ll. 23-26)

As Broadbent notices, the poet is really 'a magus determined to control the mystery' (31). Far from being humble, the poet's ode embodies the manner in which he would outdo 'the star-led Wizards' in his quest for poetic control. His desire is evident: 'And join thy voice unto the Angel choir, / From out his secret Altar toucht with hallow'd fire' (27-28). This ambition to join his voice to the celestial choir is an indication of the poem's direction, a movement seeking heavenly harmony, a forsaking of the baser elements intrinsic with the 'darksome House of mortal Clay' (14).

The vehicle to obtain this harmony is the 'music' of heaven which, '(as tis said) / Before was never made, But when of old the sons of morning sung, / While the Creator Great / his constellations set, / And the well-balanc't world on hinges hung' (*Nativity Ode*, 118-123). This striking image which recalls the creation of the world in its pre-lapsarian perfection can also be found in Ovid's account of creation in *The Metamorphoses*:

> nullus adhuc mundo praebebat lumina Titan, ...
> nec circumfuso pendebat in aere Tellus
> ponderibus librata suis ...
> hanc Deus et melior litem Natura diremit; ...
> dissociata locis concordi pace ligauit.   (I, 10, 12-13, 21, 25)[12]

Whereas this image of the balanced world is also found in Job 38: 6-7, the Ovidian reference places particular stress on creation and harmony. Further to this, and perhaps more striking, is the poet's assertion that 'if such holy song / Enwrap our fancy long / Time will run back and fetch the age of gold' (*Nativity Ode*, 133-135). Ovid's golden age, utopian in nature, is created out of the peace and harmony imposed by the god. Thomas Greene has pointed out that 'each imitative work contains by definition what might be called a revivalist initiative, a gesture that signals the intent of reanimating an earlier text or texts situated on the far side of a rupture'.[13] The strong echoes of Ovid's classical myth of creation and its golden age may hint at part of Milton's intent, a reanimation of the heavenly music to create a poetic age of gold.

An indication of this intent can be found in the subdued picture of nature in the poem. Nature is not perfected through a Christian Incarnation, as Arthur Barker asserts,[14] but suppressed through shame—'Confounded, that her Maker's eyes / Should look so near upon her foul deformities' (*Nativity Ode,* 43-44)—and by force—'Th'old Dragon under ground, / In straiter limits bound, / Not half so far casts his usurped sway' (*Nativity Ode,* 168-170). Nature is tamed and hushed by the harmony imposed on it:

> The Winds, with wonder whist,
> Smoothly the waters kiss't,
> Whispering new joys to the mild Ocean,
> Who now hath quite forgot to rave,
> While Birds of Calm sit brooding on the charmed wave.
>
> The Stars with deep amaze
> Stand fixt in steadfast gaze.   (*Nativity Ode,* ll. 64-70)

As in Ovid, Milton's image of nature is controlled and subdued. This is an important theme in the tale of Orpheus:

> qua postquam parte resedit
> dis genitus vates et fila sonantia movit,
> umbra loco venit: ...
> ut satis inpulsas temptavit pollice chordas
> et sensit varios, quamvis diversa sonarent,
> concordare modos, hoc vocem carmine movit:
> "ab Iove, Musa parens, (cedunt Iovis onmia regno,)
> carmina nostra move!   (*Metamorphoses* X, 88-89, 145-148)[15]

In *The Metamorphoses,* all nature is subdued by the power of Orphic song —all nature, that is, but the Maenads whose sexual potency is scorned by Orpheus. Bacchic love or sexual passion, symbolised by the Maenads, must then be subdued along with nature for Milton's poem to proceed. This, then, becomes the problem in re-working the Orphic myth.

The mute presence of the Mother in the poem underscores this concern with subduing sexual passion. She is given a brief allusion where she is syntactically subordinate to 'the Son of Heav'n's eternal King / Of wedded Maid, / and Virgin Mother born' (*Nativity Ode,* 2-3). The emphasis is on the Mother's chastity and her silence is a prelude to a larger silencing of maternal nature in the poem as a whole. In *Elegia Quinta*'s age of gold nature was free of sexual shame: 'Exuit invisam Tellus rediviva senectam. / Et cupit amplexus, Phoebe, subire tuos' (55-56).[16] In *The Nativity Ode,* however, Nature tries 'To hide her guilty front with innocent Snow' (39) as 'It was no season then for her / To wanton with the Sun, her lusty Paramour' (35-36). The amorous Earth must give way to silence as all nature is

hushed by the technical control of the poet/magus. Once the sexual passion
of maternal nature is quieted, the figure of Peace is introduced to promote a
new order of harmony:

> She crown'd with Olive green, came softly sliding
> Down through the turning sphere,
> His ready Harbinger,
> With Turtle wing the amorous clouds dividing,
> And waving wide her myrtle wand,
> She strikes a universal Peace through Sea and Land.
>
> (*Nativity Ode*, ll. 47-52)

Peace resembles strongly two figures from *The Metamorphoses* that have
great import in the tale of Orpheus. Hymen, god of marriage, who half-
heartedly presided over Orpheus and Eurydice's wedding, brought ill-for-
tune to that couple:

> Inde per inmensum croceo velatus amictu
> aethera digreditur Ciconumque Hymenaeus ad oras
> tendit et Orphea nequiquam voce vocatur.
> adfuit ille quidem, sed nec sollemnia verba
> nec laetos vultus nec felix attulit omen ...
> nam nupta per herbas
> dum nova naiadum turba comitata vagatur,
> occidit in talum serpentis dente recepto.
>
> (*Metamorphoses* X, 1-5, 8-10)[17]

Milton's Peace presides over the poem much like Hymen, but now the
blessing Peace brings is given without hesitation. Further, Peace also
resembles Venus in Orpheus' song:

> vecta levi curru medias Cytherea per auras
> Cypron olorinis nondum pervenerat alis:
> agnovit longe gemitum morientis et albas
> flexit aves illue, utque aethere vidit ab alto.   (X, 719-720)[18]

However, instead of promoting sexual licentiousness as Venus did in *The
Metamorphoses*, Milton's Peace 'divides' the 'amourous clouds' and
'strikes' a new harmony, particularly a sexual one. Ovid also pictures the
harmony of creation as an act of division and exclusion:

Hanc deus et melior litem natura diremit.
nam caelo terras et terris abscidit undas
et liquidum spisso secrevit ab aere caelum.
aqae postquam evolvit caecoque exemit acervo,
dissociata locis concordi pace ligavit.   (*Metamorphoses* I, 21-25)[19]

As Ovid's god imposed a new order upon nature, so too does Peace strike a new harmony to control nature and for 'her fears to cease' (*Nativity Ode*, 45).

The effects of the imposition of peace by separation and exclusion are immediate. Now the sexual imagery used is not encumbered by the shame and guilt that nature possessed. It is a peace of continence—or of chaste love that now controls nature:

> His reign of peace upon the earth began:
> The Winds, with wonder whist,
> Smoothly the waters kiss't,
> > Whispering new joys to the mild Ocean,
> Who now hath quite forgot to rave.   (*Nativity Ode*, ll. 63-67)

Milton's poem requires that a sexual harmony be enforced because 'infantile sexuality poses a threat which must be mastered or repressed'.[20] This threat is only overcome in the *Nativity Ode* by the organising power of the singer and his song. Poetic control becomes the only manner in which the forces of the Maenads can be suppressed.

Spenser's love-lorn Colin Clout is a prime example of the threat of sexual passion to self mastery. Colin breaks his pipe and ends his singing (*Shepheardes Calender*, 'January' 71-72)[21] because he is unable to harmonise himself with the world around him. Colin Clout's failure to control his sexual passion allows Milton to ridicule the poetic impotency brought on by failure in love in a pointed allusion:

> The Shepherds on the Lawn,
> Or ere the point of dawn,
> > Sat simply chatting in a rustic row
> Full little thought they then,
> That the mighty Pan
> > Was kindly come to live with them below;
> Perhaps their loves, or else their sheep,
> Was all that did their silly thoughts so busy keep.
> > > > (*Nativity Ode*, ll. 85-93)

Such impotency is immediately struck out of Milton's poem with his description of the 'music sweet' (*Nativity Ode*, 93) which accompanies the Babe's birth. Indeed, the music Milton envisions can return the world to the perfection, sexual and otherwise, that the age of gold once promised:

> And speckl'd vanity
> Will sicken soon and die,
>   And leprous sin will melt from earthly mold,
> And Hell itself will pass away,
> And leave her dolorous mansions to the peering day ...
>
> And Heav'n as at some festival,
> Will open wide the Gates of her high Palace Hall.
>   (*Nativity Ode*, ll. 136-140, 147-148)

However, restoration of the age of gold at this point would deny the orthodox doctrine of salvation through Christ's sacrifice and this is not Milton's intent:

> But wisest Fate says no,
> This must not yet be so,
> The Babe lies yet in smiling Infancy,
> That on the bitter cross
> Must redeem our loss.   (*Nativity Ode*, ll. 149-153)

This thought renews the need to rout Apollo, the source of old pagan harmony, to leave the Orphic Christ in control of the new poetic music.

As Peace struck physical shame and guilt from the world, the Babe's birth blasts all threat of dissonance from poetic music:

> The wakeful trump of doom must thunder through the deep,
>
> With such a horrid clang
> As on Mount Sinai rang ...
> The aged Earth aghast
> With terror of that blast,
>   Shall from the surface to the centre shake.
>   (*Nativity Ode*, ll. 156-158, 160-163)

Casting out cacophony with cacophony, this booming prophecy leads us back to the peaceful manger scene: 'And then at last our bliss / Full and perfect is, / But now begins' (*Nativity Ode*, 165-167). But bliss only begins now because the 'old Dragon' (168) feels its power ebbing: 'In straiter limits bound, / Not half so far casts his ursurped sway' (*Nativity Ode*, 169-170). The 'old Dragon' of Revelation xii, Satan, even takes on the figure of the serpent slain by Apollo: 'Illa quidem nollet, sed te quoque, maxime Python, / tum genuit, populisque novis, incognita serpens, / terror eras' (*Metamorphoses* I, 438-440).[22] However, as much as Ovid's Apollo was able to defeat the serpent he was unable to master the powers of sexual passion as his boast snubbing Cupid turns to punishment in his pursuit of Daphne (*Metamorphoses* I, 450-567). The 'greater sun', Milton's Apollonian Christ, overcomes the power of Cupid, thus showing his superiority. Now the mere birth of the Babe silences the old music and poetry of sexual shame and deception: 'The Oracles are dumb, / No voice or hideous hum / Runs through the arched roof in words deceiving' (*Nativity Ode*, 173-175). The old Apollo himself becomes the defeated Sphinx, 'With hollow shriek the steep of Delphos leaving' (*Nativity Ode*, 178), as the 'dreaded Infant', by the very fact of his birth, now appears to have answered the Sphinx's 'riddle' about human life.

With Apollo fled, his singer must also be replaced. Milton's hinted recollections of Orpheus' death at the hands of the vengeful Maenads recalls the consequences of his failure to maintain control over all nature:

> A voice of weeping heard, and loud lament:
> From haunted spring and dale
> Edg'd with poplar pale,
>   The parting Genius is with sighing sent;
> With flow'r-inwov'n tresses torn
> The nymphs in twilight shade of tangled thickets mourn.
>   (*Nativity Ode*, ll. 183-188)

Milton's words echo closely the scene in *The Metamorphoses*:

> Rivers too, men say,
> Were swollen with their tears, and Naiads wore,
> And Dryads too, their mourning robes of black
> And hair dishevelled. All around his limbs
> Lay scattered. Hebrus' stream received his head
> And lyre ...
> And gained Methymna's shore on Lesbos' isle.
> There, as his head lay on that foreign sand,
> Its tumbled tresses dripping.
>   (XI, 47-51, 55-57, trans. Melville)

But the *Nativity Ode*'s echoed lament for Orpheus is introduced to show that 'Our Babe, to show his Godhead true, / Can in his swaddling bands control the damned crew' (227-228). The Babe, in other words, empowers the singer to restore Orphic song to its state before the Maenads came. In effect, the god of song (Apollo) and his son (Orpheus) give way to the new Orphic music of a 'greater sun' or Phoebus, and his poet who rushes to 'prevent [the magi] with thy humble ode' (*Nativity Ode*, 24).

The new 'Orphic' song begins with an exposure of the banished gods who are characters traditionally associated with sexual aberration and human sacrifice. Peor and Baalim (197) are infamous in their Old Testament guise connected with whoredom and sacrifice (Numbers, 25: 1-3). Ashtaroth, the Phoenician Aphrodite (Hughes, 222, n. 438), is exposed in an incestuous relationship as 'Heav'n's Queen and Mother both' (*Nativity Ode*, 201). The Tyrian maids crying for Thammuz (*Nativity Ode*, 204) are to be found in Ezekiel 8: 14, where idol worship is condemned. But Thammuz is also better known as Adonis (Hughes, 48, n. 204), who becomes, in Orpheus' own exposure of Venus' guilty passion, the 'child of his sister and his grandfather' (*Metamorphoses* X, 521). Isis, the sister and wife of Osiris, is recalled as another version of 'guilty' love, and Orus as the incestuous product of their marriage (Hughes, 49, n. 212). If the 'dreaded Infant's hand' (*Nativity Ode*, 222) seems to have little in common with the babe in the manger, it is because Milton himself succeeds where Orpheus fails; he not only exposes the sexual tyranny of the gods, but he routs them with the power of his song and his 'dreadful' little muse.

Much earlier in the poem, this conclusion was anticipated in the description of the Babe as Pan, the shepherd god (*Nativity Ode*, 88-90). In Ovid's story of Midas, Pan challenges the music of Apollo:

> Pan ibi dum teneris iactat sua carmina nymphis
> et leve cerata modulatur harundine carmen
> ausus Apollineos prae se contemnere cantus.
>
> (*Metamorphoses* XI, 153-155)[23]

In Milton's poem the Babe is able to chase Apollo from his shrine, reversing Ovid's story of Midas where Apollo's 'strains so sweet' won the day over Pan (*Metamorphoses* XI, 170). The Babe's ultimate victory is thus over the songs of this fallen tradition, filled with sexual guilt, which Apollo and Venus represent.

However, the major difficulty with the *Nativity Ode* is that Milton 'has scarcely met the problem of theodicy'.[24] That problem centres on death, and the triumph of the Christian story is, paradoxically enough, the death of the incarnate deity so that man might live. But so long as Milton sees the Christian story in terms of Orphic poetry, he can barely glance at the prospect of 'the bitter cross'. For the real triumph of his Orphic Christ is that he avoids the fate of the original Orpheus, death at the hands of the Maenads.

The very terms of his success in *The Nativity Ode* would seem to dictate their inevitable collapse in a poem about the Crucifixion. However, Milton begins *The Passion* in blissful self-confidence. The opening lines of *The Passion* ring with the nostalgia of self-quotation:

> Erewhile of Music and Ethereal mirth,
> Wherewith the stage of Air and Earth did ring,
> And joyous news of heav'nly Infant's birth,
> My muse with Angels did divide to sing. (ll. 1-4)

The sexual, poetic and ethical perfection of *The Nativity Ode* extends itself into this passage with its remembrance of music, mirth and muses singing with angels. However, Milton knew that the 'dreaded Infant' who conquered nature by inspiring the poet's song would have to complete his mission on Earth before such harmony could become permanent and that the end of that mission was the 'passion' of death. For this reason, the darkness which surrounded the guilt and shame-ridden gods in *The Nativity Ode* returns: 'But headlong joy is ever on the wing, / In Wintry solstice like the short'n'd light / Soon swallow'd up in dark and long outliving night' (*The Passion*, 5-7). Immediately, the reader is thrust into a fallen world whose ethical assumptions were created in *The Nativity Ode*. Milton continues to use classical and Christian models to describe the now-grown Infant as he renews his role as successor to the Orphic tradition.

Milton begins by explicitly flaunting his imitation of Ovid's Orpheus in *The Passion*. However, he now imitates Orpheus as the singer of sexual guilt and shame who cannot avoid the grief of death: 'For now to sorrow must I tune my song, / And set my Harp to notes of saddest woe' (8-9). This differs from the singer/poet of *The Nativity Ode* who sought to transcend such haunted music. It resembles Ovid's description of the downcast Orpheus after losing Eurydice: 'ut satis inpusas temptavit pollice chordas / et sensit varios, quamvis diversa sonarent / concordare modos' (*Metamorphoses* X, 145-147).[25] Orpheus embarks on his song of grievous sorrow which reflects his now fundamentally changed attitude, or rather, his self-defeating song of holding grief at bay by mocking Venus' grief.

The song of grief which Milton undertakes, after briefly describing the Saviour's death, is in a very different tone from that which began the poem. Instead of mourning the imminent death of the Saviour, Milton's lament echoes Ovid's treatment of Orpheus. For the singer's grief at Christ's death is immoderate and self-absorbed, much like the grief which Orpheus' father, Apollo, had warned the bereaved Cyparissus about: 'quae non solacia Phoebus / dixit! ut hunc, leviter pro materiaque doleret, / adumonuit!' (*Metamorphoses* X, 132-134).[26] Cyparissus, of course, had only killed his beloved stag, and 'resolved to die himself' (131). But Orpheus seeks to divert his own grief over the loss of Eurydice by mocking those who can't follow their own advice. In Orpheus' song Apollo contradicts his own advice when he mourns his dead lover, Hyacinth: 'semper eris mecum memorique haerebis in ore. / te lyra pulsa manu, te carmina nostra sonabunt, / flosque novus scripto gemitus imitabere nostros' (*Metamorphoses* X, 204-206).[27] Milton's speaker most obviously cannot mock Christ as Orpheus mocks his father. Rather, like Apollo, the focus of his plaint turns self-centred; for it turns on the grief of the poet, not on the pain of its subject. 'Me' and 'my' abound in this passage:

> Me softer airs befit, and softer strings
> Of Lute, or Viol still, more apt for mournful things.
> Befriend me Night, best Patroness of grief,
> Over the Pole thy thickest mantle throw,
> And work my flatter'd fancy to belief,
> That Heav'n and Earth are colour'd with my woe;
> My sorrows are too dark for day to know:
> The leaves should all be black whereon I write,
> And letters where my tears have washt, a wannish white.
>   (*The Passion*, ll. 27-35)

He is conscious, from the outset, of having to 'tune my song, / And set my Harp to notes of saddest woe' (8-9). And so it is hardly surprising that this reluctant Orpheus should say of Calvary that 'these latter scenes confine my roving verse, / To this Horizon is my *Phoebus* bound' (*The Passion*, 22-23). For the plight of this God of 'poetry' threatens the poet himself.

Orpheus' only means of diverting grief—by exposing its folly in others—catches up with him in the end. So, too, Milton's Orphic singer becomes his own parodic Apollo before he ends the song to avoid the fate of Orpheus:

> Yet on the soft'ned Quarry would I score
> My plaining verse as lively as before;
> For sure so well instructed are my tears,
> That they would fitly fall in order'd Characters.   (ll. 46-49)

For Apollo's tears were 'order'd' into characters after the death of Hyacinth: 'ispe suos gemitus foliis inscribit, et AI AI / flos habet inscriptum, funestaque littera ducta est' (*Metamorphoses* X, 215-216).[28] The necessity of Christ's death catches the Ovidian singer by surprise, as it were, since the inverse logic of the story not only keeps the poet alive, but makes him seem as ridiculous as Apollo was made to look. In Ovid's story, the god is mocked, but it is the poet who dies. In Milton, on the other hand, the poet who survives the God is hardly a substitute for deity.

The problem, restated in Christian terms, is precisely this renunciation of power in the God's humble death which threatens the singer's poetics of 'control': 'Yet more; the stroke of death he must abide, / Then lies him meekly down fast by his Brethren's side' (20-21). And so the Orphic singer tries to imagine that Christ merely played a role: 'Poor fleshly Tabernacle entered, / His starry front low-rooft beneath the skies; / O what a Mask was there, what a disguise!' (17-19). For that reason, perhaps, he never looks in the direction of the cross; neither is there a body in evidence in *The Passion*, only 'that sad Sepulchral rock / That was the Casket of Heav'n's richest store' (*The Passion*, 43-44). In effect, the Orphic poet can only lose control if he happens to look on death.

Grief is hardly as 'easily beguil'd' in *The Passion*, then, as the singer concedes in his final allusion. Though he might 'work my flatter'd fancy' (31) to believe that 'th'infection of my sorrows loud / Had got a race of mourners on some pregnant cloud' (55-56), he is aware that, like Ixion, he is guilty of fathering a monstrosity, much as the centaurs were begotten on a cloudy imitation of Juno (Melville, *Metamorphoses*, 444, n. 211). Not surprisingly, the immoderate grief of the singer ends in a memory of sexual guilt that was only temporarily deferred in the Orphic Hymn to the Nativity.

Finally, *The Passion* concludes in the *Poems* of 1645 with a confession that implies a true awareness of the problems raised: 'This Subject the Author finding to be above the years he had, when he wrote it, and nothing satisfied with what was begun, left it unfinisht' (63). In that volume, he draws a line under his Latin imitations of Ovid, writing 'Paid' to his debt and to a particular line of development:

> Haec ego mente olim laeva, studioque supino,
> Nequitiae posue vana trophaea meae.
> Scilicet abreptum sic me malus impulit error,
> Indocilisque aetas prava magistra fuit;
> Donec Socraticos unbrosa Academia rivos
> Praebuit, admissum dedocuitque iugum.

Protinus, extinctis ex illo tempore flammis,
Cincta rigent multo pectora nostra gelu;
Unde suis frigus metuit puer ipse Sagittis,
Et Diomedeam vim timet ipsa Venus.   (Hughes, 61)[29]

The references to Venus, Cupid, and the flames in his breast recall his old attraction to the Ovidian art of parody, that 'trifling purpose' which led him to write in Latin with much of the same cleverness (or 'perverse spirit') of the Master. The *Nativity Ode*, though grave and dignified, was itself a means of keeping his breast 'rigid under a thick case of ice', of battling down the threatening power of Venus. Only in *The Passion* would he discover that his classical influences fundamentally betrayed his Christian faith. Hence the failure of his Orphic 'Passion'.

This failure of *The Passion* nonetheless signals a new beginning for Milton's poetry, even if it does not quite end the reliance on Ovidian imitation. But in his final poems of elegiac exorcism, Milton now realizes that Ovid can no longer serve as a model for his poetic growth. This does not mean that Milton refused to use Ovidian situations and characters, only that he refused to imitate Ovidian thought and style any longer to create his poetry. The poet of the *Nativity Ode* and *The Passion* proves himself to be partial still to Ovidian music. However, as Milton retracts his faith in Orphic 'harmony', he must find a new poetic direction. This new bearing owes as much to the playful Ovid in Milton as it does to his Christianity.

Notes

1   *John Milton: Complete Poems and Major Prose*, edited by Merritt Y. Hughes (New York, 1957), 693. All subsequent references to and translations of Milton's poetry and prose will be to this edition.
2   Davis Harding, *Milton and the Renaissance Ovid* (Urbana, 1946), 41.
3   Linda Hutcheon, *A Theory of Parody* (London, 1985), 10.
4   Louis Martz, *Poet of Exile: A Study of Milton's Poetry* (New Haven, 1980), 33.
5   Douglas Bush, *John Milton* (London, 1980), 31.
6   L.B. Broadbent, 'The Nativity Ode', in: Frank Kermode (ed.), *The Living Milton* (London, 1960), 12.
7   D.M. Rosenberg, *Oaten Reeds and Trumpets: Pastoral and Epic in Virgil, Spenser, and Milton* (London, 1981), 135.
8   Patricia Vicari, 'The Triumph of Art, The Triumph of Death: Orpheus in Spenser and Milton', in: John Warden (ed.), *Orpheus: The Metamorphoses of a Myth* (Toronto, 1982), 215.
9   'These are my gifts for the birthday of Christ—gifts which the first light of its dawn brought to me' (Hughes, trans., 53).

10 'I sang the giants in a graver theme / And bolts victorious in Phlegra's plains. / But now I need a lighter strain, to sing / Of boys beloved of gods and girls bewitched / By lawless fires who paid the price of lust'. *Ovid: The Metamorphoses*, translated by A.D. Melville (Oxford: 1986), 229.

11 'Now, O child of the goddess, with your darts no less powerful than fire, your bow is beyond all doubt dreadful to me. Your Altars shall smoke with my sacrifices, and, as far as I am concerned, you shall be sole and supreme among the gods' (Hughes, trans., 61).

12 'No sun as yet poured light upon the world, ... / Nor in the ambient air yet hung the earth, / Self-balanced, equipoised ... / This strife a god, with nature's blessing, solved; ... / he fastened in its place / Appropriate peace and harmony' (Melville, trans., 2).

13 Thomas Greene, *The Light in Troy: Imitation and Discovery in Renaissance Poetry* (New Haven, 1982), 37.

14 Arthur Barker, 'The Pattern of Milton's *Nativity Ode*', *The University of Toronto Quarterly* 10 (1940-41): 180.

15 'when the bard, / The heaven-born bard, sat there and touched his strings, / Shade came in plenty. Every tree was there ... / and when he tried his strings / And, as he tuned, was satisfied the notes, / Though different, agreed in harmony; / He sang this song: "From Jove, great Mother Muse, / Inspire my song: to Jove all creatures bow"' (Melville, trans., 183).

16 'The reviving earth throws off her hated old age and craves thy embraces, O Phoebus' (Hughes, trans., 39).

17 'Thence through the boundless air Hymen, clad in a saffron mantle, departed and took his way to the country of the Ciconians, and was summoned by the voice of Orpheus, though all in vain. He was present, it is true; but he brought neither the hallowed words, nor joyous faces, nor lucky omen ... The outcome of the wedding was worse than the beginning; for while the bride was strolling through the grass with a group of naiads in attendance, she fell dead, smitten in the ankle by a serpent's tooth'. *Ovid: Metamorphoses*, translated by Frank Justus Miller, Vol. 2 (Cambridge, Mass., 1968), 65.

18 'Borne through the middle air by flying swans on her light car, Cytherea had not yet come to Cyprus, when she heard afar the groans of the dying youth and turned her white swans to go to him' (Miller, trans., 115).

19 'This strife a god, with nature's blessing, solved; / Who severed land from sky and sea from land, / And from the denser vapours set apart / The ethereal sky' (Melville, trans., 2).

20 Richard Halpern, 'The Great Instauration: Imaginary Narratives in Milton's *Nativity Ode*', in Mary Nyquist and Margaret W. Ferguson (eds), *Re-Membering Milton* (London, 1987), 13.

21 *Edmund Spenser's Poetry*, edited by Hugh Maclean (London, 1968), 436.

22 'Indeed the earth, against her will, produced / A serpent never known before, the huge / Python, a terror to men's new-made tribes' (Melville, trans., 12).

23 'There Pan sang his songs, / Flaunting among the gentle nymphs, and played Light airs upon his pipes, and dared to boast / Apollo's music second to his own' (Melville, trans., 238).

24 Gale H. Carrithers, 'Poems (1645): On Growing Up', *Milton Studies* 15 (1981): 161.

25 'When he'd tried his strings / And, as he tuned, was satisfied the notes, / Though different agreed in harmony' (Melville, trans., 202).

26 'What words of comfort did not Phoebus give! / What warnings not to yield to grief so sore, / So ill-proportioned' (Melville, trans., 198).

27 'You shall stay / For ever in remembrance on my lips, / And you my lyre and you my song shall hymn. / A new flower you shall be with letters marked / To imitate my sobs' (Melville, trans., 205).

28 'himself inscribed upon the flower his lament, / AI AI, AI AI, and still the petals show / The letters written there in words of woe' (Melville, trans., 205).

29 'These are the monuments to my wantonness that with a perverse spirit and a trifling purpose I once erected. Obviously, mischievous error led me astray and my undisciplined youth was a vicious teacher until the shady Academy offered its Socratic streams and taught me how to escape from the yoke to which I had submitted. From that hour those flames were extinct and thenceforward my breast has been rigid under a thick case of ice, of which the boy himself fears the frost for his arrows, and Venus herself is afraid of my Diomedean strength' (Hughes, trans., 61).

20

'VARNISH ON A HARLOT'S CHEEK': JOHN MILTON AND THE HIERARCHIES OF SECULAR AND DIVINE LITERATURE

THOMAS N. CORNS

Some religions are characterised by their inclusiveness, by the ways in which new gods are added to their pantheons without displacement of the old. Thus the gods of ancient Rome constituted an open set into which newer Asiatic deities could be and were incorporated. Of course the ancient gods survive in several modes within the Christian era; at the level of theory, however, and in the context of bible history, the Judaeo-Christian tradition asserts a monotheistic primacy which excludes and represses; displacement, not cooption, is at its core.

In Hebrew sacred text, in a frequently reiterated phrase, 'the Lord thy God is a jealous God', so that 'ye shall not go after other gods, of the gods of the people which are round about you ... lest the anger of the Lord thy God be kindled against thee, and destroy thee from off the face of the earth' (Deut. 6: 14-15). Hebraic godliness often assumes the form of exclusion and separateness from other traditions, which extend to broader cultural issues. Again, Ecclesiastes ends with an assertion of the simplicities of holiness, which may be disentangled from redundant complexities of unnecessary text: 'And further ... my son, be admonished: of making many books there is no end; and much study is a weariness of the flesh. Let us hear the conclusion of the whole matter: Fear God, and keep his commandments: for this is the whole duty of man' (Ecclesiastes 12: 12-13).

The notional simplicities of Ecclesiastes find little place in most of Milton's early poetry, though the jealous God receives appropriate celebration, most substantially in the *Nativity Ode*. 'The hand of the Lord was heavy upon them of Ashdod, and he destroyed them'; in the temple of Dagon his graven image has its hands and head cut off, so that 'only the stump of Dagon was left to him' (I Sam. 5: 5-6). These images of vengeful iconoclasm plainly inspired English Protestantism. In the *Nativity Ode*, the impact of the incarnation of Christ is to eject the false gods from their holy places, among them the classical pantheon as well as the false gods of ancient Israel.

But in a curious juxtaposition that same expulsion, though it acts out the rejections of the primary tradition, is represented in the very different idiom in which the ancient gods survive, at the level of metaphor or even typology, into the European Renaissance. Thus the infant Hercules is retained as a transcended analogue to the infant Christ:

> Nor all the gods beside,
> Longer dare abide,
>   Not Typhon huge ending in snaky twine:
> Our babe to show his Godhead true,
> Can in his swaddling bands control the damned crew.[1]

Perhaps we may pause to puzzle over the epithet qualifying his godhead: is Christ's godhead termed 'true' to differentiate it from the false godhead of Zeus, slayer of Typhon (a manoeuvre which shall see Milton execute again in *Paradise Lost*)? The chief influences, though, as scholars have long noted, are Italianate mythologising and that rather curious tradition of regarding Hercules as a type for Christ.

It is easy to find analogous cases of the appropriation of profane (in the sense of pagan) mythologies into Christian discourse, elsewhere in the *Nativity Ode* and in Milton's poems of the 1630s. Thus, Christ is perceived somewhat improbably by Hebrew shepherds as 'the mighty Pan' (*Nativity Ode*, 89; it was a familiar identification with Spenserian analogues and a very early source). In *Comus* he is '[c]elestial Cupid' embracing his 'Psyche' in the environs of 'Jove's court' (1003-1004, 1). In 'Lycidas' 'all-judging Jove' rubs alongside St Peter, and the grim Fury keeps company with Neptune, Orpheus and Camus, the allegorised figure of English higher education.

None of this is surprising, though the sudden change in this aspect of his poetry after *Poems 1645* functions both in terms of political and cultural ideology. Milton before 1637 seems to me best perceived as an essentially non-dissident figure, comfortable with the aesthetic of the Caroline court, though the evidence of 'Lycidas', even without the headnote added in 1645, shows a degree of radicalisation, presumably after the gory events of 1637 itself, something of a climactic year in the personal rule of Charles I.[2]

In terms of cultural ideology, Milton's movement in his later poems is from the riot of Italianate syncretism towards a starker neoclassicism which looks past the mediations of medieval and Renaissance strategies of incorporation to seek out afresh classical models for vernacular literature. In some ways, Milton is the cardinal figure in English neoclassicism; cardinal in the sense that on his oeuvre hinges the shift from a cultural ideology which incorporates paganism and pagan idioms into Christian celebration to a cultural ideology, much closer to the exclusion implicit at the level of theory in the Judaeo-Christian tradition, an ideology which asserts the primacy of Christian and especially sacred discourse and which devalues and relegates profane literary traditions to a place beneath the Christian hierarchy of literary idioms.

There is another, more strictly puritan element to be considered: at the heart of English religious radicalism of the mid-seventeenth century there lies a profound and vigorous philistinism. It manifests itself in a myriad forms. In part it rests in the assertion of the immediate obligations of the active over the contemplative life, documented, perhaps, in Marvell's recognition that this is the age for the 'forward Youth' to forsake the muses for 'th'unused Armour'.[3] It manifests itself, too, in a preference for humble godliness and, at times, in a suspicion of education and its associated sophistication. Hence, too, a radical contempt of any who speak beyond the assurance and guidance of the spirit within. In its extremest manifestation prayer and celebration arrive at a pronounced minimalism, as in George Fox's recommendations of 1658 for Quaker worship: 'none go beyond the measure of the spirit of God ... if you have anything ... to speak, in the life of God stand up, and speak it, if it be but two or three words, and sit down again ...'[4] The learned and eloquent minister becomes for Quakers the embodiment of church corruption: in the words of Benjamin Furly (1663), 'They put you [ministers] to the university to learn the art of speaking-by-rote, and trading in words; and when any of you hath been a competent time there, and is grown pretty cunning at cutting out of discourses, wresting plain words, and handling your tongue deceitfully, then you are fitted for the work of the ministry'.[5]

The exigencies of prose polemic forced Milton quite early to come to terms with the disjunction between his pre-war aesthetic and the austerities of militant and radical puritanism (though, as we shall see, his educational tract argues rather differently). Thus, in the antiprelatical pamphlets, while still asserting his own culture and learning (as in his *Apology* of 1642), he must necessarily defend the rights of tradesman preachers in order to resist the episcopalian claim that Long Parliament is incapable of keeping the lower classes in order. This he intermittently does as early as *The Reason of Church-Government* (1642). By 1659 and the time of *The Likeliest Means to Remove Hirelings* Milton's position is deeply sceptical about the relationship of learning and godliness. As he observes, 'the scriptures [are] translated into every vulgar tongue, as being held in main matters of belief and salvation, plane and easie to the poorest: and such no less then thir teachers have the spirit to guide them in all truth'.[6]

I should like to suggest that the redefined relationship of sacred and profane discourses to be discerned in Milton's epics is overdetermined by the pressures of aesthetic, religious and political ideology. In *Paradise Lost*

Milton the radical, Milton the puritan, Milton the neoclassicist disentangles the sacred and profane and asserts the primacy of the former. Just as the Quaker may speak no more than the spirit prompts, so the words of the poem have their validation in the nightly ministration of a sacred, Christian muse. Again, the subject matter of his poem transcends the subject matter of classical epic, while he nevertheless satisfies its formal requirements, following closely the Virgilian structural paradigm. Hence his reiterated assertion that he offers an alternative notion of the heroic, in terms of godly fortitude and in contrast with 'fabled knights / In battled feigned' (9: 30-31). His is the 'higher argument' that justly merits the 'heroic name' (40-42).

'Feigned' and 'fabled', words scarcely used in *Poems 1645*, are potent terms in *Paradise Lost* in his strategy of subordinating classical mythology and allusion, rather than incorporating it in the syncretic manner of his earliest work. Thus the hell of his epic is 'worse / Than fables yet have feigned, or fear conceived, / Gorgons and Hydras, and Chimeras dire' (2: 626-628). The bower of Adam and Eve transcends that of Pan or Silvanus both in its aesthetic quality and in the quality of its unfabled modality, both more 'sacred and sequestered' and not 'feigned' (4: 706; cp. 9: 439-443), just as Eve surpasses in both respects the beauty of Venus, 'the fairest goddess feigned / Of three that in Mount Ida naked strove' (5: 380-381).

In *Of Education* (1644), a tract that he evidently thought well enough of to reissue in 1673, Milton had conceived of his academy for the production of a puritan elite for the newly reformed England in terms of the synthesis of all cultural discourses. The polymath polyglot graduates he would produce are to relieve their labours and acquire a different kind of wisdom from the profane literatures of the classical world, without compromise to his avowed objective: 'The end ... of learning is to repair the ruins of our first parents by regaining to know God aright, and out that knowledge to love him, to imitate him, to be like him, as we may the neerest by possessing our souls of true vertue, which being united to the heavenly grace of faith makes up the highest perfection' (*CPW* 2: 366-367). Clearly, knowledge advances the individual towards spiritual perfection, and the learned who have learned, in Baconian fashion, to value content as well as style have a spiritual strength above 'any yeoman or tradesman competently wise in his mother dialect only' (370).

But in *Paradise Lost* Raphael relates to Adam that some learning is in effect idle curiosity; speculation about the stars, for example (8: 66-178). 'Be lowly wise', is Raphael's advice (173), and it plainly echoes other explanations about the real simplicities of the difficult problems which beset Adam and Eve. (*Of Education* in contrast had advocated for Christian

gentlemen in the making a leisurely perusal of 'the History of *Meteors*'—
CPW 2: 393.) That starker perspective on the non-sacred and the inessential
finds definitive rehearsal in the Son's dismissal of secular or profane culture and learning in *Paradise Regained*. In a passage replete with paradox
and an incident wholly of Milton's devising, in an argument deeply derivative of Plato's *Republic* and wholly independent of the Gospel source,
Milton has the Son dismiss all profane art and learning in terms which
assert the transcendence of the simple truths of the biblical tradition. In
place of the profane celebration of their ridiculous gods, in 'swelling epi-
thets thick-laid / As varnish on a harlot's cheek' (4: 343-344), there is the
wisdom of sacred discourse which 'men divinely taught' disclose '[i]n their
majestic unaffected style'; in them 'is plainest taught, and easiest learnt'
whatever moral truths are necessary for godly living and for salvation (357-
361).

Milton's Quaker friend Thomas Elwood believed himself to have sown
the idea of the brief epic in Milton's imagination, a notion Milton apparently encouraged (*Poems*, 1063). In some ways, *Paradise Regained* is his most
Quakerish work. In part, this may be seen in the defiant brevity of the hero;
the Son's brusque treatment of Satan ('Me worse than wet thou find'st not',
4: 486) shares a common idiom with the robust responses of George Fox to
his many interrogators. The cultural politics of *Paradise Regained* embody
the final stage of the long argument in Milton's writing between the discourses of the sacred and the profane, an argument won definitively by the
simplicities of the holy, in the paradox of the triviality of the complexities
of profane discourse in which the very syncretism of that discourse reduces
it to a virtuouso's cabinet of curiosities. Again, the idiom is that of Ecclesiastes: 'many books / Wise men have said are wearisome':

> Incessantly, and to his reading brings not
> A spirit and judgment equal or superior,
> (And what he brings, what needs he elsewhere seek)
> Uncertain and unsettled still remains,
> Deep-versed in books and shallow in himself,
> Crude or intoxicate, collecting toys,
> And trifles for choice matters, worth a sponge;
> As children gathering pebbles on the shore.   (4: 321-330).

So far in this essay I have suggested an unambiguous schematisation in
which Milton is represented as progressing (if that is not too whiggish a
word) from a Renaissance syncretism towards a rather puritanical subordination of pagan discourse to Christian. But Milton rarely admits of such

simplicities, often manifesting what I have elsewhere termed an ideological plurality.[7] So, too, in this aspect. Had *Paradise Lost* really been a valedictory work, had it constituted Milton's final statement, perhaps it would have been otherwise. But the early 1670s witnessed a flurry of publishing activity on his part. After *Paradise Regained* came the second edition of *Paradise Lost*. And there came, too, in 1673 *Poems, &c. upon Several Occasions. By Mr. John Milton: Both English and Latin, &c. Composed at several times. With a small Tractate of Education To Mr. Hartlib*. The volume returns to circulation his early (and now seemingly transcended) education programme. It reissues, too, those poems which he had published in 1645. The phrase *'Composed at several times'* had graced the titlepage of the 1645 volume, avowing its multifacetted and internally contradictory character. Milton emphasises the point further in the new edition by adding the phrase *'upon Several Occasions'*. But the phrase does not assert the authority of his later compositions over his earlier ones. Sir Thomas Browne, perhaps disingenuously, had declared in *Religio Medici*, 'I could never divide my selfe from any man upon the difference of an opinion, or be angry with his judgement for not agreeing with mee in that, from which perhaps within a few days I should dissent my selfe'.[8] Milton, however, disagrees with Milton, and in the great publishing retrospective he commits himself to in the early 1670s those differences, those sentiments uttered on several occasions, are returned to circulation on an even footing. The Son of *Paradise Regained* may disavow the pebbles on the shore; Milton in his final reissues takes out the pebbles that once pleased him so much and displays them for the readers' admiration. The ancient gods (like James I and those Jacobean bishops variously commemorated in his early verse) return to life, strutting the same stage as the puritanical and iconoclastic Son of his brief epic.

Notes

1   'On the Morning of Christ's Nativity', lines 224-228, in *The Poems of John Milton*, edited by John Carey and Alastair Fowler (1968; London, 1980); all references are to this edition.

2   See John Leonard, '"Trembling Ears": the historical moment of "Lycidas"', *Journal of Medieval and Renaissance Studies* 21 (1991): 59-81; Kevin Sharpe, *The Personal Rule of Charles I* (New Haven, 1992), especially 758-65.

3   Andrew Marvell, 'An Horatian Ode upon Cromwell's Return from Ireland', lines 1-8, in *The Poems and Letters of Andrew Marvell*, edited by H.M. Margoliouth, revised Pierre Legouis with the collaboration of E.E. Duncan-Jones (Oxford, 1971).

4   In Douglas V. Steere (ed.), *Quaker Spirituality: Selected Writings* (London, 1984), 131 (the quotation is from an Epistle).
5   Quoted by Richard Bauman, *Let Your Words Be Few: Symbolism of Speaking and Silence among Seventeenth-Century Quakers* (Cambridge and New York, 1983), 39.
6   *Complete Prose Works of John Milton*, edited by Don M. Wolfe *et al.* (New Haven, 1953-82), 7 (rev. ed.): 302. All references are to this edition (*CPW*).
7   Thomas N. Corns, '"Some rousing motions": the plurality of Miltonic ideology', in Thomas Healy and Jonathan Sawday (eds), *Literature and the English Civil War* (Cambridge, 1990), 110-126.
8   Sir Thomas Browne, *The Major Works*, edited by C.A. Patrides (Harmondsworth, 1977), 65.

21

EPIC ENDS AND NOVEL BEGINNINGS IN PARADISE LOST

ANDREW MONNICKENDAM

This essay will attempt to locate *Paradise Lost* between two extremes that initially seem as irreconcilable as the sacred and the profane: the epic and the novel. However, it should be stated that the cornerstone of this paper is precisely the belief that there are important parallels between the two pairs. The epic was the sacred model for many centuries when the emphasis on the collective implications of verse outweighed the personal concerns which would later be expressed through two of the most individualistic forms of expression: the personalised poetry of Romanticism and the novel. Using the most basic terms, we can describe *Paradise Lost* as sacred, in that it deals with God's relationship with the universe, and profane in that it centres on physical pleasure and alienation; it is also an epic poem—hardly anyone would deny that—as well as being novelistic, if not a full novel, for reasons that will become clear during the next pages. I will argue that there is considerable overlap but no confusion, even though one of the character-istics of Milton criticism has been to exclude overlap of any sort, as illus-trated by the continual use of superlatives. Milton is the first, the last, the worst; he wrote the last epic; he is the first of the masculinists, and so on. Such descriptions are unsatisfactory. Presumably St. Paul precedes Milton in time and exceeds him in importance; both the Romantics and the Victor-ians employed the epic as a form of narrative, as anyone made to enjoy *The Keeping of the Bridge*, or *Sohrab and Rustum* as a foretaste to Tennyson can testify. To the reply that these are minor epics, relics of the distant past which Milton himself had rejected in the invocation in Book IX, comes the riposte that what must accompany a diachronic study is the foregrounding of the importance of genres. Thus, in the background, we will place Bakh-tin's definition of *novel* as primarily a form of discourse, and in the fore-ground we will place Charles Martindale's *John Milton and the Transform-ation of Ancient Epic* and Ian Watt's *The Rise of the Novel* as media through which we may illumine what is, if not dark, at least a grey area.[1]

Many students and scholars get very upset by the question of sources. This is quite understandable when we consider that the weighty Longman edition spreads the poem's first six lines over two pages allowing the editor to include nearly seventy lines of clarification beneath the text. Such schol-arship encourages Milton's opposition, led, in this instance, by the New Critics, to arrive at the understandable conclusion that it is much simpler to

concentrate on the words on the page. This line of thinking gains ground
when 'clarification' of textual difficulties, in this case the image of the
fallen angels as 'autumnal leaves', is as follows:

> But M. adds the concrete precision of an actual locality again, near
> Florence. If he visited *Vallombrosia* he would know that (as its name
> partly suggests) it was shaded by extensive deciduous woods. The use
> of *shades*, by metonymy, for foliage or woods is a characteristic of
> M.'s diction.[2]

Thus scholarship is essential not only to clarify extended similes, untangle
Latinate syntax, explain the significance of lists, but also to illustrate the
extent to which Milton uses and abuses geography and botany. The editor
himself seems to have taken on the role of Milton as tutor, chastising his
inattentive nephews. Such analysis leads us to the conclusion that this
marked excess of classical scholarship shows how our secular age is unable
to cope with the conventions of the epic, itself confirming the belief that
Paradise Lost maintains its relevance primarily for the most bookish of
literary scholars interested more in the past than the present. It is also evidence of a critical stance towards Milton which may be labelled Bentley-
ism. By this I mean that commentators often behave as if Milton were on
trial for his ethical standpoint and argue that he cannot have meant what he
said, perhaps should have said something else, or in the case of the New
Critics, got it all wrong. None of these positions, it has been confirmed, is
tenable once the importance of genre as a concept is brought forward and
sustained. This essay will try to be constructive by, first, proposing alternative applications for the scholarship of sources, and second, by trying to
look into the future, beyond the seventeenth century.

Charles Martindale's analysis relocates the question of sources within a
modern framework that permits intertextual freedom, something absent, as
we have just seen, from Fowler's edition. Sources are not necessarily
sources. He argues that Renaissance poets frequently

> incorporate in their works what are in effect passages of free transla-
> tion of appropriate classical poetry (or even on occasion prose). In
> doing so they were carrying over into adult life what they had been
> taught to do as schoolboys by way of translation and imitation of the
> classics (17-18).

If Shakespeare incorporates Ovid into *The Tempest* using his scanty knowledge of Latin or Greek, as Ben Jonson outlandishly upheld, it follows that

Milton must have incorporated practically everything classical to create in *Paradise Lost* his personal vision of the literary Rococo. Martindale refutes the scholarship of sources by insisting that Milton is simply carrying on a tradition and logically cannot be labelled an obscurantist. Furthermore, if we accept that Milton is not simply citing other texts but incorporating them, instead of engaging in discussions on sources or dallying with the idea of plagiarism, we eventually admit that it all boils down to intertextuality. Another, similar strategy is Martindale's insistence that we not only have to focus correctly on the limited idea of allusion, but pay much greater attention to epic structure. Consequently source hunters often cry 'Eureka!' when in fact they have not discovered anything at all. That is to say that if we look for parallels between *Paradise Lost* and epic poetry, we will naturally find a myriad. Far from being a positive achievement, with it comes the realisation that the more we find, the more we face the possibility that all that have been uncovered are features common to the epic genre. A typical Martindale phrase would be that the so-called debate in Book II is a 'conventional feature of epic' (4); that Satan's first address to Beelzebub is simply 'a rhetorical formula' (15). Martindale's approach, however convincing it appears, leaves us with the doubt as to whether intertextuality has achieved much. If we now insist on the structure of genres rather than on sources, conceivably the textual knowledge required increases rather than diminishes. Although that still remains an open question, what Martindale's genre-orientated thesis does achieve is to redirect our study of epic poetry. For example, the fourth invocation, with its insistence on 'tedious havoc', should no longer be seen as a refutation of epic poetry, but as a formula that reinforces epic poetry's patriotism without condoning its methods. In other words, in the seventeenth century, modern politics and warfare, represented by republicanism and the New Model Army, can no longer be sustained by outmoded images of Royalist Arthurian chivalry. What Milton is possibly proposing in addition is a renovation of the genre, if it is not to be relegated to something purely exotic or mythical.

Let us go farther. Martindale's analysis implies that far from being the dull authoritarian Puritan who wrote an equally dull, authoritarian poem, in *Paradise Lost* Milton provides us with plenty of evidence for the post-structuralist thesis. The breakdown of the hierarchical relationship between text and source suggests that it is not Milton who writes *Paradise Lost* but that it is Milton who is written by *Paradise Lost* and its supposed sources, or to paraphrase Mary Nyquist's title, Milton is 're-membered'.[3] If that seems to be going too far, perhaps the Bakhtinian definition of epic poetry will be acceptable:

> The world of the epic is the national heroic past: it is a world of 'be-
> ginnings' and 'peak times' in the national history, a world of fathers
> and of founders of families, a world of 'firsts' and 'bests'. The import-
> ant point is not that the past constitutes the content of the epic. The
> formally constitutive feature of the epic as a genre is rather transferral
> of a represented world into the past.[4]

This might initially contradict earlier remarks on the nature of the epic, in
spite of Bakhtin's statement that epic contains 'a represented world' rather
than a depiction of the past itself. This implies that even though the epic
deals with moments of crisis, these flow into the present and future; consequently there is such a thing as history. Only in this way could the epic,
as a genre, have any relevance to its contemporary readers in a society
which had already disestablished the church and which would become increasingly secular.

I will now move on to Ian Watt's analysis of the novel, and will concentrate my attention on three aspects: the hero, internalisation and sexuality.
Epic acts require a hero to carry them out, and even to die for a just national cause if that is required. When we turn to *Paradise Lost* as the last epic
poem, its description as such falls to pieces. Addison, for example, states
that '... he that looks for a Hero in it, searches for that which Milton never
intended'.[5] Those dissatisfied with that remark can choose from the following list: God, the Son, Adam, Abdiel, Satan or Eve. The poem's opening
words on '... man's first disobedience', when added to the poem's concluding words on man's solitary state put forward Adam as the major candidate,
yet there seems nothing sufficiently epic or tragic in the lapsed gardener,
nothing of the calibre required for catharsis. There are two paths we can
follow at this junction. One is to turn in the direction of those who argue
that the calibre required is present elsewhere. Blake and his followers put
forward the case for the fallen prince whose nobility has been destroyed by
a reactionary, authoritarian state. The other path requires a readjustment of
the initial term, the hero. Watt searches for indications which would explain
why the novel rose in the eighteenth century in the way it did, at the
expense of other genres, including the epic. The new bourgeois readership
could not tolerate 'reading epic (which) meant a continuous effort to
exclude the normal expectations of everyday life—the very expectations
which the novel exploited' (256). This ties in with twinning the rise of the
novel with the rise of individualism, reinforcing the notion that the novel
was often concerned with the people and events of 'everyday life', unlike
the epic, which 'was masculine, bellicose, aristocratic and pagan' (254).

How many of those features can be found in Adam? The marriage novel was popular because marriage was a momentous event, especially for female readers, representing the only moment in life in which the possibility of choice was offered. Yet, it cannot be forgotten that the novel often concerned itself with the life and scandals of the aristocracy, not only in the historical novel but also in female writers such as Maria Edgeworth or Jane Austen, who wrote for a typically middle-class audience. This situation still vexed George Eliot in 1856, becoming one of the concerns of her essay *Silly Novels by Lady Novelists*,[6] continuing well into the twentieth century, as illustrated by Elizabeth Taylor's *Angel*.[7] Watt insists that the eighteenth century novelists were innovative in leaving behind past models or sources and insisting on individual experience. If we look at *Paradise Lost*, we could put forward the view that the only individuals who reflect everyday experience are Adam, and arguably Eve. Therefore, my first conclusion is that Watt's thesis ignores the ideological importance of Milton's bland hero, reflecting instead a relationship between life and literature more appropriate to Balzac or other nineteenth-century writers than to the eighteenth-century writers he analyses.

Perhaps this conjecture can most convincingly be upheld by examining three important features of Watt's analysis of *Robinson Crusoe* and subsequently relating them to Milton. First, Watt makes a great deal of the Scotsman's 'book-keeping conscience' (65). If we turn to Adam's thoughts when he considers his future now that Eve has eaten the apple, in Book IX, 896-916 and 921-959, it is easy to read his words as a proof of great love, but it is just as easy to maintain that in these two speeches he gradually forgets his book-keeping conscience, overcome, as he is, by what Crusoe did not have to encounter, female charm. Mercantilism is present even in one of Milton's most excruciating puns, 'Should God create another Eve, and I/Another rib afford ...' (Book IX, 911-912) How would he have weighed up the pros and cons if Lilith had been around? Second, Watt deals with the knotty problem of the relationship between man and nature and productivity; he asserts that

> Calvinism tended to make its adherents forget the idea that labour was God's punishment for Adam's disobedience by emphasizing the different idea that untiring stewardship of the material gifts of God was a paramount religious and ethical obligation (76).

This neat formula would have helped Milton (and Adam) in their rather half-hearted attempt to convince Eve, in a world in which heroes cannot hunt in the style of Adonis, that what their heroic duties consist of is not labour at all but stewardship. No place is more adequate for that supposition than a garden, a combination of the natural and the plastic. Third, Watt affirms that 'the idea of contract played an important part in the theoretical development of political individualism' (66). The Old Testament, and Genesis in particular, is based on a rather similar idea, that of another sort of contract: the covenant. Adam, Eve, and Noah, are all subject to agreements, with obligations and rights on both sides, though not necessarily on equal terms, as Job would later find out. Does it have to be stated that the Ten Commandments actually have to be written down (twice) by God's agent? It is widely accepted that Protestant individualism found more inspiration in the Old Testament than in other religious writings. However, Watt's analysis did not consider the proposition that the idiosyncrasies of his prototypal novelistic hero are most clearly delineated in Milton's virtuous, rural, Adam. Consequently, the break between epic poem and novel was not so abrupt as Watt and his disciples claim. The continuity between the genres still leaves unanswered, for the moment, the question of why the change required a different mode of operation for the heroic bland steward and his descendants.

Let us now turn to the second question from Watt, that of internalisation. Terry Eagleton accounts for Hamlet's condition in the following manner:

> ... the resultant 'decentring' of his identity satirically questions the violent closure of bourgeois individualism as much as that of Claudius' court ... that individualist conception of the self will itself enter into crisis. This is why many commentators have discerned something peculiarly 'modernist' in Hamlet ... he stands at the tentative beginnings of a history which may now ... be drawing to a close.[8]

Shakespeare's Hamlet is therefore a new kind of hero, distant from his predecessor in the history plays or the Roman plays through his insistence on being an individual, to the extreme of preferring the role of poet manqué to that of epic hero such as Fortinbras, as well as preferring to address Gertrude and Claudius as mother or uncle rather than King or Queen. If we add to all that, Hamlet's rejection of Ophelia, we reach the conclusion that, according to Eagleton, Hamlet suffers from the modern disease of alienation. Everything is internalised. Watt, citing Weber, calls this 'historically unprecedented "inner isolation"' (92). The modern condition, if Hamlet, Crusoe and so on are good examples, makes its presence felt in *Paradise Lost,* too. Satan's importance for the Romantics was a consequence of his alienation and internalisation. Nothing can be more internalised than his remark that 'The mind is its own place, and in itself / Can make a heaven of hell, hell of heaven' (Book I, 254-255). Moreover, it is commonly asserted that the impossibility of the Satanic enterprise, backed up by Milton's own remarks, notably 'Who durst defy the omnipotent to arms' (Book I, 50), is a clear example of absurdity. Placing individualistic concerns in opposition to omnipotence or omniscience may or may not be fruitless, but surely it is the opposition as such which is part and parcel of the internalisation of the modern hero or anti-hero. Consequently Satan is simultaneously a chivalric hero and a close relative of modern, novelistic heroes. Indeed, nothing can prove the Watt thesis better than Satan's final internalisation: his metamorphosis into another beast. In a similar way, Eve's mind is poisoned by his thoughts, when 'Squat like a toad' (Book IV, 800) he whispers to her during her sleep. This is not the only example of the process. Christine Froula analyses Eve's awakening thus:

> As her narrative shows, she has internalized the voices and values of her mentors: her speech reproduces the words of the 'voice' and of Adam and concludes with an assurance that she has indeed been successfully taught to 'see' for herself the superiority of Adam's virtues to her own, limited as far as she knows to 'beauty' briefly glimpsed in the pool.[9]

To what extent it is legitimate to bracket together the internalisation produced by Satan, Adam, Milton and God depends on the politics one adheres to, though the gender-based interpretation has become increasingly powerful in recent years. Adam's conformist personality makes him the ideal candidate for the hero of the bourgeois novel, evident both in his rejection of solitude in favour of love and in his petty, post-coital bickering with Eve. But alienation, a word used by Milton at the beginning of Book IX, is a process of internalisation sufficiently comprehensive to include alienation from God, Nature, one's partner and one's self.

Internalisation is an umbrella term which is used to include just about everything. To this accusation we can reply, along with Pascal, that 'alienation (is) evidence of the essential truth of the fall-myth'.[10] Furthermore, if God is harmony, the only alternative is alienation. But perhaps it is more useful at this point to move away from metaphysics and return to narratology. From the moment of her awakening, Eve has internalised the thoughts of others, and, it cannot be overemphasised, has given them precedence over the words of God. How do we internalise narrative? With *Paradise Lost*, there should be no problem whatsoever, as its didactic purpose is so firmly spelled out in the first invocation. However, if Eve, to a certain extent, the helpless Eve, internalises the venom of 'the toad', how do we as descendants of *Paradise Lost* respond to reading novels? Perhaps the genre itself is so ideologically weighted that it cannot be contested within its own framework. Thus, Lennard Davis argues that there can be no such thing as the political novel.[11] The Glasgow writer James Kelman specifies that his own idiosyncratic narrative form is an antidote to the ideologically weighted third person narrative, otherwise referred to, and most appropriately in a discussion of Milton, as the omniscient narrator.[12] These last two hypotheses are responses to our contemporary culture, and are therefore distant in time from *Paradise Lost.* However, a strong connection exists. For their response would confirm that the novel is such a powerful construct that it excludes any form of contestation from within the genre. In much the same way, the basis of Eve's fall is the assimilation of internalised ideas which she has no possibility of refuting. In addition, we are obliged to reorient our analysis of the importance of discourse, for, I repeat, internalised discourse is capable of refuting demonstrable proof. This is surely what has occurred when she is persuaded that what she sees in the pool is not her self but her reflection, as well as when her internalisation of Satan's logic overrules the dictates of God.

The third topic, sexuality, cannot be separated from marriage and closure whether we are dealing with *Paradise Lost* or the classic realist novel. Even though archetypal novels such as *Robinson Crusoe, The Life and Opinions of Tristram Shandy* and *Clarissa* do not automatically convey the need for closure-by-marriage, marriage-by-closure, it would be indisputable that marriage is the subject of the novel, making *Pamela* the model to follow. Milton's position in the marriage debate is contradictory: for some he is the great oppressor, for others a broad-Augustinian, something of a liberal. Undoubtedly Milton's insistence on pre-lapsarian sex is an unusual occurrence, as is its side by side mutuality. Its paradisal nature places it close to Catherine Belsey's assertion that

> ... only sexual love, the sexual act, self-evidently requires the undivided attention of subjects to each other, depends on the complicity to share the same experience, and promises the reassurance that that implies. Hence the value attached to simultaneous orgasm.[13]

James Grantham Turner's exhaustive study of contemporary sexuality suggests that Milton's Eve is partially the result of 'personal Proustian dreams of vanished happiness and an ideal mistress ...' (272). The complexity of the situation results from Milton having described within such a short space of time a completely satisfactory, natural sexual act, followed by a sexual act that although immediately satisfying leads to the first case of *post coitum omne animal tristum*. Which is closer to marriage? Which is closer to modern life? The ideal of marriage, as expounded by Milton in Book IV, places great faith in the possibility of attaining something reasonably like the ideal.

The description of the 'blissful bower' and the night under the starry sky, Book IV, 689-775, draws together the points concerning mercantilism, internalisation and sexuality. It is precisely here that Milton is at his most aggressive, attacking a large number or targets in a short period of time. Those who champion celibacy, Milton labels 'hypocrites' (Book IV, 743), emphasising sexual pleasure with a forcefulness reminiscent of the Wife of Bath. But it has to be remembered that Milton is expressing his militant anti-Catholicism and opposition to Gnostic doctrine, and that what is being promoted is not licence, but 'wedded love'. Wedded love is the universal panacea which binds families together, prevents adultery, as well as being more apt for the modern age:

> Far be it, that I should write thee sin or blame,
> Or think thee unbefitting holiest place,
> Perpetual fountain of domestic sweets,
> Whose bed is undefiled and chaste pronounced,
> Present, or past, as saints and patriarchs used.
> Here Love his golden shafts employs, here lights
> His constant lamp, and waves his purple wings,
> Reigns here and revels; not the bought smile
> Of harlots, loveless, joyless, unendeared,
> Casual fruition, nor in court amours
> Mixed dance, or wanton mask, or midnight ball,
> Or serenade, which the starved lover sings
> To his proud fair, best quitted with disdain.   (Book IV, 758-770)

Wedded love, in what must have been a rather risqué image, is located as 'the holiest place'. Unless Milton is being parodic here, this is the paradise which can be glimpsed or regained in a stable marriage. The allusions to masks and the courts have biographical and historical applications to Milton's earlier career and his republicanism. At the same time they surely have an important role in describing Satan, the lustful onlooker, in the middle four books. Furthermore, the simile of the city dweller, along with repeated allusions to Ceres, promotes the image of Satan as rapist. Satan's desire for Eve, which, according to Enoch, culminates in copulation and the birth of Cain, might not be realised in *Paradise Lost*, but if she does not yield to him physically, she is certainly seduced by his power of persuasion. A century on, as a result of a similar set of circumstances, Céciles Volanges acknowledges to the Marquise de Mertreuil that

> If it is always as difficult as this to defend oneself, one needs a good deal of practice! It is true that Monsieur de Valmont has a way of saying things so that one is hard put to think of a reply.[14]

The reason why there should be parallels with Laclos, writing in 1782, Richardson's Lovelace (*Clarissa* was written some thirty years before), and Milton's seducer, is a good test of the veracity of Watt's thesis. I have suggested that the link between the early novel and everyday life is not nearly so strong as Watt (and his followers) would make us believe. This, in turn, can only confirm the hypothesis that thematically the bourgeois novel has strong roots in Milton that are carried forward ideologically in their championing of marriage and the family, but definitely not in the prominence he gives to sexual pleasure, the description of which is more or less removed from the canonical novel, nor in his republicanism. A further important feature of Milton's views on marriage is of particular relevance here. The description of the couple retiring for the night, 'hand in hand alone they passed/Onto their blissful bower' (Book IV, 689) emphasises mutuality, a state which is broken when labour is divided in a very entangled/disentangled image, '... from her husband's hand her hand/Soft she withdrew.' (Book IX, 385/6) Hands will not be joined after the expulsion from Eden, a metonym which reinforces not only the importance of marriage but also argues very strongly for humanism, thus casting a rather peculiar slant on Milton's religious views. Christopher Hill, for example, questions Milton's orthodoxy, suggesting that we should consider his possible anti-trinitarianism or mortalism.[15] Rather than being doctrinal quibbles, these questions acquire considerable significance at the poem's close. What can be made of the couple's solitude? However much faith might be individualised or internalised, the future, as recounted in the poem's final two books, is of a world of such intense suffering that Adam seriously doubts divine strategy. In other words, if the novel ideologically promotes values such as marriage, conformity, or patriotism, Adam and Eve are deprived of the promise of a happy family, as well as all those creature comforts which marriage novels provide for their loving couples.

Despite the fact that there is a strong thematic continuity, we cannot forget the radical difference in the matter of language between a standard novel and an epic poem. Ian Watt, again:

... the function of language is much more largely referential in the novel than in other literary forms; the genre itself works by exhaustive presentation rather than by elegant concentration (31).

Watt's thesis here follows the course of those which target *Paradise Lost* as the last of the major epics; the heroic poem is said to be obsolete for its classical learning and for its language. If that argument is correct, it is only fair to add that Milton himself agrees. In the passage on the 'blissful bower' we have been referring to, it is not only 'court amours' which are immaterial to modern life but also court culture, especially the dying strains of anachronistic poetry. The future is glimpsed in the change of form that occurs after the fall. Rhetoric and the soliloquy, as employed by Satan or Adam, are replaced by brevity and sincerity, as illustrated by Eve's one line admission of guilt—'The serpent me beguiled and I did eat' (Book X, 162), or by the brief dialogues or, more tellingly for the modern age, by silence at the poem's close. It does not take much imagination to see the linguistic contrast as part of the binaries of male/female or power (including Milton and God)/the suppressed. Such a supposition only confirms that epics are potentially, if not always, the expression of national sovereignty. This ideology has simply been passed on, in the last three centuries, to the modern epic, otherwise known as the novel.

   In conclusion, I should like to place my findings within the paradigm of the sacred and the profane. To argue against such an important thesis as Watt's might be a case of literary hubris, but I consider his analysis to be over-hasty in its separation of genres and ideas. Watt condemns the epic to the past and assigns the novel to the age of capitalism. However, rather than this being a question of black and white, before and after, I have argued that there is a transition period, in the centre of which we find *Paradise Lost*. Many of the concerns of the realist novel are found there. What is perhaps even more surprising is that many of its concerns, marriage, the family, a stable income, are presented in a much less optimistic form by Milton. That is to say that if the novel becomes the sacred text of the modern world, it is arguably in a bowdlerized version. Milton would have to be considered profane for several reasons: first, his idealisation of sexual pleasure, second, his illustration that instead of living 'happily ever after' marriage leads to quarrelling, third, his fervid belief that 'Mr Right' will not be a smooth-talking aristocrat. Such a conclusion takes us a long way from the more obvious dismissal of monarchy and the court that runs the whole length and breadth of the poem.

Notes

1   Charles Martindale, *Milton and the Transformation of the Ancient Epic* (Beckham, 1986); Ian Watt (1957), *The Rise of the Novel* (Harmondsworth, 1963).
2   John Milton (ed. Fowler), *Paradise Lost* (London, 1971), n. 62.
3   Edited by Mary Nyquist and Margaret W. Ferguson, *Re-membering Milton* (New York, 1987).
4   Mikhail Bakhtin, *The Dialogical Imagination*, translated by Caryl Emerson (Austin, 1981), 13.
5   *The Spectator*, February 9, 1712.
6   George Eliot, 'Silly Novels by Lady Novelists', *Westminster Review*, lxvi (1856) 442-461. Reprinted in George Eliot, *Selected Critical Writing* (Oxford, 1992).
7   Elizabeth Taylor, *Angel* (London, 1957).
8   Terry Eagleton, *Shakespeare* (Oxford, 1986), 75.
9   Christine Froula, 'When Eve Reads Milton: Undoing the Critical Economy', *Critical Enquiry* 10 (1983): 329.
10 James Grantham Turner, *One Flesh: Paradisal Marriage and Sexual Relations in the Age of Milton* (Oxford, 1987), 5.
11 Lennard Davis, *Resisting Novels* (London: 1987), 224-239.
12 Kirsty McNeil, 'Interview with James Kelman', *Chapman* 57 (1989), 1-9.
13 Catherine Belsey, 'Love and Death in "To his Coy Mistress"', in Richard Machin (ed.), *Post-structuralist Readings of English Poetry* (Cambridge, 1988), 18.
14 Chauderlos de Laclos (1782), *Les Liaisons Dangereuses*, translated by P.W.K. Stone (Harmondsworth, 1961), 225.
15 Christopher Hill, *Milton and the English Revolution* (London, 1977), 285-323.

22

THE POLITICS OF WOMEN'S PROPHECY IN THE ENGLISH REVOLUTLON

ELAINE HOBBY

This essay reverses the relationship between the secular and the spiritual assumed by many other contributions to this volume. Rather than discussing the reworking of profane matters for sacred ends, I shall be examining the ways in which a number of mid-seventeenth-century women prophets made use of the divine for secular ends, or, perhaps, the ways in which, these women claim, they were made use of by the Divine for His secular ends, as God required them to prepare the way for Christ's return to earth. These pamphleteers considered themselves to be prophets in the Old Testament sense of the word: they were interpreters of God's word, with a bounden duty to make his will known to the world. This results in some extraordinary, but little-known, documents, in which Bible language and allusion are used to produce radical critiques of state structures and the politics of education, as God's prophets work to invent understandings of gender and of sexuality not limited to the traditional symbols of Eve, Mary, the adulterous woman and the Whore of Babylon.

Understanding of the significance of these prophecies is helped by some information about the historical context of their production. First, there is the fact that the 1650s witnessed a huge upsurge in published women's writing: whereas before 1650, in the 175 years since the beginning of printing, we know of only about 80 texts written by women that had appeared in print—and a significant number of these were translations, or were the products of a single figure, the prolific Lady Eleanor Douglas (earlier Davies)—the 1650s alone saw published some 130 works by more than 70 women.[1] The majority of these were religio-political pamphlets of the kind I am discussing here. Women's undertaking such work is less surprising than it might at first appear, since it has been shown that large numbers of women in the period were active in the churches and the radical sects; indeed, that the women members of many congregations outnumbered the men.[2] As a result of such activism, many women, especially Baptists and members of the Society of Friends (Quakers) were arrested and imprisoned, and it is from prison that most of these early pamphlets were written. From the beginning, then, the prophecies I am discussing here were clearly works intended to achieve something: their authors had been gaoled for their words and deeds, and they were keen to defend themselves,

using the explanation that they were divinely inspired to justify their possibly criminal behaviour.

In these pamphlets, women take the most holy of texts, the Bible itself,
and make it re-signify to justify their political activities. That the Bible
could not serve to vindicate them without some active adaptation of its
contents is made clear if we remember St Paul's oft-cited instructions: 'Let
your women keep silence in the churches: for it is not permitted unto them
to speak; but they are commanded to be under obedience, as also saith the
law. And if they will learn anything, let them ask their husbands at home:
for it is a shame for women to speak in the church' (I Cor. 14: 34-35); and
'Let the woman learn in silence with all subjection. But I suffer not a
woman to teach, nor to usurp authority over the man, but to be in silence'
(I Tim. 2: 11, 12). The familiarity to seventeenth-century women of these
passages, with their insistence on the authority of husbands and the silence
of wives, is demonstrated by the frequency with which their meaning is
discussed in the prophecies of the day. The licence to engage in such a
debate was provided by another biblical text, God's promise that in the Last
Days, 'I will pour out of my Spirit upon all flesh: and your sons and your
daughters shall prophesy, and your young men shall see visions, and your
old men shall dream dreams. And on my servants and on my handmaidens I
will pour out in those days of my Spirit, and they shall prophesy' (Acts 2:
17, 18). The Bible, it was clear to those women, is not a univocal text, and
in the pamphlets I am concerned with, they set out to use these gaps and
contradictions, these spaces for argument, to turn the Holy Book to their
own temporal ends.

Quite how widespread this kind of activity was during the Common-
wealth period is indicated by the presence in the Commons Journals of
repeated orders to soldiers to clear away bands of clamouring women from
the doors of the House. The best-documented of such petitioning women
are the Levellers who published their demands to Parliament for the release
of John Lilburne. The terms of that appeal are a clear instance of the way in
which evocation of the Bible—evocation, that is, of the one book most
people could be assumed to be familiar with—was used to give validity to
secular activity. The *Women's Petition* of 1651 reads:

> What shall we say? Our hope is even departed, and our expectation of
> Freedom (the fruits of our bloud shed, and expense of our estates) is
> removed far away; yea, the hope of our Liberty is cut off like a
> Weavers thumb. We have for many years (but in especial since 1647)
> chattered like Cranes, and mourned like Doves; yea with many sighs
> and tears have we presented our several complaints against God's and

our enemies; but we are hitherto so far from gaining redress, as that our eyes behold them still exalted to bear Rule over us: and thus for felicity, we reap bitter grief; for freedom, slavery; for true judgement, justice and mercy, injustice tyranny and oppression; because the Head of Tyranny was cut off in 1648 (was expected to dy, and be dead) still liveth in and by his ordained members of Injustice and Oppression; and the Norman Laws of the Oppressors still bear Dominion over us.[3]

Today's reader might be struck by the vividness of the similes here: they feel they have been severed like the weaver's thrum (the side threads used to attach a piece of cloth to the loom: 'thumb' is a printer's error), and in recent years have 'chattered like Cranes, and mourned like Doves'. What would have been immediately apparent to the reader of 1651 is that in using these terms, the women are comparing themselves to Hezekiah who, facing imminent death, called on God in parallel terms to allow him to live long enough to see the promised freedom of his people come into being (Isaiah 38: 12-14). They, like Hezekiah, see the present political situation as unbearable; like Hezekiah, they are hoping for God to send a prophet to grant them a reprieve and to instruct them, 'Prepare ye the way of the Lord' (Isaiah 40). Their enemies—parliament, the Levellers' oppressors—are also God's enemies, and this gives them the right and duty to speak, as a group united by a holy purpose to oppose those parts of the body politic that, in this metaphor, are part of the executed king's corpse, and responsible, as he was, for 'injustice, tyranny and oppression'.

The use of vivid, Bible-inspired imagery to support disruption of women's required silence is evident in many pamphlets of the period. One of the most interesting examples appears in Mary Cary's utopian imagining of the new world which Christ's second coming might be hoped to bring, in her *A New and More Exact Mappe*, 1651. In describing women's current position, she says:

they are generally very unable to communicate to others, though they would do it many times in their families, among their children and servants: and when they would be communicating to others into whose company they come, though sometimes some sprinklings come from them, yet at other times they find themselves dry and barren.[4]

To take the word 'barren' and make it mean not 'unable to bear children', women's conventional role, but 'unable to speak', is to transform the term in ways akin to the functioning of 'barrenness' in the bible. There, Sarai's, Rebekah's, and Rachel's feelings of inadequacy for not having babies (Genesis 16, 25: 21, 30: 1, 23) are followed by Isaiah's instruction to the 'barren' to 'break forth into singing ... For thy Maker is thine husband' (Isaiah 54: 1-5). This is further echoed in the New Testament in Peter's explanation that true followers of Christ will 'neither be barren nor unfruitful in the knowledge of our Lord' (II Peter 1: 8).

The prophetical works of the 1650s are saturated with this method of using the Bible as a metaphorical but holy, and so indisputable, source of guidance in pressing temporal concerns. In 1655, for instance, Hester Biddle published simultaneously her *Wo to thee City of Oxford* and *Wo to the Towne of Cambridge*. There, she presents herself as one of the 'Saints', God's chosen ones, who are empowered to 'Judge the earth'. The Judgement she delivers is not only an indictment of the material corruptions of the university cities and their graduate products, but also one constructed from a patchwork of biblical allusions:

> Praises, praises to the Lord, that he is raysing up his own Saints to Judg the earth: and many now do witness their Judgments true, but to the wicked Judgments are terrible and none but them cometh to see the fresh springs of eternal life, but they that live in the life of them that gave them forth, and there they will come to see the filthiness of these two wicked Cities, how they ly wallowing in their blood, and their blood shall be required at their own hands, for they that come forth of *Oxford & Cambridge*, they are such as *Isaiah* was sent to, to cry woe against, greedy dumb-dogs that never have enough, and love greeting in the Market-places, and long prayers in the Synagogues and the upper seats at feasts, and be called of men Masters; they are filthy bruitbeasts which maketh my people to err, therefore the ground is cursed for your sakes: thorns and thistles shall it bring forth for your sakes until you return to *Adams* first estate.[5]

God's curse on Adam in Genesis 3: 18 for his disobedience is the 'thorns and thistles' here threatened to university graduates if they fail to 'return to *Adams* first estate': a state of being which is not the literal nakedness that Adam had abandoned, but the obedience to God's will which would lead them to eschew the fascination with social hierarchy that is 'the filthiness of these two wicked Cities'. The central, bizarre image in this passage, of university men performing greeting-rituals akin to those of dogs sniffing one another's genitals, is both an apposite way of presenting the offensiveness of such concern for status, and rather alarmingly funny. To create the picture, Biddle has brought together two distinct parts of the Bible: Isaiah's condemnation of faithless watchmen who 'are all dumb dogs ... greedy dumb dogs which can never have enough' (Isaiah 56: 10-11), with Christ's condemnation of 'Scribes and Pharisees, hypocrites', false teachers who 'love the uppermost rooms at feasts, and the chief seats in the synagogues, and greetings in the markets, and to be called of men, Rabbi' (Matthew 23: 6-7). In her reworking of God's message, Biddle turns the Bible into an explicit commentary on the powerstructures of her own society, and an inescapable command to overturn them.

Such remakings of the word of God could lead to disruptions in the family structures which St Paul required women to confine themselves to. In 1660, for instance, the Quaker Alice Curwen, whose husband Thomas was in prison for non-payment of tithes, was called by God to travel to Massachusetts to challenge the persecution of radicals that had begun there. Unable, she felt, to depart on her mission immediately, she waited until 'the Lord delivered my Husband out of Prison, in which time my little Children were grown up, all except the youngest, which the Lord took away from me', and then declared her intention. Her account of this episode makes clear the extent to which an argument about the 'correct' interpretation of God's wishes could have decidedly practical results:

> I laboured with my Husband day and night to know his Mind, because it was much with me, that we were to Travail together; but he did not yet see it to be required of him at that time, but gave me liberty in Obedience to the Invisible Power, though the thing was hard, because it was shewed me at first, that we should Travail together; but the Lord made me willing to leave all (that was near and dear to me) and I went on my Journey towards London, and after some time had with Friends there, I made Preparation to go to Sea, and having got my Bed and Clothes on board the Ship, it pleased the Lord (in whom was and is my Trust) to send my Husband to go along with me.[6]

This was not a woman who was content to 'ask of her husband at home' the meaning of holy messages.

A similar assumption that God's meaning could, if truly interpreted, lead a woman to unorthodox behaviour, is found in a Baptist conversion narrative referring to events that took place at about the same time. Here, Sarah Davy, whose life has been one of great loneliness and isolation, describes herself as being invited to accept as God's loving gift her powerful attraction towards another of her own sex. The text is at its most secular —its most insistently erotic in its implications—at the points where it is also most certain of its holy source as it insists 'the Lord was pleased ... it pleased the Lord':

One day the Lord was pleased by a strange providence to cast me into
the company of one that I never saw before, but of a sweet and free
disposition, and whose discourse savour'd so much of the Gospel, that
I could not but at that instant bless God for his goodness in that providence, it pleased the Lord to carry out our hearts much towards one
another at that time, and a little while after, the Lord was pleased to
bring us together again for the space of three dayes, in which time it
pleased God by our much converse together, to establish and confirm
me more in the desires I had to *joyn with the people of God in society*,
and *enjoy Communion* with them according to the *order of the Gospel*,
she was of a society of the *Congregational* way called *Independants* ...
I was cleerly convinc't in my judgment that this was the way which
came nearest to the rule of the Gospel, and the commands of Christ,
then were our hearts firmly united, and I blessed the Lord from my
soul for so glorious and visible an appearance of his love.[7]

In various and complex ways, then, women during the aftermath of
revolution invented ways of making worldly meanings of sacred texts,
despite the biblical proscription of women's speaking. The most interesting,
because most complex, of such reinterpretations that I want to consider in
this essay is a text published from prison in Exeter by two women, Priscilla
Cotton and Mary Cole, to justify the activity for which they had been incar-
cerated: that of speaking out in public. In their prophecy they address 'the
People and Priests of England', attacking the hierarchical structure of their
society and presenting their own imprisonment as evidence that God's will
is being thwarted. I will quote the text at some length—the passage ex-
cerpted here forms the last two pages of an eight-page octavo pamphlet—
because the mischief and inventiveness of their turning scripture to profane
ends cannot be appreciated without the full spendour of the way the argument develops. I have adjusted their spelling and punctuation in the interests of clarity, and indicated the location of some of the biblical passages
they allude to:

Come down thou, therefore, that hast built among the stars by thy arts
and learning; for it's thy pride and thy wisdom that hath perverted thee.
Thou has gone in the way of Cain, in envy and malice, and ran greedily after the reward of Balaam, in covetousness; and if thou repent not,
shalt perish in the gainsaying of Kore. For if a son or a daughter be
moved from the Lord to go into the assembly of the people in a message from the Lord God, thou canst not endure to hear them speak
sound doctrine, having a guilty conscience; and fearing they would

declare against thy wickedness, thou incensest the people, telling them
that they are dangerous people, Quakers, so making the people afraid
of us; and incensest the magistrates, telling them that they must lay
hold on us, as troublers of the people, and disturbers of the peace, and
so makes them thy drudges to act thy malice, that thy filthiness may
not be discovered, and thy shame appear. But God will make them in
one day to forsake thee, and leave and fly from thee, though for the
present thou lordest it over magistrates, people, meetinghouse, and all,
as though all were thine. And thou sittest as a queen and lady over all,
and wilt have the pre-eminence, and hast got into the seat of God, the
consciences of the people, and what thou sayest must not be contra-
dicted. If thou bid them fight and war, they obey it; if thou bid them
persecute and imprison, they do it. So that they venture their bodies
and souls to fulfil thy lusts of envy and pride, and in thy pride thou
contemnest all others. Thou tellest the people, women must not speak
in a church [I Corinthians 14: 34], whereas it is not spoke only of a
female, for we are all one both male and female in Christ Jesus [Gala-
tians 3: 28]; but it's weakness that is the woman by the scriptures forbidden, for else thou puttest the scriptures at a difference in themselves, as still it's thy practice out of thy ignorance. For the scriptures
do say that all the church may prophesy one by one [I Corinthians 14:
31], and that women were in the church, as well as men, do thou judge.
And the scripture saith, that a woman may not prophesy with her head
uncovered, lest she dishonour her head [I Corinthians 11: 5]. Now,
thou wouldst know the meaning of that 'head'; let the scripture answer,
I Corinthians 11: 3, 'the head of every man is Christ'. Man in his best
estate is altogether vanity, weakness, a lie. If therefore any speak in the
church, whether man or woman, and nothing appear in it but the wisdom of man; and Christ, who is the true head, be not uncovered—do
not fully appear—Christ the head is then dishonoured. Now, the
woman, or weakness, that is man, which in his best estate or greatest
wisdom is altogether vanity, that must be covered with the covering of
the spirit, a garment of righteousness, that its nakedness may not
appear, and dishonour thereby come. Here mayst thou see from the
scriptures, that the woman or weakness, whether male or female, is
forbidden to speak in the church. But it's very plain, Paul, nor Apollos,
nor the true church of Christ, were not of that proud, envious spirit that
thou art of, for they owned Christ Jesus in man or woman. For Paul bid
Timothy to help those women that laboured with him in the gospel;
and Apollos harkened to a woman, and was instructed by her [Acts 18:
26]; and Christ Jesus appeared to the women first, and sent them to

preach the resurrection to the apostles [Mark 16; Luke 24]; and Philip had four virgins that did prophesy [Acts 21: 9]. Now thou dost respect persons, I know, and art partial in all things, and so judgest wickedly; but there is no respect of persons with God. Indeed, you yourselves are the women that are forbidden to speak in the church, that are become women; for two of your priests came to speak with us. And when they could not bear sound reproof and wholesome doctrine that did concern them, they railed on us with filthy speeches—as no other they can give to us, that deal plainly and singly with them—and so ran from us. So, leaving you to the light in all your consciences to judge of what we have writ, we remain prisoners in Exeter gaol for the word of God.[8]

The logics of this playful but angry argument need teasing out. The intellectuals who have 'built among the stars by their arts and learning' are still, sadly, recognisable figures, those figured today as 'living in ivory towers'. To the reader of 1655, another kind of echo is also apparent: here is Isaiah's insistence that the 'virgin daughter of Babylon' 'Come down, and sit in the dust' and stop yearning to be 'a lady ... that art given to pleasures'; he reproves her, 'thy wisdom and thy knowledge, it hath perverted thee' (Isaiah 47). The university-educated priests, therefore, are linked to a Bible figure of a people (metaphorically female) who have fallen away from God. This is continued by a direct allusion to Jude's condemnation of the kind of ungodly men who try to turn God-given wisdom to lascivious ends: 'Woe unto them!', he says, 'For they have gone in the way of Cain, and ran greedily after the error of Balaam for reward, and perished in the gainsaying of Core' (Jude 11). The reference to Balaam here might have struck Cotton and Cole as particularly apposite: in Numbers 22, Balak calls on Balaam to misuse the divinely granted power that his curses have material effects, and damn the Israelites. Balaam is finally prevented by God's direct intervention; but before this, his female ass also tries to hinder his evil-doing: just as the women in prison here attempt to redirect church ministers' use of their verbal abilities.

The particular social results of the priests' unholy behaviour are then speclfied: church ministers incense both magistrates and the common people against God's prophets, resulting in persecution and imprisonment. This is complicated, however, by a metaphorical point of reference: in behaving like this, the women say, the priests are trying to ensure that their 'filthiness may not be discovered, and [their] shame appear'. These images of revealed filth and shamefulness appear frequently in the Bible as descriptions of 'female' figures, the adulterous woman and the Whore of Babylon, who are excoriated in explicitly sexual and often misogynistic terms, and taken to represent the ungodly in general or, in this period, the kinds of hierarchical and 'idolatrous' practices associated with the Roman Catholic church.[9] In using a 'female' symbol to stand for the male church ministers, the women begin a move that the succeeding lines continue: a destabilising of the referents of gender-specific terms, with the result that the 'women' commanded by St Paul to be silent in the churches can be proved to be the male church ministers who have caused Cotton and Cole to be imprisoned. This unyoking of gendered terms from gendered subjects is also emphasised in their assertion that the priests in their self-importance are sitting 'as a queen and lady over all': they are 'lording' it over the people, using class privilege to maintain control and gain status.

What it is impossible to miss when reading through the steps of this argument is the pleasure the women take in its cleverness. In making reference to the points in Paul's First Letter to Corinthians and in the Acts of the Apostles where there are mentions of women's presence and practice in church, these writers might be thought to have proved their point: there were women in the first churches, and they held a vocal and active role. Such a proof would be perhaps too boring to these playful prophets. Addressing intellectuals, as they are, they play an intellectual game at the point where they muse, 'Now, thou wouldst know the meaning of that "head"'. As they work their way through a network of biblical cross-references they perform, tongue-in-cheek, the kind of 'proof' of interpretation that contemporary Bible commentaries indulged in. In such readings, words do not mean what they seem to mean, but are symbols: 'woman' means not 'female', but 'weakness' in a spiritual sense. In order to appreciate fully how contrived this argument is, it is necessary to recognise how deliberate these acts of interpretation are. The metaphorical meaning Cotton and Cole give to the word 'head', for instance—'the head of every man is Christ'—is something of a cheat, and a naughty one, because the verse relied on, I Corinthians 11: 3, actually continues, 'the head of every man is Christ; and the head of every woman is the man'. This would not be a convenient clause to quote, so they omit it, speeding on to use their series of remakings of the term 'head' to produce the apparently unassailable, and very funny, conclusion: 'Here mayst thou see from the scriptures ... you yourselves are the women that are forbidden to speak in the church'.

These imprisoned women refuse one form of the learning—the class-bound and book-based achievements of university graduates and in particular church ministers—and promote another, which they present as God-inspired. The purpose of their witty manipulations of scripture is, crucially, not a display of their own artistry, but to bring to light what is, in their eyes, truly holy: the need to change the secular organisation of society so as to make it conform to God's aims. This reorganisation includes a change in legal structures, an abolition of class and gender hierarchies, and a licence for all members of society to think and to speak, insofar as their visions can be justified as coming from the true Head, that is, from Christ. This would be a society that refuses to 'respect persons'—refuses to make hierarchical differences between people—because 'there is no respect of persons with God'. In the meantime, the authors 'remain prisoners in Exeter gaol for the word of God': their use of God's holy word has had decidedly material effects, even as their ability to use the Word or, they would claim, be used by it—sets them free to think and write.

The hard-won semi-freedom of the revolutionary years did not last, and it was of course changes in the social fabric, rather than in the word of God, that caused this. The Restoration of the Monarchy brought with it a breakdown in the assumption that the Bible could be used as a source of secular truths in the way the prophets used it, and the form of argumentation had to change. This was not a change that came about overnight, however. In 1662, Hester Biddle, who chastised the University towns in 1655 and never gave up insisting on the intimate links between God's will and social structures, was arrested whilst speaking in a Quaker meeting. At her trial, she both made use of the proofs of women's right to speak which were so often cited in the revolutionary years, and continued to insist on her right, as God's prophet, to interpret his Word and to form, through him, independent judgements. Even as she was sent to prison, she questioned the magistrate's right to judge her, and delivered her own verdict on him: the freedom he once found, she claims, in working with the 'godly' in earlier times, is something he is much the poorer for losing:

> She asked for her accusers; Then stood up one whose name was Lovel a Vintner, the Judge asked him, whether he took this woman out of the Meeting, and what she was doing: Lovel said, He took her upon a form speaking; and the Judge said, What a woman speak! The Jury and some of the Bench said, They never heard of a Woman to speak before; she asked them, If they had not read the scriptures, she told them Phoebe was a Prophetess, and Philip had four Daughters that had prophesied, and Paul wrote to his Brethren that they should take care of the women that were fellow labourers with him in the Gospel. The Judge said, That was a great while agoe; she told him, It was when the Church was in her Beauty and Glory ... The Judge said, She should ask of her Husband at home; she said, If her husband should be a Drunkard, or a sot, what should she learn of him, to be as wicked as he was? R Brown [the judge] asked, If her husband were so? She said, No, but

if he were so, what could she learn? But Christ is my Husband, and I learn of Him (said she). Alderman Brown said, she had left her Husband two years, and went with a young man into other lands; she told him, That was not his business to judge at this time, nor was it fit for him to accuse her, but she went with three Women as she was moved of the Lord ... Richard, Dost thou not remember that thou Prayedst in the Camp by Abingdon, and was that an unlawful Meeting? was that not a good Day with thee? I am afraid thou wilt never see such another.[10]

These revolutionary women played with meaning in a deadly serious way, using the divine to secular, but truly holy, ends.

Notes

1   See Elaine Hobby, *Virtue of Necessity: English Women's Writing 1649-1688* (London, 1988); Elaine Hobby, '"Discourse so unsavoury": Women's published writings of the 1650s', in Isobel Grundy and Susan Wiseman (eds), *Women Writing, History 1640-1740* (London, 1992), 16-32; Maureen Bell, George Parfitt and Simon Shepherd, *A Biographical Dictionary of English Women Writers 1580-1720* (New York and London, 1990); and, with reservations about its accuracy, Patricia Crawford, 'Women's published writings 1600-1700' in Mary Prior (ed.), *Women in English Society 1500-1800* (London, 1985), 211-282.

2   Keith Thomas, 'Women and the Civil War Sects', *Past and Present* 13 (1955): 42-62; Claire Cross, 'The Church in England 1646-1660', in G.E. Aylmer (ed.), *The Interregnum* (London, 1972), 99-120; Mabel Brailsford, *Quaker Women 1650-1690* (London, 1915); Phyllis Mack, *Visionary Women: Ecstatic Prophecy in Seventeenth-Century England* (Berkeley and Oxford, 1992).

3   *The Women's Petition* (London, 1651). For discussions of such petitioning, see Ellen MacArthur, 'Women Petitioners and the Long Parliament', *English Historical Review* 24 (1909): 698-709; Patricia Higgins, 'The reactions of women, with special reference to women petitioners', in Brian Manning (ed.), *Politics. Religion and the English Civil War* (London, 1973).

4   Mary Cary, *A New and More Exact Mappe* in her *The Little Horns Doom and Downfall* (London, 1651), 238.

5   Hester Biddle, *Wo to thee City of Oxford*, 1655. A modern edition appears in Elaine Hobby, '"Oh Oxford Thou Art Full of Filth": The Prophetical Writings of Hester Biddle, 1629[?]-1696', in: Susan Sellers (ed.), *Feminist Criticism: Theory and Practice* (New York and London, 1991), 157-169.

6   Alice Curwen, *A Relation of the Labour, Travail and Suffering* (London, 1680), 3.

7   Sarah Davy, *Heaven Realiz'd* (London, 1670). There are substantial extracts in Elspeth Graham *et al* (eds), *Her Own Life: Autobiographical Writings by Seventeenth-Century Englishwomen* (London and New York, 1989), 165-179.

8   Priscilla Cotton and Mary Cole, *To the Priests and People of England We Discharge Our Consciences, and Give Them Warning* (London, 1655). This pamphlet is also discussed in Elaine Hobby, 'Handmaids of the Lord and Mothers in Israel: Early Vindications of Quaker Women's Prophecy', in Thomas N. Corns and David Loewenstein (eds), *The Emergence of Quaker Writing* (London, 1995).

9   See especially Hosea 1-2; Isaiah 1: 21, 57: 7-13; Jeremiah 3: 1-4.4; Ezekiel 16, 23; Revelation 17, 18.

10   *A Brief Relation of the Persecutions and Cruelties that have been Acted upon the People called Quakers* (London, 1662), 35-37.

23

'LEWD, PROFANE SWAGGERERS' AND CHARISMATIC PREACHERS: JOHN BUNYAN AND GEORGE FOX[1]

ELSPETH GRAHAM

I

Working from the now familiar assumption that oppositional terms are mutually dependent, I should like, in this essay, to trace ways in which, in the 1650s and 1660s in England, constructions of faith and right relation to the Word demand an exclusion of certain forms of verbal and sexual profanity, while simultaneously depending on these as the informing repressed of nonconformist spiritual discourse. Although my aim is not to make a sustained application of any recent theoretical writing, in referring to the mutual dependence of oppositional terms I, of course, nod at a long and complex series of theoretical arguments and developments: from structuralism to Derridian deconstruction; at Foucauldian and New Historicist impacts on Renaissance study.

Here, I am, however, interested in a particular cluster of oppositions: ecstasy and the vile; masculine authority and feminine excess; speaking the Word and being spoken by profane or perverse words; control of the Symbolic and control by the Symbolic. It seems most appropriate, then, to gesture more directly, if still briefly, at two particular twentieth-century writers, before I turn to the seventeenth century. I think firstly of Genet—the influencing shadow behind Foucault who in turn shadows Derrida. Genet's quest to attain ecstasy, to achieve the sublime, is conducted through an embrace of the profane and explicitly dissolves the opposition sacred/profane. Expression of revulsion in Genet co-exists with a spiritualising, a religious, vocabulary.[2] Desire and disgust, fear and idealisation are articulated simultaneously. The sacred—for Genet a sublime sacred, quite different from that of conventional piety—is achieved through the collapse of categories of high and low, vile and heavenly, beauty and ugliness, pain and joy.

Psychoanalytically informed writing, too, tells us of the proximity of such states. So, I mention secondly, the writings of Julia Kristeva who, in *Powers of Horror: An Essay on Abjection*, describes that aspect of primary narcissism which she calls 'abjection' as involving archaic confrontations with the M/Other, before that M/Other is yet definable as Other, or is nameable, or can be conceived of as distinct or separate.[3] Abjection thus concerns the 'alterations, *within subjectivity* implied by the confrontation with the feminine' (*Powers of Horror*, 58). In a further, tantalising aside Kristeva adds:

> I shall set aside in this essay a different version of the confrontation of the feminine, one that, going beyond abjection and fright, is enunciated as ecstatic. (*Powers of Horror*, 59)

Ecstasy is the psychic flipside of archaic horror with its attendant pulses of disgust, anxiety and fascination. Both are situated in the see-saw realm where inner and outer, high and low, subject and object are undecided and undecideable (*Powers of Horror*, 135). More directly, Kristeva writes:

> Abjection accompanies all religious structurings and reappears, to be worked out in a new guise, at the time of their collapse. (*Powers of Horror*, 17)

This leads me to the particular collapse of consensus over political and religious structures and meanings that characterises the mid-seventeenth century in England.

The collapse of categories of spiritual attainment and profanity was not, of course, an explicit or even desired goal of English nonconformists in the 1650s and 1660s; quite the contrary. (Men such as Bunyan and Fox took care to distinguish themselves from the Ranters of the 1640s whose antinomian beliefs, habits of cursing and theory and practice of sexual freedom come close to this.) What we see in the development of the sects and in the written accounts of charismatic leaders such as Bunyan and Fox is how the breakdown of consensus over religious and political meanings, or as importantly, ways of being, after the execution of Charles I, the law-giving Father, leads to urgent attempts not only to find a tenable position within religious discourses which offers a personally secure subjectivity, but also to find positions of authority over others, as leaders of congregations and groups with evangelical aims. Such attempts to find authoritative positions representing exemplary attainment of access to truth were constructed equally in opposition to rival claims. These highly volatile and fragile positions become for the thousands seeking truth a focus for unleashed free-flowing desire. At the same time, figures such as Bunyan and Fox, through their activities as preachers and through their self-representations, struggle to embody the function of the law. They simultaneously regulate the self and the congregations over which they have authority, mobilising desire and seeking to organise it. They construct themselves as subjects and objects of desire. But structures of exclusion work in conjunction with the operation of structures of desire and identification. The confrontation with and exclusion of a variety of threats (whether members of congregations, rivals, opposing beliefs or aspects of the self) become associated with the organisation of desire. It is in this twin functioning of desire and exclusion that I am interested.

II

The importance of Bunyan's achievement of right relation to God's Word has often been recognised as involving a process of realigning himself in relation to written and spoken words more generally. After his first calling, during a game of cat, Bunyan describes how he continues in his unreformed ways:

> Now therefore I went on in sin with great greediness of mind, still grudging that I could not be satisfied with it as I would. This did continue with me about a month, or more; but one day, as I was standing at a neighbour's shop window, and there cursing and swearing, and playing the madman, after my wonted manner, there sat within the woman of the house, and heard me, who, though she was a very loose and ungodly wretch, yet protested that I swore and cursed at that most fearful rate, that she was made to tremble to hear me; and told me further, That I was the ungodliest fellow for swearing that ever she heard in all her life; and that I, by thus doing, was able to spoil all the youth in a whole town, if they came but in my company.[4]

Here, sin is equated with cursing and swearing: abuse in words is abuse of words and the Word. This is linked implicitly with issues of gender. Bunyan explains his addiction to swearing as an attempt to gain authority: 'I knew not how to speak unless I put an oath before, and another behind, to make my words have authority' (*GA*, 28). The bracketing of utterance in profanity gives it power. It is the power of vehemence, but it is also a power that is culturally inscribed in complex ways. Since swearing is conventionally associated with masculine power it might seem obvious to link Bunyan's swearing with an attempt to assert a masculine forcefulness. The text seems to imply this. In his reaction to the woman's reproof, Bunyan instantly links his swearing with an implicit failure of paternal teaching: the wrong line of masculine authority has been passed to him: 'I wished with all my heart that I might be a little child again, that my father might learn me to speak without this wicked way of swearing' (*GA*, 27). Henceforth his movement towards becoming a righteous Father is commensurate with finding a righteous language—a language of true authority. In his later friendship with Mr Gifford, from whom he learns new ways of reading the Bible, we could hypothesise a revised version of a child-father relationship.

But in this earlier passage describing the neighbour's reproof of Bunyan for swearing, the gender issues are more complex. It is the response of a *woman* which shames Bunyan. Interestingly, the woman is not virtuous, but 'very loose and ungodly'. As in the episode where Bunyan encounters by chance the poor women of Bedford sitting at a door and speaking of their love in Christ, women's voices seem to provide a corrective mirroring or magnification of Bunyan's own. The poor women were more marginal, more excluded than Bunyan himself, yet gave evidence of a more deeply experienced spirituality than that represented in Bunyan's 'brisk talk[ing] ... in the matters of religion' (*GA*, 37). Swearing likewise is revealed to him as a false verbal authority. Indeed, his facility in cursing, the retrospective voice of Bunyan suggests, likened him to a madman. It is lack of control that characterised his language. He is as 'loose' or unbounded in his likeness to a madman, or as he elsewhere puts it, to Tom o' Bedlam, as the wretch of a woman in her ungodliness. The swearing is all the worse for exceeding the looseness of a loose woman.

The text gives us this. Extra-textual information confirms that gendered issues are at play and that verbal abuse is a complex cultural issue. In the seventeenth century swearing was illegal: it could be a civil or criminal offence, or an offence to be taken to church courts. Bunyan's terminology does not give us a precise indication of what form of swearing he engaged in. His references to 'cursing', 'swearing' and 'oaths' might suggest blasphemy (religious profanity) or obscenity (which always has sexual and social implications) or both. However, historical work on court records reveals a general seventeenth-century preoccupation with verbal offences of all kinds.

Largely, however, those offences which came to adjudication were women's offences. Eighty-five per cent of court charges of scolding, which is frequently connected with cursing and mocking, were made against women, and very often charges were brought by women. 'Scold' was a term in common law and implied a cursing, disorderly, turbulent, chiding person. The clear legal concern was with the social disruptivenss of the scold: an especially worrying offence in a period where communities, whether urban or rural, were small. Men when accused of such crimes were more often charged with a comparable offence of 'barratry'. A barrator was defined as someone who engaged in brawling and who set others at odds. The terms 'barrator' and 'scold' are apparently close, but actual cases suggest that charges of barratory almost always involved financial corruption. The gendering of these adjacent crimes, then, reflects the gendering of issues of reputation and notions of honesty. While the social disruptiveness of both men and women is a serious matter, damage to one's own or another's reputation involves sexual slurs in relation to women, but slurs on economic honesty in relation to men.[5]

Bunyan's swearing, then, and the reproaches of the 'loose woman' point to a cluster of anxieties surrounding his potential identification as a criminal and as a social outcast. For the Calvinist, already anxious about the very real possibility—even likelihood—of eternal spiritual exclusion from God, this compounds a sense of loss. In Bunyan's case it latches onto another form of social exclusion—that of his status as a tinker. (It is possible to read all of Bunyan's confrontations with authorities of various sorts as a series of conflicts over his calling. Such issues are at the centre of his trial in which Bunyan is referred to as 'a pestilent fellow' who is 'a breaker of the peace', and which in part hinges on different applications of the notion of calling. To Bunyan and his wife it signifies his calling to God and to preach; to the Justices it signifies his occupation, his calling as a tinker. The low social status of Bunyan's inherited occupation, the seriousness of giving up one's calling, and unruly and socially disruptive speaking—here Bunyan' preaching—are all crucial matters informing debate at the trial.) If the ungodly woman's reproof calls such fears of exclusion into play, it also aligns him with women as outsiders through the feminine nature of the charge levelled at him. In his renunciation of swearing he temporarily aligns himself with the feminine in order then to dissociate himself from the looseness and excess associated with the feminine as well as from a series of social and spiritual threats. The crisis of this moment is social, spiritual, gendered and sexual. These are all tied closely to the verbal, and are associated with Bunyan's need henceforth to refigure himself as subject in control of language.

Relinquishing swearing, the first stage to a reforming or reconstructing of the self through a reconstructed language, is followed by a long process wherein Bunyan has to learn to control and to read language. As Roger Pooley puts it:

> *Grace Abounding* is one long journey in interpretation, in learning how to read the words of God in the Bible and in direct revelation. For a long time the words seem hostile, blows more often than comforts.[6]

Indeed, words almost literally strike Bunyan:

> Then would the former sentence fall like a hot thunderbolt upon my
> conscience ... (*GA*, 163)
> Then did that scripture seize upon my soul ... (*GA*, 182)
> ... that piece of a sentence darted in upon me ... (*GA*, 204)

Isolated phrases and pieces of disembodied text alternately strike and uplift
Bunyan. He learns—partially at least—to integrate understanding of biblical
verses into a more fluid reading of the message of grace contained in the
New Testament, and to read the Old Testament through the message of
God's promise in Christ in the New Testament. Bunyan's reading or interpretative skills develop alongside his preaching skills. It is perhaps his
achievement of authority over his congregation at Bedford that marks his
progress as much as his gaining of more subtle and sophisticated hermeneutic skills. From being merely 'a brisk talker ... in the matters of religion'
he becomes a charismatic preacher. To preach, to take on the role of Father
to his congregation, is to contain the self through exclusion of profane
language and perverse reading, and simultaneously to take control of the
representation of the self through a narrative of the self that both articulates
the threat of the profane and the mastery of it. (The writing of *Grace
Abounding to the Chief of Sinners* is, of course, instrumental in establishing
Bunyan as coherent yet split subject-Father, the source of his own self.)

The issue of slander which marks a powerful moment of disequilibrium
near the end of *Grace Abounding to the Chief of Sinners* is, in this context,
an especially threatening one. Joan Webber has demonstrated the importance of the figure of the slanderer in 'Puritan' writing.[7] Typically, she suggests, the slanderer is a figure who accuses the Puritan of private vices. For
Bunyan the issue of slander is rather more complex. The public and private
are not easily separable in the forming of a nonconformist preacher's identity. Nor, I would argue, is the issue of slander—associated with the other
forms of verbal offence I have referred to, barratry, scolding and cursing—
ever a purely personal issue in a culture where issues of reputation and
social acceptability are so important. If Bunyan's subjectivity is reformed
through the publication (in writing and preaching) of the process of reconstructing his subjectivity—a subjectivity that is always under threat—and
this reconstruction itself is concerned with establishing boundaries that
mark out wrong relation to words, the figure of the slanderer, who attacks
the subject by taking control of words from him, by speaking him in the
very terms that need to be expelled or denied, is the most potent of all
attackers. Those words which have had to be articulated in order to be

excluded are, of course, words of temptation to the abject. Swearing, conventionally, speaks what is taboo. A clear division between the tabooed or profane and the right defends against the abject. Yet we see constantly in Bunyan how such distinctions, though made, are made only to be subverted and remade. And the makings of laws of distinction between the profane and the spiritual are so meshed with searching for a tenable subjectivity, that we witness the wrenchings of the abject as a pull within subjectivity. It is perhaps not surprising that intense moments of insight into relation with the Word and words are signalled sometimes by 'flashed' references to the feminine. (The religious books brought to him as a dowry by his wife; the poor women in the doorway; the loose woman who admonishes him for swearing.) Nor is it surprising that the struggle against the dizzying terrors of the abject are, at times, clearly linked with the bodily:

> I felt also such a cloging and heat at my stomach, by reason of this my terror, that I was, especially at some times, as if my breast bone would have split in sunder; then I thought of that concerning Judas, who by his falling headlong, burst asunder, and all his bowels gushed out (Act i.18) (GA, 164).

In his search for a tenable subject position that confers him authority—linguistically and socially—Bunyan is, then, constantly entangled in negotiations of a configuration of issues: social, spiritual and sexual. In the passage describing his response to slanderous accusations (GA, 307-317) we see an extraordinary conflation of these. Reference to circulating rumours (loose words without an acknowledged author) that Bunyan is a witch, highwayman, or Jesuit (GA, 307) bring together precisely those possibilities of exclusion that underlie his struggles throughout the text. 'Highwayman' suggests lawlessness, criminality, and a lack of masculine honesty; 'Jesuit' implies extreme spiritual illegitimacy and a sinister ability to tempt others; and 'witch', an accusatory term most commonly applied to women, imputes diabolic power and carries implications of sexual misdemeanour and deviance.

Bunyan's atypically hysterical tone in the following paragraphs has frequently been noticed. The charges of sexual misdemeanour mobilise the threat of the profane and the abject which Bunyan has sought to define himself against and to expel through his long conversion process. Issues of sexuality, truth and words are conjoined in the attacks on him. Before he denies the sexual allegations, he explores the appropriate verbal stance to take:

> So, then, what shall I say to those who have thus bespattered me?
> Shall I threaten them? Shall I chide them? Shall I flatter them? Shall I
> intreat them to hold their tongues? No, not I, were it not for that these
> things make them ripe for damnation, that are the authors and abettors,
> I would say unto them, Report it, because it will increase my glory.
>
> Therefore I bind these lies and slanders to me as an ornament, it
> belongs to my Christian profession to be vilified, slandered, reproached
> and reviled ... (*GA*, 311-312).

Although Bunyan does goes on to abuse his abusers, he first speculatively
tests out verbal possibilities in relation to the abject, so that the passage
ultimately comprises a simultaneous and uneasy taking on of the profane
(through identification with Christ and as a Christian) and warding off of it,
through attack on and vilification of others. He 'bind[s] these lies and
slanders' to him in an attempt to assimilate the profane or perverse to the
self, but also in order to draw a boundary between himself and the vile—to
divide the sacred from the profane.

At an earlier stage in his conversion process Bunyan had pondered the
Old Testament distinctions between clean and unclean meat:

> I was almost made about this time, to see something concerning the
> beasts that Moses counted clean and unclean. I thought those beasts
> were types of men; the clean types of them that were the people of
> God; but the unclean, types of such as were the children of the wicked
> one. Now, I read that the clean beasts chewed the cud; that is, thought
> I, they show us we must feed on the Word of God. They also parted
> the hoof; I thought that signified we must part, if we would be saved,
> with the ways of ungodly men ... (*GA*, 71).

If establishing the place of the abject and the vile in relation to the sacred is
necessary to any religious structure, Bunyan, in this passage, is engaged in
a particularly direct reformulation of those distinctions, codified in Levi-
ticus as dietary taboos, to correspond with doctrines of Election and Reprobation. *Grace Abounding to the Chief of Sinners* as a whole is concerned
with a more complex series of decisions about what belongs to the self and
what does not, which involved Bunyan in raising the spectre of the abject in
an attempt to separate from it. The abject or profane circulates around the
self which seeks to distance itself from it. Uneasy and complex negotiations
of the pull of the vile with all its destabilising possibilities underlie Bunyan's self-manoeuvrings and perhaps also contribute to his power as a charismatic preacher.

III

I turn finally to the rather different negotiation of structures of the profane and the sacred and a different articulation of charismatic authority in the *Journal* of the Quaker leader, George Fox.[8] Quakerism was an essentially ecstatic movement, based on belief in what was variously referred to as the Inner Light or Spirit or Christ or Truth. The notion of Christ within, along with the concept of the living Word, led easily into the millennial notion that Christ had actually come in Quakers, and even to direct identification with Christ. In Quakerism, the place of the vile cannot easily be separated from the place of the sacred since it is an antinomian religion, in which there is no authority of the law to create clear demarcations. Typically, in Quaker writings, many boundaries are blurred—those between individuals, between biblical text and human voice, between biblical and worldly history and the personal histories of individual lives. Since Friends are living embodiments of God's word—human texts—religious manoeuvrings are as often enacted through behaviour as articulated verbally. In George Fox's *Journal* we encounter moments where the fascinating pull of the abject and its relation to the sacred are negotiated through highly symbolic, and mysterious, performance.

In his record of the year 1651, for instance, Fox writes of how, after he was released from Derby prison, he travelled towards his home county of Leicestershire where hostile rumours circulated that he had been taken 'up above the clouds and after found again full of gold and silver' (*Journal*, 71). As he travelled south he saw the three steeples of Lichfield Cathedral which 'struck at [his] life'. He is commanded by the Lord to go to Lichfield. The following passage describes what then occurred:

> I went over hedge and ditch till I came within a mile of Lichfield. When I came into a great field where there were shepherds keeping their sheep, I was commanded of the Lord to pull off my shoes of a sudden; and I stood still, and the word of the Lord was like a fire in me; and being winter, I untied my shoes and put them off; and when I had done I was commanded to give them to the shepherds and was to charge them to let no one have them except they paid for them. And the poor shepherds trembled and were astonished.
>
> So I went about a mile till I came into the town, and as soon as I came within the town the word of the Lord came unto me again to cry, 'Woe unto the bloody city of Lichfield!'; so I went up and down the streets crying, 'Woe unto the bloody city of Lichfield!' Being market day I went into the market place and went up and down in several places of it and made stands, crying, 'Woe unto the bloody city of

Lichfield!', and no one touched me nor laid hands on me. As I went down the town there ran like a channel of blood down the streets, and the market place was like a pool of blood.

And so at last some friends and friendly people came to me and said, 'Alack George! where are thy shoes?' and I told them it was no matter; so when I had declared what was upon me and cleared myself, I came out of the town in peace about a mile to the shepherds: and there I went to them and took my shoes and gave them some money, but the fire of the Lord was so in my feet and all over me that I did not matter to put my shoes on any more and was at a stand whether I should or no till I felt freedom from the Lord to do so (*Journal*, 71).

How might we interpret the meanings of this extraordinary passage ? Certain aspects of it are conventional enough in the (unconventional) context of Quaker writing and activity. Fox's running through the streets of Lichfield without his shoes may be seen as a version of the Quaker practice of going naked as a sign. His cries of 'Woe unto the bloody city of Lichfield!', like Hester Biddles' pamphlet *Wo to thee city of Oxford, thy wickedness surmounteth the wickedness of Sodome* (1659), an attack on the place of education of church ministers and thus home of conventional Protestant theology, demonstrates the Quaker tendency to associate metonymically what they saw as corrupted beliefs with actual locations. And Fox himself in his rationalisation of his behaviour, at the end of this passage, points to the fact that Lichfield had been the scene of many Christian martyrings. But the emphasis on the passage is as much on his transactions with the shepherds and the removal of his shoes as it is with his cries against Lichfield. Several speculative interpretations suggest themselves. Fox, as a child had worked with sheep, and as William Penn tells us in his Preface to the original edition of the *Journal*, had shown a particular aptitude for shepherding (*Journal*, xxxix). Later, as we know from Fox himself (*Journal*, 2), he was apprenticed to a shoemaker in Leicestershire. It is possible, then, to read aspects of this passage (which contributes to Fox's inspired apprehension of divine truth and to his establishment, both through the experience and the relation of it, in his ministry) as an enactment of personal transitions in his life. The ritualised financial transaction between him and the shepherds may serve to mark his metaphoric return to the work of his childhood through his taking on the role of shepherd to his followers: through payment of a debt to actual shepherds he acknowledges his metaphoric relation to them. Since, however, Fox had abandoned his occupational calling as apprentice shoemaker, and as we have seen in relation to disputes over Bunyan's calling, this was a serious matter, defining the individual as

socially and personally unfixed, shoes are likely to have powerful resonances for Fox. The staging of the ritual perhaps enacts a settling of his
vocation. The ritualised payment for his shoes may even represent a paying
of a debt to his previous master, since Fox had commented that, 'While I
was with him, he was blessed; but after I left him he broke, and came to
nothing' (*Journal*, 2) or it may have an indirect and loose association with
debts owed by Cromwell's army to Leicester shoemakers who had provided
shoes for soldiers but had not been paid for them. (Fox is perhaps showing
himself to be more trustworthy than the Army Grandees?) Or, the purity of
Fox's motivations may be suggested by this implicit rebuttal, symbolised
by his financial integrity in fulfilling the conditions he has himself set up
for the shepherds, of the rumours mentioned at the outset of his account of
the episode. The story of his ascension to the clouds, to be found on his
descent full of gold and silver, contains imputations of corruption or financial gain. Fox performs his defence. A rather different and wider interpretation might further suggest, in Fox's need to buy back his own shoes from
the shepherds, the working out of a broad cultural shift. In the Ranter Abiezer Coppe's *A Second Fiery Flying Roule* he describes an episode in which
a beggar asks for money.[9] Coppe is mentally split by different responses to
the beggar which can be identified with the conflicting demands of his
financially thrifty and cautious Puritan upbringing and his later more extravagant Ranters beliefs, which included a clear sense of the suffering of the
poor. In the passage from Fox's *Journal* a similar acting out of the habits of
thought of a newly emergent capitalism might be suspected.

More directly biblical meanings to the key elements in this highly-
charged episode are equally relevant. Taking off shoes has a variety of sig-
nificances in the Old and New Testaments: in property transactions the
handing over of a shoe can (as in Ruth 4.7) mark the sealing of an agree-
ment or bond; shoes are removed during mourning or in sacred places; or
taking off shoes may signify freeing the self from restriction or hostility.
The bathing of feet clearly represents notions of atonement or of exaltation
through abasement. Blood, likewise, is a potent spiritual symbol, evoking
not only the history of Christian martyrs, but the originating passion of
Christ.

In the description of Fox's inspired behaviour, then, a great many possible meanings are brought together in a highly condensed, symbolic form.
His actions in the fields and in Lichfield itself serve to mark a series of
eruptions of the holy and the corrupt which are not patterned or organised
through clear demarcations. Rather they enacted through a ritual performance in which blurrings of bodily boundaries (implied by the vision of
Fox's shoeless feet running through streams of blood), personal history, the

almost fetishistic transaction over his shoes, Christian history and a specific city in the English Midlands serve to mark out the separation of divinely inspired Quaker belief from competing Protestant structures of belief. The formation of Quaker doctrine is achieved through the personal dismantlings and physical articulations of powerful, attractive and mysterious figures such as Fox. He, like Bunyan, was accused of being a witch, but also inspired devotion and extraordinarily courageous emulation. He attracted fear and fascination. Fox's *Journal*, however, reveals a quite different formulation of the sacred and profane from Bunyan's *Grace Abounding to the Chief of Sinners*. Whereas Bunyan uneasily struggled to bind the corrupt to him, in order to distinguish himself from it, Fox's writing describes his living-out of the contesting forces of the sacred and profane in moments of ecstatic embodiment of their simultaneous interrelation and moment of separation.

Notes

1   Thanks to colleagues and postgraduate students at Liverpool John Moores University, especially Matthew Jordan and Tamsin Spargo, for their helpful suggestions and comments on an earlier version of this essay.

2   See, for instance, Jean Genet, *Our Lady of Flowers* (originally published as *Notre Dame de Fleurs*, secretly in Paris, 1943) and remarks such as: 'I am waiting for heaven to slam me in the face. Saintliness means making good use of pain. It's a way of forcing the devil to be god', *The Thief's Journal (Journal du Voleur*, Geneva, 1948). This quotation given and translated by Edmund White, *Genet* (London, 1993), 7.

3   Julia Kristeva, *Powers of Horror: An Essay on Abjection*, first published as *Pouvoirs de l'horreur* (Paris, 1980), translated by Leon S. Roudiez (New York, 1982).

4   John Bunyan, *Grace Abounding to the Chief of Sinners* (1666), edited by Roger Sharrock (Oxford, 1962) paragraph 26. References to *Grace Abounding*, abbreviated to *GA*, given henceforth in the text of the essay, refer to paragraph numbers.

5   See Laura Gowring, 'Language, Power, and the Law: Women's Slander Litigation in Early Modern London' and Martin Ingram, '"Scolding Women Cucked or Washed": a Crisis in Gender Relations in Early Modern England?', in Jenny Kermode and Garthine Walker, eds, *Women, Crime and the Courts in Early Modern England* (London, 1994).

6   Roger Pooley, *English Prose of the Seventeenth-Century 1590-1700* (London and New York, 1992), 77.

7   Joan Webber, 'Donne and Bunyan: The Styles of Two Faiths', in Stanley E. Fish, ed., *Seventeenth-Century Prose* (Oxford, 1971), 501.

8   George Fox, *Journal* (1694), edited by John L. Nickalls (Cambridge, 1952).

9   Abiezer Coppe, *A Second Fiery Flying Roule* (1649) in Nigel Smith, ed., *A Collection of Ranter Writings from the Seventeenth Century* (London, 1993), 101-103.

24

THE RESTORATION POETRY OF JOHN NORRIS

FRANS KORSTEN

It is one of the commonplaces of English literary history that, in the second half of the seventeenth century, the sacred was divorced from the profane, that the sacred and profane became separate modes. After the Restoration there was a clear decline in religious poetry, and the nature of religious poetry underwent a considerable change as well.[1] It is my concern here to examine the poetry of John Norris against the background of this development. The body of Norris's poetry is small: seventy-five poems in English and a few in Latin, nearly all of them written before the Glorious Revolution and before he became John Norris of Bemerton. In 1687 there appeared *A Collection of Miscellanies, Consisting of Poems, Essays, Discourses and Letters*, which, before the middle of the eighteenth century, had gone through ten editions.[2] The *DNB* entry on Norris does not contain a single reference to his poetry, but in the past forty years his poems have received serious attention from a number of scholars and critics. In 1954 Maren-Sofie Röstvig presented Norris as an exponent of the classical tradition of retirement poetry and she claimed that several poems reveal a distinctly Epicurean bent. In 1955 Geoffrey Walton came with a generally favourable treatment of Norris's poetry, from which Norris appeared as one of the last Metaphysicals, and Walton alleged that Norris did not merely form the tail-end of the Metaphysical tradition, but that he to some extent renewed it. In 1971 John Hoyles offered a synthesis in that he tried to show that the philosophy, the theology and the poetry all had a common basis. Hoyles also called Norris the last of the Metaphysicals in the seventeenth century. Richard Acworth's full-length study of Norris (1979) concentrated mainly on the philosophy and, as to the poetry, he largely adopted the line taken by Walton and Hoyles.[3] In surveys and histories of literature and philosophy, Norris mostly appears as a late survivor from an earlier, richly imaginative, period in an increasingly rationalistic age. Thus, in his *History of English Philosophy*, Sorley calls Norris the antithesis of Locke, and he contrasts Norris's mysticism with Locke's critical empiricism.[4] My contention is that, certainly as far as the poetry is concerned, Norris was much more a child of the Restoration period and of the Enlightenment that he has been made out to be. There are undeniable links with earlier ways of thinking and feeling, and earlier modes of expression, but yet I think that Norris was more of a 'modern' than a late Metaphysical, and that much of his poetry illustrates the enervation of the sacred, and the encroachment of the profane upon the sacred.

I will first examine Norris's views on poetry and after that deal in some detail with the poetry itself, also paying attention to the specific nature of his religious poetry. How much of a 'modern' Norris—the Tory High Anglican clergyman—was, becomes clear from the prose essays and discourses on moral and philosophical subjects in his *Collection of Miscellanies*.[5] Summing up the 'hindrances to knowledge', Norris mentions all the familiar causes given in the late seventeenth and the early eighteenth century: prejudices, a wrong perception of things, ambiguity of terms and phrases and 'an overfond and superstitious deference to Authority, especially that of Antiquity' (119). Norris attached much importance to clear thinking as a means of achieving not only intellectual but also moral improvement. He was the first official critic in England of Locke's *Essay Concerning Human Understanding*; five months after the appearance of the *Essay*, he published a reaction which was not directed against Locke's theology, but against his epistemology. Norris rejected Locke's theory of the origin of ideas as based on sense-impressions and maintained instead that our ideas derive directly from God and that we see all things in God. In taking up this position Norris was in the 'sacred' camp, opposing the 'profane' modern philosophy, but on the other hand he greatly appreciated Locke as the right kind of thinker.[6] The 'Advertisement from the Authour to the Reader' and the preface 'To the Reader' preceding the poems contain interesting material on Norris's conception of poetry. He expresses the then widely-heard complaint that poetry 'has of late mightily fall'n off from the beauty of its idea, and from its ancient majesty and grandeur'.[7] Most recent and contemporary poetry is criticised by him as 'light, frothy stuff, consisting either of mad extravagant rants, or slight witticisms, and little amorous conceits' (32). He solemnly remarks that poetry was once 'the best institute for the moralizing and governing the passions of mankind' (33), and he wishes to restore poetry to its former prestige. He himself hopes to contribute to this by starting from what he calls 'substantial massy sense' and by then making that massy sense 'yield to the softness of Poetry' (34). However, in spite of this plea for greater seriousness and substance, it is clear that Norris rated philosophy and theology far more highly than poetry. Often there is an apologetic note in his remarks about his involvement with poetry: 'I do not think it an employment beneath the character of a scholar' and 'I can't find in my heart to repent me of those few blank hours bestow'd in this exercise' (34).

Norris had the mind and sensibility of a thinker and a systematiser, rather than of a poet. His poetry often makes the impression of consisting of ideas versified and decorated with images and figures of speech. The *Collection of Miscellanies* contains a number of paraphrases of the Psalms that bring this out very well. What happens to the Psalm texts could perhaps best be described as a kind of embroidering, a deliberate application of 'the softness of Poetry', which often results in a rather adjectival and circumstantial poetry. Several poems were supplied with annotations by Norris himself and these annotations, containing lengthy explanations of his method and his intentions, make clear how much 'put together' some of his poems are.[8] The close correspondence between the prose essays and the discourses on the one hand and the poetry on the other confirms the impression of ideas in a poetical dress. The opening sentence of Psalm 137—'By the rivers of Babylon, there we sat down, yea, we wept, when we remembered Zion'—has in *The 137th Psalm Paraphrased to the 7th Verse* been elaborated and expanded into 'Beneath a reverend gloomy shade / Where Tigris and Euphrates cut their way / With folded arms and heads supinely laid / We sate, and wept out all the tedious day' (179).

As a starting-point for my discussion of Norris's poetry I would like to quote some passages from John Hoyles's *The Waning of the Renaissance*. Hoyles characterizes Norris's poems as 'strongly and homogeneously marked by the Metaphysical tradition' (122), and he regards Norris as 'closely involved on the one hand with the line of Donne, Herbert, Marvell and Vaughan, and on the other with the emerging forces and forms of the Enlightenment' (76). Hoyles finds the metaphysical nature of Norris's poetry especially in the informal tone and the metaphysical wit. It seems to me that Hoyles overstates the importance of the link between Norris and the metaphysical poets. Of course, there are traces of the earlier poetical mode. One of Norris's most succesful poems, in my view, is *The Conquest:*

In power of wisdom to contend with Thee
Great God, who but a Lucifer would dare?
Our strength is but infirmity,
And when we this perceive, our sight's most clear:
But yet I will not be excell'd thought I,
In love, in love I'll with my Maker vy.
I view'd the glories of Thy seat above,
And thought of every grace and charm divine,
And further to increase my love
I measured all the heights and depths of Thine
Thus there broke forth a strong and vigorous flame,
And almost melted down my mortal frame.

But when Thy bloody sweat and death I view,
I own—dear Lord—the conquest of Thy love.
Thou dost my highest flights outdo,
I in a lower orb and slower move.
Thus in this strife's a double weakness shewn,
Thy love I cannot equal, nor yet bear my own.   (127)

In the account of an individual's engagement with God, the ultimate admission of smallness and inadequacy and the intimacy of tone, this poem is clearly reminiscent of a number of Herbert poems. Occasionally Norris's poetry has an epigrammatic quality that is quite effective. *The Complaint*, an otherwise undistinguished poem about a favourite Norris theme—the vanity of man's hopes and the fruitlessness of his pursuits—ends with a biting couplet which in a way also points forward to the eighteenth-century manner:

But now our appetites you vex and cheat,
With real hunger and phantastick meat.   (86)

The light-dark antithesis, the body-soul dichotomy, the soul's longing for a flight to God are all features we recognize from the poetry of Marvell, Vaughan and Traherne. So Hoyles clearly does have a point, but yet the differences seem to me to be both larger and more important than the similarities.

Norris was suspicious of wit, and on the whole his poetry is not remarkable for denseness of texture, lightfootedness, lyrical grace, dramatic intensity or rich ambiguity. There is a looseness about several of his poems which affects such various levels as rhyme, rhythm, imagery and argumentation. Norris's fondness for Pindaric Odes did not help in this respect, and his poetry regularly falls short of the Augustan standards of polish and decorum. The second part of the poem *The Passion of Our Blessed Saviour* describes Christ's victory over his doubts and fears in Gethsemane in terms that would have raised many Augustan eyebrows:

Thrice He sent for His release
Pathetick embassies of peace:
At length, His courage overcame His doubt,
Resolv'd He was, and so the bloody flag hung out.   (39)

Norris's use of certain words like the adjective 'sweet' is sometimes indiscriminate, and causes a blurring of outlines.[9] Compare for a moment the role played by the word 'sweet' in Herbert's poem *Vertue*, where 'sweet' is an integral part of the central opposition enacted in the poem. Often emotions are described or recorded rather than rendered. Thus in *The Impatient* the 'black night' (128), in which the speaker pines for the bright glories of the future state, strikes one as a manner of speaking and not as the lived-through anguish of some of Herbert's poems. In the following passage from *Seraphick Love*, the ecstasy seems largely a matter of statement:

> To Thee, Thou only fair, my soul aspires
> With holy breathings, languishing desires.
> To Thee m'inamoured, panting heart does move,
> By efforts of ecstatic love.   (64)

Of course, all this is not simply a question of inadequacy on Norris's part. In the Restoration period ambiguity, obscurity, individual peculiarities and matters of mere personal relevance came to be disapproved of, and Norris's poetry fits in with this development. His poems reflect the tendency towards the general and the abstract, away from the concrete and individual.[10] Norris was singled out by a critic as one of the few late seventeenth century poets who 'regard natural objects closely and with enjoyment',[11] but this is a rather surprising statement when one thinks of the generalised descriptions of scenery and landscape; there is hardly any specific locale in his poems.

The way in which the body-soul dichotomy figures in Norris's poems is also a case in point. There is a general and almost automatic denigration of the body in Norris's poetry. Characteristically, the soul is mostly either the speaker or the addressee, the body has no voice and is referred to in terms like 'envious flesh', 'dregs of sense', 'this dark house of clay', 'this gross vehicle'.[12] This is not unexpected from someone who was so much oriented towards reaching real bliss and full knowledge in the afterlife, and it also helps to account for the strikingly unsensuous character of his poetry. Whereas in the poetry of the first half of the seventeenth century the sacred did not in any way exclude the bodily and the sensuous, with Norris the sacred has become ethereal and disembodied. A glance at Marvell's poetry brings out this point very clearly. There is an obvious thematic similarity between Norris's *The Refinement* and Marvell's *A Dialogue between the Soul and Body*; incidentally, Norris's poems contain various echoes from Marvell's *Miscellaneous Poems* which had been published in 1681.[13] Yet Norris's poem has nothing of the concreteness and the dramatic unsolvable conflict between the antagonists of Marvell's poem. In *The Refinement* the suggested solution is that of rarefying and refining the body out of all existence.

With respect to the interests and themes of his poems, too, Norris would seem to belong much more to the early phases of the Enlightenment than to an earlier tradition. It is true, there was a side to Norris, which I hesitate to call mystical, but which nevertheless made him to some extent an unusual figure in his day. A poem like *Seraphick Love* must have struck many of his contemporaries as odd and perhaps even embarrassing, as is also suggested by his being nicknamed 'Seraphick Norris'.[14] It is clear that his imagination was fired by visions of the splendour of eternal life—the frequency of words like 'blessed','bliss' and 'blissful' testifies to this pre-occupation—and in a poem like *The Prospect* the rapture about the envisaged entry into the realm of eternal light is evident. Yet for all that, Norris's religion has a distinct Restoration colour. Of the seventy-five English poems about one-third could be called religious poems, the rest consisting mainly of moral essays and philosophical meditations, though the boundary between the religious poems and the rest is not always very sharp. A High Anglican in church-political terms, Norris was theologically a latitudinarian who had been influenced by Neoplatonist ways of thinking—in 1682 he published a translation of Hierocles—and by the philosophy of the Cambridge Platonist Henry More.[15] Norris's religion does not often give the impression of deep spirituality. For Hierocles moral virtue and intellectual knowledge were closely linked, and this idea is also discernible in Norris's writings. As I said before, Norris was convinced that clear thinking would lead to moral improvement, and it is telling that the words 'mind' and 'soul' often seem to be used indiscriminately by him. The God of Norris's poems is the Creator rather than the Saviour, and Norris's attitude towards sin and death clearly evinces his theological optimism. In the poem *The Complaint* the following lines occur: 'Do we for this long life a blessing call / And tremble at the name of death?' (85); but Norris's trembling seems to be a rather theoretical trembling because in his poems and essays death is not presented as in any way daunting or problematical. There is nothing like the crippling sense of unworthiness and the undermining fear and uncertainty about death to be found in some of Donne's poems and sermons, and Norris does not seem to have any doubts about being admitted to eternal life. Sin has no place in Norris's religious poetry; in one of his essays he calls sin 'unreasonable', and 'the height of folly',[16] and we are obviously not far from the deist position here.

More than once he describes God in terms of harmony and proportion, and he sees harmony and proportion in the universe too; there is no sense of mystery and wonder about the created world, as is the case with

Vaughan. And harmony and proportion is what he alleges to be the ideal for poetry as well. A fair number of Norris's religious poems can be seen against the background of what has come to be known as physico-theology, or the habit, on the part of many late seventeenth and early eighteenth-century scientists and philosophers, to refer the glory of creation to the Creator, and to posit the harmony of science and religion.[17] The following extracts provide an illustration of this:

Before great Love this monument did raise,
This ample theatre of praise.
Before the folding circles of the sky
Were tun'd by Him who is all harmony.

Hymn to Darkness (80)

Throughout the works divine I cast my eye,
Admire their beauty and their harmony,
I view the glorious host above,
And Him that made them, praise and love,

My Estate (126)

They only can this tribute duely yield
Whose active spirits range abroad,
Who traverse o'r all Nature's field
And view the great magnificence of God.
They see the hidden wealth of Nature's store
Fall down and learnedly adore;

To Dr. Plot, On His Natural History Of Staffordshire (183)

The Restoration side of Norris is also strongly present in his retirement poems. Maren-Sofie Röstvig has dealt with them—and with their classical models—at some length, but I would add that these poems present an un-ascetic view of retirement, mostly a not very arduous retirement-à-deux. Some of these poems such as *Sitting in an Arbour* and *The Retirement* openly express a self-centred and almost hedonistic attitude, a rather surprising position for the pious Anglican clergyman. I referred earlier to a group of Norris's poems as 'moral essays' and also in this respect the poetry has an almost eighteenth-century ring about it. In poems like *The Consolation*, *To Himself* and *Content* he moralises about such well-worn themes as 'our discontent is from comparison', 'be satisfied with your lot and do not aim too high' and 'all human endeavour is vain'. The presence, in the *Collection of Miscellanies*, of a translation of Horace's Tenth Ode of

the Second Book, the Golden Mean ode, confirms the impression of a pru-
dentialist stance.

Occasionally Norris achieves a manner of his own as a poet. His paraphrase of the second chapter of the Song of Songs, from verse 10 to 13, has
a freshness, gaiety and charm which is quite striking. However, mostly such
success concerns only parts of poems or single lines. In the last stanza of
The Prospect the speaker rapturously imagines the final moment of coming
home to God:

> Now for the greatest change prepare,
> To see the only great, the only fair.
> Vail now thy feeble eyes, gaze and be blest;
> Here all thy turns and revolutions cease,
> Here's all serenity and peace:
> Thou'rt to the centre come, the native seat of rest.
> There's now no further change, nor need there be
> When one shall be variety.   (178)

The poem *Beauty*, describing the beauty of creation and defining God as
beauty, is piously but laboriously expository, up to the last stanza, when it,
unexpectedly, catches fire:

> But do not thou, my soul, fixt here remain,
> All streams of Beauty here below
> Do from that immense ocean flow,
> And thither they should lead again.
> Trace then these streams, till thou shalt be
> At length o'erwhelmed in Beauty's boundless sea.   (193)

The Resignation, a poem about the duty of submission to God's will, even
though with clenched teeth, has this arresting line:

> Nature shrank in, and all my courage dy'd.   (163)

Yet on the whole one cannot make large claims for Norris's poetry. It
reflects many of the current views and attitudes of the late seventeenth
century, and in its manner it is even more representative. His work is largely outside the framework of the specifically biblical, Protestant poetics
posited by Barbara Lewalski as 'informing a major strain of English seventeenth-century religious lyric'.[18] In some respects Norris's position was
exceptional at the time, but he did not give an exceptional poetical express-

ion to it. His poems clearly show the effects of the new Restoration conception of poetry, and both in matter and in manner they chiefly belong to the early Enlightenment. I have already referred to the popularity of the *Collection of Miscellanies* and in the first half of the eighteenth century several poets were interested in his poetry and borrowed from it.[19] Viewing his poetry against the background of the sacred and the profane in the seventeenth century, one can conclude that there is a narrowing down and shrinking of the sacred, and a shift from individual and urgently felt religiosity towards a more generalised morality.

Notes

1   See, for instance, Geoffrey Walton, *Metaphysical to Augustan. Studies in Tone and Sensibility in the Seventeenth Century* (London, 1955), 153, and John N. Wall, *Transformation of the Word* (Atlanta, 1988), 368.

2   The 10th edition appeared in 1749. For the text of Norris's poems I have used the edition of Alexander B. Grosart of 1871, *The Poems of John Norris of Bemerton*.

3   Maren-Sofie Röstvig, *The Happy Man. Studies in the Metamorphosis of a Classical Ideal*, 2 Vols (Oslo, 1954); Geoffrey Walton, *op. cit.*; John Hoyles, *The Waning of the Renaissance 1640-1740. Studies in the Thought and Poetry of Henry More, John Norris and Isaac Watts* (The Hague, 1971); Richard Acworth, *The Philosophy of John Norris of Bemerton (1657-1712)* (Hildesheim-New York, 1979). For the argument that there was a later metaphysical tradition, to which also John Norris could be said to belong, see T.A. Birrell, 'Sarbiewski, Watts and the Later Metaphysical Tradition', *English Studies* 37 (1956): 125-132.

4   W.R. Sorley, *A History of English Philosophy* (Cambridge, 1937), 130-131.

5   See especially 'Of the Advantages of Thinking', *A Collection of Miscellanies: Consisting of Poems, Essays, Discourses and Letters, Occasionally Written*, 4th ed. (London, 1706).

6   *Cursory Reflections upon a Book call'd An essay concerning human understanding (1690)*, edited by Gilbert D. McEwen, Augustan Reprint Society No. 93 (Los Angeles, 1961).

7   Grosart, *op. cit.* 31. The 'Advertisement from the Authour to the Reader' and the preface 'To the Reader' contain many points that are also to be found in Sir Thomas Pope Blount's authoritative *De Re Poetica: Or, Remarks upon Poetry* (London, 1694).

8   The line 'Drawn by the bent of the aethereal tide' in the poem *The Elevation* gets the following comment: 'This is in allusion to the Cartesian hypothesis of vortices or whirl-pools of subtile matter. The mystic sense is this, that the higher a seraphic soul advances in the contemplation of the supreme Good, the stronger he will find its attractions', Grosart, *op. cit.*, 108.

9   See, for instance, the poem *A Pastoral upon the Blessed Virgin* (87-94).

10   For these and related questions concerning Restoration poetics see Blount, *op. cit.*, and the 'Introduction' to Irène Simon (ed.), *Neo-Classical Criticism* (London, 1971).

11   H.N. Fairchild, *Religious Trends in English Poetry* (New York, 1939, repr. 1964), Vol. 1, 210.

12   Cf. the poems *Seraphick Love, On a Musician Supposed to be Mad with Musick, The Discouragement* and *The Refinement*. For Norris's slighting references to the body see also the 'Annotations' to the poem *The Elevation* (104-105).

13   Especially in poems like *Satiety, The Prospect* and *The Refinement* there are echoes from Marvell's *The Garden* and *A Dialogue between the Soul and Body*.

14   See C.E. Doble *et al.* (eds), *Hearne's Remarks and Collections* (Oxford, 1885-1921), Vol. 10, 445.

15   See Rosalie L. Colie, *Light and Enlightenment* (Cambridge, 1957); Norris expressed his great admiration for More in his poem *To Dr. Henry More. An Ode.*

16   Quoted by Acworth, *op. cit.*, 74.

17   See R.S. Westfall, *Science and Religion in Seventeenth-Century England* (New Haven, 1958).

18   Barbara K. Lewalski, *Protestant Poetics and the Seventeenth-Century Religious Lyric* (Princeton, 1979), 4.

19   Herbert Drennon shows the influence of Norris on Henry Needler ('Henry Needler and Shaftesbury', *PMLA* 46 [1931]: 1095-1106), and on James Thomson ('James Thomson and John Norris', *PMLA* 53 [1939]: 1094-1101); Maren-Sofie Röstvig clearly proves that Mary Chudleigh borrowed from Norris (*op. cit.* Vol. 1, 416-430); Grosart indicates both Thomas Gray's and Robert Blair's indebtedness to Norris.

25

ROCHESTER, BEHN AND THE MARTYRDOM OF LUST

EDWARD BURNS

The baroque can be said to lack gravity, in both senses of the word. From an English point of view it has always been taken to lack seriousness, the weightiness of a Renaissance style, which in the visual arts, of course, we did not have. What we had was a Baroque that, from its origins in Royalist eulogy to its self-subverting social eclecticism as a libertine style, has been dismissively characterised as an escapism which dwindleed, or floresced, into a flamboyant promiscuity. The late seventeenth-century Baroque of the English poets Rochester and Behn belongs to the libertine appropriation and subversion of those styles originally introduced to Britain in order to glorify James I and his and his heir's fantasies of order. In this subversion the visual emblems of power and the glorious (if directionless and diffuse) weightlessness of movement characteristic of apotheoses of the monarch—in, for example, Rubens's ceilings for Inigo Jone's Whitehall Banqueting house—becomes for Rochester writing of Charles II a scandalous cartoon of the Baroque:

> Nor are his high desires above his strength:
> His scepter and his prick are of a length; ...
> Restless he rolls about from whore to whore,
> A merry monarch, scandalous and poor.[1]

Behn's royalism would never allow her to profane the monarch thus. But both Rochester and Behn seem to me to find a gravity in an exploration of the weightlessness of style achieved in Baroque painting and architecture. There, bodies and buildings simultaneously impinge on our awareness both as material things and as imaginative constructs that mockingly deny our mundane need to fix them in place. In Rochester's and Behn's poetry a tottering architecture of conceit can be built on the pinhead of an irretrievable moment. Such a poem therefore can be read as both trivial—in that its occasion is an episode in a defiantly casual life—and grave, in that what becomes apparent is an illumination within that moment of the facticity of the body, and the precariousness of its life in a desire for other bodies. In this, despite the comparative restraint of the language she uses, Behn is perhaps the more profane. Rochester plays these two interdependent, mutually defining concepts off against each other, in order to create a space for the sacred, a space where the experience of the body can be given a privileged meaning. Behn, however, continually disrupts the economies and procedures by which the Baroque sacralises experience, to provide a sense of the fluidly and spatially unstable profane.

The sacred and profane are, as this suggests, interdependent concepts. The term 'profane' in modern English usage, can overlap in meaning with 'the obscene', a word formed from a parallel spatial metaphor, that which is 'off the scene', inadmissible to sight or hearing. But the obscene or 'off scene' confers no particular value on what is 'on scene', other than decency or respectability. The meaning of the word profane is also constructed through a spatial contrast—outside or away from the 'fane', the temple, the sacred space. The spatial model implies a transgressible line, and invites us to imagine its transgression. To invoke one idea in secular poetry is to imply the existence of and to some extent to validate the other.

Rochester can be both obscene, and though undeniably indecent, still acknowledge the existence of the sacred. 'A Ramble in St James's Park' is one of his most explicitly misogynist poems—albeit that the misogyny is so spectacularly overt and its occasion made so obviously insufficient that the poem's anger turns against itself and what might start as an exorcism ends in a masochistic circularity, where misogyny is itself undone and inverted. 'And may no woman better thrive', the last couplet has it, 'who dares profane the cunt I swive' (46). Sacralising the cunt also puts bounds around it, appropriates it maybe, certainly takes it from the women's control. But it also puts it into a different kind of space, a sacred space, under neither gender's jurisdiction. The invading penis, always seen by Rochester as somehow 'breaking' in, is thus simultaneously seeking sanctuary and blaspheming. In the lyric 'The Mistress', an attempt to sacralise the lover's own interior space, as the receptacle of his languishing soul, fails farcically and is discarded—it 'haunts my breast, by absence made / The living tomb of love' (88). But the sacred can be invoked to define a space of authentic emotion and belief, a space again outside the jurisdiction of either, able to contain and confer meaning on the violent moment:

> Alas! 'tis sacred jealousy,
>   Love raised to an extreme:
> The only proof 'twixt her and me
>   We love and do not dream.   (89)

Behn shares a superficially similar appropriation of a language of the sacred as euphemism and frame for penetrative sexual acts and apparent emotional trauma. But there are two major differences between her use of such language and Rochester's. One is that for Behn the act itself, the 'sac-rifice', is performed both in the literal narrative of seduction and in the pseudo-classical analogy used to mask and to simultaneously reveal it, as happening *outdoors*. The other is that the violence implied in sacrifice is separated from it, and explored in analogies of combat and archery, con-ducted in glances and words, which precede and surround the sexual act itself. The first of these characteristics marks Behn's refusal to demarcate a sacred space; the second has the consonant effect of rendering the actions and roles of sexual combat diffuse, detaching them from a fixed focus on the body of the kind on which Rochester's ideas of sexual martyrdom insist. Here are two stanzas of pastoral seduction from 'The Disappoint-ment':

> But he as much unus'd to Fear,
>   As he was capable of Love,
>   The blessed minutes to improve,
>   Kisses her Mouth, her Neck, her Hair;
>   Each Touch her new Desire Alarms,
>   His burning trembling Hand he prest
>   Upon her swelling Snowy Brest,
>   While she lay panting in his Arms.
>   All her Unguarded Beauties lie
> The Spoils and trophies of the Enemy.
>
> And now without Respect or Fear,
>   He seeks the Object of his Vows,
>   (His Love no Modesty allows)
>   By swift degrees advancing-where
>   His daring Hand that Altar seiz'd,
>   Where Gods of Love do sacrifice.
>   That Awful Throne, that Paradice
>   Where Rage is calm'd, and Anger pleas'd,
>   That Fountain where Delight still flows,
> And gives the Universal World Repose.[2]

The martial image of the shepherd's approach is subverted not only by unambiguously labelling him 'the enemy', but by the gradual increase in the size of the shepherdess's cunt, from that which is accessible to a mere human hand, to the dizzyingly inclusive Baroque vision of the 'fountain where Delight still flows'—'still' meaning always, but also perhaps pun-ningly creating a power that is mystically still and in movement at the same

time—to give 'the Universal World Repose'. But what is sacrificed on the
altar? The shepherd's failure is the nymph's disappointment;

> She does her softest Joys dispence,
> Off'ring her Virgin-Innocence
> A Victim to Loves Sacred Flame;
> While the o'er-Ravish'd Shepherd lies
> Unable to perform the Sacrifice.   (67)

The priest himself is the victim. In Behn's 'To my Lady *Morland* at
Tunbridge' a Christian ceremony becomes a pagan sacrifice. Again she uses
the word 'altar', and implies that the event is sited outdoors, rather than
bounded within the sacred space of a church—her sacrifices are often either
outside or ambiguously located, in an again typically Baroque confusion or
conflation of outside and inside. The officiating priest becomes a martyr to
love:

> 'Twas at the Altar, where more Hearts were giv'n
> To you that day, then were address'd to Heav'n.
> The Rev'rend Man whose Age and Mystery
> Had rendred youth and Beauty Vanity,
> By fatal Chance casting his Eyes your way,
> Mistook the Bus'ness of the Day,
> Forgot the Gospel, and began to Pray.
> Whilst the Enamour'd Crowd that near you prest,
> Recieving *Darts* which none could e'er resist,
> Neglected the Mistake o'th'Love-sick Priest.   (62)

Martyrdom, unlike the experience of the visionary, is an essentially
social transaction, as a glance at any picture of sacrifice or martyrdom will
show. It requires a martyr, martyrers, a witnessing crowd, some believing,
some unbelieving, some waverers about to be persuaded and a heavenly
audience which is also poised with some kind of reward. We ourselves are
also there—a kind of posterity who are also present within the illusionistic-
ally registered past moment. Rochester and Behn differ significantly in their
placing of the poem within this network of act and gaze, in ways continuous with their different use of the 'sacrifice' motif. Rochester's 'To the
Postboy' is a poem of self-picturing, but the picture is so punishingly unflattering that it seems also a kind of self-martyrdom. It is so difficult, as
more than one commentator on the poem has remarked, to imagine a poet

writing this way of himself, that one's instinct is to ascribe the poem to another.[3] The poem is short enough to be quoted in its entirety:

> Son of a whore, God damn you! can you tell
> A peerless peer the readiest way to Hell?
> I've outswilled Bacchus, sworn of my own make
> Oaths would fright Furies, and make Pluto quake;
> I've swived more whores more ways than Sodom's walls
> E'er knew, or the College of Rome's Cardinals.
> Witness heroic scars—Look here, ne'er go!—
> Cerecloths and ulcers from the top to toe!
> Frighted at my own mischiefs, I have fled
> And bravely left my life's defender dead;
> Broke houses to break chastity, and dyed
> That floor with murder which my lust denied.
> Pox on't, why do I speak of these poor things?
> I have blasphemed my God, and libeled Kings!
> The readiest way to Hell—Come, quick!
> Boy   Ne'er stir:
> The readiest way, my Lord, 's by Rochester.   (130-131)

The poem alludes to an incident of a drunken brawl instigated by Rochester in which one of his party, Major Downs, was killed while trying to defend the group from the local forces of law and order. The occasion opens up to a moment of seeing; Rochester looms ghostlike and wounded, like an apparition of the risen Christ. He is confirmed, fixed, named by the poem, but in a context where the wounds are a mark of the death of his reputation. The wounds and scars are 'real' both in the economy of the text—they are readable signs with a stable referent—and in an invited placing of the poem in terms of our anecdotal knowledge of the 'real' poet. The ambiguity of that seventh line emphasises this double point. It is an invitation to ourselves and to the boy—the roles overlap, as the boy is not constructed as an independent subject until the speech prefix for last two lines of the poem[4]—to bear witness to scars which in themselves bear witness to his presence before us, like the wounds of the risen Christ when he appeared to Thomas, and to his distinctly unheroic past. So we can read the line as a simple inversion of word-order, so saying that the heroic scars are witnesses. What is at issue here is the status and nature of the wound, and its relation to the structure of witnessing and suffering that the martyrdom analogy sets up.

These are wounds on a male body. Perhaps one should point out that, whatever the misogynistic verbal violence unleashed against them, in

Rochester women are never hurt or marked, even in terms of the conventional 'love's arrows' metaphor. Rather, their physical resilience and capacity for sexual pleasure converts the phallic projectiles of male desire into extensions of the women's own capacity for enjoyment. In the 'Mock Song' Rochester parodies a poem by Sir Car Scroope. Scroope addresses his mistress, Cary Frazier, in the conventional terms of love's martyrdom:

When killed with grief Amyntas lies,
    And you to mind shall call
The sighs that now unpitied rise,
    The tears that vainly fall,
That welcome hour that ends his smart
    Will then begin your pain,
For such a faithful, tender heart
    Can never break, can never break in vain.   (136)

Rochester answers with a poem impersonating Cary, the addressee, and transforms the pain Scroope self-pityingly and vengefully wishes on her into an infinite and ecstatic pleasure:

'Were all my body larded o'er
    With darts of love, so thick
That you might find in every pore
    A well-stuck standing prick,
Whilst yet my eyes alone were free,
    My heart would never doubt,
In amorous rage and ecstasy,
    To wish those eyes, to wish those eyes fucked out'.   (136-137)

Bernini's famous sculpture of St Theresa in Ecstasy always tends to be evoked at moments like this—Cary's 'amorous rage and ecstacy' is a self-generated secular equivalent. This reverse of sacred parody is similar to the parallel Alice B. Toklas makes in recommending her 'Haschich Fudge'; 'ecstatic reveries and extensions of one's personality on several simultaneous planes are to be complacently expected. Almost anything St Theresa did, you can do better ...'[5] St Theresa is of course ecstatically wounded, and the Baroque convention of the pleasure-giving wound may give us pause. On the male body a wound is a mark of the history of that male subject, memorialised as a scar—as in Rochester's 'heroic scars ...' On the female body the wound closes, the body can seemingly receive an intense and distinct pleasure without its leaving a specific trace. Behn does wound her women, but it would be wrong to say that she wounded the female *body*, or that it was the male body doing the wounding. In Behn the 'wounds' may be caused by reading, as in 'On a Copy of Verses made in a Dream, and sent to me in a morning before I was awake'—

>   ... if by Chance such Wounds you make,
> And in your Sleep such welcome Mischiefs do;
>   What are your Pow'rs when you're awake,
> Directed by Design and Reason too?   (60)

These wounds are not in themselves to be read, at least by onlookers, though in 'Love Reveng'd', in a somewhat compressed involution, the eyes must read on themselves the wound that they have invited and which is inscribed on them: 'Oh how she burns, but 'tis too late, / For in her Eyes she reads her Fate' (96). Behn's martyrs and witnesses are more mobile than the fixed focuses of Rochester's theatre of sexual martyrdom—comically, fluently so. There is a kind of mutuality in the martyrdom in a poem like 'To Lysander at the music meeting'. Lysander is a kind of angel, but he is also a Sebastian lounging, as Baroque Sebastians, unlike their high Renaissance predecessors, almost always are.

> It was too much, ye Gods, to see and hear;
> Receiving wounds from both the Eye and Ear:
> One Charme might have secur'd a Victory,
> Both, rais'd the Pleasure even to Extasie ...
> Your bosom now and than (sic) a sigh wou'd move,
> (For *Musick* has the same effects with Love.)
> Your Body easey and all tempting lay,
> Inspiring wishes which the Eyes betray,
> In all that have the fate to glance that way ...
> So look young Angels, Listening to the sound,
> When the Tun'd Spheres Glad all the Heav'ns around:
> So Raptur'd lie amidst the wondering Crowd,
> So Charmingly Extended on a Cloud.
>   When from so many ways Loves Arrows storm,
> Who can the heedless Heart defend from harm?   (94)

Baroque Sebastians lounge, because they are presented after the event; they are waiting for a group of women, St Irene and her companions to come and heal them. So instead of the arrows marking the direction of an ambiguously desiring violent male gaze, as in the high Renaissance versions, they mark the benign desire of an anticipated female gaze. There is a kind of mutual pathos here, as again, Aphra's eyes wound and are wounded.

Finally I feel that Behn's literalism about direction and placing under-cuts the potential physicality of the wounding metaphor. The speaker of 'The Invitation' informs 'Damon' that

> ... whilst you did prepare your Charmes,
> On purpose *Silvia* to subdue:
> I met the arrows as they flew,
> And sav'd her from their harms.   (55)

So she tells him he might as well make the best of it. The geometrical pre-cision of Behn's placing, as in the composition of a Baroque picture, sug-gests weightless disembodied bodies, whose wounds are lightly worn, trans-ferrable, provisional, and under the management of the acting subject rather than *vice versa*. Perhaps, compared to Rochester, she is the profane of the two in that she moves away from, lingers outside the temple, and never really enters it. A shifting between the planes of elaborate narrative analogy and literal anecdote, in the intiguingly elaborate structures of the 'Musick-Meeting' and 'Lady *Morland*', unsettles the the relation between the wound or scar and its referent and/or origin. She does not allow a stable heroic or sacred space—which Rochester always does—where special meanings are possible, nor does she present texts which are wounded or scarred, as his are, by the marks of an insistent personal history. Behn's achievement is unlike that of any other comparable figure in its uneasy fit with those meta-phors of weight, gravity, permanence, and their compatible opposites of rupture, lesion, rift, which provide our discursive frame for the text that displays its heroic scars. In Behn, the weightlessness is all.

Notes

1   Rochester, *The Complete Poems*, edited by David M. Vieth (Yale, 1968), 79. All further references are to this edition.
2   *The Works of Aphra Behn: Volume I; Poetry*, edited by Janet Todd (London, 1992), 66, ll. 31-50. All further references are to this edition.
3   See my 'Rochester, Lady Betty and the Postboy', in *Reading Rochester*, edited by Edward Burns (Liverpool, 1995).
4   This is in the manuscript, though the often added prefix 'Rochester' for the start of the poem is not.
5   *The Alice B. Toklas Cook Book* (London, 1954), 259.

INDEX

Aesop 215

Ambrose, St. 123n, 195

Andrewes, Lancelot 107, 213, 217, 237

Aneau, Barthlémy 227

Aretino, Pietro 8-10, 12, 15n

Aristotle 163, 165

Ascham, Robert 25, 31n, 186

Askew, Anne 20

Austen, Jane 287

Aytoun, Robert 48, 59n

Bacon, Sir Francis 84

Bakhtin, Mikhail 283, 286, 294n

Balbulus, Notker 188

Balzac, Jean Louis Guez de 231-234, 236n, 287

Bartas, Guillaume du 207, 208

Bede, St. 203

Behn, Aphra 329-332, 334-336

Bellay, Joachim du 227

Benci, Francesco 68, 70, 73

Bible xi, xii, 18, 20, 36, 65, 106-108, 111, 115, 121, 122, 186, 216, 232, 243, 244, 295-299, 302-304, 310, 311

    Acts 200, 296, 301-303; *Colossians* 120, 125n; *Corinthians, I* 105, 116, 121, 126n, 301, 303; *Corinthians, II* 175, 177; *Deuteronomy* 275; *Ecclesiastes* 18, 20, 275, 279; *Ephesians* 3, 120, 121, 123n, 125n, 149n, 175, 177; *Ezekiel* 208, 268, 306n; *Galatians* 105, 301; *Genesis* 114, 115, 123n, 176, 216, 217, 288, 297, 298; *Hosea* 306n; *Isaiah* 176, 177, 215, 297-299, 302, 306n; *Jeremiah* 129, 306n; *Job* 100, 175, 262, 288; *John* 111, 112, 163, 176, 178, 251, 252; *Jude* 196, 216, 302; *Leviticus* 314; *Luke* 110-112, 116, 119, 175, 302; *Malachi* 176; *Mark* 110-112, 145, 302; *Matthew* 25, 105, 110, 111, 113, 114, 119, 177, 195, 200n, 252, 299; *Numbers* 268, 302; *Peter, I* 111, 121, 126n; *Peter, II* 298; *Philippians* 215, 257; *Psalms* 8, 11, 14n, 20-23, 36, 47, 48, 57, 131, 176, 196, 197, 199, 232, 321; *Revelation* 175, 177, 267, 306n; *Romans* 166, 168, 175, 177, 178; *Ruth* 317; *Samuel, I* 275; *Song of Songs* 111, 117, 118, 247, 250n, 326; *Timothy, I* 120, 123n, 125n, 215, 296; *Timothy, II* 123n, 177

Bible, translations of

    Coverdale 20, 37; *Geneva* 123n, 177, 182n, 215; *King James* 107, 215, 216; *Vulgate* 20, 24-27

Biddle, Hester 298, 299, 304, 305n, 316

Blake, William 286

Breton, Nicholas 70

Brouwer, Christoph 188

Browne, Sir Thomas 167, 204, 208, 218n, 280, 281n

Buchanan, George 46, 47, 59n

Bunyan, John 308-314, 316, 318

Burns, Robert 58

Busby, John 65

Calvin, Jean 142

Camden, William 187, 206

Campensis, Joannes 20, 25, 31n

Camphuysen, Dirck Rafaelsz 230-233, 236n

Canisius, Henricus 190, 192

Cary, Mary 297, 305n

NOTES ON CONTRIBUTORS

DOMINIC BAKER-SMITH was educated at Cambridge where he later became a lecturer in English. In 1976 he was appointed to a chair at Cardiff and since 1981 he has been Professor of English at the University of Amsterdam. He has written widely on English and Neo-Latin writers of the Renaisaance, and his study *More's Utopia* was published in 1991. He is currently editing Erasmus's expositions of the Psalms for the Toronto *Collected Works of Erasmus*.

MARK BERGE is currently involved in researching a PhD thesis on the Orcadian writer, George Mackay Brown, at the University of Manitoba, Canada. He has recently published an article on silence and irresolution in *King Lear* in *Reclamations of Shakespeare*, edited by Ton Hoenselaars (Amsterdam: Rodopi, 1995). He is also the editor of *Treeline*, an Internet journal for Canadian short fiction and poetry on the World Wide Web.

EDWARD BURNS is Senior Lecturer in English at the University of Liverpool, where he teaches Renaissance and seventeenth-century literature, and English Drama. His publications include *Restoration Comedy: Crises of Desire and Identity* (Mcmillan, 1987), *Character* (Macmillan, 1990) and *Reading Rochester* (Liverpool, 1995). He is currently editing *I Henry VI* for the third edition of the Arden Shakespeare, and working on a book on Shakespeare and magic.

THOMAS N. CORNS is Professor and Head of the School of English and Linguistics at the University of Wales, Bangor. His recent publications include *Uncloistered Virtue: English Political Literature, 1640-1660* (Oxford, 1992) and *Regaining 'Paradise Lost'* (London, 1994), and he is the editor of *The Cambridge Companion to English Poetry, Donne to Marvell* (Cambridge, 1993).

PAUL J.C.M. FRANSSEN lectures in the English Department of the University of Utrecht, specialising in Renaissance and eighteenth-century British literature. His PhD was on *The Mystic Winepress: A Religious Image in English Poetry, 1500-1700* (Utrecht, 1987) and he has since published essays on Spenser, Shakespeare, Herbert, Milton and Pope as well as Oscar Wilde and Salman Rushdie.

ELSPETH GRAHAM is Principal Lecturer in Literature and Cultural History at Liverpool John Moores University. She edited (with Hilary Hinds, Elaine Hobby and Helen Wilcox) *Her Own Life: Autobiographical Writings by Seventeenth-Century Englishwomen* (Routledge, 1989) and has published articles on seventeenth-century autobiography and women's writing, Bunyan and Milton, and feminist literary theory.

ACHSAH GUIBBORY is Professor of English at the University of Illinois at Urbana-Champaign. Her publications include *The Map of Time: Seventeenth-Century English Literature and Ideas of Pattern in History* and essays on Donne, Jonson, Bacon, Herrick, Browne, Cowley and Dryden. She is the holder of a John Donne Society Distinguished Publication Award, and is currently completing a book on *Literature and the Cultural Significance of Religious Conflict, Donne to Milton.*

ELIZABETH HEALE teaches Renaissance literature at the University of Reading. She has published a book on Spenser—*The Faerie Queene: A Reader's Guide*—and among her recent publications is an article on the 'Devonshire' manuscript of early Tudor poetry. She is currently working on a book on Wyatt and courtly poetry of the Henrician period.

THEO VAN HEIJNSBERGEN is a Lecturer in the Department of Scottish Literature at the University of Glasgow. His research focuses mainly on sixteenth-century Scottish poetry within its wider European context. His publications include an essay on the love lyrics of Alexander Scott, and a contribution on the Bannatyne manuscript to *The Renaissance in Scotland*, edited by A.A. MacDonald, Michael Lynch and Ian B. Cowan (Leiden, 1994).

M. THOMAS HESTER is Alumni Distinguished Professor of English at North Carolina State University. He is the author of *Kinde Pitty and Brave Scorn: John Donne's Satyres* (Duke, 1982), editor and translator (with R.V. Young) of *Justus Lipsius' 'Epistolica Institutio'* (Southern Illiois, 1995) and editor/co-editor of forthcoming volumes of Donne's Prose, Prose Letters and, in het Donne Variorum Edition, the Satires. He is also the founding co-editor of the *John Donne Journal.*

ELAINE HOBBY is Reader in Women's Studies in the Department of English and Drama at Loughborough University. She has been working on seventeenth-century women's writing since 1978, and does not intend to stop. Her current research includes the preparation of an edition of Jane Sharp,

The Midwives Book (1670) for the Oxford University Press Brown Women Writers' Series.

JEFFREY JOHNSON is Associate Professor of English at College Misericordia in Dallas, Pennsylvania. He is a contributing editor for Volume VIII of the *Donne Variorum* and has published articles on Donne, Herbert and Vaughan.

ARTHUR F. KINNEY is Thomas W. Copeland Professor of Literary History at the University of Massachusetts, Amherst. He is the founding editor of *English Literary Renaissance* and Massachusetts Studies in Early Modern Culture. He is presently working on a full-length study of *Macbeth* and editing *The Witch of Edmonton* for the New Mermaid series.

FRANS KORSTEN is Professor of English Literature at the University of Nijmegen. He has published on seventeenth and eighteenth-century literature and the history of the book, including *A Catalogue of the Library of Thomas Baker* (1990).

ALASDAIR A. MACDONALD is Professor of English Langauge and Literature of the Middle Ages at the University of Groningen. He is the author of a number of articles on late-medieval and Renaissance English and Scottish literature, and co-editor of: *The Renaissance in Scotland* (Leiden, 1994); *Loyal Letters: Studies on Mediaeval Alliterative Poetry and Prose* (Groningen, 1994); *Pagans and Christians* (Groningen, 1995); *Centres of Learning: Learning and Location in Pre-modern Europe and the near East* (Leiden, 1995).

JEREMY MAULE is Fellow in English at Trinity College, Cambridge, with research interests in English Renaissance poetry and prose. He is the founding General Editor of 'Renaissance Texts from Manuscript', and is currently preparing an edition of the spiritual autobiographies of two 'Scripture Women of Colchester' from the 1630s, Rose Thurgood and Cecily Johnson.

ANDREW MONNICKENDAM is Senior Lecturer in English literature at the Universitat Autònoma de Barcelona. He has published articles principally on Scottish literature, and Milton and intertextuality. He is currently working on the application of hypertext systems to the teaching of literature.

JOHN R. ROBERTS is Professor of English at the University of Missouri-Columbia and is the author of annotated bibliographies of criticism on

Donne, Herbert and Crashaw. He has also edited collections of original essays on Crashaw and on the seventeenth-century English religious lyric and has published essays on Donne, Southwell and Herbert.

LORRAINE ROBERTS is Associate Professor at Saint Mary's College of Minnesota and has written essays on Southwell and Crashaw. Her most recent essay, 'The "Truewit" of Crashaw's Poetry', appears in *The Wit of Seventeenth-Century Poetry*, edited by Claude J. Summers and Ted-Larry Pebworth (University of Missouri Press, 1995).

JONATHAN SAWDAY is Senior Lecturer in the Department of English at the University of Southampton. He is co-editor of *Literature and the English Civil War* (Cambridge, 1990) and author of *The Body Emblazoned: Dissection and the Human Body in Renaissance Culture* (Routledge, 1995). He is currently editing *Pericles* for the Arden Shakespeare.

PAUL R. SELLIN is 'oud-hoogleraar, Engelse letterkunde na 1500' at the Vrije Universiteit, Amsterdam, and currently Professor Emeritus, Department of English, University of California, Los Angeles. A specialist in Renaissance Neo-Latin literary criticism, Anglo-Dutch relations, Milton and Donne, his books include *'So Doth, So Is Religion': John Donne and Diplomatic Contexts in the Reformed Netherlands, 1619-1620* (Columbia, Missouri, 1988).

W.A. SESSIONS is Regents' Professor of English at Georgia State University. He has recently completed three book manuscripts: a critical biography of Henry Howard, Earl of Surrey; the Bacon volume for the Twayne series under the editorship of Arthur Kinney; and an annotated bibliography of twentieth-century works on Francis Bacon in the G.K. Hall Essential Authors series under the editorship of James Harner.

MARIJKE SPIES is Professor of Dutch Literature before 1700 at the Vrije Universiteit, Amsterdam. Her main research interests are rhetoric and the sixteenth-century Dutch so-called rhetoricians' literature. Recent essays include a study of the Mennonites and Dutch literature in the seventeenth century, and she is currently working on a book on Dutch culture around 1650.

PAUL G. STANWOOD, Professor of English at the University of British Columbia, is president of the John Donne Society of America (1995). He is the author of many essays and reviews on Renaissance poetry and prose, a selection of which appears in *The Sempiternal Season: Studies in Seventeenth-Century Devotional Literature*, and *John Donne and the Theology of Language* (co-authored with Heather Ross Asals). He has edited texts by John Cosin, William Law, Richard Hooker and Jeremy Taylor.

GARY A. STRINGER is Professor of English at the University of Southern Mississippi. He has published essays on various Renaissance topics and is General Editor of the Variorum Edition of the Poetry of John Donne.

RICHARD TODD teaches English literature at the Vrije Universiteit Amsterdam. His publications in the field of early modern literature include *The Opacity of Signs: Forms of Interpretative Activity in George Herbert's 'The Temple'* (Columbia: University of Missouri Press, 1986) and articles on the Sidney-Pembroke psalter and Dutch analogues, and on Carew's epitaph on Donne.

CLAIRE WARWICK has just been awarded her PhD, for which she studied at Selwyn College, Cambridge. Her future plans concern a study of the literary representation of the beloved in love poetry, both secular and sacred. She is currently working for Chadwyck Healey on the Patrologia Latina database while looking for an academic job.

HELEN WILCOX is Professor of English Literature at the University of Groningen. Her publications include (as co-editor) *Her Own Life: Autobiographical Writings of Seventeenth-century Englishwomen* (Routledge, 1989), *George Herbert: Sacred and Profane* (Amsterdam, 1995), (as editor) *Women and Literature in Britain, 1500-1700* (Cambridge, 1996), and articles on Shakespeare, George Herbert, seventeenth-century devotional poetry and early modern women's writing.